American English File

Teacher's Book 3

Clive Oxenden
Christina Latham-Koenig

with Brian Brennan

OXFORD
UNIVERSITY PRESS

Paul Seligson and Clive Oxenden are the
original co-authors of *English File 1* (pub. 1996)
and *English File 2* (pub. 1997).

OXFORD
UNIVERSITY PRESS

198 Madison Avenue
New York, NY 10016 USA

Great Clarendon Street, Oxford OX2 6DP UK

Oxford University Press is a department of the University of Oxford.
It furthers the University's objective of excellence in research,
scholarship, and education by publishing worldwide in

Oxford New York

Auckland Cape Town Dar es Salaam Hong Kong Karachi
Kuala Lumpur Madrid Melbourne Mexico City Nairobi
New Delhi Shanghai Taipei Toronto

With offices in

Argentina Austria Brazil Chile Czech Republic France Greece
Guatemala Hungary Italy Japan Poland Portugal Singapore
South Korea Switzerland Thailand Turkey Ukraine Vietnam

OXFORD and OXFORD ENGLISH are registered trademarks of
Oxford University Press.

© Oxford University Press 2008

Database right Oxford University Press (maker)

Photocopying

Editorial Director: Sally Yagan
Publisher: Laura Pearson
Managing Editor: Anna Teevan
Project Editor: Maria A. Dalsenter
Design Director: Robert Carangelo
Project Leader: Bridget McGoldrick
Manufacturing Manager: Shanta Persaud
Manufacturing Controller: Faye Wang

ISBN: 978 0 19 477449 9

Printed in China

10 9 8 7 6 5 4 3

This book is printed on paper from certified and well-managed sources.

Acknowledgments

Cover design by: Jaclyn Smith

The authors would like to thank all the teachers and students around the
world whose feedback has helped us to shape this series.

Special thanks to Beatriz Martin for her help with the Communicative
photocopiable activities.

Finally, very special thanks from Clive to María Angeles, Lucia, and Eric, and
from Christina to Cristina, for all their help and encouragement. Christina
would also like to thank her children Joaquin, Marco, and Krysia for their
constant inspiration.

*The publisher and authors are grateful to those who have given permission to
reproduce the following extracts and adaptations of copyright material:*

pp. 26 and 205 *We Are Family*. Words and Music by Bernard Edwards and
Nile Rodgers © 1979 Bernard's Other Music and Sony/ATV Songs LLC. All
rights for Bernard's Other Music administered by Warner-Tamerlane
Publishing Corp. All rights on behalf of Sony/ATV Songs LLC administered
by Sony/ATV Music Publishing, 8 Music Square West. Nashville, TN 37206.
All rights reserved. Used by permission.

p. 32 *Ka-ching*. Words and Music by Shania Twain and Robert John Lange
© 2002 Out of Pocket Prod. Ltd. and Loon Echo, Inc. All rights for Out of
Pocket Prod. Ltd. administered by Universal Music – Z Tunes Llc. (ASCAP).
All rights for Loon Echo, Inc. administered by Universal Music – Z Songs
(BMI). All rights reserved. Used by permission.

pp. 61 and 206 *You Can Get It If You Really Want*. Words and Music by
Jimmy Cliff © 1970 Island Music Ltd. (PRS). Copyright renewed. All rights
administered in the US and Canada by Universal – Songs of PolyGram
Int., Inc. (BMI). All rights reserved. Used by permission.

pp. 75 and 207 *Our House*. Words by Carl Smyth. Music by Chris Foreman
© 1982 EMI Music Publishing Ltd. All rights for the US and Canada
controlled and administered by EMI Blackwood Music, Inc. All rights
reserved. International copyright secured. Used by permission.

pp. 91 and 208 *Sk8er Boi*. Words and Music by Avril Lavigne, Scott Alspach
(Scott Spock), Lauren Christy, and Graham Edwards © 2002 Almo Music
Corp., Avril Lavigne Publ. Ltd., Warner-Tamerlane Publ. Corp., Mr. Spock
Music, Rainbow Fish Publ., WB Music Corp., Ferry Hill Songs, Hollylodge
Music, Tix Music and Copyright Control. Rainbow Fish Publishing, Mr.
Spock Music and Hollylodge Music administered by Warner-Tamerlane
Publishing Corp. All rights for Ferry Hill Songs and Tix Music administered
by WB Music Corp. All rights for Avril Lavigne Publ. Ltd administered by
Almo Music Corp. (BMI). All rights reserved. Used by permission.

pp. 113 and 209 *Holding Out For A Hero*, from the Paramount Motion
Picture *Footloose*. Words by Dean Pitchford. Music by Jim Steinman.
© 1984 by Ensign Music. International copyright secured. All rights
reserved. Used by permission.

pp. 121 and 210 *Ironic*. Words and Music by Alanis Morissette and Glen
Ballard © 1994 Songs of Universal, Inc., Universal Music Corp., Vanhurst
Place Music, Aerostation Corp. All rights for Vanhurst Place Music
administered by Universal Music Corp. (ASCAP). All rights reserved.
Used by permission.

*The publisher would like to thank the following for their kind permission to
reproduce photographs and other copyright material:* Allstar p. 156 (The Color
Purple/Warner Brothers, Some Like it Hot/United Artists); Alamy pp. 139
(Digital Archive Japan), 157 (Eiffel Tower/Direct Photo); Corbis Images pp.
154 (men/Benelux), 172 (Rosie Ruiz/Bettmann), 206 (weight lifter/Janni
Chavakiszefa, ballet dancer/Gary Salterzefa); Getty Images pp. 151 (young
couple/Ian Sanderson), 153, 154 (women/Martin Ried), 155 (Zia Soleil), 157
(Kenneth Branagh/Time Life Pictures), 207 (Hulton Archive); The Kobal
Collection p. 156 (Cleopatra/20th Century Fox, Gandhi/Columbia/Goldcrest,
The Piano/Jan Chapman Productions/CIBY 2000); NHPA pp. 157 (cat/Yves
Lanceau), 174 (cheetah); Oxford University Press pp. 151 (older
couple/Medio Images), 174 (skeleton/Image Source); Picture Alliance p. 172
(Ben Johnson); Rex Features p. 174 (snail)

Illustrations by: Phil Disley pp. 141, 145, 150, 152, 185; Martina Farrow pp.
205, 208; Gavin Reece p. 178; Colin Shelbourn pp. 138 (computer, skiing),
143, 146, 159, 175, 176, 181, 184, 191, 195; Andy J. Smith p. 138 (snake);
Duncan Storr p. 209; Kath Walker pp. 140, 142, 144, 147, 148, 158, 160,
177, 179; Annabel Wright p. 210

Picture research by: Cathy Blackie, Terry Taylor

Syllabus checklist

		Grammar	**Vocabulary**

Pronunciation	Speaking	Listening	Reading
/ʊ/ and /u/, understanding phonetics	talking about eating habits	an interview with a chef	Food: fuel or pleasure?
/ɔr/ and /ər/	telling a story talking about sports	an interview with a soccer referee	When you hear the final whistle
word stress, adjective prefixes and suffixes	families	psychologist talking about position in the family song: *We are family*	We are family
saying numbers	money questionnaire	song: Ka-*ching* understanding a news program	My life without money
sentence stress, strong adjectives	How long…?	an interview with an American living in Ecuador	It was just a vacation, but it changed my life
stress in compound nouns	talking about road safety	a trip from London to the south of France; road safety	Race to the sun
sentence stress	talking about cell phones talking about manners	an interview about politeness	Culture shock
-eigh, -aigh, -igh	matching people with their jobs	interview with a musician	Do I really look like this?
sentence stress	talking about abilities	psychologist talking about learning new skills; song: *You can get it if you really want*	Never give up
/ʌ/ or /yu/?	talking about education	interview about a TV show	So school these days is easy? Think again
sentence stress	describing your dream house	people's dream houses song: *Our house*	Houses you'll never forget
/s/ or /z/?	talking about friendship things you used to do, have, etc.	interview about *Friends Reunited* people talking about friendship	Do you need to "edit your friends?"

		Grammar	Vocabulary

Pronunciation	Speaking	Listening	Reading
-ough and *-augh*	planning a new city	an expert talking about how to slow down in life	Slow down, you move too fast
sentence stress, *the*, /θ/ or /ð/?	topics men and women talk about men v women	two journalists talking about a spa song: *Sk8er Boi*	A gossip with the girls?
word stress	talking about work imagining doing other jobs	an interview with Jessica, the librarian	From librarian to political reporter… In a month!

Pronunciation	Speaking	Listening	Reading
consonant sounds: /g/, /dʒ/, /k/, /ʃ/, /tʃ/	shopping questionnaire talking about complaining	understanding a radio program about bad service	Making a complaint – is it worth it?
sentence stress	movie questionnaire	an interview about working with Steven Spielberg	Famous movies that moved us (literally!)
word stress	talking about a person you admire	a radio contest about heroes and icons song: *Holding out for a hero*	Heroes and icons of our time

Pronunciation	Speaking	Listening	Reading
sentence stress	How lucky are you?	the conclusions of stories about bad luck and good luck song: *Ironic*	Bad luck? Good luck? Can we make our own luck?
intonation in tag questions	a police interview roleplay	interview with a detective	Jack the Ripper – case closed?
review of sounds, linking	talking about TV habits	people talking about objects they couldn't live without	Couple turns on after 37 years without power.

What do intermediate students need?

The intermediate level is often a milestone for students: at this point, many students really begin to "take off" in terms of their ability to communicate. Some students, however, may see the intermediate level as a "plateau" and feel that they are no longer making the progress they were before. Students at this level need fresh challenges to help them realize how much they know and to make their passive knowledge active, together with a steady input of new language.

Grammar, Vocabulary, and Pronunciation

At any level, the basic tools students need to speak English with confidence are Grammar, Vocabulary, and Pronunciation (G, V, P). In *American English File 3* all three elements are given equal importance.

Each lesson has clearly stated grammar, vocabulary, and pronunciation aims. This keeps lessons focused and gives students concrete learning objectives and a sense of progress.

Grammar

Intermediate students need

- to review and extend their knowledge of the main grammatical structures.
- to practice using different tenses together.
- student-friendly reference material.

At this level, there is as much emphasis on consolidating and putting into practice known grammar as learning new structures. We have tried to review known grammar in fresh and stimulating contexts, and new structures are presented clearly and memorably. The **Grammar Banks**, at the back of the Student Book, give students a single, easy-to-access grammar reference section, with clear rules and example sentences, plus two practice exercises for each grammar point.
⬭ Student Book page 130.

The oral grammar practice exercise in the Student Book encourage students to use grammatical structures in controlled and freer contexts.

The photocopiable Grammar activities in the Teacher's Book can be used for practice in class or for self-study.
⬭ Teacher's Book page 140.

Vocabulary

Intermediate students need

- systematic expansion of topic-based lexical areas.
- to "build" new words by adding prefixes and suffixes.
- practice in pronouncing new lexis correctly.
- to put new vocabulary into practice.

Every lesson in *American English File 3* has a clear lexical aim. Many lessons are linked to the **Vocabulary Banks**, which help present and practice high-frequency, topic-based vocabulary in class and provide a clear reference bank designed to aid memorization. The stress in multisyllable words is clearly marked, and phonetic script is provided where necessary.
⬭ Student Book page 144.

Students can practice using the vocabulary from all the **Vocabulary Banks** in context with the MultiROM and the *American English File* Student Website. There is also a photocopiable activity to review the vocabulary from each File.
⬭ Teacher's Book page 195.

Pronunciation

Intermediate students need

- practice in pronouncing sounds and words clearly.
- to be aware of rules and patterns.
- to be able to understand the phonetic symbols in their dictionary.
- an awareness of word and sentence stress.

Clear *intelligible* pronunciation (not perfection) should be the goal of students at this level. Research shows that correct pronunciation of individual sounds and syllable stress plays a key role in effective oral communication. Pronunciation is given a great deal of importance in *American English File 3*, and every lesson has a pronunciation focus that often prepares students for a speaking activity.
⬭ Student Book page 10.

American English File has a unique system of sound pictures, which give clear example words to help students identify and produce the sounds. If your students have not used *American English File* before, the Teacher's Book provides clear guidance on how to introduce the sound pictures system.
⬭ Teacher's Book page 15.

The pronunciation focus is linked to the **Sound Bank**, a reference section where students can see and practice common sound–spelling patterns.
⬭ Student Book page 157.

Throughout the book, there is also a regular focus on word and sentence stress, where students are encouraged to copy the rhythm of English. This will help students pronounce new language with greater confidence.

Speaking

Intermediate students need

- topics that will motivate them to speak.
- the key words and phrases necessary to discuss a topic.
- to feel their pronunciation is clear and intelligible.
- practice in more extended speaking.
- time to organize their thoughts before speaking.

The ultimate aim of most students is to be able to *speak* English. Every lesson in *American English File 3* has a speaking activity where students get the chance to put into practice grammar, vocabulary, and pronunciation that has been worked on earlier in the lesson. Many of these activities have a planning stage and students are also encouraged to use some key phrases provided in **Useful language**.
⬭ Student Book page 71.

Photocopiable Communicative activities can be found in the Teacher's Book. These include pair and group activities, mingling activities, and games.
⬭ Teacher's Book page 169.

Listening

Intermediate students need

- interesting, integrated listening material.
- confidence-building, achievable tasks.
- practice in "getting the gist" and listening for detail.
- practice in dealing with authentic spoken language.

Listening is still a problem for many students at intermediate level, and *American English File 3* addresses this with motivating and integrated listening texts and tasks that are challenging in terms of speed, length, and language difficulty, but that are always achievable. Longer listenings are broken into separate parts with different tasks, to avoid memory overload. The Teacher's Book often suggests alternative ways of dealing with a listening, such as pausing and listening in sections. Students are exposed to a wide variety of accents, including some non-native speakers of English.
⊃ Student Book page 91.

American English File 3 also contains seven songs that we hope students will find enjoyable and motivating. For copyright reasons, five of these are cover versions.

Reading

Intermediate students need

- engaging topics and stimulating texts.
- exposure to a wide variety of authentic text types.
- challenging tasks that help them read better.

Many students need to read in English for their work or studies or will want to read for pleasure about their interests. Reading is also vital in helping to extend students' vocabulary and to consolidate grammar. The key to encouraging students to read **outside** class is to give them motivating material and tasks **in** class that help them develop their reading skills. In *American English File 3* reading texts have been adapted from a variety of real sources (newspapers, magazines, the Internet) and have been chosen for their intrinsic interest, which we hope will stimulate students to react and respond.
⊃ Student Book page 73.

The **Review & Check** sections include a more challenging text that helps students to measure their progress.
⊃ Student Book page 19.

Writing

Intermediate students need

- clear models.
- an awareness of register, structure, and fixed phrases.
- a focus on "micro" writing skills.

Worldwide, people are writing in English more than ever, largely because of the importance of e-mail and the Internet. *American English File 3* has one Writing lesson per File, where students study a model before doing a guided writing task themselves. These writing tasks focus on both electronic and "traditional" text types, and provide consolidation of grammar and lexis taught in the File.

There is also always a focus on a writing "micro skill", for example, punctuation, spelling, or connecting expressions.
⊃ Student Book page 97.

Practical English

Intermediate students need

- to consolidate and extend their knowledge of functional language.
- to know what to say in typical social situations.
- to get used to listening to faster, more colloquial speech.

Students will need to use English if they travel to an English-speaking country or if they are using English as a *lingua franca*. The seven *Practical English* lessons review and extend common situations (for example, introducing yourself and others, or making polite requests) and go on to introduce and practice the language for new situations (for example, expressing opinions or apologizing). These lessons also highlight other useful "Social English" phrases such as *I'm allergic to…* To help these everyday situations come alive, there is a story line involving two main characters, Mark (American) and Allie (British), that continues from *American English File 2*. Don't worry if you or your students haven't used the previous level – there is a summary of the story so far in the first episode.
⊃ Student Book page 16.

The Practical English lessons are also on the *American English File 3* Video, which teachers can use instead of the Class Audio CD for these lessons. The video will make the lessons more enjoyable and will help students to role-play the situations.

Extracts from the video (the first conversation from each lesson) are also on the MultiROM.

Review

Intermediate students need

- regular review.
- motivating reference and practice material.
- a sense of progress.

Intermediate students need to feel that they are increasing their knowledge and improving their skills. At the end of each File there is a **Review & Check** section. **What do you remember?** reviews the grammar, vocabulary and pronunciation of each File. **What can you do?** provides a series of skills-based challenges and helps students measure their progress in terms of competence. These pages are designed to be used flexibly according to the needs of your students.
⊃ Student Book page 18.

The photocopiable Communicative, Grammar, and Vocabulary activities also provide many opportunities for recycling.
⊃ Teacher's Book pages 138, 169, 195.

Study Link

The Study Link feature in *American English File 3* is designed to help you and your students use the course more effectively. It shows *what* resources are available, *where* they can be found, and *when* to use them.

The Student Book has these Study Link references:

- from the Practical English lessons ⊃ MultiROM.
- from the Grammar Bank ⊃ MultiROM and Website.
- from the Vocabulary Bank ⊃ MultiROM and Website.
- from the Sound Bank ⊃ MultiROM and Website.

These references lead students to extra activities and exercises that link with what they have just studied.

The Workbook has these Study Link references:

⊃ the Student Book Grammar and Vocabulary Banks.
⊃ the MultiROM.
⊃ the Student Website.

The Teacher's Book has Study Link references to remind you where there is extra material available to your students.

Student Book organization

The Student Book has seven Files. Each File is organized like this:

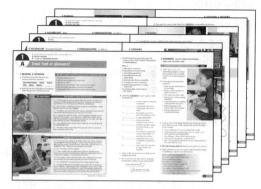

A, B, and C lessons Three four-page lessons that form the core material of the book. Each lesson presents and practices **Grammar** and **Vocabulary** and has a **Pronunciation** focus. There is a balance of reading and listening activities, and lots of opportunities for spoken practice. These lessons have clear references to the Grammar Bank, Vocabulary Bank, and Sound Bank at the back of the book.

Practical English One-page lessons that teach functional language (making suggestions, apologizing) and also social English (useful phrases like *Just a minute*). The lessons link with the *American English File 3* Video.

Writing One-page lessons that focus on different text types and writing "micro" skills, like punctuation and spelling.

Review & Check A two-page section – the left- and right-hand pages have different functions. The **What do you remember?** page reviews the **Grammar**, **Vocabulary**, and **Pronunciation** of each File. The **What can you do?** page provides **Reading**, **Listening**, and **Speaking** "Can you…?" challenges to show students what they can achieve.

The back of the book

In the back of the Student Book you'll find these three Banks of material:

Grammar Bank (pages 130–143)
Two pages for each File, divided into A–C to reflect the three main lessons. The left-hand page has the grammar rules and the right-hand page has two practice exercises for each lesson. Students are referred to the Grammar Bank when they do the grammar in each main A, B, and C lesson.

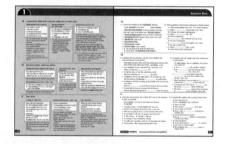

Vocabulary Bank (pages 144–155)
An active vocabulary resource to help students learn, practice, and review key words. Students are referred to the Vocabulary Bank from the main lessons.

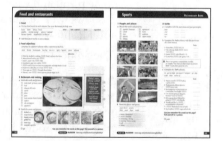

Sound Bank (pages 157–159) A three-page section with the *English File* sounds chart and typical spellings for all sounds. Students are referred to the Sound Bank from the main lessons.

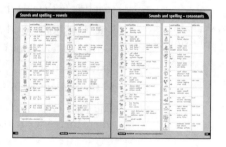

You'll also find:

- **Communication activities** (pages 116–121) Information gap activities and roleplays.
- **Audioscripts** (pages 122–129) Scripts of key listenings.
- **Irregular verbs** (page 156)

More for students

Workbook Each A–C lesson in the Student Book has a three-page section in the Workbook. This provides all the practice and review students need. Each section ends with:

- **More Words to Learn**, which reminds students of new vocabulary from the lesson that is not in the Vocabulary Bank.
- **Listening**, which gives students extra listening practice based on the theme of the lesson. The material is on the audio CD portion of the MultiROM.

Each **Practical English** lesson has a one-page section in the Workbook, and includes "Practical English reading."

MultiROM

The MultiROM has two functions:

- It's a CD-ROM, containing review of **Grammar, Vocabulary, Pronunciation, Practical English** (with extracts from the Video), and **Dictation** activities.
- It's an audio CD for students to use on a CD player or computer. It has the audio material for the Workbook listening activities.

Student Website

www.oup.com/elt/americanenglishfile/3

Extra learning resources, including:
- grammar activities
- vocabulary puzzles
- pronunciation games
- Practical English activities
- interactive games

More for teachers

Teacher's Book The Teacher's Book has detailed lesson plans for all the lessons. These include:

- an optional "books-closed" lead-in for every lesson.
- Extra idea suggestions for optional extra activities.
- Extra challenge suggestions for ways of exploiting the Student Book material in a more challenging way if you have a stronger class.
- Extra support suggestions for ways of adapting activities or exercises to make them more accessible for weaker students.

All lesson plans include keys and complete audioscripts. Extra activities are color-coded in green so you can see where you are at a glance when you're planning and teaching your classes.

You'll also find over 60 pages of photocopiable materials in the Teacher's Book:

Photocopiable Grammar activities see pages 138–161

There is a photocopiable Grammar activity for each A, B, and C lesson.

Photocopiable Communicative activities see pages 169–192

There is a photocopiable Communicative activity for each A, B, and C lesson.

Photocopiable Vocabulary activities see pages 195–202

There is a photocopiable Vocabulary activity for each File.

Photocopiable Song activities see pages 205–210

All the photocopiable material is accompanied by clear instructions and keys.

The Teacher's Book also includes the answer key for the workbook (see pages 211–220).

Video This is a unique "teaching video" that links with the Practical English lessons in the Student Book. The video has a story line that features Mark (American) and Allie (British). Each video section can be used with the tasks in the Student Book Practical English lessons as an alternative to using the Class Audio CD. It shows students language in clear contexts and will help them role-play each scene. Extracts of the video also appear on the MultiROM.

Class Audio CDs These three CDs contain all the listening materials for the Student Book.

Test Generator This CD-ROM includes over a thousand questions organized both in ready-to-print tests (in PDF format) and in question banks, where they can be selected and edited into tests customized to your students' needs. The CD-ROM also includes the audio for the listening sections of the tests.

Teacher Website

www.oup.com/elt/teacher/americanenglishfile

This gives you extra teaching resources, syllabus information, etc.

1
A

G present tenses: simple and continuous; action and non-action verbs
V food and restaurants
P /ʊ/ and /u/, understanding phonetics

Food: fuel or pleasure?

File 1 overview

This first File (**1A–1C**) focuses on the present, the past, and the future. The first lesson, **1A**, reviews the simple present and present continuous, and introduces the concept of action and non-action verbs. The second lesson, **1B**, brings together the three past (narrative) tenses, which were taught separately in the previous level of *American English File*. Finally, the third lesson, **1C**, contrasts the three future forms: *going to*, *will*, and the present continuous (for future).

Lesson plan

In this first lesson SS review the simple present and continuous. SS also learn to distinguish between action and non-action verbs (sometimes called static and dynamic verbs). This distinction will help them use other continuous forms correctly later. The topic of the lesson is food, first looking at different attitudes toward food around the world, and then at a British chef's experience of opening a restaurant in Chile. Pronunciation focuses on the difference between the /ʊ/ and /u/ sounds, and emphasizes the usefulness of knowing phonetics by showing SS how they can use their dictionary to find or check the pronunciation of "irregular" words.

If you would like to begin the first lesson without the book, there is a photocopiable "getting to know you" activity on pages 169 and 170 (instructions on page 162), and two photocopiable review grammar activities on pages 138 and 139 (key on page 136).

Optional lead-in (books closed)

- Write **FOREIGN RESTAURANTS** on the board. Then elicit from SS the different kinds of foreign restaurants in their town, e.g., *Italian*, *French*, etc. Write them on the board (eliciting the spelling from SS if you want to review the alphabet), and ask SS which they think are the most popular and why.
- Then ask them if they think food from their country is popular abroad, and if yes, which dishes in particular.

1 READING & SPEAKING

a ● Books open. Focus on the question and give SS a few minutes in pairs to think of some food and dishes. Make sure SS are clear about the difference between *food* (meat, fish, pasta, etc.) and *dishes* (beef stew, sushi, pizza, curry, etc.).

● Get responses from different pairs and write their ideas on the board. Accept all appropriate suggestions. You could also include drinks.

Some possible suggestions
The US: burger, apple pie; **China:** fried rice, noodles; **France:** cheese (e.g., Roquefort), pâté; **Italy:** pasta, pizza; **Japan:** sushi, seaweed; **Mexico:** fajita, chili con carne.

b ● Focus on the title of the lesson and elicit or explain the meaning of *fuel* in this context (= something that gives you energy) and *pleasure* (= something that makes you happy). Explain that they are going to read part of an article where women from different countries were interviewed about their attitudes toward food and diet.

● Now focus on the photos and ask SS to tell you what food they can see.

● Focus on questions 1–6, and make sure SS understand them, especially questions 5 and 6. Point out that *cut down* = eat less of something, and that *diet* in this context = the food people eat regularly. SS may already know the other meaning of *diet* = to eat less food in order to lose weight.

● Tell SS to read all Alice's answers once before trying to match them to questions 1–6 (by writing the numbers in the boxes). Then they do the same for Jacqueline. Remind SS of the importance of guessing the meaning of unknown words from context. Have SS compare their answers with a partner's and then check answers.

| Alice Freeman | A 6 | B 3 | C 4 | D 2 | E 5 | F 1 |
| Jacqueline Fabre | A 3 | B 5 | C 6 | D 4 | E 1 | F 2 |

c ● Focus on the task. Have SS read the article again and answer questions 1–9 with the correct initial. Check answers. You could encourage SS to justify their answers by referring to the article.

1 Both	6 Alice
2 Jacqueline	7 Both
3 Alice	8 Jacqueline
4 Jacqueline	9 Both
5 Jacqueline	

d ● Focus on the highlighted words and phrases, and the definitions 1–10. Give SS a few minutes to match them, individually or in pairs, and check answers. Model and drill pronunciation.

1 eat out	6 fat
2 honey /ˈhʌni/	7 dishes
3 servings	8 whole wheat
4 heat up	9 soup /sup/
5 takeout	10 stew /stu/

Extra support

You could go through the whole article with the class (with the paragraphs in order) clarifying the meaning of other new words and expressions.

Extra challenge

Put SS in pairs, **A** and **B**. Write questions 1–6 on the board and have SS close books. **A** then tells **B** from memory how Alice answered the questions, and **B** does the same for Jacqueline. Tell SS to answer in the third person. Monitor to make sure that SS remember to add -*s* to simple present verbs and to use *doesn't* for negatives.

e • Now ask the whole class whose diet they think is healthier and why. Accept all opinions but ask SS to justify them.

> This is a matter of opinion. Both have reasonably healthy diets, but Jacqueline's is more varied and she enjoys food more. On the other hand, Alice eats less fat and sugar.

f • Focus on the speech bubbles. SS now use questions 1–6 from **1b** to interview each other in pairs. Encourage them to ask for and give more information, e.g., if they don't cook, they should say why they don't, etc.

Extra idea

You could have SS interview you first. Show them by your answers how much detail you want them to give.

• Get responses from the whole class to see if they agree about question 6. In a multilingual class, compare what is happening in their countries.

2 GRAMMAR present tenses: simple and continuous; action and non-action verbs

a • **1.1** Focus on the photo of sushi and elicit from SS what it is (a Japanese dish of small cakes of cold rice often wrapped in seaweed and sometimes with raw fish). Ask them if they have ever tried it, etc.

• Explain that SS will hear Rumiko, a Japanese woman, answering questions 2–6 from the article.

• Tell SS that when they listen the first time they should not write anything but just try to get a general understanding of what Rumiko says and to decide if food is "fuel or pleasure" for her.

• Play the recording once. When the recording is finished, ask the whole class *Do you think food for her is fuel or pleasure?* Ask SS to justify their opinions.

> Probably more pleasure, as she likes cooking, enjoys eating out, and likes the variety of food and restaurants.

b • Now focus on the questions. Play the recording again, pausing between questions to give SS time to take notes of the answers (or to answer them orally with a partner). Play the recording one more time if necessary and then check answers.

> 1 Just a cup of coffee in the office. She doesn't get up early enough to have breakfast.
> 2 In sushi restaurants and ones that serve organic food.
> 3 She works late, her kitchen is too small, and her boyfriend is a better cook than she is.
> 4 She drinks a lot of coffee.
> 5 No, she doesn't need to because she has a healthy diet and exercises regularly.
> 6 She thinks it's getting worse, more westernized. As a result, people are getting fatter.
> 7 No, she doesn't. She likes the fact that there are more different kinds of restaurants and food / more variety when you eat out.

1.1 CD1 Track 2

(audioscript in Student Book on page 122)
I = interviewer, R = Rumiko
I Rumiko, what do you eat on a typical day?
R I don't usually have breakfast because I can't get up early enough to eat! I normally just buy coffee and drink it in the office.
   I usually have lunch in a restaurant near the office with people from work. When I was younger, I used to go to fast-food restaurants and have pizza, or fried chicken and French fries. Now I prefer eating something healthier, so I go to sushi restaurants or restaurants that serve organic food. And for dinner I eat out a lot, too.
I Do you ever cook?
R Well, I like to cook, but I work very late every day and also my kitchen's too small. My boyfriend's a better cook, anyway.
I Do you ever eat unhealthy food?
R Well, I don't eat a lot of sweet things but I drink a lot of coffee every day. I think I'm addicted to caffeine.
I Are you trying to cut down on anything right now?
R No. I eat healthily and I exercise regularly, so I don't think I need to cut down on food.
I Are people's diets in your country getting better or worse?
R Oh, probably worse. I think the diet in Japan today is much more westernized than before and that's why some people are getting fatter. But personally, I like the fact that there are more different kinds of food and restaurants now. I enjoy the variety, it makes eating out much more fun.

Extra support

If there's time, you could have SS listen again with the audioscript on page 122 so they can see exactly what they understood / didn't understand. Translate / explain any new words or phrases.

c • Focus on the instructions. Give SS a minute, in pairs, to choose the correct form. Check answers, having them explain why (in their L1 if necessary). For 2 and 5, they may simply "feel" that *prefer* and *like* are right without being able to explain why. This would be a good moment to explain about action and non-action verbs (see **Grammar notes** on page 14).

> 1 I don't usually have (It's a habitual action)
> 2 I prefer (non-action verb, not normally used in the continuous)
> 3 I drink (It's a habitual action)
> 4 people are getting (It's an action in progress at the moment)
> 5 I like (non-action verb, not normally used in the continuous)

d • Tell SS to go to **Grammar Bank 1A** on page 130. If your SS have not used the *American English File* series, explain that all the grammar rules and exercises are in this part of the book.

• Go through the examples and read the rules with the class.

Grammar notes

Simple present

- At this level SS should be clear about the form and use of the simple present.
- Remind SS of the difference in pronunciation of the third person -*s*, i.e., /s/ (verbs ending in an unvoiced consonant, e.g., *cooks, eats*), /z/ (verbs ending in a vowel sound or voiced consonant, e.g., *plays, has*), and /ɪz/ (verbs where you add -*es*, e.g., *watches, finishes*).
- Remind them too of the irregular pronunciation of (he / she / it) *says* /sɛz/ and *does* /dʌz/.

⚠ The simple present is also occasionally used to refer to the future, e.g., *The next train leaves at 7:30*. This use is not dealt with here.

Present continuous

- SS who don't have a continuous form in their language may need reminding that this is the form they must use when they are talking about actions in progress now.
- Remind SS of the other use of the present continuous for future arrangements. This will be reviewed fully together with the other future forms in **1C**.

Action / Non-action verbs

- We have called them action / non-action verbs as we think this helps to make the difference clearer for SS. There are several verbs, apart from *have*, which can be both action and non-action, e.g., *think* (**action** = mental activity; **non-action** = have an opinion) and also *see, look, feel*. At this level it may be best to use *have* as one clear example.

- Focus on the exercises for **1A** on page 131. SS do the exercises individually or in pairs. Check answers either after each exercise or after they have done both. Where relevant, have SS tell you why the wrong sentences are wrong.

> **a 1** They always have breakfast
> **2** She's taking a shower.
> **3** We need an answer
> **4** I'm studying a lot now
> **5** She doesn't eat
> **6** They are always late.
> **7** Are you going out
> **8** He never replies
> **9** It depends on the weather.
> **b 1** are you having
> **2** does he do
> **3** Are you going away
> **4** Do you want
> **5** is she cooking

- Tell SS to go back to the main lesson on page 5.

e • Focus on the question prompts. Elicit the questions from the class to make sure they use the right form and drill pronunciation, having SS copy the rhythm by stressing the "information" words.

> What do you usually have for breakfast?
> How many cups of coffee do you drink a day?
> Where do you usually have lunch?
> How often do you eat out a week?
> Do you prefer to eat at home or to eat out?
> Do you need to buy any food today?
> Are you hungry? Do you want something to eat?
> Are you currently taking any vitamins or food supplements?
> Are you currently trying to eat in a healthy way?

Extra support

You could write the full questions on the board and underline the stressed words to help SS get the rhythm right.

- Monitor as SS work in pairs, making sure they are using the simple present and present continuous correctly. The focus here should be on accurate practice of the grammar rather than on fluency.

3 VOCABULARY food and restaurants

a • Focus on the quiz. Quickly go through the questions, and then set a time limit of about five minutes for SS to answer in pairs.

Extra idea

You could divide the class into teams and make this a competition.

- Check answers and write them on the board, getting SS to spell some of the words.

> **Possible answers**
> **1 red** - apple / strawberry / cherry, **yellow** - banana / lemon / grapefruit, **green** - apple / pear / grapes
> **2** meat, fish, eggs, etc.
> **3** cheese, cream, yogurt, etc.
> **4** toast, bread, cereal, eggs, croissant, etc.
> **5** cookies, candy, fruit, potato chips, nuts, chocolate, etc.
> **6** lettuce, tomatoes, carrots, onions, beans, potatoes, etc.
> **7** plate, spoon, knife, fork, salt, pepper, tablecloth, olive oil, vinegar, glass, etc.

b • Tell SS to go to **Vocabulary Bank** *Food and restaurants* on page 144.
- Focus on section **1a Food**, and have SS do it in pairs. Check answers and model and drill pronunciation. Draw SS' attention to the fact that the phonetic transcription is given for words where the spelling–pronunciation relationship is unusual.

meat	fish / seafood	fruit	vegetables
duck	shrimp	peaches	beans
sausage	salmon	strawberries	lettuce

- Now do **1b**. Give SS time to add words. Then write the column headings on the board, and elicit words from SS. Drill pronunciation.

Extra idea

When you check answers to **1a**, copy the chart on the board. Then elicit SS' extra words (**b**) and write them on the board in the chart for other SS to copy any new words.

- Now get SS to do section **2 Food adjectives**. Correct answers.

1 Homemade	5 Take-out
2 spicy	6 low-fat
3 raw	7 fresh
4 frozen	8 sweet

- You may want to teach some opposites of *sweet* (*sour*, *salty*, *bitter*).
- Finally, have SS do section **3 Restaurants and cooking**, and check answers.

a 1 plate   2 fork   3 glass   4 salt and pepper
  5 napkin   6 knife   7 spoon   8 appetizers
  9 main courses   10 desserts
b 11 fried eggs   12 boiled rice   13 baked potatoes
  14 grilled fish   15 steamed vegetables
  16 roast chicken

- SS may ask what the difference is between *baked* and *roast*, as both mean cooked in the oven. *Roast* always means cooked with fat, and is used especially for meat and potatoes. *Baked* is used for bread, cakes and most sweet things, and also fruit or vegetables.
- Finally, focus on the instruction "Can you remember the words on this page? Test yourself or a partner."

Testing yourself

- For **Food** SS can cover the columns and try to remember the words in each category. For **Food adjectives** they can try to remember the adjectives by covering the **Adjective** column and reading the sentences. They can uncover, one by one, to check. For **Restaurants and cooking** they can cover the words and look at the pictures and try to remember the words.

Testing a partner

- Alternatively, SS can take turns testing each other. **B** closes the book and **A** defines or explains a word for **B** to try and remember, e.g., **A** *What do you call food that you buy at a restaurant and take home to eat?* **B** *Take-out food.* After a few minutes, SS can change roles.
- In a monolingual class, SS could also test each other by saying the word in their L1 for their partner to say in English.

Study Link SS can find more practice of these words and phrases on the MultiROM and on the *American English File 3* Website.

- Tell SS to go back to the main lesson on page 6.

c ● Here the words and phrases from the **Vocabulary Bank** are put into practice.
- Put SS into pairs, preferably face to face. Focus on the questions. SS take turns asking and answering the questions. The student who is asked a question should return it using *What / How about you?*
- Monitor and help with any new food words SS may want to use.
- If there's time, get some quick responses from the class.

Extra idea

You could have SS ask you the questions in **3c** first before asking each other.

4 PRONUNCIATION /ʊ/ and /u/, understanding phonetics

Pronunciation notes

There are two focuses here. First, SS work on distinguishing between two similar sounds and they look at the typical spellings for these sounds. Then there are exercises to show them how useful it is for them to be able to understand the phonetic transcription of words given in dictionaries.

a ● Focus on the sound pictures. If your SS are not familiar with them, explain that the sound pictures give a clear example of a word with the target sound and help them remember the pronunciation of the phonetic symbol (there is one for each of the sounds of American English).
- Elicit the two words (*bull* and *boot*) and point out the difference between the two sounds.

b ● Now focus on the words and give SS a few minutes, in pairs, to put them in the correct column. You could suggest that the best way is to practice saying each word with one sound and then with the other sound and see which sounds correct. Tell SS to be careful with double *o* words as this combination of letters is sometimes pronounced /ʊ/ and sometimes /u/.

Extra support

You could play the recording first for SS to hear the words <u>before</u> they try to put them in the correct column. You could also tell SS how many words go in each column.

c ● **1.2** Play the recording once for SS to check their answers. Then play it again, pausing after each word for SS to repeat.

1.2	CD1 Track 3
bull /ʊ/	boot /u/
cook	food
cookies	fruit
good	juice
sugar	mousse
	soup
	spoon

d ● Now tell SS to go to the **Sound Bank** on page 157. Explain that here they can find all the sounds and their symbols and also the typical spellings for these sounds plus some more irregular ones.
- Focus on *bull* and *boot*, and the different words and spellings. Point out again that SS have to be careful with words with double *o*, as some are pronounced /ʊ/ and others are pronounced /u/.

Study Link SS can find more practice of English sounds on the MultiROM and also on the *American English File 3* Website.

- Tell SS to go back to the main lesson on page 6.

e ● Now focus on the information box and read it with SS. Emphasize that understanding phonetic symbols means that they can check the pronunciation of new words in a dictionary, as well as their meaning.

f ● **1.3** Focus on the task. Tell SS to look at the phonetics, individually or in pairs, and to try and figure out the exact pronunciation of each word. They can look at the **Sound Bank** on page 157 to check the pronunciation of individual symbols.

● Before you play the recording, elicit from the class how they think each word is pronounced. Play the recording word by word, and have SS listen and repeat after the recording.

1.3	CD1 Track 4
1 knife fruit salmon	
2 sausage lettuce sugar	
3 yogurt menu diet	

Extra idea

Have SS cover the words and just look at the phonetics and practice saying the words.

g ● **1.4** Give SS a moment to read the six sentences. Then play the recording once all the way through for SS to hear them. Then play it again, pausing after each sentence for SS to repeat. Finally, have SS practice saying the sentences themselves (quietly) before asking individual SS to say them.

1.4	CD1 Track 5
1 The first course on the menu is lettuce soup.	
2 What vegetables would you like with your steak?	
3 Do you want yogurt or chocolate mousse for dessert?	
4 I take two spoonfuls of sugar in my coffee.	
5 Sausage isn't very good for you.	
6 Would you like some fruit juice?	

5 LISTENING

a ● Do this as an open class question and see what SS think. Give your opinion too!

b ● **1.5** Focus on the instructions and the photos. Tell SS that when they listen the first time, they should just try to get a general understanding of what Kevin says and to try to number the photos in the order that they are mentioned. When they listen the second time SS will be questioned more on details.

Extra support

Before you play the recording, you could pre-teach a few key words or phrases you think your SS might not know.

● Play the recording once for SS to number the photos 1–5. Check answers having SS tell you what each photo shows.

1 A Frederick's, Kevin's restaurant
2 C An English breakfast
3 E a trifle (typical English dessert, made with fruit, cake and cream)
4 B tennis at Wimbledon
5 D a restaurant kitchen (with only men working there)

c ● Focus on the questions and quickly go through them. Play the recording again. You could pause after each question is answered and give SS time to answer each question. When the recording is finished, have SS compare with a partner. You may need to play the recording (or part of it) again before checking answers.

1 Because he liked the country, and Chileans are open to new things.
2 Frederick is his father's name and his middle name.
3 Because they don't expect the English to be good cooks.
4 English breakfasts and desserts, e.g., trifle. They are all very popular.
5 One. Many reasons: women don't like the unsocial hours, and they don't like the atmosphere – there's a lot of shouting – and it's very hot.
6 The language.

Extra support

After checking answers, you could have SS listen again with the audioscript on page 122 so they can see exactly what they understood / didn't understand. Translate / explain any new words or phrases.

1.5	CD1 Track 6

(audioscript in Student Book on page 122)
I = interviewer, K = Kevin
I Kevin, why did you decide to open a restaurant in Chile?
K I'd always wanted to have my own restaurant. I'd visited Chile as a tourist and loved it, and I thought it would be a good place because Chileans are pretty open to new things, new ideas. So I opened Frederick's.
I Why did you call the restaurant Frederick's?
K Because Frederick's my father's name. It's my middle name, too.
I What kind of food do you serve?
K Mainly international dishes like pasta, steak and French fries, risotto – but we also serve several English dishes as well.
I Were Chilean people surprised when they heard that an English chef was going to open a restaurant here?
K Yes, they were – very! I think people don't usually expect the English to be good cooks.
I Is your chef English?
K No, he's Chilean – but I've taught him to make some English dishes.
I What kind of English dishes do you have on your menu?
K Well, we're open in the morning, so we serve traditional English breakfasts, eggs, sausage, toast, and so on, and then we have a lot of English desserts at lunchtime, for example, trifle – that's a popular English dessert made with fruit and cake and cream.
I Are the English dishes popular?
K Yes, especially the desserts and cakes. I think people here in Chile have a very sweet tooth.
I I hear that you've met a lot of famous people in your career as a chef.
K Yes, I used to cater for the tennis tournament at Wimbledon, and I've also worked for the royal family. I've met a lot of famous people who are very interesting, from every point of view.

> I You said earlier that your chef was a man. Do you have any women working in your kitchen?
>
> K Yes, one, but the rest are all men. In fact, I think that's typical all over the world – there are far more men than women in restaurant kitchens.
>
> I Why do you think that is?
>
> K I think there are a lot of reasons. The most important reason is probably the unsocial hours. Most women don't want a job where you have to work until late at night. Then there's the atmosphere. Women don't like being shouted at, and there's a lot of shouting in restaurant kitchens. It's also usually extremely hot and I think women don't like that either.
>
> I Do you think you'll stay in Chile?
>
> K Yes! I love Chile and its people, and the climate is perfect. The language is the most difficult thing for me, but the Chileans are very understanding.

d • Have SS answer the questions with a partner and then get their responses or simply ask the whole class. You could also tell them about the restaurants that you like.

6 SPEAKING

a • Tell SS that they are going to give their opinion about various topics related to food. Focus on the phrases in **Useful language**. Elicit / explain what they mean and drill the pronunciation.

• Focus on the instructions, and divide SS into groups of three if possible. Give them enough time to think of reasons and examples.

b • Monitor while SS are debating, and encourage them to use the phrases for agreeing and disagreeing. Don't overcorrect, but make a note of any errors that you may want to focus on when they finish speaking.

Extra support

Start by saying what you think about sentence 1, giving examples if you can, and then get SS to agree or disagree with you and say why.

Extra photocopiable activities

Grammar
present tenses: simple and continuous page 140
Communicative
A time for everything page 171 (instructions page 162)

HOMEWORK

Study Link **Workbook** pages 4–6

G past tenses: simple, continuous, perfect
V sports
P /ɔr/ and /ər/

If you really want to win, cheat

Lesson plan

In this lesson SS review past tenses. In *American English File 2* they learned the past continuous and the past perfect in separate lessons, so this is the first time they are brought together. The topic is sports, and the two angles are cheating in sports and what happens to athletes when they retire. The vocabulary focus is on words and phrases connected with sports, and the pronunciation focuses on two more sounds which SS often have problems with, /ɔr/ and /ər/.

Optional lead-in (books closed)

Ask SS what *to cheat* means, and elicit a translation / explanation (= to act in a dishonest way to get an advantage for yourself). Then elicit typical ways in which people cheat, e.g., on an exam or in a card game.

1 GRAMMAR past tenses: simple, continuous, perfect

a ● Books open. If you didn't do the lead-in, make sure SS understand the meaning of *cheating*. Then do this as an open class question and elicit sports and different ways of cheating, e.g., taking drugs.

b ● Focus on the photos and ask SS what they can see. Elicit / teach the word *sword* /sɔrd/ (in picture 3).
   ● Focus on the task, have SS read the article, and then ask the class to say how the three people cheated.

> Diego Maradona used his hand to score the winning goal.
> Fred Lorz traveled in somebody's car for part of the marathon.
> Boris Onischenko changed part of his sword; it turned on the "hit" light without his hitting his opponent.

   ● Elicit or explain / translate any vocabulary that is causing problems, and tell SS that they will be doing sports vocabulary later in the lesson.

c ● Focus on the highlighted verbs in the first text. Elicit that *was playing* is past continuous, *protested* is simple past, and *had scored* is past perfect.
   ● Then have SS underline an example of each tense in the other two texts. Check answers.

> **2 simple past:** won, finished, was, took, started, didn't win
> **past continuous:** was waiting, were cheering, was shouting
> **past perfect:** had traveled
> **3 simple past:** protested, said, examined, made, could, went, called
> **past continuous:** was competing, was winning, was showing, was scoring
> **past perfect:** had changed, hadn't hit

d ● Give SS time in pairs to match the tenses to the rules. Check answers.

> **1** simple past   **2** past continuous   **3** past perfect

e ● Tell SS to go to **Grammar Bank 1B** on page 130. Go through the examples and read the rules with the class.

Grammar notes

Simple past
   ● SS should be clear about the use of the simple past for completed past actions. However, they will probably need to review the irregular verbs, which are on page 156. Encourage SS to highlight the ones they find difficult to remember and to test themselves periodically.
   ● Remind SS of the different pronunciations of the *-ed* ending (regular verbs): /t/ (verbs ending in an unvoiced consonant, e.g., *looked, finished*), /d/ (verbs ending in a vowel sound or voiced consonant, e.g., *played, phoned*), and /ɪd/ (verbs ending in /t/ or /d/ + *-ed*, e.g., *protested, started, ended*).

Past continuous
   ● Remind SS that this is the past equivalent of the present continuous. It is used for actions in progress in the past that are often "interrupted by a short completed action" (simple past.), e.g., *I saw an accident when I was driving here this morning.*
   Sorry, we were watching a movie when you called and we didn't hear the phone.

Past perfect
   ● This tense was previewed in *American English File 2* but may be new for some of your SS. If so, you will need to make the form and use clear. We use the past perfect when we are talking in the past and we want to refer to an action that happened earlier, e.g., *When I got home I saw that somebody had broken the window* (i.e., the window was broken before I came home). Refer SS to the irregular past participles on page 156 as this tense requires the participle form.
   ⚠ It is important to point out to SS that in some cases the simple past or past perfect are both possible.

Using past tenses together
   ● Tell SS that these three tenses are often used together when we tell a story or anecdote in the past. Most verbs tend to be in the simple past (First, … Then …, etc.), but we often use the simple past in conjunction with either or both the past continuous and past perfect, e.g., *I got home late and my wife had already finished her dinner and was watching the news on TV.*

   ● Focus on the exercises in **1B** on page 131. SS do the exercises individually or in pairs. Check answers either after each exercise or after they have done both.

a 1 were watching
   2 had left
   3 had studied
   4 was driving
   5 had only had
b 1 did the accident happen, was driving, hit
   2 had already started, called
   3 took, went
   4 had finished, had gone
   5 lost, was talking

- Tell SS to go back to the main lesson on page 9.

f • Focus on the instructions. If necessary, let SS quickly read the texts again.
- Put SS in pairs and make sure they cover the texts. Give them a few minutes to remember and retell the stories between them using the three narrative tenses. Then have three different pairs tell their story.

Text 1: was playing, scored, protested, allowed, showed, had scored
Text 2: won, was waiting, were cheering, started, had traveled
Text 3: was competing, was winning, protested, examined, discovered, had changed

2 SPEAKING

a • Focus on the instructions and make sure SS understand they are going to tell a true story about something that happened to them.
- Give SS time to choose which story they are going to tell, and to plan it. Encourage them to think about the vocabulary they are going to need, especially verbs.
- Monitor and help SS with their planning and with any specific vocabulary.

Extra idea

Model the activity first by telling them a story of your own. Pause from time to time and encourage SS to ask you questions.

b • Put SS in pairs (or groups of three). Monitor while they are telling their stories but don't correct too much as the aim here is to encourage fluency, and SS are unlikely to use all the tenses perfectly.
- If SS are enjoying the activity (and you have time), you could have them change partners and tell their story again, or tell one of the other stories.

3 LISTENING

a • Either do this in pairs or as an open class question, eliciting disadvantages on the board. You could also ask SS if they can think of any advantages.

Possible disadvantages
Players and fans often insult them; people focus on the mistakes they make, not on the right decisions; they have to travel a lot, etc.

b • **1.6** Focus on the photo and the instructions. Give SS a few minutes to read the questions first. Then play the recording once. Have SS compare with a partner. Then check answers.

1 b 2 c 3 b 4 a 5 a 6 b 7 a

c • Play the recording again. Pause after each of the referee's answers, and tell SS in pairs to try to remember the question and as much detail as they can of his answer. Give them time to discuss this. Then elicit the interviewer's question and the referee's answer in as much detail as possible.
- Ask the whole class the last question. Encourage SS to give reasons to justify what they say.

Extra support

If there's time, you could have SS listen to the recording with the audioscript on page 122 so they can see exactly what they understood / didn't understand. Translate / explain any new words or phrases.

1.6   CD1 Track 7
(audioscript in Student Book on page 122)
I = interviewer, JA = Juan Antonio
I What was the most exciting game you refereed?
JA Oh, it's difficult to choose *one* game as the most exciting. I remember some of the Real Madrid–Barcelona games, for example, the first one I ever refereed. The atmosphere in the stadium was great. But really it's impossible to pick just one – there have been so many.
I Who was the best player you ever saw?
JA During my career I've met many great players. It's very difficult to say who was the best, but there's one player who stands out for me, not just for being a great soccer player but also for being a great human being, and that was the Brazilian international player Mauro Silva, who used to play here in Spain.
I What was the worst experience you ever had as a referee?
JA The worst? Well, that was something that happened very early in my career. I was only 16 and I was refereeing a game and the home team lost. After the game, I was attacked and injured by the players of the home team and by the spectators. After all these years I can still remember a mother who had a little baby in her arms and was trying to hit me. She was so angry with me that she nearly dropped her baby. That was my worst moment, and it nearly made me stop being a referee.
I Do you think that there's more cheating in soccer than in the past?
JA Yes, I think so.
I Why?
JA I think it's because there's so much money in soccer today that it has become much more important to win. Also, the game is much faster than it used to be, so it's more difficult for referees to detect cheating.
I How do soccer players cheat?
JA Oh, there are many ways, but for me the worst is what we call "simulation." Players pretend there has been a foul when there has been no foul at all. For example, sometimes a player falls down and says someone pushed him or hit him when, in fact, nobody has touched him. In my opinion, when a player does this, he's cheating not only the referee and the players of the other team, but also the

spectators. The spectators pay money to see a fair contest, not to watch people cheat!

I What's the most difficult thing about being a referee?

JA Ah, the most difficult thing is to make the right decisions during a game. It's difficult because you have to make decisions when everything's happening so quickly – soccer today is *very* fast. Also, important decisions often depend on the referee's *interpretation* of the rules. Things aren't black and white. And of course, making decisions would be much easier if players didn't cheat.

I So, in your opinion, fair play doesn't exist anymore.

JA No, I didn't mean that. I think fair play does exist – the players who cheat are still the exceptions.

4 VOCABULARY sports

a ● Focus on the quiz, and have SS do it in pairs or small groups. Set a time limit, e.g., two minutes. Check answers, making sure SS can say the numbers correctly.

> **1** 90 minutes (+ added time for stoppages).
> **2** Two.
> **3** Six.
> **4** Every four years.
> **5** 42.195 kilometers or 26 miles 385 yards.
> **6** Eighteen.
> **7** 400 meters.

b ● Tell SS to go to **Vocabulary Bank** *Sports* on page 145. Have SS do section **1 People and places** individually or in pairs. Check answers, and model and drill the pronunciation.

> **a 1** players **2** fans **3** referee **4** spectators
> **5** coach **6** team **7** captain **8** stadium
> **9** sports arena
> **b 1** court **2** field **3** pool **4** track **5** course
> **6** slope

● In **1a** point out that the *coach* is the non-playing person in charge of a sports team. He / She is in charge of training, tactics, and team selection.

In **1b** point out that you usually use both words to describe the place where you play a sport, e.g., *tennis court, soccer field*, etc.

● Then do the same for section **2 Verbs**.

⚠ Point out that in **b** and **c**, SS should write the verbs in the Verb column **not** in the shaded spaces in the sentence. By doing this they can later use the sentences to test their memory.

> **a** beat, beat, beaten   lose, lost, lost
> win, won, won   tie, tied, tied
> **b 1** beat **2** lost **3** tied **4** won
> **c 1** warm up **2** train **3** get injured **4** get in shape
> **5** score **6** go **7** play **8** do

● Finally, focus on the instruction "Can you remember the words on this page? Test yourself or a partner."

Testing yourself

For **People and places a** SS can cover the words and then look at the photos to try to remember the words. In **b** they can cover the words on the list and look at the sports to remember the places. In **Verbs** they can cover the past tense / past participle forms and the **Verb** columns and try to remember the verbs.

Testing a partner

See **Testing a partner** on page 15.

Study Link SS can find more practice of these words on the MultiROM and on the *American English File 3* Website.

● Tell SS to go back to the main lesson on page 10.

c ● In this activity, words from the **Vocabulary Bank** are put into practice. Focus on the instructions. Give SS a few minutes to answer the questions in pairs. Get responses from as many pairs as possible. Encourage SS to give you their information in sentences, e.g., *The team is Flamengo. They're a soccer team in the first division. They play in a stadium called…*

5 PRONUNCIATION /ɔr/ and /ər/

Pronunciation notes

The focus is on two sounds that are often mispronounced because of the sometimes irregular relationship between sound and spelling. The biggest problem is *-or*, which is sometimes /ɔr/ and sometimes /ər/.

a ● Focus on the sound pictures and elicit the words and sounds: *horse* /hɔrs/ and *bird* /bərd/.

● Give SS a few minutes to put the words in the right column. Warn them to be careful with the *-or* words, which may go in one column or the other.

b ● **1.7** Play the recording once for SS to check their answers. (See audioscript below.)

> | **1.7** | CD1 Track 8 |
> |---|---|
> | horse /ɔr/ | bird /ər/ |
> | shorts | were |
> | four | serve |
> | score | world |
> | sport | girl |
> | warm up | hurt |
> | court | shirt |
> | | worse |

c ● Tell SS to go to the **Sound Bank** on page 157. Go through the different spellings. Emphasize that *-or* is usually pronounced /ɔr/, but that there are a few very common words where it is pronounced /ər/, e.g., *world, work, word*, and *worse / worst*.

Study Link SS can find more practice of English sounds on the MultiROM and also on the *American English File 3* Website.

● Tell SS to go back to the main lesson on page 10.

d • **1.8** Focus on the sentences and give SS time to practice saying them individually or with their partner.

• Then elicit the first sentence from a student or SS and then play the same sentence on the recording to see if they said it correctly. Do the same for the rest of the sentences. Then, if necessary, use the recording for SS to listen and repeat.

1.8   CD1 Track 9

1 I got hurt when I caught the ball.
2 Her serve's worse than the other girl's.
3 It was a tie. The score was 4–4.
4 It's the worst sport in the world.
5 We warmed up on the court.
6 They wore red shirts and white shorts.

---

6 SPEAKING

• This topic-based speaking activity takes into account that not all SS are interested in sports! Focus on the instructions and the chart, and point out the two alternative "choices."

Extra support

Have SS interview you with the first few questions from whichever group you belong to. Elicit extra questions to show possible follow-up questions.

• Monitor while SS interview each other. Correct any pronunciation errors with the vocabulary they just learned, and help them with any new vocabulary they need. Make a note of any common mistakes, and if necessary, have a correction spot at the end of the activity.

• Get some responses from a few individual SS.

7 READING

a • Focus on the photos and captions, and elicit that they were all top athletes who have now retired.

• Focus on the questions, and explain *reach their "peak"* (= be at their best). Have SS ask and answer in pairs.

• Get responses and give SS information about what these people do now.

At time of going to press, **Michael Jordan** is in advertising and owns several businesses including his own clothing line and fragrance.
Muhammad Ali has Parkinson's disease, which doctors believe was caused by punches he received to the head. He still makes celebrity appearances.
Franz Beckenbauer is at present working on the committee that organizes the World Cup.
John McEnroe won seven "Grand Slam" titles. Since retiring from professional tennis in 1992, he has combined TV commentating with playing in "veteran" tournaments. In 2006 he made a comeback on the ATP doubles professional tour (and won the first tournament he played in).

---

b • Focus on the article and the instructions. Make sure SS understand the word *retire* (stop doing a job / sport because you are 65 / too old to play the sport).

• Give SS a few minutes to read the article once all the way through (without worrying about the meaning of individual words), and elicit that most professional athletes find it difficult to retire.

c • Go through sentences A–F to make sure SS understand them. Explain that *career*, in this context, is the time a person spends doing his / her job or field of work.

• Now explain that these are the first sentences from paragraphs 1–6. They tell you what each paragraph is about, and are known as "topic sentences." Tell SS that in order to match the "topic sentences" to their paragraphs, they must read each paragraph carefully to understand what it is about.

• Set a time limit for SS to read the text again and match the topic sentences to the right paragraphs.

• Have SS compare with a partner and then check answers.

---

1 F   **2** E   **3** C   **4** B   **5** A   **6** D

• Finally, go through each paragraph with the class and elicit / translate / explain the meaning of any new vocabulary.

d • Focus on the instructions. Tell SS to try to remember, or to guess, all the nouns, and then tell them to check their answers in the article. Elicit the answers, write them on the board, and have SS underline the stressed syllable in the multisyllable words. Then model and drill the pronunciation.

---

2 glamour	**5** failure
3 loss	**6** retirement
4 recognition	

• Finally, quickly test SS by having them cover the new words and then asking them, e.g., *What's the noun from depressed?*

e • If your class knows a lot about sports, have them do this in pairs. If not, do it as an open class question.

Extra photocopiable activities

Grammar
past tenses page 141
Communicative
What a cheater! page 172 (instructions page 162)

HOMEWORK

Study Link **Workbook** pages 7–9

G future forms: *going to*, present continuous, *will*
V family, personality
P prefixes and suffixes

1C

We are family

Lesson plan

In this lesson, the three most common future forms are contrasted. SS will have studied them all separately, but may not have had to discriminate between them. The lesson emphasizes that the future form you use normally depends on what the speaker wants to say, e.g., whether he / she wants to express a plan or pre-arranged event, or make an "instant" decision at that moment. The initial lesson context is the changing "shape" of the family and SS review and extend family vocabulary. From there they move to adjectives of personality, and the lesson ends with a listening exercise where a psychologist talks about how our personality is defined by our position in the family.

Optional lead-in (books closed)

- Review family words by doing this quiz with the class either orally or on the board.

  What do you call...
  1 your mother's brother? (my uncle)
  2 your father's sister? (my aunt)
  3 your aunt and uncle's children? (my cousins)
  4 your sister's son? (my nephew)
  5 your brother's daughter? (my niece)
  6 your wife's brother? (my brother-in-law)
  7 your husband's mother? (my mother-in-law)
  8 the person who was your wife? (my ex-wife)
- Make sure SS can pronounce and spell the words correctly.

1 VOCABULARY & SPEAKING family

a • Books open. Focus on the pictures and the question. Elicit answers and reasons from the whole class, but don't tell them if they are right yet. Then give them a minute to read the first paragraph of the article to check.

> The typical family of the future, according to the article, is the picture on the left. It is "long and thin" because families will have only one child, and people will live longer, so there will be more generations but fewer people in each.

b • SS now read the whole article and focus on the meaning of the highlighted words. When SS have matched the words and definitions, have them compare with a partner. Then check answers, and model and drill the pronunciation.

> 1 great-grandparents
> 2 an only child
> 3 single-parent families
> 4 cousins
> 5 in-laws
> 6 extended family
> 7 great-great-grandparents
> 8 half-brothers
> 9 stepmother
> 10 a couple

⚠ You may also want to teach *stepbrother / stepsister* (= the children of your stepmother / stepfather, but who don't have the same mother or father as you and are not blood relatives).

c • Put SS in pairs or groups of three. Now go through the seven predictions again, making sure SS are clear exactly what they mean. Then focus on questions 1–3 and explain that SS have to discuss each prediction using these questions.
  • Before SS start, focus on the phrases in **Useful language** and drill pronunciation, having SS underline the stressed words and syllables, e.g., I <u>think</u> so / I <u>don't</u> <u>think</u> <u>so</u> and <u>maybe</u> / <u>probably</u>.
  • Discuss the first prediction with the whole class, and find out if it is true now with younger SS, and if the class thinks it will be true in the future.
  • Now give SS time to discuss the other six predictions in pairs or small groups. Monitor and help where necessary and encourage SS to give reasons for their opinions.
  • Get responses from some pairs / groups.
⚠ Some of these predictions may refer to issues that are culturally sensitive for your SS, e.g., single-parent families or divorce.

2 GRAMMAR future forms

a • 🔊 **1.9** Focus on the instructions. Play the recording once and get responses from the class. You could pause after each conversation.

> 1 grandson / grandmother; they are talking about what he's going to do next year.
> 2 father / daughter; they are talking about what time she's going to come back.
> 3 mother / son; he is asking her if he can borrow her car.

b • Go through the sentences and check SS understand *crash* (= when a vehicle hits something, e.g., another vehicle). Make it clear that SS don't have to number sentences in order, but simply have to match two to each conversation.

Extra challenge

Have SS, in pairs, decide before they listen again which sentences are from which conversation.
Play the recording again. Check answers.

> A 1 B 3 C 1 D 2 E 3 F 2

1.9 CD1 Track 10

(audioscript in Student Book on page 122)

1 A So, what are you going to do next year, dear? Are you going to go to college?
   B No, Gran. I've already told you three times. I'm not going to college. I'm going to look for a job. I want to earn some money.
   A All right, dear, you don't need to shout. I'm not deaf. What time is it now?
   B Ten after five. I'll make you a cup of tea.
   A Oh yes, dear, that'd be very nice.
2 A See you tomorrow, then.
   B Hold on a minute. Where are you going?
   A Out. It's Friday night, remember?
   B What time are you coming back?
   A I'm not coming back. I'm staying at Mom's tonight.
   B I think you need a hat. It's going to be cold tonight.
   A Dad! Nobody wears hats anymore! Bye!
3 A Can I use your car tonight?
   B No.
   A Why not?
   B You'll crash it again.
   A I won't. I'll be really careful. I'll drive slowly. I promise.
   B OK. Here you are. But be careful.
   A Thanks. See you later.

c • Focus on the instructions. Make sure SS understand the words, especially *arrangement* (= something that will happen in the future where all the details, e.g., place / time, have been agreed). Check answers.

> **plan / intention:** C
> **arrangement:** D
> **prediction:** B, F
> **promise:** E
> **offer:** A

• From this, elicit from SS that generally speaking we use *going to* for plans and predictions, *will* / *won't* for predictions, offers and promises, and the present continuous for arrangements.

d • Tell SS to go to **Grammar Bank 1C** on page 130. Go through the examples and read the rules with the class.

Grammar notes

going to
• SS should be familiar with the form and meaning of this. The important thing to emphasize is that we use *going to* for things **we have already decided to do**, i.e., it is our plan or intention.
• *Going to* can also be used to express a prediction, e.g., *I think it's going to rain.*

Present continuous
• Emphasize that:
  – whenever we use the present continuous (for future arrangements, especially when a time / place has been agreed), *going to* is also possible. However, with the verbs *go, come, leave, meet, have* (dinner, etc.), we tend to use the present continuous.

will
Point out:
  – the use of *will* / *won't* for instant decisions at the moment of speaking, offers, and promises. A typical mistake here is to use the simple present for offers, e.g., ~~I carry your bag for you.~~
  – the use of *will* / *won't* for predictions, e.g., *I think it will rain. She won't come.*

• Remind SS that in spoken English *will* is almost always contracted to *'ll.*

⚠ For predictions, emphasize that *will* / *won't* and *going to* can both be used. However, when you can <u>see</u> that something is about to happen, it is more common to use *going to*, e.g., *He's **going to crash**.* (I can see him going toward a tree.)

• Focus on the exercises for **1C** on page 131. SS do the exercises individually or in pairs. Check answers either after each exercise or after they have done both.

> **a** 1 I'm going to study   5 I'll help
>   2 We're going   6 I'm meeting
>   3 ✓   7 I won't do
>   4 ✓   8 ✓
> **b** 1 I'll get
>   2 I'm going (to go)
>   3 we're having / we're going to have
>   4 I'll answer
>   5 She's having / She's going to have

Extra idea
Have SS read the conversations in **b** aloud to practice the rhythm.

• Tell SS to go back to the main lesson on page 13.

e • Focus on the instructions and go through the sentences. Elicit from SS the questions they need to ask (the first four are present continuous and the last four are *going to*), e.g., *Are you seeing a relative this weekend? / Are you having dinner with your family tonight? / Are you going to leave home in the near future? / Are you going to go on vacation with your family this year?* etc.

⚠ Make sure SS realize that they ask an affirmative question not a negative one for the second and last sentences.

• Now tell SS to stand up and move around the classroom asking their questions until they find someone who answers *yes* for each one, in which case they must ask for more details.
• Stop the activity and ask SS to sit down when one student has a name for all the questions, or when you think SS have had enough. Get responses.

Extra support
Drill the questions for SS to practice the rhythm. Elicit a few "extra information" questions for each one, e.g., (for the first one) *Who are you seeing? Where? Why?*, etc.

3 READING

a • Ask the whole class the question and elicit opinions.

b • Focus on the photos and the article, and stress that Wendy is the younger sister and Carnie is the older sister (you could write this on the board to remind SS).

• Now focus on the instructions. Then do the first one with the whole class. Ask them which of the two sisters they think had a more unusual hairstyle, the older (Carnie) or the younger (Wendy). If SS don't have any ideas, ask them which child they think is normally more of a rebel, the older or the younger one.

• SS continue predicting in pairs. Elicit answers from a few pairs, but don't tell them if they're right or wrong.

Extra support

If SS find it hard to predict or don't have many ideas, do this as a whole class activity before they read.

c • Now set a time limit for SS to read the article carefully to check and correct their answers. Tell them to underline the part of the text that gave them the answer.

1 C "she had bright red spiky hair."	
2 W "I always thought Carnie was really cool."	
3 C "I used to follow them, but she hated that."	
4 W "I desperately wanted to be with her."	
5 W "I sometimes think poor Wendy has spent all her life competing with me."	
6 C "I wasn't interested in studying."	
7 W "Wendy used to tell my parents."	
8 C "I used to pinch her and bite her."	
9 C "I was very jealous of Wendy."	
10 W "She always defended me."	

• Now ask SS if their predictions were right. Ask what things they think are typical in their relationship (e.g., Wendy always followed Carnie and friends, but Carnie didn't want her around) and what things they thought were surprising (e.g., Wendy always defended Carnie).

d • Focus on the instructions. Tell SS that they must try and guess the correct meaning by looking at the context. Do number 1 with the whole class. By reading the whole paragraph "*I desperately wanted to be with her and her friends...,*" it is clear that *cool* must be a positive adjective.

• Give SS a few minutes in pairs to choose the meaning of each word or phrase and then compare with their partner. Encourage them to give reasons for their choice.

• Check answers, and point out the pronunciation of *criticize* /ˈkrɪtəsaɪz/ and the adjective *close* /kloʊs/.

1 b	2 a	3 a	4 a	5 b	6 a	7 a	8 b

Extra support

You could go through the whole text with the class eliciting / explaining / translating any other new vocabulary.

e • Focus on the question. Then give SS a few minutes to discuss it in pairs, or you could discuss it with the whole class.

HOW WORDS WORK...

• This regular feature focuses on small grammar or vocabulary points that come out of a reading or listening. Go through the examples and then the rules.

• Emphasize that reflexive pronouns are made by adding *self* (or *selves* in the plural) to the possessive adjective (*my, your,* etc.). The exceptions are *himself* and *themselves*, where *self* and *selves* are added to the object pronouns.

⚠ You may want to teach SS the expression *by* + reflexive pronoun = alone, e.g., *I cooked it by myself.*

• Now focus on the exercise and give SS a minute or two to do it individually or in pairs. Check answers.

1 each other	4 each other
2 itself	5 each other
3 ourselves	6 myself

4 VOCABULARY personality

a • Focus on the instructions. If SS can't remember the adjectives, tell them to find them in the article about Wendy and Carnie. Check answers and the pronunciation of the adjectives.

1 talkative	3 shy
2 quiet /ˈkwaɪət/	4 jealous /ˈdʒɛləs/

• You could ask SS if they can remember which sister the adjectives go with (Wendy was quiet and shy, Carnie was jealous and talkative).

b • Tell SS to go to **Vocabulary Bank** *Personality* on page 146. Focus on section **1 What are they like?** and elicit / teach that the question *What's he / she like?* = What kind of personality does he / she have?

• Now give SS, in pairs, enough time to complete the sentences with the adjectives.

Extra support

Let SS use their dictionaries to help them with this section. Check answers and model and drill pronunciation.

2 Competitive	10 Independent
3 Selfish	11 Bossy
4 Aggressive	12 Affectionate
5 Charming	13 Reliable
6 Sensible	14 Sensitive
7 Sociable	15 Ambitious
8 Manipulative	16 Jealous
9 Moody	

⚠ Point out the difference between *sensible* and *sensitive* (these can cause difficulty in some languages).

• Now go through the adjectives again with the class. For each one ask SS if they think it's a positive, negative, or neutral characteristic. (You may not always agree, e.g., some people see ambitious as negative and some as positive.)

• Now focus on sections **2 Opposite adjectives** and **3 Negative prefixes**. Explain that with some adjectives of personality, the opposite is a completely different word, but for others you simply add a negative prefix. Then give SS time to do the exercises. Either correct answers after each section or after both.

2 clever – stupid
   generous – stingy
   insecure – self-confident
   lazy – hardworking
   quiet – talkative
   shy – outgoing
3 unfriendly, unimaginative, unkind, unreliable,
   unselfish, unsociable
   dishonest, disorganized
   impatient, irresponsible, insensitive

- Elicit that *un-* is by far the most common negative prefix. Explain also that *im-* is used before adjectives beginning with *p* or *m*, e.g., *impossible*, *immature*, and *ir-* before adjectives beginning with *r*, e.g., *irregular*.
- Finally, focus on the instruction "Can you remember the words on this page? Test yourself or a partner."

Testing yourself

For **What are they like?** SS can cover the list of adjectives 1–16 and read the definitions and try to remember the words. They uncover, one by one, to check. For **Opposite adjectives** SS can cover the words in the list and remember the opposite adjectives and for **Negative prefixes** they can cover the chart and look at the adjectives in the list to remember the prefixes.

Testing a partner

See **Testing a partner** on *page 15*.

Study Link SS can find more practice of these words on the MultiROM and on the *American English File 3* Website.

- Tell SS to go back to the main lesson on *page 15*.

c ● Tell SS to close their eyes and try to remember adjectives of personality they have just learned. Then tell them to open their eyes and write down the first three that come to mind.
- Now tell SS that in fact this is a personality test! This is what the adjectives they have chosen mean: the first adjective they wrote is how they see themselves, the second is how other people see them, and the third is what they are really like. (This activity is based on a real personality test.)

5 PRONUNCIATION prefixes and suffixes

a ● Focus on the adjectives, and elicit / explain that 1–4 are grouped according to their endings, and that 5 is adjectives with negative prefixes. Have SS, individually or in pairs, practice saying the adjectives and underline the stressed syllable. Do not check answers yet.

b ● **1.10** Play the recording once for SS to check and check answers. Drill the pronunciation.

1 <u>jea</u>lous am<u>bi</u>tious <u>gen</u>erous
2 <u>so</u>ciable re<u>li</u>able
3 re<u>spon</u>sible <u>sen</u>sible
4 com<u>pe</u>titive <u>tal</u>kative a<u>ggres</u>sive <u>sen</u>sitive
5 un<u>friend</u>ly inse<u>cure</u> im<u>pa</u>tient

1.10   CD1 Track 11

1 jealous   ambitious   generous
2 sociable   reliable
3 responsible   sensible
4 competitive   talkative   aggressive   sensitive
5 unfriendly   insecure   impatient

- Now play the recording again, pausing after each group for SS to repeat. Elicit that neither the endings (or suffixes) *-ous*, *-able*, etc. nor the prefixes (*un-*, *im-*, etc.) are stressed. You could point out the schwa sound in the endings *-ous* = /əs/, *-able* and *-ible* = /əbl/.

c ● Now give SS time to practice saying the adjectives correctly.

6 LISTENING & SPEAKING

a ● Focus on the question, and get a show of hands for each position in the family to create class statistics to see how many oldest children, etc., there are.

b ● **1.11** Focus on the instructions and the chart. Point out that they should listen for four more adjectives for each column, and that they will hear the recording at least twice.
- Play the recording once all the way through, pausing between sections if necessary.

c ● Have SS compare with a partner. Then play the recording again, pausing after each kind of child for SS to add to / check their answers and to listen for more details.
- Check answers, and ask SS for extra examples / information.

Oldest children	Middle children	Youngest children	Only children
self-confident	independent	charming	spoiled
ambitious	competitive	affectionate	selfish
responsible	sociable	relaxed	organized
bossy	jealous	lazy	responsible
aggressive	moody	manipulative	imaginative

1.11   CD1 Track 12

(audioscript in Student Book on page 122)
A = announcer, P = presenter, N = Norah

A   It's eight o'clock and time for *Breakfast Time*.
P   Good morning, everyone. Our guest this morning is the writer Norah Levy. Norah's here this week promoting her new book *We are family*, which is all about how our position in the family affects our personality. Welcome, Norah.
N   Thank you.
P   Now is this really true, Norah? That our position in the family affects our personality?
N   Sure. OK, other factors can influence your personality too, but your position in the family is definitely one of the strongest.
P   So tell us a little about the oldest child in a family – the firstborn.
N   Well, the oldest children get maximum attention from their parents and the result is that they're usually pretty self-confident people. They make good leaders. Did you know that fifty-two percent of the US presidents were firstborn children? Firstborn children are often ambitious and they're more likely to go to college than their

brothers or sisters. They often get the top jobs, too. Oldest children are often responsible people, because they often have to take care of their younger brothers or sisters. The downside of this is that sometimes this means that when they're older they worry a lot about things. They can also be a little bossy, or even aggressive, especially when they don't get what they want.

P What about the middle child?

N Well, middle children are usually independent and competitive.

P Competitive?

N Yes, because they have to fight with their brothers and sisters for their parents' attention. And they're usually sociable. They like being with people, probably because they've always had other children to play with. However, on the negative side, middle children are often jealous of their brothers and sisters, and they can be moody.

P And the youngest children?

N If you're the youngest in a family, you'll probably be very charming, very affectionate, and a pretty relaxed person. This is because parents are usually more relaxed when they have their last child. On the other hand, youngest children are often a little lazy. This is because they always have their older brothers and sisters to help them. And they can be pretty manipulative. They use their charm to get what they want.

P OK, that's all very interesting. Now, I'm an only child. People often have the idea that only children like me are spoiled. Is that true?

N Well, it's true in many cases! Only children are the only ones. They don't have to share with anyone, so they're often spoiled by their parents and their grandparents. As a result, they can be somewhat selfish. They think of themselves more than of other people.

P OK. Well, that sounds like a good description of me! Is there any good news?

N Oh, yes, there is. On the positive side, only children are usually very organized and responsible, and they can be very imaginative, too.

P Well, thank you, Norah, and good luck with the book. And now it's time for the news headlines…

Extra support

If there's time, you could have SS listen again with the audioscript on page 122 so they can see exactly what they understood / didn't understand. Translate / explain any new words or phrases.

d • Focus on the instructions. Demonstrate the activity by telling SS about yourself and someone in your family, and saying if the information is true for you or not.

• Then put SS in pairs and have them do the same. Monitor and help with vocabulary if necessary. Don't overcorrect but encourage SS to communicate.

• Get a few pairs to report back to the class, asking if they agree with what the psychologist said.

7 1.12 ♫ SONG We are family

This song was originally made famous in 1979 by the group Sister Sledge. If you want to do this song in class, use the photocopiable activity on page 205.

1.12 CD1 Track 13
We are family

Everyone can see we're together
As we walk on by
And we flock just like birds of a feather
I won't tell no lie
All of the people around us they say
"Can they be that close?"
Just let me state for the record
We're giving love in a family dose

We are family
I got all my sisters with me
We are family
Get up everybody, sing
We are family
I got all my sisters with me
We are family
Get up everybody, sing

Living life is fun and we've just begun
To get our share of this world's delights
High hopes we have for the future
And our goal's in sight
No we don't get depressed
Here's what we call our golden rule
Have faith in you and the things you do
You won't go wrong, oh no
This is our family jewel

We are family…, etc.

Study Link SS can find a dictation and a Grammar quiz on all the grammar from File 1 on the MultiROM and more grammar activities on the *American English File 3* Website.

Extra photocopiable activities

Grammar
future forms page 142
Communicative
Future questions page 173 (instructions page 163)
Vocabulary
Describing game page 195 (instructions page 193)
Song
We are family page 205 (instructions page 203

HOMEWORK

Study Link **Workbook** pages 10–12

Function Introducing people, meeting people again
Language *Let me introduce you to…, It's great to see you again,* etc.

Lesson plan

This is the first in a series of seven **Practical English** lessons where SS learn and practice functional language. There is a story line, which is a continuation of the story in the **Practical English** lessons in *American File 1* and *2*. However, the story can stand alone, so it is not a problem if your SS have not used these books previously. These lessons feature two main characters, Mark Ryder, an American, and Allie Gray, who is English. They both work for a music company, MTC.

In the first part of the lesson SS meet Allie, who gives a quick summary of how she met Mark and what happened between them. She explains that they are now going to be working together in the Paris office of MTC, where she will be Mark's boss. Mark is about to arrive for his first day in the office.

Study Link These lessons are on the *American File 3* Video, which can be used instead of the Class Audio CD for this lesson (see Introduction page 9). The main functional section of each episode (normally the first section, but in **File 1** the second section) is also on the MultiROM with additional activities.

Optional lead-in (books closed)

Introduce the lesson by giving SS the information in the first paragraph above. If all or some of your SS used *American File 2*, ask them if they remember Mark and Allie and elicit as much information about them as you can.

THE STORY SO FAR

1.13

- SS listen to Allie introducing herself and talking about how she and Mark met and what happened previously. Focus on the photos of Allie and Mark, and then on sentences 1–7.
- Play the recording once all the way through, and tell SS not to write anything, just to listen. Then play it again, pausing if necessary for SS to mark the sentences T or F. Have them compare answers with a partner before you check answers, and elicit why the F sentences are false.

1 F (a year ago)
2 T
3 F (They work for MTC.)
4 F (for a conference)
5 T
6 F (Allie is going to be Mark's boss.)
7 T

1.13 CD1 Track 14
(audioscript in Student Book on page 123)
ALLIE
My name's Allie Gray and I'm from Cambridge in England. I met Mark about a year ago. He's from San Francisco. We both work for MTC, a music company. I was working in the London office and he came there on business. We got on really well and we really liked each other.
Anyway, at the end of his trip, he invited me to go to a conference in San Francisco. We had a great time again. And then something amazing happened. When I was in San Francisco, I was offered a job in our new office in Paris.
When I told Mark, he told me that he was going to work in the Paris office, too!
There's just one little thing. His job is marketing director, but mine is managing director, so I'm going to be his boss. I've been in Paris for three weeks now, and I love it. Mark arrived from San Francisco yesterday. He's coming into the office this morning.

Extra support

Let SS listen again with the audioscript on page 123 so they can see exactly what they understood / didn't understand. Elicit / explain / translate any new words or phrases.

MEETING PEOPLE

a ● **1.14** Tell SS to cover the conversation with their hand or a piece of paper. Focus on the photos and tell them that the people all work in the Paris office. The SS are going to listen to them being introduced to Mark and they have to listen to find out what their jobs are.

Extra support

Before you play the recording, you could elicit / give possible jobs in a (music) company and write them on the board, making sure you include the jobs mentioned: managing director, sales director / head of sales, PR (public relations) director, marketing manager, personnel manager, secretary, designer, receptionist, personal assistant (PA), etc.

- Play the recording once all the way through. Then play it again, pausing after each person is introduced to give SS time to write their jobs in. Check answers.

Allie is the managing director.
Mark is the marketing director.
Nicole is Allie's personal assistant.
Jacques is the PR director.
Ben is the designer.

- Elicit also that Jacques and Nicole are French, and Ben is English.

b ● Now have SS uncover and look at the conversation. In pairs, they should read it and see if they can remember or guess the missing words. Stress that they shouldn't write the words in the conversation. Ideally, they should write in pencil in the margin.

c ● Play the recording again for them to check. Then go through the conversation line by line and check answers. Find out how many SS had guessed the words correctly. Where they had not guessed correctly, see if their alternative also fits.

1.14   CD1 Track 15

M = Mark, N = Nicole, A = Allie, J = Jacques, B = Ben
M **Hi**. I'm Mark Ryder.
N Ah, you're the new marketing director.
M That's right.
N I'm Nicole Delacroix. I'm Allie's personal assistant. **Welcome** to Paris!
M Thank you.
N I'll just tell Allie you're here. Allie? Mark Ryder's here. OK. You're from San Francisco, **aren't** you?
M Yes, I am.
A Hello, Mark.
M Allie! It's **good** to see you again. How are you?
A Very well. Did you have a good **journey**?
M Yes, fine, no problems.
A Let me **introduce** you to the team. You've **met** Nicole, my personal assistant?
M Yes, we've said hello.
A **This** is Jacques Lemaître, our PR director.
J How **do** you do?
M Mark Ryder. How do you do?
A And this is Ben Watts, our designer.
B Hi, Mark.
M Great to **meet** you, Ben.
B We've **heard** a lot about you.
M Really? All good, I hope.
A OK. Shall we go to my office?

---

d ● Now focus on the key phrases (highlighted in the conversation) and the task. Elicit / explain that *How do you do?* is the most formal way to greet someone when you shake hands with them at a first meeting. It is not a real question (it really means *nice to meet you*), and the normal response is to "echo" the question *How do you do?* (= nice to meet you too) or use another expression like *Pleased to meet you. How do you do?* is nowadays mostly used in formal (e.g., business) contexts. *Pleased / Nice / Good / Great to meet you* are very common ways of greeting people you have just met in a more informal context.

e ● **1.15** Play the recording, pausing after each highlighted phrase for students to repeat. Encourage them to copy the rhythm and intonation.

1.15   CD1 Track 16

M = Mark, N = Nicole, A = Allie, B = Ben
M Hi. I'm Mark Ryder.
N Welcome to Paris!
N You're from San Francisco, aren't you?
M It's good to see you again.
A Did you have a good journey?
A Let me introduce you to the team.
A You've met Nicole, my personal assistant?
A This is Jacques Lemaître, our PR director.
M How do you do?
M Great to meet you, Ben.
B We've heard a lot about you.

28

Extra support

You could have SS read the conversation in pairs to practice rhythm and intonation.

f ● Have SS stand up in pairs. Tell them they are going to move around introducing each other to other pairs. When they introduce their partner, they should say what his / her name is, what he / she does, and where he / she is from (make sure they know all this information about each other). A typical exchange (where Student A is Ana and Student B is Marco) would be:
Student **A** *Hello. This is Marco. / Let me introduce Marco. He's from Lima and he's in college. His major is biology.*
Students **C** and **D** *Nice to meet you.*
Student **B** *And this is Ana…*

Extra support

You could elicit this exchange and write it on the board so SS remember what they have to say.

● Encourage SS to use different phrases, e.g., *Great to meet you / We've heard a lot about you,* etc. and let the activity go on until each student has introduced his / her partner at least twice.

SOCIAL ENGLISH It's a secret

a ● **1.16** Focus on the photo and ask *Where do you think they are?* (Walking in Paris, by the Seine.) Then focus on the question and elicit ideas. Play the recording once all the way through and check the answer. Ask SS why they think Allie and Mark want to do this.

They want to keep their relationship a secret.

b ● Focus on the instructions. Go through the questions and then play the recording again. Have SS compare answers, and then play it one more time if necessary. Check answers, and elicit / explain the meaning of any words or expressions SS didn't understand, e.g., *weird* (= strange).

| 1 A | 2 B | 3 M | 4 B | 5 M | 6 M |

1.16   CD1 Track 17

(audioscript in Student Book on page 123)
M = Mark, A = Allie
A What a lovely view! The river's beautiful, isn't it?
M Paris is so romantic. I can't believe we're here together at last.
A Yes, it's weird.
M Weird? It's wonderful. I really missed you.
A Me too.
M Why don't we sit down?
A So, did you like the office?
M Yes, it's great. How do you get on with everyone?
A OK. But we'll see. I've only been here three weeks. What did you think of them?
M I thought Jacques was very nice, and Nicole…
A What about Nicole?
M She was very friendly.
A You know we have to keep things a secret.
M What things?

A You know, us. Our relationship. I don't want the people in the office to know we're together.

M No, of course not. But it isn't going to be easy.

A No, it isn't. How's the hotel?

M It's OK, I guess, but it's not like having my own place. I have to find an apartment.

A Don't worry. It won't take you long. What are you thinking?

M Do you really want to know? I was wondering what kind of a boss you'll be.

A Well, you'll find out tomorrow.

Extra support

Let SS listen one more time with the audioscript on page 123 so that they can see exactly what they understood / didn't understand. Help them with any new vocabulary or expressions.

c ● **1.17** Now focus on the USEFUL PHRASES. Give SS a moment to try to complete them, and then play the recording to check.

1.17   CD1 Track 18

M = Mark, A = Allie

M Why **don't** we sit down?

M I **have** to find an apartment.

A Don't worry. It won't **take** you long.

M I was **wondering** what kind of a boss you'll be.

A **Well**, you'll find out tomorrow.

Extra idea

Ask SS if they can remember who said each phrase (and in what context), e.g., Allie says *Don't worry. It won't take you long.* (about finding an apartment).

d ● Play the recording again, pausing for SS to repeat. In a monolingual class, elicit the equivalent expressions in SS' L1.

HOMEWORK

Study Link **Workbook** page 13

1
WRITING
DESCRIBING A PERSON

Lesson plan

This is the first of seven Writing lessons; there is one at the end of each File. In today's world of e-mail communication, being able to write in English is an important skill for many SS. We suggest that you go through the exercises in class, but assign the actual writing (the last activity) for homework, although SS may also want to do the planning in class.

In this lesson SS consolidate the language they have learned in **File 1** by writing an informal e-mail describing a friend.

a ● Focus on the two e-mails and the instructions. Set a time limit for SS to read them and answer the questions. Check answers.

> 1 Because a friend of Claudia's, Amanda, wants to stay in her house in New Jersey. Stephanie wants to know a little more about Amanda, and if Claudia thinks she would get along with Stephanie's family.
> 2 Yes, Claudia recommends Amanda.

b ● Now focus on the five underlined spelling mistakes and have SS correct them in pairs. Check answers by having SS spell the words correctly. Write them on the board.

> studying   friends   responsible   listening   usually

c ● Focus on the instructions. Give SS a few minutes to reread Claudia's e-mail and answer the questions. SS can do this orally or in writing. Check answers.

> 1 extroverted, sociable, hardworking, responsible, independent
> 2 going out, seeing movies, listening to music
> 3 She's a little messy, her English isn't very good

Extra idea

You could ask SS a few more comprehension question about Amanda, e.g., *How old is she? What does she do? What do you know about her family?*, etc.

d ● Focus on the chart and the highlighted expressions. Have SS fill it in, while you copy it on the board. Then check answers and write them in the right place.

Anna is	extremely very / really pretty a little	messy.

● Finally, focus on the **Useful language** box and go through the expressions.

WRITE an e-mail

Go through the instructions. Then either have SS plan and write the e-mail in class (set a time limit of 20 minutes) or have them just plan in class, or assign both the planning and writing for homework.

Before SS hand in their e-mails, have them exchange them with another student to read and check for mistakes.

Extra idea

If you decide to have SS do their planning in class, you could also get them to tell a partner about the friend they are going to write about, using the paragraph ideas 1–4 to help them.

REVIEW & CHECK

The File finishes with two pages of review. The first page, **What do you remember?**, reviews the grammar, vocabulary, and pronunciation. These exercises can be done individually or in pairs, in class or at home, depending on the needs of your SS and the class time available. If SS do them in class, check which SS are still having problems or any areas that need further review. The second page, **What can you do?**, presents SS with a series of skills-based challenges. First, there is a reading text (which is of a slightly higher level than those in the File) and two listening exercises. Finally, there is a speaking activity that measures SS' ability to use the language of the File orally. We suggest that you use some or all of these activities according to the needs of your class.

GRAMMAR

1 did you get	6 had changed
2 bought	7 'm meeting / 'm going to meet
3 Do you like	8 finish
4 hit	9 'll pick you up
5 was driving	10 'll love / 're going to love

VOCABULARY

a 1 seafood (not an adjective)
  2 fried (not a kind of meat)
  3 roast (a way of cooking – the others are cutlery)
  4 field (not a person but a place)
  5 beat (verb, not a place)
  6 affectionate (the others are adjectives with a negative meaning)
  7 moody (the others are adjectives with a positive meaning)
  8 family (it's a "group" – the others are individual members)
b 1 spicy 2 appetizer 3 tie 4 injured
  5 stepfather 6 selfish 7 stingy
c 1 for, out 2 for 3 up 4 along

PRONUNCIATION

a 1 course (/kɔrs/)
  2 food (It's /u/.)
  3 worse
  4 moody (It's /u/.)
  5 frozen (/ˈfroʊzn/)
b <u>me</u>nu, refe<u>ree</u>, im<u>pa</u>tient, <u>so</u>ciable, irre<u>spon</u>sible

CAN YOU **UNDERSTAND THIS TEXT?**

a 1 F **2** DS **3** T **4** T **5** F **6** F **7** DS **8** T
9 DS **10** T
b nutritionist = an expert on diet
rejects = doesn't want
solid = the opposite of liquid
craves = wants very much
choking = not being able to breathe because you have
something in your throat
in advance = before you do something

CAN YOU **UNDERSTAND THESE PEOPLE?**

a 1 b **2** b **3** c **4** a **5** c
b 1 Mark Reid **2** 040155 **3** Sunday **4** 6–7 **5** 5

1.18 CD1 Track 19

1 A I'm going to have some coffee. What do you want?
B I'll have some orange juice.
A What about Sally and Tim?
B Get them some orange juice, too. They said they were thirsty.
A Are you sure? I thought Sally wanted tea?
B No, she wanted something cold.
A OK, fine.

2 A Let's stop and have something to eat.
B I don't want anything to eat, but let's stop. I'd like some water and I need to use the restroom.
A Aren't you hungry? It's lunchtime – I'm starving.
B No, I really don't want anything.
A You're not on a diet, are you?
B No, but I'm not feeling 100 percent. It must be something I ate last night.

3 A It's a shame Robertson isn't still playing for us. He was much better than the players we have now.
B Yeah, he was amazing.
A What happened to him, do you know?
B He retired. I think he opened a restaurant.
A No, that was Gallagher. He opened a restaurant in Buffalo.
B Oh yeah, that's right. I remember now. Robertson's working as a coach in Tampa. With the junior team, the 16-year-olds.
A Oh really? Well, I think he'd be a good coach.

4 A Where are you going?
B Just for a run. I won't be long.
A Well, don't be late for lunch. Remember my mother's coming.
B Oh right. Anyone else or just your mother?
A Your sister's coming. Don't you remember?
B Oh yeah, that's right. I'm glad Ann's coming. I think she'll get along well with your mother. Do you need any help with lunch?
A I'm OK for now, but I will later. So don't be too long.
B OK, I'll be about 20 minutes.

5 A We have to get Olivia a present. It's her birthday next week.
B Why don't we just give her some money?
A Oh come on! that's so impersonal. It's her 21st birthday and she's our only granddaughter.
B Well, you choose something for her then.
A That's so typical. Then I have all the work of going and finding something.
B Well, then give her money, like I said before. We're not her generation. We don't know what kind of things she likes.
A Speak for yourself. I think I'll get her a sweater.
B Oh, she never wears sweaters.
A Oh, you're so helpful!

1.19 CD1 Track 20

A Hartford Sports Center. Good afternoon.
B Hello. I'd like to reserve a tennis court for Sunday, please.
A Are you a member?
B Yes, the name's Reid – R-E-I-D. Mark Reid.
A What's your membership number, please?
B It's 040155.
A OK, thanks. Here we are. A court for Sunday. Let's see. What time did you want it for?
B From eight to nine in the evening.
A Hmm... I'm afraid they're all full then. We have one from five to six or six to seven.
B Six to seven, then.
A OK, Mr. Reid, that's court number 5 reserved from six to seven.

G present perfect and simple past
V money, phrasal verbs
P saying numbers

2A Ka-ching!

File 2 overview

Lesson **2A** looks at money and numbers and reviews the most common uses of the present perfect and contrasts this tense with the simple past. **2B** introduces SS to the present perfect continuous, through the context of life changes. SS also learn how to use "strong" adjectives, e.g., *tiny, delicious*. In the final lesson of the file (**2C**), comparative and superlative adjectives and adverbs are reviewed and practiced, and the vocabulary of transportation is introduced through the contexts of comparing forms of traveling and road safety.

Lesson plan

In this lesson SS review the present perfect and the simple past and learn common words and phrases to talk about money. A song about today's money-obsessed society introduces some common words related to money, and a conversation where two people are arguing about money provides the context for the grammar review. In the second half of the lesson, SS read about a woman who has decided to live without money. Finally, they practice saying and understanding numbers, fractions, and percentages, etc.

Optional lead-in (books closed)

Put SS in pairs and give them three or four minutes to brainstorm some titles of pop songs that are about money. Write the titles of the songs on the board and for each one ask who sang it.

Some suggested titles: *Money* (Pink Floyd), *Money, Money, Money* (Abba), *Material Girl* (Madonna), *Can't buy me love* (The Beatles), *Money makes the world go round* (from *Cabaret*), *Money for nothing* (Dire Straits), *If I were a rich man* (from *Fiddler on the Roof*), etc.

1 VOCABULARY & LISTENING money

a ● **2.1** This song was originally recorded by the Canadian singer Shania Twain in 2002. For copyright reasons this is a cover version.

● Books open. Tell SS that they are going to listen to a song about money. Focus on the title (*Ka-ching!*) and tell SS that when they've heard the song they will know what it means.

● Now focus on the words in the list and ask SS which ones they know. Tell them not to worry about the words they don't know as they will focus on their meaning later, when they see them in context in the song.

● Play verse one and then pause the recording to give SS time to write in the missing words. Play the verse again if necessary. Then play the second verse and give SS time to try and write in the missing words. Check answers (marked in bold in the audioscript).

2.1   CD1 Track 21

We live in a [1] **greedy** little world
that teaches every little boy and girl
to [2] **earn** as much as they can possibly,
then turn around and spend it foolishly.
We've created us a [3] **credit card** mess
we [4] **spend** the money that we don't possess.
Our religion is to go and [5] **blow** it all,
so it's shopping every Sunday at the [6] **mall**.

All we ever want is more,
a lot more than we had before.
So take me to the nearest store. (Ka-ching!)
Can you hear it ring? (Ka-ching!)
It makes you want to sing. (Ka-ching!)
It's such a beautiful thing – Ka-ching!
(Ka-ching!) Lots of diamond rings, (Ka-ching!)
the happiness it brings, (Ka-ching!)
you'll live like a king,
with lots of money and things.

When you're [7] **broke** go and get a [8] **loan**.
Take out another [9] **mortgage** on your home,
consolidate so you can [10] **afford**
to go and spend some more when you get bored.

All we ever want is more, etc.

Ka-ching!

● Finally, ask SS what *Ka-ching* is. (It's the sound of a cash register.)

b ● Put SS into pairs. Tell them to look at words 1–10 in the song and try to match them to their definitions A–J. Emphasize that the words in parentheses (noun, verb, etc.) will help them make sure they choose the right word. Check answers. Model and drill the pronunciation of *mortgage* /ˈmɔrgɪdʒ/ and elicit that the *t* is silent.

A spend	F credit card
B loan	G earn
C afford	H greedy
D mall	I blow
E broke	J mortgage

c ● Give SS time to read the song and to understand it, and play the recording again. Help with any difficult words and phrases, e.g., *foolishly* (= not intelligently), *a mess* (= when everything is untidy, not in its place), *possess* (= own, have), *consolidate* (= put all your debts together).

● Now focus on the three summaries of the song. Explain / elicit the meaning of *obsessed* (= when you are obsessed with something you think about it all the time). Tell SS to choose what they think is the correct summary of the song. Check answers.

2

d ● Tell SS to go to **Vocabulary Bank** *Money* on page 147 and to do section **1 Verbs**. Emphasize that they will have to put some of the verbs into the past tense. Set a time limit and then check answers. Model and drill pronunciation.

1 inherited	**6** can't afford	**11** invested
2 save	**7** charged	**12** earn
3 borrowed	**8** took out	**13** is worth
4 lent	**9** cost	
5 waste	**10** owe	

● Now focus on section **2 Prepositions** and emphasize that SS must write the preposition in the preposition column, <u>not</u> in the shaded space in the sentence. (This is so they can test themselves later.) Check answers.

1 for	**2** back	**3** in, by	**4** on	**5** to	**6** from	**7** for

● Next, focus on section **3 Nouns** and give SS time to do the exercise. Check answers and model and drill the pronunciation of the words / phrases where necessary.

1 coin	**4** tax	**7** ATM
2 bill	**5** loan	
3 salary	**6** mortgage	

● Finally, focus on the instruction "Can you remember the words on this page? Test yourself or a partner."

Testing yourself

For **Verbs** SS can cover the list of verbs and the right-hand list of sentences and read sentences 1–13 to try to remember the verbs. They uncover, one by one, to check. For **Prepositions** they cover the **Preposition** column and read the fill-in-the-blank sentences and remember the prepositions. For **Nouns** they can cover the list and words 1–7 and try to remember the nouns.

Testing a partner

See **Testing a partner** on page 15.

Study Link SS can find more practice of these words on the MultiROM and on the *American English File 3* Website.

● Tell SS to go back to the main lesson on page 21.

2 GRAMMAR present perfect and simple past

a ● Put SS in pairs. Focus on the cartoon and conversation and give SS time to read the conversation and complete it with Ben's sentences. Tell SS that they have to guess Ben's last line.

b ● **2.2** Play the recording once for SS to check and correct their answers. Pause just before you get to the last line and elicit ideas from the class as to what Ben says.

2.2   CD1 Track 22

S = Shelley, B = Ben

S Is that a new camera?
B Yes. I bought it yesterday.
S What's wrong with our old camera?
B It's old.
S Old? How long have we had it? A year?
B We've had it for at least three years. Maybe longer.
S Three years? I'm sure we bought it last year. Look. We can't afford a new camera.
B Why not?

S Have you seen this?
B No. What is it?
S The gas bill. It arrived this morning. And we haven't paid the phone bill yet. Take it back to the store and get your money back.
B I can't.
S Why not?
B Because I've already used it.

---

c ● Focus on the instructions. Remind SS that the form of the present perfect is *have* + past participle. In pairs, give SS a couple of minutes to underline four examples of the present perfect and three of the simple past. Check answers and write the seven sentences on the board.

Present perfect	**Simple past**
How long have we had it?	I bought it yesterday.
We've had it for at least three years.	I'm sure we bought it last year.
Have you seen this?	It arrived this morning.
We haven't paid the phone bill yet.	

● Now tell SS to answer questions 1–4 in pairs. Tell them to look at the examples on the board to help them. Check answers using the examples on the board to exemplify the rules.

1 simple past (e.g., *We bought it last year.*)
2 present perfect (e.g., *We've had it for three years.*)
3 present perfect (e.g., *Have you seen this?*)
4 simple past (e.g., *It arrived this morning.*)

d ● Tell SS to go to **Grammar Bank 2A** on page 132. Read the examples and go through the rules with the class. Model and drill the example sentences.

Grammar notes

● In **Grammar Bank 2A** the main uses of the present perfect are pulled together and contrasted with the simple past. This is all review from Level 2, but it is the first time SS have compared the two tenses in such detail. If you know SS' L1, some careful use of L1 / L2 contrast could help here.

Simple past

● The most important point to emphasize is that when we use the simple past, **a specific time in the past** is mentioned, e.g., *Did you see the game last night?*, or understood between the speakers, e.g., *Did you see the game?* (We both know it was last night.) So, a question beginning *When...?* will normally be in the simple past.

● Typical mistakes: ~~Have you see the match last night?~~ ~~What time have you arrived?~~

Present perfect

● SS will need more help with the various uses of this tense.

● The most important point to emphasize is that we use this tense for a past action where no specific time is mentioned or understood, e.g., *I've been to Paris twice* or when there is a connection with the present, e.g., *I've worked here for two years.* (I'm still working here.) This second use is especially hard to remember for most nationalities, who would tend to use a present tense in their L1.

- Remind SS of the difference between *been* and *gone*.
  He's been to Berlin = He has visited Berlin and come back.
  He's gone to Berlin = He is in Berlin now.
- Typical mistakes: ~~I've been to Paris last year. I work here for two years.~~
- Refer SS to the **Irregular Verbs** list on page 156 and test them periodically on the past and participle forms.

- Focus on the exercises for **2A** on page 133. Have SS do exercise **a** individually or in pairs. Check answers. Then do the same for exercise **b**.

a 1 he hasn't arrived yet
 2 We haven't seen each other
 3 Have you ever written
 4 She's never been to
 5 I lent him $50
 6 I've known them for ten years
 7 What year did you graduate
 8 We have already been
 9 she hasn't replied yet
 10 They've lived in that house
b 1 have you been, started, lived, moved, 've lived
 2 Has your brother found, 's already started
 3 Have you ever been, went, was, cost

- Tell SS to go back to the main lesson on page 21.

3 SPEAKING

- This questionnaire practices the contrast between the simple past and present perfect and also provides an opportunity for free-speaking.
- Put SS in pairs and focus on the questionnaire and the example speech bubbles. Make sure SS understand *recently* and drill the pronunciation /ˈrisəntli/.
- Point out that the questions in the questionnaire are in the present perfect because they are asking about your whole life until now (*Have you ever..?*) or about the recent past but without specifying a day or time (*Have you .... recently?*).
- However, if the answer is "Yes" then the "follow-up" questions asking for more information should be in the simple past, because you are now referring to a specific time in the past, e.g., *When (did you lose your credit card)? What happened?*
- Elicit all the questions to check that SS remember the past participles that they need to use.
- You could either have one student ask all the questions and then SS change roles or SS can take turns asking each other a question and the same question can be repeated using *What about you?*
- Stop the activity when the time limit is up or if you think the activity is running down. If there's time, get SS to report and find out, e.g., how many people in the class have sold something on the Internet. However, don't let this stage go on too long.

Extra support

You could model the activity first by having SS choose a couple of questions to ask you and eliciting follow-up questions.

4 READING

a ● Focus on the three sentences and give SS a moment to choose the one that best describes their attitude to money. Find out with a show of hands the number of SS who have chosen each sentence.

b ● Now focus on the photo of Heidemarie and the questions. Elicit some suggestions from the class (e.g., because she doesn't want to work, she begs in the street, she steals from shops, etc.).
 ● Set SS a time limit to read the whole article once (e.g., three or four minutes). Then check answers.

She wants to prove that money is not important; what is important is what kind of person you are.
She does things for other people and in exchange they give her what she needs to live.

c ● Now tell SS to read the article again. When they have finished, they answer questions 1–8 either in pairs or individually. Check answers. Elicit / explain the meaning of *house-sit* (= look after another person's house while they are away, like babysit).

1 She was a psychotherapist.
2 Some clothes and a few personal belongings.
3 She set up a "swapping circle."
4 First she house-sat, now she lives in a student residence.
5 Yes, but she doesn't get paid.
6 She asks friends or she does something for someone.
7 That all jobs are equally important and that we shouldn't judge people according to how much they earn.
8 She gave it away.

d ● SS now focus on the highlighted phrasal verbs, which they have to match to the dictionary definitions 2–4. Stress that although the verbs are in different tenses in the article, they should write them next to the definitions in the base form. Check answers.

2 turn up **3** give away **4** set up

e ● In pairs, SS answer the questions. Then have SS report their opinions to the class and try to find out what the class as a whole thinks about each question.

5 VOCABULARY & PRONUNCIATION
saying numbers

Pronunciation notes

Even though SS should already "know" numbers 1–1,000, this is an area where plenty of practice is always needed as it is never easy to understand and say numbers in a foreign language. Native speakers sometimes mishear the *thirteen / thirty* difference and ask for clarification.

a ● **2.3** Have SS write the missing numbers (in figures). Check answers by writing the numbers on the board in two columns to reflect the exercise.

15	750	75,000	1,000,000
50	1,500	750,000	7,500,000
100	7,500		

- Elicit from the class how each number is pronounced before playing the recording and pausing before the next one.
- Point out:
  - the difference in stress between *fifteen* and *fifty* (*sixteen* / *sixty*, etc.) and the use and unstressed pronunciation of *and* /n/ in *seven hundred and fifty*.
  - that after a number we say *million*, not *millions*, e.g., *seven million, ten million*, etc.

2.3	CD1 Track 23

fifteen
fifty
a hundred/one hundred
seven hundred and fifty
one thousand five hundred
seven thousand five hundred
seventy-five thousand
seven hundred and fifty thousand
a million/one million
seven and a half million

- Now have SS practice saying the numbers themselves.

b • **2.4** Focus on the task. Have SS try to fill in the blanks and let them compare answers with a partner. Then play the recording for SS to check / correct their answers. Finally, check answers by writing the missing words on the board (see **bold** words in audioscript below).
- Point out:
  - with prices, e.g., $8.99, we usually say *eight ninety-nine*.
  - the use and pronunciation of *percent* to express percentages.
  - the use of . (= point) in decimals.
  - the use of the indefinite article with fractions, e.g., *a half*.
- Give SS more practice by letting them repeat after the recording and by testing each other (**A** points at a figure and **B** says it, and vice versa).

2.4	CD1 Track 24

two **fifty** · **seven point** three five
eight **euros** and · a **half**/one **half**
  ninety-nine cents · a **third**/one **third**
three **pounds twenty** · a **quarter**/one **quarter**
fifty **percent** · three **fourths**/three
zero **point** five · **quarters**
three point nine · six **and** a half

c • Focus attention on the numbers and have SS practice saying them in pairs before asking individual SS for answers or letting all SS call the numbers out.

6 LISTENING & SPEAKING

a • **2.5** Here SS listen to a news bulletin that features a whole range of numbers.
- Focus on the task. Play the recording the first time for SS to simply count the number of news items and get a very general understanding of the bulletin.

There are four (a road accident, a protest by transit workers, unemployment figures, house prices).

Extra challenge
Have SS also say briefly what each news item is about.

b • Focus on the questions and give SS time to read them. Then play the recording again, this time in sections (item by item), and have SS answer the two questions on each item. Play the recording (or parts of it) again if necessary. Then check answers.

1	17	5	138,000
2	85 mph (miles an hour)	6	6.9 million
3	hundreds	7	a third
4	8.5%	8	$226,000

Extra support
If there's time, you could have SS listen to the recording with the audioscript on page 123 so they can see exactly what they understood / didn't understand. Translate / explain any new words or phrases.

2.5	CD1 Track 25

(audioscript in Student Book on page 123)
Good evening. I'm Rafael Perez with the six o'clock news. At least 17 people have been injured in an accident on the freeway near San Francisco. The police said that the truck that caused the accident was traveling at about 85 miles an hour, well over the 65-mile-an-hour speed limit. Meanwhile, hundreds of transit workers have walked off the job in protest against the transit authority's pay offer. The unions have asked for a raise of 8.5 percent over two years. There will be a meeting between their leaders and city officials later today.
Just released, the latest unemployment figures show that the total number of unemployed people, 6.9 million, is essentially unchanged this month. Over the year unemployment has gone up slightly from 4.6 to 4.8 percent, which means 138,000 more unemployed for the year. The secretary of labor says some of this increase has been caused by the shutdown of auto plants in the Midwest.
In real estate, agents are predicting that housing prices will continue to go up this year, making it extremely difficult for first time buyers to get into the housing market. It's estimated that house prices have increased by one third over the last five years. The average price of a single-family home in the US is now about $226,000. And, now the weekend weather report...

c • Either do this in pairs and then get answers from the whole class, or do it as a whole class activity and try to reach agreement on each figure.

Extra photocopiable activities

Grammar
present perfect and simple past page 143
Communicative
Numbers quiz page 174 (instructions page 163)

HOMEWORK

Study Link Workbook pages 14–16

35

2
B Changing your life

G present perfect continuous
V strong adjectives: *exhausted*, *amazed*, etc.
P sentence stress, strong adjectives

Lesson plan

People changing their lives through travel provides the context for introducing SS to the present perfect continuous (with *for* and *since*). They listen to a woman who took a year off from teaching to study art in Ecuador, and they read about two other women whose lives were changed forever by a vacation. The vocabulary focus is on using strong adjectives, like *furious* and *exhausted*, and the pronunciation focuses on sentence stress. At the end of the lesson SS learn a second use of the present perfect continuous to talk about recently finished actions, e.g., *"What have you been doing? You look exhausted." "I've been taking tests all day."*

Optional lead-in (Books closed)

- Ask the class if they know any foreigners living in their country.
- Then ask how long they have lived there and how well they speak the language.
- Finally, ask if they have any problems and what they are (e.g., adapting to different customs, food, etc.).

1 LISTENING

a ● Books open. Put SS in pairs and have them quickly discuss the three questions before asking the whole class for their ideas.

b ● Focus on the photos and have SS read the three lines about Angela. Elicit / explain that *took a year off* = stopped working for a year. Then have SS say what they can see in each photo.

c ● **2.6** Tell SS that they are going to listen to Angela talking about her life in Ecuador. Before SS listen, focus on questions 1–7 and make sure SS understand them.

- Focus on the questions. Then play the recording once, but tell SS just to listen.

d ● Give SS a few minutes to compare with a partner what they have understood so far. Then play the recording again for them to try to understand more details. Play all (or part of) the recording again if necessary. Check answers.

1 Because she has always been interested in the culture and language of Latin America.
2 She wanted a break from teaching and she wanted to study the art of the Andean countries.
3 At the university.
4 Listening.
5 They're happy to find that a foreigner loves the Ecuadorian culture and wants to learn about it.
6 It's a great way to meet people and earn money to pay for classes.
7 The people – their hospitality is amazing.

Extra support

If there's time, you could play the recording again while SS read the audioscript on page 123 so they can see what they understood / didn't understand. Translate / explain any new words or phrases.

2.6 CD1 Track 26

(audioscript in Student Book on page 123)
I = interviewer, A = Angela
I So, how long have you been living here?
A For about six months now.
I Why did you choose Ecuador?
A Because I have always been interested in the culture and language of Latin America.
I Why did you want to take a year off?
A Basically I wanted a break from teaching. I love teaching children but I needed a change. Also, I've been drawing and painting since I was a child and I took art classes in college. I've always wanted an opportunity to study the art of the Andean countries, such as Peru and Ecuador.
I What have you been doing here since you arrived?
A Well, I've been taking some art classes at the university and getting to know some of the local artists. Luckily, many of them speak a little English, as I don't know much Spanish yet. But I am learning the language as quickly as I can.
I Is Spanish a difficult language to learn?
A Not really. A lot of words are similar in English and Spanish. Listening is probably the most difficult thing for me. I often have to ask people to repeat things more slowly.
I Are the other students in your classes helpful when you don't understand something?
A Yes, very. I think they're happy to find that a foreigner loves the Ecuadorian culture and wants to learn about it.
I You also teach English?
A I've been teaching for about three months now. It's a great way to meet people and of course earn a little money to pay for my classes!
I What's the best thing about living in Ecuador so far?
A The people! The hospitality of the people here is absolutely amazing.

---

2 GRAMMAR present perfect continuous with *for / since*

a ● **2.7** Focus on the task and play the extracts from the interview with Angela twice. Check answers.

1 living 2 drawing, painting 3 doing
4 taking 5 teaching

2.7   CD1 Track 27

2.7   CD1 Track 27
1 So, how long have you been living here?
2 Also, I've been drawing and painting since I was a child and I took art classes in college.
3 What have you been doing here since you arrived?
4 Well, I've been taking some art classes at the university and getting to know some of the local artists.
5 I've been teaching for about three months now.

b ● Have SS look at sentences 1–5 and answer the three questions. You could do this as a whole class activity. Check answers.

1 action verbs
2 continuous / repeated actions
3 one that is still happening

c ● Tell SS to go to **Grammar Bank 2B** on page 132. Go through the examples and rules for the present perfect continuous *for unfinished actions*. (NOT recent continuous actions). The second half of the grammar will be dealt with in the second part of the lesson.

Grammar notes

Present perfect continuous (with *How long...?* and *for / since*)

● For many SS, including those who used *American English File* before, this will be the first time they have seen the present perfect continuous.

● Point out to SS that in the same way that there is a "simple" and "continuous" form of the present and the past, there are also two forms of the present perfect (simple and continuous).

● The most important difference between the two forms for SS at this point is that with *How long…?* and *for / since* we normally use the continuous form with action verbs (e.g., *learn, go, play, do, wait,* etc.) and the simple form is used with non-action verbs (e.g., *be, have, know*).

⚠ Two common verbs that can be used in either form are *live* and *work*.

● Some typical mistakes:
  – getting the form wrong, e.g., forgetting to include *been*: ~~How long have you learning English?~~
  – depending on their L1, some SS may try to use the present tense instead of the present perfect continuous, e.g., ~~I am learning English for a long time.~~
  – using the continuous form of the present perfect with non-action verbs, e.g., ~~I've been knowing my best friend for fifteen years.~~
  – confusing *for* and *since*.

● Elicit that *'ve* = have and *'s* = has.

● Now get SS to do exercise **a** only on page 133 (not **b**, which they will do later in the lesson) individually or in pairs. They will need to write the sentences in a notebook. Then check answers.

a 1 How long have they been going out together?
2 I've been studying English for two years.
3 He hasn't been feeling very well recently.
4 You've been reading that book for months!
5 Have you been waiting (for) a long time?
6 We haven't been spending much time together.
7 How long has she been living there?
8 I've been renting this house for three years.
9 The elevator hasn't been working since 10 o'clock.
10 Has she been working here (for) a long time?

● Tell SS to go back to the main lesson on page 25.

3 PRONUNCIATION sentence stress

Focus on the information box, which reminds SS about this basic rule regarding stress patterns in English.

Pronunciation notes

As SS should already know, in English, words that are stressed more strongly are the ones that carry information, e.g., I WENT to the MOVIES on FRIDAY NIGHT. These are typically verbs, nouns, adjectives, and adverbs. The other "non-information" words (e.g., personal pronouns, articles, and small words like *to, of, on, as,* etc.) are pronounced less strongly, and these words often get shortened when we speak, e.g., *the* becomes /ðə/. It is this mixture of stressed and unstressed words that gives English its rhythm and SS need plenty of practice until correct stress and rhythm becomes instinctive.

a ● **2.8** Tell SS that they are going to hear a dictation of five present perfect continuous sentences. The first time they listen, they should try to write down any words they hear (these will probably be the stressed information words). Then they look at the words they have and try to remember or guess what the complete sentence is. The second time they listen, they try to fill in any blanks they have. These will probably be unstressed words. Play the recording again if necessary. Check answers and write the sentences on the board.

2.8   CD1 Track 28
1 I've been studying English for six years.
2 Have they been living in Korea for a long time?
3 How long has your brother been working for that company?
4 How long have you been teaching Spanish?
5 My husband hasn't been sleeping very well recently.

b ● **2.9** Play the recording for SS to listen and repeat, copying the rhythm. Encourage them to pronounce the stressed (underlined) words more strongly and not to stress the other words.

B

2.9 CD1 Track 29

1 I've been <u>living here</u> for <u>two years</u>.
2 <u>How long</u> have you been <u>learning English</u>?
3 She's been <u>working</u> in <u>Italy</u> since <u>October</u>.
4 <u>How long</u> have you been <u>waiting</u>?
5 It's been <u>raining all night</u>.
6 We've been <u>looking</u> for a <u>an apartment</u> for <u>ages</u>.

4 SPEAKING

In this speaking activity, SS practice using both the present perfect simple and continuous.

a ● Focus on the instructions and give SS time to write true information (e.g., *tennis* in the first circle) in as many of the circles as they can. Go around the class making sure they have completed at least six of the circles.

b ● Focus on the instructions and the ⚠ box. Emphasize that they should make the *How long…?* questions using the bold verbs. With an action verb, e.g., *play*, *do*, etc., they should use the present perfect continuous. With non-action verbs, they should use the present perfect simple, e.g., *How long have you known your best friend?* NOT ~~How long have you been knowing…~~

● Remind SS that with the verb *live* you can use either of the present perfect forms.

Extra support

Go through the circles before you start and elicit whether the verbs are action or non-action and the question that SS should ask in each case. You could demonstrate the activity yourself by copying a couple of circles on the board (one with an action verb, the other with a non-action verb) and writing something true in them. Then the class could ask you three questions about each one.

● Put SS in pairs. Focus on the speech bubbles. SS now compare their information and take turns choosing one of their partner's circles and asking him / her about the information in it. Remind them that one question must be *How long…?*

● Monitor and help or take part yourself if there is an odd number of SS.

● Bring the activity to a close before it starts running down. If there's time, get one person in each pair to report an interesting piece of information about their partner.

5 READING

a ● Focus on the question and elicit ideas, e.g., a vacation could relax you and make you feel happier, you could meet someone who becomes a good friend, a vacation could make you decide to go and live in the place where you had the vacation, etc.

b ● Focus on the task and go through the instructions. Then either read the introduction out loud or have SS read it.

● Put SS in pairs, **A** and **B**. Set a time limit for SS to read their text (e.g., three or four minutes). Tell them not to worry about unknown words at this stage.

c ● SS now take turns telling their partner about the woman in their text using the four questions as a guide. Monitor and help SS.

Victoria
1 She's working at Monkey World (which takes care of apes that have been mistreated).
2 She was working as a manager at a chain store.
3 She went on a working vacation in Borneo. She worked with apes and enjoyed it. When she came back, she found it difficult to return to her old life. She decided to go back to college to study biology.
4 She's really happy now. She feels that she's doing something important, not wasting her life.

Sally
1 She's living on the Greek island of Lipsi.
2 She was living in London, working for a large financial services company. She had a good salary and social life but she didn't enjoy getting up early or the bad weather.
3 She went to Lipsi, a Greek island, for a vacation with a friend and loved it – the people, the weather, the food, the mountains. She decided to apply for a job with the travel company that organized her vacation. She got a job as a tourist guide on the island.
4 She's very happy there. She can't imagine living in London again.

d ● SS now read each other's texts.

Extra support

You could check SS' general understanding of both texts by asking individual SS the questions in **c**, first about Victoria, then about Sally.

e ● Focus on the task. Still in pairs, SS look at each highlighted word in turn and try to guess its meaning. Then they match it to its dictionary definition. Check answers and model and drill pronunciation where necessary, e.g., *applied* /əˈplaɪd/, *tiny* /ˈtaɪni/.

1 trivial	6 the Tube
2 insane	7 delicious
3 keeper	8 applied for
4 apes	9 blazing
5 mistreated	10 tiny

f ● Ask these two questions to the whole class and elicit opinions.

6 VOCABULARY & PRONUNCIATION
strong adjectives

a ● Focus on the column headings and the two examples from the reading texts (1 and 2). *Tiny* and *delicious* are examples of "strong" adjectives, i.e., adjectives that are used instead of using *very* + a normal adjective. Strong adjectives are more expressive than normal adjectives and are used especially in conversation. Emphasize that you <u>can't</u> use *very* with these adjectives (although you can use *really* or *absolutely*).

● Give SS time to read the sentences, which all contain a strong adjective. From the context or their previous knowledge, SS should be able to write synonyms for each one by writing the normal adjective. SS could work in pairs or they could compare answers when they finish.

38

- Check answers and model and drill pronunciation where necessary.

3 angry	8 big
4 afraid / frightened / scared	9 cold
5 tired	10 dirty
6 hot	11 good
7 hungry	12 bad

b ● SS now cover exercise **a** and from memory complete the responses with a strong adjective.

c ● **2.10** Play the recording for SS to check their answers and ask SS to tell you how the strong adjectives are stressed (they are stressed strongly).

2 furious 3 tiny 4 exhausted 5 filthy 6 terrified

```
2.10                                          CD1 Track 30
1  A  Are you hungry?
   B  Yes, I'm starving.
2  A  Was your mother angry?
   B  Yes, she was furious.
3  A  Is her apartment small?
   B  Yes, it's tiny.
4  A  Are you tired?
   B  Yes, I'm exhausted.
5  A  Is the floor dirty?
   B  Yes, it's filthy.
6  A  Are you afraid of spiders?
   B  Yes, I'm terrified of them.
```

- Play the recording, pausing after each exchange for SS to repeat the questions and responses. Encourage SS to copy the strong stress on the strong adjectives.

d ● Sit SS in pairs, **A** and **B**, preferably face to face. Tell them to go to **Communication** *Are you hungry? Yes, I'm starving!* **A** on page 116, **B** on page 119.

- Give SS a few moments to read their instructions and then demonstrate the activity with a student **B** (you take the part of student **A**).

- Point out that when a pair has finished the activity they should repeat it, this time trying to respond as quickly as possible and trying to stress the strong adjective strongly.

- Tell SS to go back to the main lesson on page 27.

7 GRAMMAR present perfect continuous (for recent continuous actions)

a ● Have SS look at the pictures. Ask them the two questions and elicit answers, e.g., *The woman looks angry and the man, too. Maybe they've been arguing,* etc.

b ● **2.11** Play the recording for SS to check their ideas and to complete sentences 1–3. Play the recording again, stopping after each conversation. Check answers.

1 Sharon and Kenny **have been arguing.**
2 The man **has been reading by the pool** (without any sunscreen on).
3 The man and woman **have been sightseeing** and **walking all afternoon.**

```
2.11                                          CD1 Track 31
(audioscript in Student Book on page 123)
1  A  Hello?
   B  Hi, Sharon. It's me... Kylie.
   A  Oh. Hi, Kylie.
   B  Hey, you sound awful – what's been happening?
   A  Oh, nothing. Well, OK... Kenny and I have been arguing.
   B  What about? What's he been doing this time?
   A  He's been sending text messages to his ex-girlfriend again.
   B  No!
   A  I knew this vacation was a mistake. I shouldn't have come.
2  A  You are so red! How long have you been sunbathing? All morning?
   B  I haven't been sunbathing. I've been reading.
   A  Yes, but in the sun! Didn't you put any sunscreen on?
   B  No.
   A  You'd better go and put some lotion on now. You're going to feel terrible tonight...
3  A  You two look exhausted. What have you been doing?
   B  We've been sightseeing in the town. We've been walking all afternoon.
   C  Yes, my feet are killing me.
   A  Well, come and sit down and have a nice cup of coffee.
```

Extra support

Ask more questions to check comprehension, e.g., *Who's Sharon talking to?* (Kylie, maybe a friend or her sister.) *What has Kevin been doing?* (Sending text messages to his ex-girlfriend.), etc.

c ● Tell SS to go to **Grammar Bank 2B** on page 132. Go through the rules for present perfect continuous for recent continuous actions.

Grammar notes

Present perfect continuous (for recent continuous actions)

- Here SS learn another use of the present perfect continuous, to talk about recent continuous actions that have often just stopped, e.g., if you call a friend you haven't seen for a while, the conversation might be:
What have you been doing? I haven't seen you for a couple of weeks.
I've been taking exams. (= he / she either just finished or the exams are still in progress)

- Have SS do exercise **b** on page 133 individually or in pairs. Check answers.

b 1 Have ... been crying, 've been watching
2 's been barking
3 haven't been sleeping
4 've been shopping
5 have ... been doing, 've been playing

Extra idea

Give SS more practice of the rhythm of the present perfect continuous by getting them to read the conversations in pairs.

39

- Tell SS to go back to the main lesson on page 27.

d • Focus on the task and give SS time to think of a possible reason why they are *exhausted*, *filthy*, etc. Emphasize that their reason must be expressed using "*I've been* _____ *-ing.*"

- Demonstrate the activity yourself with a student. First, focus on the exchange in speech bubbles. Then have the student choose an adjective and ask you a question. (*Hi. You look .... What have you been doing?*) Then invent an answer with the present perfect continuous, and elicit more questions (*Why?*, etc.).

- Put SS in pairs and they take turns having mini-conversations using alternate adjectives. **A** asks **B** using *exhausted* and **B** asks **A** using *filthy*, etc. When they finish, they start at the beginning again but this time **B** starts, using *exhausted*.

Extra photocopiable activities

Grammar
present perfect continuous page 144
Communicative
How long have you been doing it? page 175 (instructions page 163)

HOMEWORK

Study Link Workbook pages 17–19

2C

G comparatives and superlatives
V transportation and travel
P stress in compound nouns

Race to the sun

Lesson plan

In this lesson SS review comparative and superlative forms and learn common words and phrases connected with travel and transportation. In the first half of the lesson, the context is a race from London to the South of France to see which form of transportation (car, plane, or train) is the quickest, cheapest, and most comfortable. In the second half of the lesson, the topic changes to safety and SS read and listen about some research that was done to determine which activities done while driving are the most dangerous (e.g., talking on the phone, opening a bag of chips, etc.). This leads to SS talking about various aspects of road safety, such as speed limits and drinking and driving. The pronunciation focus is on word stress in compound nouns, e.g., *traffic jam*, *rush hour*, etc.

Optional lead-in (books closed)

- Do a quick class survey by writing these three questions on the board:
  1 How do you get to class?
  2 How long does it take you?
  3 Do you normally have a good or bad trip?
- First, have SS ask the questions to the SS sitting nearest them. Remind SS that you can say *by car / train / subway*, etc. and either *on foot*, or more usually *I walk*.
- Then find out with a show of hands which is the most popular form of transportation and who has the shortest and the longest trip. Also try to establish who has the best or easiest trip and who has the worst.

1 READING

a • Books open. Put SS in pairs and have them ask each other the two questions. Get some responses from the class about which is the most popular of the three forms of transportation.

b • Focus on the title of the article and make sure SS understand *race*. Tell SS that they are going to read about a race that was organized between three journalists who traveled either by train, car, or plane from London to the South of France. Tell SS to look at the map and the photos. Explain that many people in Britain go on vacation to the South of France and that people argue about what is the best way to get there – by train, car, or plane. Tell SS that they are going to read about the trips by plane and train and that later they will listen to the car driver's trip.

- Have SS read the introduction to the article. Check they understand the meaning of *discount airline* (= a cheap airline that sells tickets on the Internet) and the phrasal verb *set off* (= to start a trip) and then have SS in pairs answer the questions. (Try to avoid SS seeing that these questions are partially answered in exercise 2 on page 29!) Elicit some opinions from the class.

c • Explain the task and give SS a moment to look at the article to find out (but not to call out!) which paragraph they think is the first one for the plane. Elicit that the answer is paragraph D.
- Now set a time limit for SS to read the two scrambled texts and put the paragraphs in order. When they think they have completed the task, they should check their answers with another student. Check answers.

The plane	The train
1 D 2 A 3 C 4 G	1 E 2 H 3 B 4 F

Extra support

You could now go through the text with the SS, reading the two trips aloud paragraph by paragraph. After each paragraph, ask SS which words told them that it was a plane or train trip, and focus on any other words related to travel in general, which SS could underline.

Traveling in general
travel, set off, suitcase, luggage, taxi, ticket, trip, seat
Plane
airport flew (fly) airline check-in window seat seat numbers security gate (48) board / get on (a plane) took off (take off) land
Train
station platform dining car

d • Focus on the instructions and have SS read about the two trips again, this time in the right order and to answer the questions by writing **T** or **P** in the boxes. Set a time limit and when SS finish, get them to compare their answers with a partner's, and then check answers.

1 P 2 T 3 P 4 T 5 T 6 P 7 P 8 P 9 T 10 T

Extra idea

You could have SS underline or highlight five words or phrases they want to remember from the text. Have them compare their words / phrases with a partner and then get some feedback from the class.

HOW WORDS WORK...

- Focus on the examples and the explanation. Point out that:
  – *How long does it take… (+ verb)?* is often used to ask how much time is needed to complete a particular trip, e.g., *How long does it take to get downtown from here? It takes half an hour. How long does it take to fly from New York to London? It takes eight hours.*
- To ask somebody about their trip add *you* to the question:
  A: *How long does it take **you** to drive to work in the morning?*
  B: *It takes **me** about half an hour.*

41

- We often use *How long does it take?* <u>without</u> a second verb, e.g.,

  A: *Let's go to Boston by train.*

  B: *OK. How long does it take?*

  A: *About four hours.*

- This construction can also be used to ask about other things, not just trips, e.g., *How long does it take to learn to speak a foreign language?*

- Focus on the task. Put SS in pairs and have them ask and answer the two questions. Encourage them to use *It takes me...* in their answers rather than just answering with a figure.

Extra support

If you think your SS need more practice of this structure, you could write some prompts on the board, e.g., *cook pasta, boil an egg, fly to Miami, walk downtown*, etc.

2 LISTENING

a ● **2.12** Tell SS that they are now going to hear about the trip of the third person, the car driver, in the race to the South of France. Look again at the photo of Martin's car on page 28.

⚠ If this is a different lesson from when you did exercise **1 READING**, it would be a good idea to have SS tell you what they can remember about the people who traveled by train and plane.

- Focus on the pictures of Martin's trip and the task. Then play the recording all the way through for SS to try to number the pictures in order.

Extra idea

Alternatively, you could pause the recording after each section and elicit which picture goes with it.

1 C	2 D	3 E	4 A	5 F	6 G	7 B

b ● Have SS read through sentences 1–9 and then play the recording again for SS to mark the sentences T or F. Play the recording (or part of it) again if necessary. Have them compare their answers with a partner's and then check answers. For false sentences elicit the correct information.

1 F (There was no rush hour traffic.)
2 T
3 T
4 T
5 F (It takes an hour and a half.)
6 T
7 F (It's 130 km/h.)
8 T
9 F (It's 960 km.)

2.12   CD1 Track 32

(audioscript in Student Book on page 123)

I left at six. It was still dark when I put my suitcase in the car and drove off. It was fast and easy to go through London because it was Saturday, so there was no rush hour traffic. Soon I was on the highway heading toward Folkestone on the south coast. I stopped at a gas station for a cup of coffee and a sandwich. I didn't buy any gas because it's much cheaper in France.

I arrived in Folkestone at 8:10. The problem with traveling by car from England to France is that Britain is an island. There are 35 kilometers of water between England and France. You can get across it by ferry, but there's a much better and quicker way – the Channel Tunnel.

The Channel Tunnel is only a train tunnel, not a road tunnel, and so you have to put your car on a train. The trip takes an hour and a half, and drivers have to sit in their cars because there are no seats on the train for passengers. I arrived at the terminal and joined the line of cars waiting for the next train.

At 10:30 the train arrived in Calais and I drove my car off the train and onto the road – a French road. It was nice to drive on the right again, although that was not so easy with an English car.

The traffic in Calais was really bad. Finally I got out of Calais and onto the highway to the South of France. The speed limit on French highways is 130 kilometers an hour and the road was clear, so now I could travel quickly. But first I stopped at a gas station to fill up.

Gas is cheaper in France than in Britain but, on the other hand, you have to pay to travel on French highways. In Britain they are free.

It's 960 kilometers from Calais to Avignon, and the trip on the highway was boring. I listened to my favorite music to pass the time and I stopped again for lunch. At eight o'clock I finally arrived in Avignon. I found my hotel and I was looking forward to a delicious French meal.

c ● **2.13** SS listen to the last part of Martin's trip and complete the chart. Check answers, and ask SS if they guessed correctly in exercise **1a**.

By car			
14 hours	£200	6	10

2.13   CD1 Track 33

At eight o'clock I finally arrived in Avignon. I found my hotel and I was looking forward to a delicious French meal. It took me 14 hours to get there, and cost a total of £200. I gave the trip ten out of ten for convenience but only six for comfort. I was exhausted.

Extra support

If there's time, you could have SS listen to the recording with the audioscript on page 123 so they can see exactly what they understood / didn't understand. Translate / explain any new words or phrases.

d ● Do this as a whole class activity. Agree on a city (preferably a good distance away). Elicit the different ways of traveling there and write them on the board, e.g., by car, by bus, by train, by plane. Elicit how long the trip takes by each form of transportation and discuss which way is the best / worst.

3 GRAMMAR comparatives and superlatives

a ● Focus on the task. Have SS do this in pairs or individually and then compare answers in pairs. Check answers.

1 ✗ the quickest way
2 ✓
3 ✗ as cheap...as
4 ✓
5 ✗ less expensive than
6 ✗ the most comfortable hotel
7 ✓
8 ✓

b ● Tell SS to go to **Grammar Bank 2C** on page 132. Read the examples and go through the rules with the class.

Grammar notes

Comparatives and superlatives

● SS will almost certainly have been taught the basic rules regarding comparative and superlative forms of adjectives and adverbs, so this grammar focus should be mainly review and consolidation. SS may still mix up comparative and superlative forms, e.g., ~~This is the older building in the town,~~ and make mistakes with the rules for forming comparatives and superlatives.

● Typical mistakes include:
 – Always using *more* and *most*, e.g., ~~more big, the most fast,~~ etc.
 – mixing up comparative and superlative forms, e.g., ~~This is the older building in the town.~~
 – confusing *as* and *than*, e.g., ~~The train isn't as cheap than the bus.~~
 – omission of the definite article, e.g., ~~He's best player in the team.~~
 – confusing adjectives and adverbs, e.g., ~~You drive more quick than me.~~

● Have SS do the exercises on page 133 in pairs or individually. Check answers either after each exercise or after both.

a 1 as **2** the **3** than **4** ever **5** in **6** most
 7 as **8** more **9** as **10** him
b 1 hotter **2** the most competitive **3** the laziest
 4 better **5** the most boring **6** earlier
 7 the worst **8** the most ambitious **9** safest
 10 farther

● Tell SS to go back to the main lesson on page 30.

c ● Put SS in pairs. Focus on the task and demonstrate what SS have to do.

● First, SS have to decide, e.g., which is the safest of the three forms of transportation, e.g., *Traveling by car is the safest. Traveling by motorcycle is safer than traveling by bike.* Then they compare them again using each of the other two adjectives.

Extra challenge

Have pairs compare with another pair to see if they agree, and get them to defend their choices.

4 VOCABULARY transportation and travel

a ● All the words appeared in the reading or listening texts. Give SS a couple of minutes to put them in the right column. Check answers.

train	car	plane
dining car	highway	check in
platform	rush hour	gate
station	speed limit	take off

b ● Tell SS to go to **Vocabulary Bank** *Transportation and travel* on page 148 and do section **1 Plane**, either individually or in pairs. Check answers and model and drill pronunciation.

1 baggage claim	6 land
2 check-in counter	7 take off
3 suitcase	8 luggage
4 gate	9 aisle
5 boarding card / pass	

● Point out that *baggage* and *luggage* mean the same (i.e., bags and suitcases), but that *luggage* is the more common word to use, and *baggage* the more technical word (used by the air industry). You may also want to teach the verb *check in*.

● Now get SS to do section **2 Train**. Check answers. Elicit and drill the pronunciation.

● Point out that you can just use *station* instead of *train station*.

10 ticket office	13 platform
11 (train) station	14 (rail) car
12 the subway	

● Tell SS to do section **3a Road**. Check answers and pronunciation.

15 bus	20 car
16 highway	21 helmet
17 bike	22 motorcycle
18 van	23 streetcar
19 truck	24 taxi

● SS do **3b**. They could compare their answers in pairs before you check answers.

1 gas station	8 speed limit
2 traffic light	9 public transportation
3 seat belt	10 pedestrian area
4 rush hour	11 bike lane
5 car crash	12 taxi stand
6 parking ticket	13 parking lot
7 traffic jam	

● Point out that the strong stress normally falls on the first syllable in compound nouns, e.g., <u>seat</u> belt.

● Finally, tell SS to do section **4 Travel**. Check answers. Elicit the pronunciation of the words and model and drill if necessary.

1 Travel	2 trip	3 journey	4 flight

● SS often confuse *travel* with *trip*, so emphasize that *travel* is often used as a verb and never as a countable noun. You can't say *a travel*.

● *travel* does exist as an uncountable noun, e.g., *travel broadens your mind*, but it may be better not to focus on this at this level so as not to confuse SS.

- Finally, focus on the instruction "Can you remember the words on this page? Test yourself or a partner."

Testing yourself

For **Plane, Train and Road a** SS can cover the words and look at the pictures and try to remember the words. For **Road b** they can cover the list and the compound nouns 1–13. They look at the clues and remember the phrases, uncovering one by one to check. For **Travel** they cover the definitions and look at the words on the list and try to remember what they mean.

Testing a partner

See **Testing a partner** on page 15.

Study Link SS can find more practice of these words on the MultiROM and on the *American English File 3* Website.

- Tell SS to go back to the main lesson on page 30.

5 PRONUNCIATION & SPEAKING stress in compound nouns

Explain to SS that compound nouns are very common in English. A compound noun is a two-noun phrase, but the first noun functions as an adjective that describes the second noun, e.g., a bus stop, a credit card. Sometimes they are one word, e.g., sunglasses, and occasionally they are hyphenated.

a • **2.14** Focus on the task and play the recording for SS to repeat the compound nouns one by one. Then ask SS which of the two words carries more stress (the first one).

2.14	CD1 Track 34
traffic light	pedestrian area
boarding pass	gas station
parking lot	rush hour
car crash	seat belt
bike lane	traffic radar
parking ticket	speed limit
traffic jam	ticket office

b • Put SS in pairs and tell them to answer the questions, which use the compound nouns.
- Tell SS to take turns asking the questions. Monitor that SS are stressing the compound nouns correctly.
- If there's time, ask a few SS for their responses.

6 LISTENING & SPEAKING

a • Focus on the instructions and check that SS understand all the vocabulary, e.g., *a bag of chips, a can of soda*, etc. Give SS a few minutes to read the article and do questions 1 and 2. Get some responses from the class.

b • **2.15** Focus on the task and play the recording for SS to number the activities 1–6. To add suspense, you could pause the recording just before the expert says which thing is the most dangerous, second most dangerous, etc., and elicit from the class what they think is going to be next.
- Check answers.

---

1 Opening a bag of chips or a can of soda.
2 Picking up a specific CD from the passenger seat.
3 Making a call on your cell phone.
4 Listening to your favorite music.
5 Talking to other passengers.
6 Listening to music you don't know.

- Find out if anyone guessed the top three correctly.

c • Now SS listen for more detail. Tell SS to read questions 1–8. Play the recording again, pausing where necessary to give SS time to write the answers.
- Have SS discuss what they heard with their partner and play the recording again if necessary before checking answers.

1 Concentrate 100% on controlling the car.
2 Because you need both hands to do it (and you take your hands off the wheel for a second or two).
3 They take their eyes off the road for one or two seconds.
4 Their control of the car.
5 More quickly and less safely.
6 They drive more aggressively.
7 They don't pay (enough) attention to what is happening on the road.
8 Because it doesn't distract you as much.

- Finally, ask SS if any of the results surprised them.

2.15   CD1 Track 35

(audioscript in Student Book on page 124)

T = TV host, E = expert

T And this evening on *Behind the Wheel* we talk to Brian Russo, who is an expert on road safety. Brian, you did some tests to find out how dangerous it is to do other things when we're driving. According to your tests, what's the most dangerous thing to do?

E Well, the first thing I have to say is that doing anything else when you're driving is dangerous and can cause an accident. Because when you're driving you should concentrate 100 percent on controlling the car and anything else you do is a distraction. The tests we did in a simulator showed that the most difficult and most dangerous thing is to try and open a bag of chips or a can of soda. The reason is that most people actually need two hands to open a bag of chips or a can of soda, so they take both hands off the wheel for a second or two. And, of course, that's the most dangerous thing you can possibly do. In fact, one of the drivers in the simulator actually crashed when he did this.

T Oh, wow. And which is the next most dangerous?

E The next most dangerous thing is to select a specific CD from the passenger seat. This is extremely dangerous too because to do this you have to take your eyes off the road for one or two seconds.

T And number three?

E Number three was making a phone call on a cell phone. What we found in the tests was that drivers drove more slowly when they did this, but that their control of the car got worse.

T Yes, I can believe that. And number four?

E Number four was listening to your favorite music. In the tests most drivers drove more quickly and less safely when they were listening to music they already knew. If the music was fast and heavy, some drivers even drove more aggressively.

T So no heavy metal when you're driving?

E Absolutely not.
T And in fifth place?
E In fifth place was talking to other passengers. The problem when we talk to other people in the car is that we pay too much attention to what we're saying or what we're hearing and not enough attention to what's happening on the road.
T So the least dangerous is listening to music you *don't* know.
E That's right. The least dangerous of all these activities is listening to unfamiliar music on the radio or on a CD player. It seems that if we *don't know* the music, then we're less distracted by it. In this part of the tests, all drivers drove safely and well.

Extra support

If there's time, you could have SS listen again with the audioscript on page 124 so they can see exactly what they understood / didn't understand. Translate / explain any new words or phrases.

d ● Give SS time to read the statements to decide if they agree or disagree with them and to think of their reasons.

e ● Put SS into small groups of three or four. Appoint a group secretary, whose job it is to read out the sentence and then invite opinions from the other SS as well as giving his / her own opinion. The secretary should also take down how many people agreed or disagreed with each statement.

Extra support

Remind SS of expressions of agreement and disagreement (see page 7) by eliciting them and writing them on the board.

● Ask SS and find out if there was a general consensus of agreement or disagreement on each statement.

Study Link SS can find a dictation and a Grammar quiz on all the grammar from File 2 on the MultiROM and more grammar activities on the *American English File 3* Website.

Extra photocopiable activities

Grammar
comparatives and superlatives page 145
Communicative
Questionnaire page 176 (instructions page 164)
Vocabulary
Split crossword puzzle page 196 (instructions page 193)

HOMEWORK

Study Link Workbook pages 20–22

PRACTICAL ENGLISH IN THE OFFICE

Function Making requests, asking permission
Language *Could you…?, Would you mind…?, Is it OK if…?,* etc.

Lesson plan

In the first part of the lesson, SS review and extend ways of asking people politely to do things and asking permission. This language is presented through a series of exchanges between people in the office. In the second part of the lesson (**Social English**), Mark has a drink after work with Ben and Nicole.

Study Link These lessons are on the *American English File 3* Video, which can be used instead of the Class Audio CD for these lessons (see Introduction page 9). The main functional section of each episode is also on the MultiROM with additional activities.

Optional lead-in (books closed)

● Review what happened in the previous episode by eliciting the story from SS, e.g., *Who works in the MTC Paris office? What are their jobs? What happened when Mark arrived in the Paris office?*
What did Mark and Allie talk about when they went for a walk in the evening? Do the people in the office know about their relationship? Do they want to keep it a secret?

● Also try to elicit the phrases they reviewed / learned in the first episode for introducing people, e.g., *Let me introduce you to the team.* You could write these with spaces on the board to help SS remember.

● If you are using the Video, you could play the previous episode again, leaving out the "Listen and Repeat" sections.

REQUESTS AND PERMISSION

a ● **2.16** Tell SS to cover the conversation with their hand or a piece of paper (or write the questions on the board and get SS to close their books). Focus on the photo and the three questions.

● Play the recording once all the way through. Then play it again, pausing after the answer to each question to give SS time to answer. Check answers. Remind SS that *time off* = time when you don't have to work.

1 To send him the concert dates.
2 To help him (open a computer document).
3 If she can have tomorrow afternoon off.

b ● Now have SS look at the conversation. In pairs, they read it and see if they can guess or remember the missing words. Emphasize that they shouldn't write the words in the conversation but in pencil alongside or on a separate sheet of paper.

c ● Play the recording again for them to check. Then go through the conversation line by line and check answers. Find out if SS had guessed the words correctly. Where they had not guessed correctly, see if their alternative also fits.

| **2.16** | | CD1 Track 36 |

J = Jacques, M = Mark, B = Ben, A = Allie, N = Nicole

J Mark? Would you mind **sending** me those concert dates?

M Of **course** not. Ben, are you busy?

B Me? Never.

M **Could** you help me? I can't open this document.

B **Sure.**

M Thanks.

A Hi, Nicole.

N Could you sign these, please?

A Sure.

N Is it **OK** if I take tomorrow afternoon off?

A I'm **sorry**, but tomorrow's really difficult.

N What about Friday afternoon?

A Friday? That's fine. Do you **think** you could **send** me the request by e-mail?

N Uh, yes, of **course.**

A Hello. Hi, Mark. Could you hold a moment, Mark? Thank you, Nicole. **Can** you come and see me when you have a moment?

d ● **2.17** Now focus on the key phrases highlighted in the conversation. Play the recording, pausing after each sentence for SS to repeat. Encourage them to copy the rhythm and intonation.

| **2.17** | | CD1 Track 37 |

J = Jacques, M = Mark, B = Ben, A = Allie, N = Nicole

J Would you mind sending me those concert dates?

M Of course not.

M Could you help me?

B Sure.

N Is it OK if I take tomorrow afternoon off?

A I'm sorry, but tomorrow's really difficult.

A Do you think you could send me the request by e-mail?

N Yes, of course.

A Can you come and see me when you have a moment?

e ● Focus on the chart and the task and give SS time to complete the chart. Get them to do this in pairs or individually and then compare answers in pairs. Check answers.

Request	Response
Would you mind (sending me those concert dates)?	Of course not.
Could you (help me)?	Sure.
Do you think you could (send me the request by e-mail)?	Yes, of course.
Can you (come and see me when you have a moment)?	
Permission	
Is it OK if (I take tomorrow afternoon off)?	I'm sorry, but…

● Point out that:

  – The expression you use in a given situation often depends on, e.g., how big a favor you are asking or how well you know the person you are talking to.

  – You can also use *Can / Could / May I* to ask for permission, e.g., *May I use your phone?*

  – The verb after *Would you mind …* must be the *-ing* form. This phrase requires a negative answer, e.g., *(No,) of course not* if you agree to the request.

  – Apart from *of course not*, the other responses can be used for all requests / permissions.

f ● Tell SS to go to **Communication *Requests*** on page 119 and focus on the task. Demonstrate if necessary. Set a time limit, then have SS move around the room, and talk to as many SS as they can.

● At the end you could find out who got the most SS to help him / her.

SOCIAL ENGLISH Office gossip

a ● **2.18** Focus first on the title and elicit / explain the meaning of *office gossip* (= talking about other people at work and their personal lives). Then focus on the photo and the task. Play the recording once for SS to answer the question. Elicit answers.

Ben, Jacques, Isabelle (Jacques's wife), and Allie.

| **2.18** | | CD1 Track 38 |

(audioscript in Student Book on page 124)

M = Mark, B = Ben, A = Allie, N = Nicole

N Have you started looking for an apartment?

M No, I haven't had time yet.

B Anyway, it's best to get to know Paris first.

M Yeah – it's a big city.

N Merci.

B Merci.

M Merci beaucoup.

N Very good, Mark!

M Thanks. That's nearly all the French I know!

B Hi, Beatrice. … Yeah… just a minute. Sorry.

N How do you like the office?

M Oh, it's great.

N And the people?

M Really friendly! I like Ben a lot. He's amazing with computers. And Jacques's a really nice guy!

N Oh, Jacques, he's very charming. Everybody likes him. And he has a lovely wife. She used to be a pop star when she was young. Have you heard of Isabelle?

M No, I'm sorry, I haven't.

N She's very pretty. Allie is very attractive, too.

M Allie? Yeah, I guess.

N Although her clothes are very English. And she's very formal. You know, today, I asked if I could have a day off, and she wanted me to send her an e-mail!

M Well, the English have their funny ways.

N Oh yeah. Oh, hello, Allie.

A Hi.

M Allie! Hi, let me get you a drink.

A Thanks. I'll have a Diet Coke™.

b ● Focus on sentences 1–6 and go through them quickly. Then play the recording for SS to mark them T or F. Play the recording again if necessary. Check answers getting SS to correct the false sentences.

1	T
2	T
3	F (She was a pop singer.)
4	F (She thinks her clothes are "very English.")
5	F (She says Allie is very formal.)
6	T

Extra support

If there's time, you could have SS listen to the recording with the audioscript on page 124 so they can see exactly what they understood / didn't understand. Translate / explain any new words or phrases.

c ● **2.19** Now focus on the **USEFUL PHRASES**. Give SS a moment to try to complete them, and then play the recording to check.

2.19   CD1 Track 39

M = Mark, B = Ben, A = Allie, N = Nicole
N Have you started **looking** for an apartment?
M I haven't had time **yet**.
B **Just** a minute.
N **How** do you like the office?
N Have you **heard** of Isabelle?
M **Let** me get you a drink.
A Thanks. I'll **have** a Diet Coke™.

Extra idea

Ask SS if they can remember who said each phrase (and in what context), e.g., *Ben says "Just a minute"* (when his phone rings).

d ● Play the recording again, pausing for SS to repeat. In a monolingual class, you could elicit the equivalent expressions in SS' L1.

HOMEWORK

Study Link **Workbook** page 23

---

2   WRITING   TELLING A STORY

Lesson plan

This second writing lesson focuses on using the past tenses practiced in **File 2** to tell a story, and also on using common connecting expressions such as *so*, *because*, and *although*. The vocabulary from lesson **2C** (**Transportation and travel**) is also repeated here. There is also a "mini focus" on finding and correcting mistakes.

We suggest that you do exercises **a–c** in class, but assign the actual writing (the last activity) for homework. If there's time, you may also want to do the planning in class.

a ● Focus on the magazine article and tell the SS to read the story once without worrying about the mistakes or the spaces. Then ask them if the people caught their flight in the end. (They did.)

● Put SS in pairs and set a time limit. Tell them to read the article again and correct the six underlined mistakes. Check answers. Elicit that *felt* is the past of *feel*, not *fall*, which is the verb here.

~~leaved~~ **left**	we couldn't ~~to~~ check in
didn't ~~knew~~ **know**	**couldn't check in**
to ~~found~~ **find**	~~felt~~ down **fell**
we ~~was~~ **were**	

b ● Put SS in the same pairs to read the text again and complete the spaces with words from the list. Check answers.

1 when	**4** After	**7** so
2 but	**5** but	**8** Although
3 so	**6** because	**9** in the end

c ● Focus on the **Useful language** box and make sure SS understand all the phrases. Then give them a few moments to decide if they refer to a trip by car or plane. Check answers.

the flight was delayed P	there was a traffic jam C
your car broke down C	you got a flat tire C
you got lost C	you forgot your passport P
you missed your flight P	your flight was overbooked P

WRITE about a nightmare trip

Go through the instructions. Then either have SS plan and write their story in class (set a time limit of 20 minutes) or have them plan their story in class and write at home, or assign both the planning and writing for homework.

Before SS hand in their stories, have them exchange them with another student to read and check for mistakes.

For instructions on how to use these pages, see page 30.

GRAMMAR

a 1 already   2 long   3 Since   4 Have   5 yet
b 1 been working   2 had, since
  3 more expensive   4 carefully as   5 the most

VOCABULARY

a 1 bank (It's a place. The others are forms of payment.)
  2 mortgage (It's a noun. The others are all verbs.)
  3 hungry (The other adjectives are all "strong" adjectives.)
  4 awful (It has a negative meaning. The other three have a positive meaning.)
  5 travel (It's a verb. The other words are nouns.)
  6 helmet (You wear it. The other three are vehicles.)
  7 train station (It's related to train travel. The other words are all related to road travel.)
b 1 filthy   2 tax   3 rush hour   4 lend   5 platform
  6 inherit   7 boarding pass / card   8 tiny
c 1 off   2 out   3 for   4 back   5 by

PRONUNCIATION

a 1 card (It's /ɑr/.)   4 cyclist (It's /s/.)
  2 tiny (It's /aɪ/.)   5 earn (It's /ər/.)
  3 charge (It's /tʃ/.)
b in**vest**, se**cur**ity, **lugg**age, pe**des**trian, **terr**ified

CAN YOU UNDERSTAND THIS TEXT?

a 1 a   2 b   3 c   4 c   5 b
b fortunate = lucky
  charity = an organization that collects money to help people who are poor, sick, etc.
  volunteer = somebody who offers or agrees to do something without being forced or paid
  orphanage = an institution where children without parents live and are looked after
  down payment = a percentage of the price of something you are buying that you pay in advance
  annoyed = made angry
  adopted = taken by a family and raised as if they were their own children
  useful = having a practical use
  definitely = certainly, without doubt

CAN YOU UNDERSTAND THESE PEOPLE?

a 1 b   2 c   3 b   4 c   5 a

b 1 $7,500   2 Three years   3 $261.45   4 8.5%
  5 March 22nd

2.20   CD1 Track 40

1 A What's the matter?
   B I can't find my credit card. I must have dropped it somewhere.
   A Well, think. When did you use it last?
   B I bought some gas on the way to work… Did I pay for lunch with the card? No, I paid cash. Oh, and this morning I went to the flower shop. I got some flowers for Sally's birthday.
   A Well, call the flower shop then. Someone might have picked it up.
2 A How long have you been teaching?
   B Well, I've been working here since last October, so that's a year and a half. And I taught for two years before that.
   A Oh, where was that?
   B A school in Peru.
   A Huh, that must have been interesting.
   B Yes, it's a fascinating place.
3 Last night's heavy snow has made most main roads impassable. Right now, the trains are still running normally but the airports are closed. So it's definitely not a good day to be traveling.
   Business news now. Wall Street closed 3 points down after yesterday's gains…
4 A How are you getting to Buffalo?
   B We *were* going to drive up Route 17. Then we heard that there was a lot of roadwork on that highway, so we decided to take Route 80 instead.
   A I thought the Thruway was faster.
   B It is, but there are too many trucks!
5 A Why does your brother rent his apartment? Why doesn't he buy one?
   B He can't afford it.
   A Yeah, but paying rent's just a waste of money. If you can afford to pay rent, you can afford to pay a mortgage.
   B Yeah, but he only has a temporary contract and his wife's unemployed at the moment.

2.21   CD1 Track 41

A Good morning, Ms. Stevens. Please, have a seat.
B Thank you.
A Now, I understand you want a small loan.
B Yes, that's right. I want to buy a new car.
A How much do you need?
B I think I'm going to need about $7,500.
A OK, and over what period of time do you want this loan?
B Three years.
A Well, let's see… Over three years the monthly payments would be $261.45.
B Hmm. What's your interest rate at the moment?
A It's 8.5%.
B And could that change?
A No, that would be fixed for the period of the loan.
B OK.
A And when would you like the money?
B As soon as possible.
A By the end of next week?
B That'd be fine. And when will I start the payments?
A Your first one will be on March 22nd.
B Fine.
A Good. Well, I'll draw up the loan agreement and you'll receive that in the mail in a couple of days.

G *must, have to, should* (obligation)
V cell phones
P sentence stress

3A Modern manners

File 3 overview

The grammatical focus of this File is on modal verbs. **3A** deals with modal verbs of obligation, **3B** looks at modal verbs of deduction or certainty (*must (be), may / might (be)* and *can't (be)*), and **3C** presents *can, could,* and *be able to* to express ability and possibility. By the end of the File, SS should have a clear understanding of how the common modal verbs work in English and when and how to use them.

Lesson plan

This lesson focuses on modern manners, which provides a context for SS to distinguish between different common ways of expressing obligation: *must / have to* and *should.* SS will have met these verbs separately, but will probably not have contrasted them before, and in this lesson the difference between a modal verb (*must, should*) and a normal verb (*have to*) is made clear. The vocabulary focus is on words and expressions related to using a phone. The pronunciation focuses on sentence rhythm.

Optional lead-in (books closed)

Do a quick survey to find out how many students in the class are carrying a cell phone. Then find out which make is the most popular. Take the opportunity to make sure everybody's phone is turned off!

1 VOCABULARY & SPEAKING cell phones

a ● Books open. Focus on the instructions, and have SS match the words and countries in pairs. Check answers.

> **1** e **2** g (In German nouns always have a capital letter.) **3** b **4** a **5** f **6** d **7** c

 ● Ask the class which names they like most / least. You could get a show of hands for this.

b ● **3.1** Now focus on the instructions and sentences A–G. Give SS a few moments to go through them in pairs and say what they think the bold words mean. Clarify the meaning of any words or phrases they don't know.
 ● Now play the recording. Pause after the first sound effect, and elicit that the sounds they are hearing are different ring tones, so the answer is D. Now continue playing the recording to the end and give SS time to compare answers. Play again if necessary and check answers.

Extra support

Alternatively, you could pause the recording after each sound effect and let SS, in pairs, choose the right sentence.

> **1** D **2** C **3** G **4** F **5** A **6** E **7** B

> **3.1**   CD1 Track 42
> **1** *Several different ring tones*
> **2** "Good-bye."
> **3** *Busy signal*
> **4** **Jack**   Please leave a message after the tone.
>   **Sandra** Oh, hi, Jack, it's Sandra. I was just calling…
> **5** *Dialing tone and ring tone*
> **6** **Jim**   Oh, hi. It's Jim. I called half an hour ago but Ann wasn't in. Is she there now?
> **7** *Texting*

 ● Have SS close their books and play the recording again. Pause after each sound effect and get the class (or individual SS) to say the sentences.

c ● Focus on the questionnaire and go through the questions with SS. If you didn't do the lead-in, check that they understand, *hands-free, turn off.*

Extra idea

Have SS ask you the questions first.

2 GRAMMAR *must, have to, should* (obligation)

a ● Focus on the picture of the man talking loudly on a cell phone in a bus. In pairs, have SS answer the questions together.
 ● Quickly check answers from SS, but don't discuss question 3 too long as SS will be talking about bad cell phone habits in **c**.

b ● **3.2** Focus on the task and questions and quickly go through them. If necessary, explain / translate *complain* and *social occasions* and any other words SS don't understand.
 ● Play the recording once, pausing after each extract for SS to do the task.
 ● Check answers.

> **A** 5 **B** 2 **C** 4 **D** 3 **E** 1

> **3.2**   CD1 Track 43
> (audioscript in Student Book on page 124)
> **1** I'm a salesperson and I work in a clothing store. What really makes me angry is when I'm waiting on somebody and suddenly their cell phone rings, and they answer the phone and start having a conversation. It's really annoying. I think that if you're in a store and talking to a salesperson, then you shouldn't answer the phone.
> **2** What most annoys me is people who use their phones on a plane. I mean, everybody knows that you have to turn off your cell phone on a plane and that you must not use it until you get off the plane. But some people turn on their phones the moment the plane lands and they start making calls. Why can't they wait another 15 minutes?

3 I hate it when people talk very loudly on their cell phones in a public place. The other day I was in the waiting room at the doctor's and there was a man there whose cell phone rang about every two minutes, and we all had to listen to him talking loudly to his wife, then to his boss, then to a garage mechanic… I think that if you're in a public place and someone calls you, you should talk really quietly or go somewhere else. And you don't have to shout – the other person can hear you perfectly well.

4 What really annoys me are people who use their phones a lot when they're with other people – like when you're out for dinner with someone and they spend the whole time talking on their cell phones or texting other people to arrange what they're doing the next day. I think it's really rude.

5 I hate people who use their cell phones in the car, even if they're hands-free. Whenever you see someone driving badly, nine times out of ten they're on the phone.

c ● Focus on the instructions and have SS, in pairs or individually, match 1–5 with A–E and then compare with a partner. Make sure SS understand *rule*, *law*, and *allowed / permitted*. Check answers.

1 D	2 C	3 B	4 A	5 E

● Finally, ask the class which of these things annoys them the most.

d ● Tell SS to go to **Grammar Bank 3A** on page 134. Go through the examples and read the rules with the class. Model and drill pronunciation where necessary.

Extra idea

In a monolingual class, you could have SS translate the example sentences and compare the forms / verbs they would use in their L1.

Grammar notes

Obligation and necessity: *have to* and *must*

● *have to* / *must* and *should* / *shouldn't* were taught separately in *American English File 2.*
In this lesson they are reviewed and contrasted in more detail.

● Some typical mistakes are:
   – saying *must to*, e.g., ~~I must to be on time tomorrow.~~
   – confusing *must not* (prohibition) and *don't have to* (not necessary / not obligatory).
   – using *must* (not *had to*) in the past tense, e.g., ~~I must study last night.~~

Advice or opinion: *should* / *shouldn't*

● The important point to emphasize here is that *should* isn't as strong as *have to* / *must* and it is normally used to express a personal opinion or give advice.

● Compare:
You should talk to your teacher about the problem.
(= I think it's a good idea.)
You must talk to your teacher about the problem.
(= I think it's very important you do this.)

● Focus on the exercises on page 135 and have SS do them individually or in pairs. Check answers either after each exercise or after they have done both.

a	1	don't have to		5	had to
	2	must		6	Did you have to
	3	didn't have to		7	shouldn't
	4	Do you have to		8	can't

b	1	shouldn't go		4	should talk
	2	they have to		5	must not/can't use
	3	don't have to			

● Tell SS to go back to the main lesson on page 37.

3 PRONUNCIATION & SPEAKING sentence stress

a ● **3.3** Focus on the sentences. Play the recording and pause for SS to repeat, copying the rhythm.

3.3	CD1 Track 44

1 You <u>must not</u> <u>use</u> your <u>phone</u> on a <u>plane</u>.
2 I <u>don't have</u> to <u>go</u> to <u>work</u> <u>tomorrow</u>.
3 We <u>have</u> to <u>take</u> an <u>exam</u> in <u>June</u>.
4 You should <u>turn</u> <u>off</u> your <u>cell</u> <u>phone</u> in <u>class</u>.
5 You <u>shouldn't</u> <u>talk</u> <u>loudly</u> on a <u>cell</u> <u>phone</u>.
6 I <u>must</u> <u>go</u> to the <u>bank</u> this <u>morning</u>.

● Point out that:
   – in (+) sentences *should* is not usually stressed and is pronounced /ʃəd/.
   – the negative forms *must not*, *don't have*, and *shouldn't* are always stressed.

● Remind SS:
   – of the silent *l* in *should* /ʃʊd/.
   – the weak form of *to* in *have to* /tə/.
   – *must* can have either a strong or weak pronunciation. It normally has a weak pronunciation unless we want to give special emphasis. Compare:
   1 I must <u>go</u> to the <u>bank</u> this <u>morning</u>.
      (= It is something I need to do.)
   2 I <u>must</u> <u>go</u> to the <u>bank</u> this <u>morning</u>.
      (= It is very important I do this.)

b ● Focus on the definition of *manners*. Have SS read it and make sure they understand it. In a monolingual class you could elicit a translation in their L1.

● Now focus on the instructions and the first sentence in **Manners or the law?** Ask SS if there is a law about not playing noisy games on a cell phone in public, and elicit that there isn't. It is just good manners, so they have to mark this sentence M.

● Have SS, in pairs, mark the rest of the sentences M or L. Check answers. (Some may vary from country to country.)

Answers (in the US)
1 M   2 L   3 L   4 L (if it is a class rule)   5 M
6 L   7 M   8 L

c ● Now for sentence 1 elicit from the class *You shouldn't play noisy games on a cell phone in public.* Have SS practice saying it a couple of times to get the rhythm right.

● SS continue in pairs making sentences with *should / shouldn't, have to, can't,* or *must not.*

> **Possible answers according to the US** (may vary in different countries)
>
> You shouldn't play noisy games on a cell phone in public.
> You must not send text messages when your car is stopped at traffic lights.
> You must turn off your cell phone on a plane.
> You must turn off your cell phone in class (if it's a school rule).
> You shouldn't talk loudly on a cell phone on public transportation.
> You must not use a handheld cell phone while driving a car.
> You shouldn't make very personal calls in public.
> You must not use your cell phone at a gas station.

4 READING

a ● Focus on the title of the article. Check if SS understand *culture shock*.

> A feeling of confusion or anxiety that you may feel when living in or visiting another country.

b ● Focus on the article and the four summaries. Give SS time (at least five minutes) to read the article and then, with a partner, choose the best summary. Check answers.

> The English and Russian ideas of good manners are different.

Extra idea

An alternative and more "interactive" way of dealing with this text would be to read the text with the class, paragraph by paragraph, asking SS to try and guess the meaning of new words from the context. After each paragraph, ask your SS questions to compare the English (or Russian) attitude to manners to that of people in their country. For example, after paragraph 1, you could ask if it is necessary in your SS' country to add words like *could you* and *please.*

c ● Now have SS read the article again and, in pairs, to mark sentences 1–10 T or F. Tell them to mark the part of the text that gave them the answer. Check answers and get SS to justify their answers.

> **1** F (She got angry because of the way he asked her to pour him some tea.)
> **2** T
> **3** T
> **4** F (He was <u>very</u> surprised, i.e., amazed.)
> **5** F (It was disgusting.)
> **6** F (She was angry.)
> **7** T
> **8** T
> **9** F (They thought she was crazy.)
> **10** T

d ● Focus on the instructions. SS should try to do the exercise from memory. Check answers.

> **1** step   **3** make   **5** translate
> **2** pour   **4** swallow

e ● Do this as an open class question and elicit ideas. Have SS say why.

Extra idea

You could have SS underline or highlight five words or phrases they want to remember from the text. Have them compare their words / phrases with a partner and then get some feedback from the class.

5 LISTENING

a ● **3.4** Focus on the instructions. Play the recording once, pausing after each speaker to give SS time to write. You could also let them compare with a partner before moving on to the next speaker. Play the recording again if necessary.

> **1** Yes   **2** Yes   **3** No   **4** Yes

b ● Focus on the seven questions. Give SS time to read them. Then play the recording again, pausing after each speaker to give SS time to write. Have SS compare with a partner. Play the recording again if necessary. Check answers.

> **1** They say it's a sign that Americans are not sincere.
> **2** No, she agrees with them, but she still likes the fact that people use this expression.
> **3** The "thank-you people."
> **4** He suggests that Americans don't know how to say anything else in Chinese.
> **5** Faster pace of life, parents not teaching good manners to children, rude behavior on TV.
> **6** They act loud and pushy when visiting other countries, dress too casually to go to nice restaurants.
> **7** No, he thinks most of them are OK.

3.4 CD1 Track 45

(audioscript in Student Book on page 124)

Clare

In a store in the US, when you go to the checkout counter to pay, the salesperson always thanks you and says, "Have a nice day." For Americans this is standard polite behavior. However, some visitors to the US find this expression "Have a nice day!" very annoying. They say it's a sign that Americans are not sincere. You know, the salesperson doesn't really care if you have a nice day or not. I understand what they mean, but personally I really like it. I prefer the people who serve me in stores and restaurants to be polite and friendly, even if they are not 100% sincere. And the Americans are very good at that.

Paul

Well, some Chinese refer to Americans as "the thank-you people," because of our constant use of the phrase. You don't usually hear the Chinese say *please* or *thank you*. It's just not part of their culture. In fact, the standard Chinese answer to "Thank you" means something like "You don't have to be that polite!" So I would say yes, we are polite and we do use *please* and *thank you* a lot. A Chinese friend suggested that this might be because Americans generally don't know any other words in Chinese, but I don't think this is really fair. I think it's more a cultural thing.

Andrea

I saw a survey the other day that said that Americans themselves feel they are not as polite as they used to be. Sixty-nine percent said that Americans are ruder now than they were 20 or 30 years ago. Many people blamed this on the faster pace of life in the US today. About 70 percent said that parents were to blame for not teaching their children good manners. They also said that kids saw too many examples of rude behavior on TV. I agree. I think we used to be polite, but we aren't anymore, especially young people.

Marcos

In my job, I've met a lot of Americans and I think they're polite in the way they talk and also in the way they respect other people's opinions. And their manners in general are good. OK, this isn't true of all Americans. Some of the tourists that come here can be pretty loud and pushy, especially if they don't get the service they want, and they don't always know or respect some of our customs. I mean, you see Americans dressed in shorts, T-shirts, and sandals trying to go into a really nice restaurant. Then they don't understand why they can't do that, even when they see that all the local people are very nicely dressed – but, in general, I think the majority are OK.

Extra support

If there's time, you could have SS listen to the recording with the audioscript on page 124 so they can see exactly what they understood / didn't understand. Translate / explain any new words or phrases.

- Now ask the class what they think, especially if they have been to the US or met American people.

6 SPEAKING

- Divide SS into groups of three or four and focus on the instructions and the questionnaire.
- Then focus attention on the section **Greeting people** and the speech bubble. Elicit opinions from the whole class about what is good / bad manners in their country when meeting people for the first time.
- Let SS continue in groups. Monitor and help with vocabulary, and correct any misuse of modals of obligation, particularly confusion between *shouldn't, must not,* and *don't have to.*
- When SS have finished, if there's time, get some comments about one topic from each section.

Extra photocopiable activities

Grammar
must, have to, should page 146
Communicative
Are they true? page 177 (instructions page 164)

HOMEWORK

Study Link **Workbook** pages 24–26

G *must, may, might, can't* (deduction)
V describing people
p *-eigh, -aigh, -igh*

Judging by appearances

Lesson plan

In this lesson, SS begin by reading and talking about how people feel about their passport photos, which leads to learning vocabulary to describe people physically. From this the topic develops into how we often judge people by their appearance. SS have to try to guess three women's jobs purely on how they look. This topic provides the context for learning modal verbs of deduction. SS have met all these modals (*can, must, might*) before, but have not used them to make logical deductions. The pronunciation focus in this lesson is on the tricky combination of letters *-eigh*, *-aigh*, and *-igh*.

Optional lead-in (books closed)

- Bring in any documents you have of yourself that have a photo, e.g., passport, ID card, driver's license, etc.
- Ask SS what they do if they need a photo for ID. Elicit that you can ask someone to take a digital photo of you, or you can go to a photo studio or a photo booth. Ask SS which they think is the best and why.
- Then show your ID card, etc. to SS. Ask them if they think it is a good photo or if you look different in the photo, and then tell them where you had it taken, if you think it looks like you, and if you like it or not and why.

1 READING

a • Books open. Focus on the questions, and, if you didn't do the lead-in, explain / translate *photo booth*. Give SS time to answer the questions in pairs. Tell them that they can show each other their photos if they have ID cards, etc. with them, but that they don't have to, especially if they truly dislike their photos!

b • Now focus on the instructions and the photos, and elicit SS' opinions as to whether the people look like their passport photos.

c • Focus on the instructions and the four questions. Make sure SS understand *vain* (= placing too much importance on your appearance). Give SS a minute to read the introductory paragraph of the article, and then get them to answer the questions in pairs. Check answers.

> 1 Because it's one of the photos of ourselves that we most often show other people.
> 2 The Italians.
> 3 The Norwegians.
> 4 The French.

- Now you could read the paragraph again with the class, eliciting / clarifying meaning of new vocabulary. Ask the class how they think people from their country feel about their photos.

d • Now set a time limit for SS to read the rest of the article. Have SS, in pairs, answer the questions, and then check answers.

> **Ruth England** is happy with hers. She took time to get a good photo of herself.
> **Michael Winner** isn't happy with his. He thinks he looks like a drug dealer.
> **Toby Young** doesn't like his because it doesn't look like him, so people don't believe the passport is his.

Extra idea

Instead of having SS read quietly, you could read the three paragraphs with the class and ask after each paragraph if the person is happy with their photo and why.

e • Focus on the instructions and the highlighted words and the two possible definitions for each one. Check answers, and if necessary, elicit an exact translation of each word. Model and drill the pronunciation. Have SS underline the stress in *embarrassed* and *hideous*.

> 1 a 2 a 3 b 4 a 5 b 6 a 7 b

HOW WORDS WORK...

- Focus on the sentences and then go through the rules. The common mistake here is for SS to use *look* with a noun (*He looks a businessman*) or *look like* with an adjective (*You look like happy*). Give SS a couple of minutes to do the exercise. Check answers.

> 1 look like 2 look 3 looks like 4 look

Extra support

If you think your SS need more practice, you could write these sentences on the board for them to complete.
1 He's forty but he only _____ thirty.
2 What's that building? It _____ a factory.
3 Your boss _____ a nice person. Is she?
4 This cake _____ delicious but it's horrible.

> 1 looks 2 looks like 3 looks like 4 looks

2 VOCABULARY describing people

a • Tell SS to go to **Vocabulary Bank** *Describing people* on page 149.
- Focus on section **1 Age** and get SS to do it in pairs. Check answers.

> 1 about 2 forties 3 mid- 4 late 5 early

Extra idea

Drill the expressions by asking SS how old various famous people are (i.e., people whose exact ages SS are unlikely to know).

- Now focus on sections **2 Height and build** and **3 Hair**. Have SS match the sentences and pictures, and check answers, either after each section or after the two sections. Model and drill pronunciation.

> **2**
> 1 A 2 C 3 B
> **3**
> 1 E 2 A 3 G 4 B 5 C 6 F 7 D

- Remind SS that:
  - we use the verb *be* with adjectives like *tall*, *short*, etc., and that we frequently use modifiers, e.g., *a little, very, really*, etc.
  - we use *have* + hair (except with the adjective *bald*), and that we don't use an article, e.g., ~~she has a long blond hair / the long blond hair.~~
  - when we describe a person physically, height, build, and hair are the aspects we tend to concentrate on. We may also mention other features (eyes, nose, etc.) but usually only if they are in some way significant, e.g., *She has beautiful eyes.*
- Finally, focus on section **4 General adjectives**, which covers adjectives that describe various degrees of attractiveness. SS should first decide if they are positive or negative, and then if they are usually used for men, women, or both. Check answers and drill pronunciation if necessary.

> attractive [+] [B]   plain [–] [B]
> beautiful [+] [W]   pretty [+] [W]
> good-looking [+] [B]   ugly [–] [B]
> handsome [+] [M]

- Point out that *ugly* is much stronger than *plain*.
- Focus on the information box and point out the difference between the two questions. You could drill the questions by asking about members of the class, e.g., *What does Victor look like?* (e.g., *He's tall, he has dark hair*, etc., *What's he like?* (e.g., *He's friendly, funny*, etc.).
- Finally, focus on the instruction "Can you remember the words on this page? Test yourself or a partner."

Testing yourself

For **Age** SS can cover sentences 1–5 and just look at the definitions and try to remember the phrases. For **Height and build** and **Hair** SS can cover the sentences and look at the pictures only and remember the sentences. For **General adjectives** they can cover the right-hand column and try to remember if the adjectives are positive or negative or if they apply to men, women, or both.

Testing a partner

See **Testing a partner** on page 15.

Study Link SS can find more practice of these words on the MultiROM and on the *American English File 3* Website.

- Tell SS to go back to the main lesson on page 41.

b ● **3.5** Now focus on the pictures. Explain that two women witnessed a robbery, and SS are going to hear them describing the man they saw to the police.
- Before they listen, put SS in pairs to describe the people. Play the recording once, and let SS discuss who they think the robber is and why. Then play the recording again. Check answers, and have SS tell you why it is the right person.

> **3**

> **3.5**   CD1 Track 46
> (audioscript in Student Book on page 124)
> **P = policeman, W1 = woman 1, W2 = woman 2**
> P   OK now, can you describe the man you saw in the bank?
> W1 Well, he was, uh, sort of medium height, you know, not short – but not tall either. And quite skinny, you know, thin.
> W2 Yes. And he had a beard and a little mustache.
> W1 No, he didn't. He had a mustache but not a beard. It's just that I think he hadn't shaved.
> W2 No, it was a beard, I'm sure.
> W1 And anyway, Doris, you weren't wearing your glasses, so you probably didn't see him very well.
> W2 Yes, I did. I saw him very well.
> P   OK, OK. So, no mustache then.
> W1 No, he had a mustache but he didn't have a beard.
> P   And what about his hair?
> W2 Dark.
> W1 Yes, short, dark hair.
> P   Straight?
> W1 No, I think it was curly. What about you, Doris?
> W2 Yes, very curly.
> P   So, dark, curly hair?
> W1 Yes. That's what we said.
> P   And what time was it when…?

Extra idea

You could give SS extra practice with the vocabulary by having them describe members of their family to each other, or by having them describe famous people for their partners to identify. Encourage them to begin with the person's age, then physical description, and then (to help them to identify the person) their job.

3 PRONUNCIATION -eigh, -aigh, -igh

Pronunciation notes

These combinations of letters can present problems for SS, but in fact their pronunciation follows some clear rules:
-eigh is almost always /eɪ/. *Height* is an exception.
-aigh is always /eɪ/
-igh is always /aɪ/

a ● Focus on the instructions and the words on the list. In pairs, SS try to put them in the right column. Get them to do this by instinct.

b ● **3.6** Play the recording once for SS to check. Then check answers and point out the spelling rules given above.

3.6		CD1 Track 47
train /eɪ/	bike /aɪ/	
in his eighties	bright	
neighbor	height	
overweight	high	
straight	light brown	
weigh	might	
	sight	

Extra support

Play the recording again, pausing after each word for SS to repeat.

c ● Focus on the questions and have the class answer them. Tell SS that a good way to remember the pronunciation of *height* is to associate it with *high*.

> *-igh* is pronounced /aɪ/, *-eigh* is usually pronounced /eɪ/. *Height* is the exception.

d ● **3.7** In pairs, SS now practice saying some sentences. Play the recording for them to listen and check. For more practice you could have SS repeat after each sentence.

3.7	CD1 Track 48
1 She has light brown hair. It's short and straight.	
2 He's medium height and slightly overweight.	
3 He's in his eighties, but his eyesight's very good.	
4 She likes wearing tight straight-leg jeans.	

Study Link SS can find more practice of English sounds on the MultiROM and also on the *American English File 3* Website.

4 GRAMMAR *must, may, might, can't* (deduction)

a ● Focus on the title of the article and ask SS if they think it is true that we judge other people by their appearance.

● Focus on the pictures and the three paragraphs. Tell SS that they are going to read part of an article from *Marie Claire*, where readers had to speculate which woman had which job, guessing only from their appearance.

● First, have SS describe the three women using the vocabulary they learned in the **Vocabulary Bank**, e.g., *She looks about 30. She's short and she has short dark hair*, etc.

● Then focus on the three jobs and have SS, in pairs, guess who does what. Ask a few SS for their responses, but don't tell them if they are right or wrong. Tell SS not to read the texts at this point.

Extra idea

You could write the three numbers on the board and get a show of hands to see how many people think, e.g., that 1 is the managing director, etc.

● Now give SS a couple of minutes to read the article and match each woman to a paragraph. Have SS compare with a partner, and then check answers, getting them to say why.

1 C	2 B	3 A

b ● Focus on the instructions and give SS a few minutes to read the article again. Have SS discuss the questions in pairs and report answers to the class.

> 1 Laura, because people think she's too small to be a policewoman. Thea, because they think she's too young and dresses too casually to be a managing director.
> 2 Sam, because when people recognize her last name they expect her to be a "typical rich kid."

c ● Focus on the task and have SS do this either individually or in pairs. Check answers.

> 1 can't be
> 2 must be
> 3 might be

d ● Now tell SS to go to **Grammar Bank 3B** on page 134. Go through the examples and read the rules with the class. Model and drill the example sentences.

Extra idea

In a monolingual class, you could have SS translate the example sentences and compare the forms / verbs they would use in their L1.

Grammar notes

modals of deduction: *must* (*be*), *may* / *might* (*be*), *can't* (*be*)

● SS are already familiar with these modal verbs in other contexts, e.g., *must* for obligation, and *can't* for permission. Here they are used in a different way to speculate and make deductions.

● Although these verbs are often used with *be* in the presentation, they can be used with any verb, e.g., *She must have a lot of money*.

● The most common mistakes are, e.g., using *must not* instead of *can't* for something that's impossible, (e.g., ~~It must not be true.~~) and using *can* instead of *might* / *may* for a possibility (e.g,. *He's speaking Spanish.* ~~He can be Spanish or South American.~~).

● Now focus on the exercises on page 135 and give SS time to do them individually or in pairs. Check answers either after each exercise or when SS have done both.

a 2 G	3 A	4 D	5 J	6 C	7 F	8 E	9 B
10 H							
b 1 might	2 can't	3 might not	4 must				
5 can't	6 can't	7 must					

e ● Now tell SS to go to **Communication *Who do you think they are?*** on page 116. Go through instructions a–d. Make sure SS remember the meaning of the jobs.

● Tell SS to speculate with each person in turn, going through all the jobs, eliminating some and leaving a couple of possibilities (e.g., *The woman in A might be a violinist or a comedian*). Then when you think they've had enough time, tell them to make a final decision for each one. Monitor while they discuss and encourage them to use *He / She can't be, might be, must be*, etc.

● Check answers, eliciting from different pairs sentences with *We think he / she must be the…*, and see if any of the pairs guessed all five right.

Extra support

You could write *We think he / she must be the...* on the board.

A is a racecar driver (Danica Patrick).
B is a comedian (Jon Stewart).
C is a university professor (Gunter Weller).
D is a boxer (Leila Ali, Muhammad Ali's daughter).
E is a violinist (Nigel Kennedy).

- Tell SS to go back to the main lesson on page 43.

5 LISTENING

a ● Focus on the instructions and on the photo. Tell SS they must talk about each of the three possible answers, using *must be*, *may/might be*, or *can't be*.

- After a few minutes, elicit sentences from each pair. If they use *can't be* or *must be*, encourage them to say why, e.g., *He can't be from Sweden. He's very dark.* **Don't tell them the right answers at this stage.**

b ● **3.8** Focus on the instructions. Play the recording for SS to check their answers to **a**. Get a show of hands to see who was right.

1 He's from Spain (although he's been living in England).
2 He's in his (late) thirties.
3 He's a musician (a flamenco guitarist).

3.8   CD1 Track 49

(audioscript in Student Book on page 124)

I = interviewer, R = Rafael

I Rafael Lloyd. A Spanish first name and an English last name?
R Yes. My mother was Spanish and my father, English.
I Is Rafael your real name then or your stage name?
R It's my real name: my mother was from Cordoba in Spain and Rafael's the patron saint of Cordoba. But it's also my stage name.
I What nationality are you?
R I'm Spanish and British. I was born in Spain and I was brought up there. I've spent a lot of time in Britain, too. I've been living in England for the last ten years.
I Oh, good. Are you bilingual?
R Yes, I am.
I And, it's a strange question, do you feel more Spanish than British or vice versa?
R Well, I think I feel more Spanish in most respects, especially as a big part of my life revolves around Spanish culture. But I do like individuality, eccentricity, and tea. I must feel a little British too, I suppose!
I Do you think you look more Spanish than English?
R Well, I think I look Spanish, but when I travel, people always think I'm from their country and people have stopped me in the street, for example, in Cairo and in Rome, to ask me for help, so I must have an international face... Maybe I should be a spy!
I When did you start learning to play the guitar?
R I started when I was nine, when my family lived in

Madrid. A teacher used to come to our apartment and give me lessons.
I I see, so how long have you been working professionally as a flamenco guitarist?
R I started when I was 17, I mean, that's when I started to get paid for my first concerts. I'm now 39, and that's, uh, 22 years?

---

c ● Focus on the instructions. Give SS time in pairs to look at the headings first to see if they can remember any of the information. Now play the recording again. Then have SS compare what they understood with their partner and make notes.

- Play the recording (or part of it) again if necessary, and then check answers. Try to elicit all the information Rafael gives for each heading.

Name: His name's Rafael Lloyd – he has a Spanish first name and an English last name. It's his real name and his stage name.
Parents: His mother was Spanish and his father's English. He was born in Spain but now he lives in England.
Languages: He's bilingual (English / Spanish).
Nationality: He *feels* more Spanish than English, partly because of his job.
He thinks he *looks* Spanish, but he says he must have an "international face" because when he is abroad people always think he's from their country – e.g., if he's in Italy, people think he's Italian.
Profession:
He's a flamenco guitarist. He started playing the guitar when he was 9, in Madrid.
He's been working as a guitarist for 22 years. He started when he was 17.

d ● **3.9** Now focus on questions 1–4. If necessary, check SS understand *make a living* and *stereotype*. Play the second part of the interview once and let SS compare what they think. Play it again if necessary, and check answers.

1 It's easier to make a living in Britain because there are fewer flamenco guitarists there.
2 In the US, Germany, and Japan (but flamenco is popular all over the world).
3 The stereotype is of someone with long, dark hair (which he used to have).
4 In Spain (where they believe more in stereotypes). He thinks the British don't judge people by their appearance.

CD1 Track 50

(audioscript in Student Book on page 125)

I = interviewer, R = Rafael

I   As a flamenco guitarist living in Britain, is it easy to make a living?

R   I think life as a musician is never easy. But I think it's easier in Britain than in Spain, because there are fewer flamenco guitarists there.

I   And where's flamenco popular, apart from in Spain?

R   Well, the biggest markets for flamenco outside Spain are really the US, Germany, and Japan, but I've found that it's popular all over the world. It has a strong identity that people relate to in every corner of the planet.

I   Now, you don't look like the stereotype of a flamenco guitarist. People imagine flamenco guitarists as having long, dark hair...

R   That's true. I used to have really long hair, but I decided to cut my hair short.

I   Are people in Britain surprised when they find out that you're a flamenco guitarist?

R   No, not really. That's one of the things I like about Britain: no one judges you on appearance.

I   And what about in Spain?

R   Well, actually, in Spain people find it much harder to believe that I'm a flamenco guitarist. I think Spanish people believe in stereotypes more than in Britain. And they judge you more on your appearance. But as soon as people hear me play the guitar, they know that I'm the real thing.

I   Could you play something for us?

R   Of course.

Extra support

If there's time, you could have SS listen to the recording with the audioscript on page 125 so they can see exactly what they understood / didn't understand. Translate / explain any new words or phrases.

e ● Do this as an open class question. Elicit ideas / opinions, and tell SS what you think.

Extra photocopiable activities

Grammar
must, may, might, can't page 147
Communicative
Spot the difference page 178 (instructions page 164)

HOMEWORK

Study Link **Workbook** pages 27–29

3 C

G *can, could, be able to* (ability and possibility)
V *-ed / -ing* adjectives
P sentence stress

If at first you don't succeed, ...

Lesson plan

The grammatical focus of this lesson is for SS to learn how to use *be able to* in the tenses / forms where *can / can't* cannot be used. The context is success and failure, and the language is presented through a magazine article about three people who have tried unsuccessfully to learn something. Later in the lesson, SS read about two women – a swimmer and a surfer – who have succeeded in their sport despite suffering enormous setbacks – they both lost a limb. The pronunciation focus is on sentence stress in sentences with *can / could / be able to*, and SS talk about different skills and whether they can do them or would like to be able to do them. The vocabulary focus reviews *-ed* and *-ing* adjectives, which SS have seen before in *American English File 2*.

Optional lead-in (books closed)

- Write on the board:

  Noun: **SUCCESS**   Opposite noun: _____
  Adj: _____   Opposite adj: _____
  Verb: _____   Opposite verb: _____

- Put SS in pairs. First, elicit the meaning of *success* (= something well done), that it's a noun, and that the stress is on the second syllable. Then have SS try to complete the chart. Check answers and drill pronunciation.

success	failure
successful	unsuccessful
succeed	fail

- Now ask SS whether they have ever tried to learn to do something, e.g., to learn a sport, and not succeeded. Get responses from the class and find out *why* the person failed to learn.

1 GRAMMAR *can, could, be able to*

a ● Books open. Write the title of the lesson on the board: *If at first you don't succeed, ...* Focus on the instructions, and have SS, in pairs, choose a sentence half to complete the sentence. Elicit answers from different pairs before telling them what the saying is:

> If at first you don't succeed, try, try again.

- Now elicit ideas for which phrase SS think is the best advice.

b ● Focus on the definition of *be able to*, and elicit that it is similar in meaning to *can*. Tell SS that now they are going to see how *be able to* is used and to compare it with *can*.

c ● Focus on the task and on sentences A–G. Set a time limit for SS to read the text and to fill the blanks with the missing phrases. Tell them to read each text first before they try to complete it.

- Have them compare their answers with a partner's and then check answers.

1 D	2 G	3 B	4 F	5 A	6 E	7 C

Extra support

Do the first text with the whole class.

d ● Focus on the instructions and the question. Then take each phrase and elicit the answers.

A present perfect	**D** simple past
B simple past	**E** gerund
C future with *will*	**F** conditional
	G simple present

e ● Tell SS to go to **Grammar Bank 3C** on page 134. Go through the examples and read the rules with the class. Model and drill where necessary.

Extra idea

In a monolingual class, you could have SS translate the example sentences and compare the forms / verbs they would use in their L1.

Grammar notes

be able to

- SS should all be perfectly familiar with the verb *can* for ability and possibility (or permission). *Can / can't* is a modal verb that has a past and conditional tense (*could / couldn't*) but has no present perfect or past perfect forms, nor does it have an infinitive or *-ing* form. In these situations *be able to* must be used.

- Typical mistakes:
  – Trying to use *can* where they should use *be able to*, e.g., ~~I want to can speak English well.~~ / ~~I won't can come to your party on Saturday.~~
  – leaving out *to*, e.g., ~~I won't be able help you.~~

⚠ There is a small difference between *could* and *was able to*. In a (+) simple past sentence, if we want to refer to something difficult that someone succeeded in doing **on a specific occasion**, we use *be able to* (or *managed to*), e.g., *Although the space was very small, he was able to (or managed to) park there.* In this context it is not possible to use *could*. With a strong class you may want to point this out.

- Now focus on the exercises on page 135 and give SS time to do them individually or in pairs. Check answers either after SS have done the first exercise or after they have done both of them.

a	1	haven't been able to	5	Will … be able to
	2	be able to	6	'd be able to
	3	won't be able to	7	'll be able to
	4	to be able to	8	not being able to
b	1	can't	5	can
	2	could	6	to be able to
	3	to be able to	7	can
	4	won't be able to	8	haven't been able to

f
- Now put SS in pairs, **A** and **B**, preferably face to face. Tell them to go to **Communication** *Guess the sentence.* **A** go to page 116, and **B** go to page 119.
- Demonstrate the activity by writing in large letters on a piece of paper the following sentence:
  Sorry. I won't be able to see you tonight.
  Don't show the piece of paper to the SS yet. Then write on the board:
  Sorry. I won't _____ you tonight.
- Tell SS that what's missing is a form of *be able to* + a verb. Tell them that they have to guess the exact sentence that you have written on a piece of paper. Elicit ideas. If they are wrong, say "Try again," until someone comes out with the right answer. Then show them your piece of paper with the sentence on it.
- Tell SS to look at instruction **a**. Give them a few minutes to complete their sentences **in a logical way**. Explain that their partner has the same sentences already completed and the idea is to try and complete the sentences in the same way. Emphasize that they have to use a form of *be able to*. Monitor and help while they are doing this. **Tell SS not to show their sentences to their partner.**
- Now tell SS **A** and **B** to focus on their instruction **a** and tell **A** to read out his / her first sentence and for **B** to tell him / her if he / she has guessed the sentence correctly. If not, he / she has to guess again. When they finish, SS **B** read his / her sentences to SS **A**, etc.
- Tell SS to go back to the main lesson on page 45.

2 PRONUNCIATION sentence stress

Pronunciation notes

The first exercise here focuses on the strong and weak pronunciations of *can* and *could*.

SS have been made aware of this before, but it is an important point as it can cause communication problems, e.g., if a student says *I can do it* (incorrectly stressing *can*), a native speaker will probably understand *I can't do it.*

The second and third exercises are to help SS get the right rhythm when they make *be able to* sentences.

a
- **3.10** Focus on the instructions and tell SS that they will hear the dictation twice.
- Play the recording, pausing between sentences to give SS time to write. Then play the recording again.
- SS may have difficulty distinguishing between *can* and *can't*. Check answers.

3.10	CD2 Track 2
1 He could read when he was four.	
2 I can't play the guitar.	
3 Where could we have dinner?	
4 I can see what you mean.	
5 We couldn't find the street.	
6 What can you do there?	

- Now remind SS that:
  – *can* and *could* are normally unstressed in affirmative (+) and interrogative (?) sentences when they are pronounced /kən/ and /kəd/. In negative (-) sentences *can't* and *couldn't* are stressed and are pronounced /kænt/ and /kʊdnt/. Emphasize the importance of <u>not</u> stressing *can* in affirmative sentences (see **Pronunciation notes**).
- Play the recording again for SS to listen and repeat the sentences.

b
- **3.11** Here SS practice the rhythm of sentences with *be able to*. Play the recording once all the way through, and then play it again, pausing after each sentence for SS to repeat it.

3.11	CD2 Track 3
1 I'd <u>love</u> to be <u>able</u> to <u>ski</u>.	
2 We <u>won't</u> be <u>able</u> to <u>come</u>.	
3 I've <u>never</u> been <u>able</u> to <u>dance</u>.	
4 She <u>hates</u> <u>not</u> being <u>able</u> to <u>drive</u>.	

c
- **3.12** Go through the instructions. Explain (or show on the board) that they will first hear an example sentence, e.g., *I'd love to be able to ski.* Then they will hear a verb (e.g., **ride a horse**). SS then have to make a new sentence using that verb, i.e., *I'd love to be able to ride a horse.* At the same time they should try to copy the rhythm of the original sentence.
- When SS are clear what they have to do, play the recording and get the whole class to respond. Repeat the activity for extra practice.

3.12	CD2 Track 4
1 I'd love to be able to ski.	
(*ride a horse*) I'd love to be able to ride a horse.	
(*windsurf*) I'd love to be able to windsurf.	
2 We won't be able to come.	
(*park*) We won't be able to park.	
(*do it*) We won't be able to do it.	
3 I've never been able to dance.	
(*speak French*) I've never been able to speak French.	
(*play chess*) I've never been able to play chess.	
4 She hates not being able to drive.	
(*cook*) She hates not being able to cook.	
(*swim*) She hates not being able to swim.	

3 SPEAKING

- Focus on the instructions and on the abilities in the circle, making sure SS understand them all.
- Now focus on the "flow chart" and show SS the two possible routes depending on the answer to the first question. To demonstrate the activity, have SS ask you about a couple of the abilities.

- Put SS in pairs, preferably face to face. If there is an odd number of SS in the class, you can take part yourself or have one group of three. Monitor and correct any misuse of *can / could / be able to*.
- Ask SS to report afterward and find out how many people, e.g., can ride a horse or can't cook, etc.

HOW WORDS WORK...

Two different meanings of *so* are looked at here.

1 Focus on the two examples and have SS match *so* to its uses. Check answers.

> **1** to emphasize an adjective or adverb
> **2** to connect a cause and result

2 Give SS a minute in pairs to decide which use of *so* is exemplified in each sentence. Check answers.

> **A** 1 **B** 2 **C** 1 **D** 1 **E** 2

- Point out that *so* (to connect a cause and result) is sometimes used in the middle of a sentence and sometimes at the beginning of a new sentence, e.g., *When we got to the station the train had already left. So, we got a taxi home.*
- You could also tell SS that *so* is often used at the beginning of a question like this: *So, what happened in the end?*

4 VOCABULARY *-ed / -ing* adjectives

a • Focus on the picture and on the questions and elicit answers. Elicit / explain / translate the meaning of the two adjectives in each case.

> **1** The woman (C) is **bored** because the man is talking too much. He (A) is **boring**.
> **2** The little girl (B) is **embarrassed** because of the way her father is dancing. He (D) is **embarrassing**.

- Point out that:
  - the *-ed* adjective is used for the person who **has** the feeling, i.e., a *boring* person makes us feel *bored*.
  - the *-ing* adjective is used for a thing (or person) that **causes** the feeling.

b • Focus on the instructions and remind SS that these are all adjectives that have both *-ing* and *-ed* forms. Give SS a couple of minutes to choose the right adjective.

c • Tell SS to look at the texts on page 44 to check answers. Make sure SS know what the correct adjective means.

⚠ *Embarrassed* can cause some difficulty in some languages.

> **1** disappointed **2** embarrassing **3** frustrating

d • Now give SS a minute to complete the adjectives in the questions with *-ed* or *-ing*. Check answers.

> **1** exciting   **6** bored
> **2** depressed   **7** embarrassing
> **3** interesting   **8** frightened
> **4** disappointed   **9** tired
> **5** tiring   **10** boring

e • Focus on the questions. Have SS ask you a couple of questions first and have them ask for more information. SS then ask and answer in pairs.

5 LISTENING

a • Focus on the instructions. Give SS a minute to match the three phrasal verbs and their meanings. Check answers.

> **1** c **2** a **3** b

Extra idea

You could quickly drill the verbs by asking SS: *Are you going to keep on learning English next year? Is there anything you just gave up? Would you like to take up a new language or sport? Which one?*

b • **3.13** Focus on the instructions and give SS a few minutes to read the seven tips. The first time SS listen they must check the **five** tips they hear the psychologist mention. Play the recording all the way through, and play again if necessary. Check answers.

> 1 3 4 5 7

> **3.13**   CD2 Track 5
>
> (audioscript in Student Book on page 125)
> **I = interviewer, P = psychologist**
> **I** Hello and welcome to this week's edition of *All about you*. Today's program's about taking up new activities, and how to succeed at them. With us is psychologist Dr. Maggie Prior. Good afternoon.
> **P** Good afternoon.
> **I** Dr. Prior, what tips can you give our listeners who are thinking of learning to do something new?
> **P** Well, first of all, I would say **choose wisely**. On the one hand, **don't choose something completely unrealistic. For example, don't decide to take up sailing if you can't swim,** or parachute jumping if you're afraid of heights. But, on the other hand, **don't generalize and think that just because you aren't very good at one sport, you won't be able to do any sports at all.** I mean, just because you were bad at gymnastics at school doesn't mean that you might not love playing tennis.
> **I** So think positive?
> **P** Definitely. And never think you'll be bad at something before you've even tried it.
> **I** OK, so, let's imagine I've started to learn to play tennis and I'm finding it very hard work.
> **P** **Well, first don't give up too quickly, keep on trying for at least a few months**. It often takes time to begin to enjoy learning something new. Another thing that can help, **if you're having problems learning something, is to give it a break and then try again, perhaps a month or two later.**
> **I** But what if I find I really don't have a talent for tennis?
> **P** I think **the important thing is not to be too ambitious. I mean, if you've never been active in sports and you decide to learn to play tennis, don't expect to become the next Wimbledon champion. Just aim to enjoy what you're doing, not to be the best in the world at it.**
> **I** But what if, even after all this, I still feel I'm not getting anywhere?

P Well, sometimes you do have to accept it and say, "OK, this really isn't my thing," and you need to give it up. But why not try something else? There are lots of other things you can learn to do. **But remember that if you take up an activity that you're really interested in, even if you aren't very good at it, you'll make new friends, because you'll be meeting other people who have similar interests.**

I So it might be good for my love life.

P Exactly.

I Dr. Maggie Prior, thank you very much.

c ● Now focus on the instructions and then play the recording again. Pause after each tip and then let SS discuss in pairs exactly what they understood. Check answers, and then play the next tip, etc.

1 Don't take up sailing if you can't swim.

3 Just because you were bad at gymnastics doesn't mean you won't love tennis.

4 Keep on trying for at least a few months. / Have a break and then try again one or two months later.

5 If you take up tennis, don't expect to become the next Wimbledon champion.

7 You'll meet other people who have similar interests to you.

Extra support

If there's time, you could have SS listen again with the audioscript on page 125 so they can see exactly what they understood / didn't understand. Translate / explain any new words or phrases.

6 READING

a ● Do this as an open class question. If you know someone yourself, tell SS about him / her.

b ● Focus on the photos and ask what's unusual about the two women.

● Focus on the instructions, and make sure SS understand the questions in the chart.

● Put SS in pairs and give them time (e.g., five minutes) to each read their article, and complete the chart.

Natalie

1 A car hit her when she was going to a training session on a motorcycle.

2 Three months after the accident.

3 Thrilled. It felt like her leg was there.

4 She qualified for the final at the Commonwealth Games in Manchester (for able-bodied swimmers).

5 She hopes to swim faster than she did before the accident.

Bethany

1 A tiger shark attacked her and tore off her arm.

2 As soon as she left hospital.

3 She was so happy she cried.

4 She finished 5th at the National Surfing Championship.

5 She accepts that she will never be world champion.

c ● When SS have finished, have them use the chart to tell each other about the person they have read about. Encourage them to give as much detail as they can. Monitor the pairs and help and correct as necessary.

d ● Focus on the instructions. Give SS time to read the text they haven't read yet and to underline five words / phrases they want to remember in either text. They can use their dictionary if they have one. Monitor and help with any problems.

e ● Focus on the instructions and have SS answer the two questions.

They are both athletes who excelled in water sports. They both lost a limb, but have both gone back to their sports and have triumphed again, competing against able-bodied people.
Natalie still wants to improve as a swimmer and her dream is to swim faster than before she had the accident. Bethany, however, has accepted that she will never fulfill her dream to be world champion.

7 3.14 ♫ SONG *You can get it if you really want*

● This song was originally made famous in 1972 by the Jamaican reggae singer Jimmy Cliff. If you want to do this song in class, use the photocopiable on page 206.

3.14	CD2 Track 6

You can get it if you really want

You can get it if you really want,
You can get it if you really want,
You can get it if you really want,
But you must try, try and try,
Try and try,
You'll succeed at last.

Persecution you must bear,
Win or lose, you've got to get your share
Got your mind set on a dream
You can get it, though hard it seems
Now

You can get it if you really want, etc.

Rome was not built in a day,
Opposition will come your way
But the harder the battle you see,
It's the sweeter the victory
Now

You can get it if you really want, etc.

Study Link SS can find a dictation and a Grammar quiz on all the grammar from File 3 on the MultiROM and more grammar activities on the *American English File 3* Website.

Extra photocopiable activities

Grammar
can, could, be able to page 148
Communicative
Find someone who… page 179 (instructions page 164)
Vocabulary
Pictionary page 197 (instructions page 193)
Song
You can get it if you really want page 206
(instructions page 203)

HOMEWORK

Study Link Workbook pages 30–32

Function Directions
Language *The easiest way is to get the metro. Take line 11 to…*

Lesson plan

In this lesson SS practice giving and understanding directions that involve taking public transportation (in this case the Paris metro). The language taught could also be used for trips by bus, e.g., *How many stops is it?*, etc.

In **Social English** Nicole takes Mark to see an apartment. While they are looking at the apartment, Allie calls Mark on his cell phone, but he tells Nicole that the caller was his daughter in the United States.

Study Link These lessons are on the *American English File 3* Video, which can be used instead of the Class Audio CD for these lessons (see Introduction page 9). The main functional section of each episode is also on the MultiROM with additional activities.

Optional lead-in (books closed)

- Review what happened in the previous episode by eliciting the story from SS, e.g., *What happened in the last episode?* (Mark chatted to Nicole in the bar after work.) *Who did they talk about?* (Ben, Jacques, and Allie.) *What did Nicole say about Allie?* (She is pretty but she dresses in a very English way. She is also very formal.) *Who arrived at the end?* (Allie.)

- Remind SS of the language that they learned in the last lesson (ways of making requests and asking permission). You could write some of the key expressions on the board with blanks for SS to complete.

- If you are using the Video, you could play the previous episode again, leaving out the "Listen and Repeat" sections.

HOW TO GET THERE

a ● **3.15** Focus on the photo and elicit that Mark is probably asking for directions. Then focus on the instructions and the three questions. Tell SS to cover the conversation with their hand or a piece of paper.

Extra idea

You could write the questions on the board and have SS listen with books closed.

- Play the recording once and check answers.

> The apartment is in Belleville. The best way to go is by metro (subway). Mark is going to drive there with Nicole.

b ● Now have SS look at the conversation. In pairs, they read it and see if they can guess or remember the missing words. Emphasize that they shouldn't write the words in the conversation, but in pencil alongside or on a separate sheet of paper.

c ● Play the recording again for them to check. Then go through the conversation line by line and check answers. Find out how many SS had guessed the words correctly. Where they had not guessed correctly, see if their alternative also fits.

- Point out the idiomatic phrase *I'll give you a lift* (third line from bottom of dialogue) which means *I'll take you in my car*. You could also mention that in American English this is usually *I'll give you a ride*.

3.15   CD2 Track 7

M = Mark, J = Jacques, N = Nicole
M Where **exactly** is it? … I'm sorry, I didn't catch that. OK. **How far** is it? … OK, OK. Merci. Au revoir.
J Any luck?
M I think I've found an apartment… How do I **get** to Belleville?
J The easiest **way** is to get the metro at Pyramides. Take line 14 and **change** at Châtelet.
M OK.
J Then take Line 11 **towards** Mairie des Lilas.
M Where do I **get** off?
J At Belleville.
M How many **stops** is it?
J Six, I think.
M Oh, right. I've found it on the map. How long does it **take** to get there?
J About half an hour.
N Have you found a flat?
M Yeah… In Belleville this time.
N When are you going to see it?
M This afternoon.
N If you can wait till six, I'll **give** you a lift. I live near Belleville, so I'm driving that way.
M That's great. Thanks.

---

d ● **3.16** Now focus on the key phrases highlighted in the conversation. Play the recording, pausing after each sentence for SS to repeat. Encourage them to copy the rhythm and intonation.

⚠ Don't worry too much about how they pronounce the French place names.

3.16   CD2 Track 8

M = Mark, J = Jacques, N = Nicole
M Where exactly is it?
M How far is it?
M How do I get to Belleville?
J The easiest way is to get the metro at Pyramides.
J Take line 14 and change at Châtelet.
J Then take line 11 towards Mairie des Lilas.
M Where do I get off?
M How many stops is it?
M How long does it take to get there?
N If you can wait till six, I'll give you a lift.

---

e ● Now have SS cover the conversation and focus on the answers. Elicit the questions from the whole class.

> 1 How do I get to Belleville?
> 2 Where do I get off?
> 3 How many stops is it?
> 4 How long does it take to get there?

You could give SS further practice of the rhythm of the phrases by getting them to read the conversation in pairs.

f ● Put SS in pairs, **A** and **B**. Tell them to go to **Communication** *How do I get there?*, **A** on page 117 and **B** on page 120. Go through the instructions and focus on the speech bubbles. Give SS time to decide on the best routes from South Station to wherever they are going to give directions to.

  ● **A** starts by asking **B** for directions. It is probably easier if **A** asks for directions for each of the places, and they then change roles, rather than asking alternately for directions. Monitor to check that SS are drawing the routes correctly.

  ● Finally, you could ask the class if anyone has ever used a US subway and if so, whether they found it easy or difficult to use.

SOCIAL ENGLISH What's going on?

a ● **3.17** Focus on the photo and ask *Who can you see? Where are they? What are they doing?* Then focus on the question and play the recording once and check answers.

> Yes, he does.

3.17	CD2 Track 9

(audioscript in Student Book on page 125)
L = landlady, M = Mark, A = Allie, N = Nicole

L This is the apartment. *Je vous laisse visiter. Je serai en bas.*
M Merci, madame. Sorry, Nicole. What did she say?
N She said that we can have a look at the flat. She's going to wait downstairs.
M Thanks. So, what do you think?
N Well, it's a long way from the station. And it's on the fourth floor. It's a pity there isn't a lift.
M Who needs one? The stairs are good exercise. Look, there's a great view from here.
N It's also very noisy.
M Sure, but it has character. It's just how I imagined an apartment in Paris.
N Everything's old, including the heating. It will be very cold in the winter.
M Oh, hi.
A (*on phone*) Well, what's it like?
M Nice – really Parisian.
A Are you going to take it?
M I think so, yeah…
A I can't wait to see it!
M Yeah…
A Are you OK? Are you on your own?
M No, I'm with the woman who owns the apartment. I'll call you back.
A OK, speak later. Love you.
M Love you too, bye. Sorry about that. That was… that was my… my daughter.
N Calling from America?
M You know. She's just taking an interest.
N Taking an interest. That's nice.

---

b ● Focus on the questions. Then play the recording again. Have SS compare answers, and then play it one more time if necessary. Check answers, and elicit / explain the meaning of any words or expressions SS didn't understand. You may need to remind students that *flat* and *lift* are the British words for *apartment* and *elevator*.

> **1 Advantages:** It has a great view, it has character, it's very Parisian.
> **Disadvantages:** It's a long way from the station, it's on the 4th floor and there's no elevator, it's noisy, everything's old (including the heating).
> **2** He tells Allie he's with the owner of the apartment because he doesn't want her to know he's with Nicole. He tells Nicole that it was his daughter on the phone because he doesn't want her to know Allie called him. Nicole probably doesn't believe him.

Extra support

If there's time, you could have SS listen to the recording with the audioscript on page 125 so they can see exactly what they understood / didn't understand. Translate / explain any new words or phrases.

c ● **3.18** Now focus on the **USEFUL PHRASES**. Give SS a moment to try to complete them, and then play the recording to check.

3.18	CD2 Track 10

M So, what do you **think**?
N It's a long **way** from (the station).
A What's it **like**?
A I can't **wait** (to see it)!
A Are you on your **own**?
M I'll call you **back**.

Extra idea

Ask SS if they can remember who said each phrase (and in what context), e.g., Mark says *So what do you think?* (When he asks Nicole about the apartment.)

d ● Play the recording again, pausing for SS to repeat. In a monolingual class, elicit the equivalent expressions in SS' L1.

HOMEWORK

Study Link Workbook page 33

Lesson plan

In this third writing lesson, SS practice writing an informal letter. Although today most people tend to send e-mails when possible, there are some circumstances, for example to say thank you, where a handwritten letter might be more appropriate. Also, SS are sometimes required to write this kind of letter in external exams. The content and style are the same as for an e-mail with just a couple of small differences.

a • Focus on the instructions. SS may remember Amanda, Claudia's friend (from **Writing 1**) who wanted to stay for a month in the US.

• Go through A–G making sure SS understand *apologize, mention*, etc. Then give SS a few minutes to decide on a logical order for the letter. Don't check answers.

b • Now have SS read the letter to see whether their order coincides with Amanda's. Check answers.

1 D	2 B	3 G	4 E	5 C	6 F	7 A

Extra idea

As you correct, ask SS a few questions about the content of the letter, e.g., after 1, *Why didn't she write earlier?* (Because she has been very busy.), after 3, *What nice things does she mention?* (The weather, how her English got better, meeting Claire and Emma.), etc.

c • Focus on the second paragraph of Amanda's letter and tell SS there are five punctuation mistakes. Elicit what kind of mistakes these might be, e.g., not using capital letters, leaving out apostrophes or putting them in the wrong place, or not using periods or commas correctly.

• Give SS a few minutes to find the mistakes, individually or in pairs. Then check answers.

> **I'm** writing to thank you for inviting me to stay with you in **July.** I had a fantastic time. The weather was perfect and I really think my **English** got better. **I** hope you think so too!

d • Give SS a moment to look back and compare the e-mails on page 17 with the letter. Elicit that an informal e-mail and an informal letter are almost identical in style / organization, etc. The only real difference is that:

– in letters you write your address. In an e-mail you don't usually do that.

– you usually begin a letter with *Dear* (name). In e-mails people often use *Hi* (name) instead of *Dear*.

– in a letter you *enclose* a photo (i.e., put it in the envelope). In an e-mail you *attach* a photo electronically.

• Finally, focus on the **Useful language** box and go through the expressions (which can be used in either informal letters or e-mails).

WRITE a letter to thank them

Go through the instructions. Then either have SS plan and write the letter in class (set a time limit of 20 minutes) or have them just plan in class, or assign both the planning and writing for homework.

Before SS hand in their letters, have them exchange them with another student to read and check for mistakes.

For instructions on how to use these pages, see page 30.

GRAMMAR

1 should join	6 don't have
2 can't be	7 must be
3 be able	8 might be / may be
4 must not / can't	9 have to
5 might not / may not	10 shouldn't drink

VOCABULARY

a 1 mid 2 length 3 straight 4 bangs 5 wears
b 1 interested 2 depressed 3 boring
   4 embarrassing 5 frustrated
c 1 off 2 back 3 up 4 like 5 in

PRONUNCIATION

a 1 fifties (It's /ɪ/.)	4 change (It's /dʒ/.)
2 height (It's /aɪ/.)	5 mustache (It's /ʃ/.)
3 brown (It's /aʊ/.)	

b disa<u>ppoi</u>nted emba<u>rra</u>ssing <u>i</u>nterested fru<u>s</u>trated
<u>ove</u>r<u>weight</u>

CAN YOU UNDERSTAND THIS TEXT?

a 1 b 2 a 3 c 4 a 5 b
b **burst into tears** = suddenly start crying
   console = make someone feel better about their
   problems
   sympathetic = understanding other people's feelings /
   problems
   I couldn't stand it = I couldn't bear / tolerate the
   situation
   deeply hurt = (made to feel) very unhappy / upset

CAN YOU UNDERSTAND THESE PEOPLE?

a 1 b 2 c 3 a 4 c 5 b
b 1 Daniel 2 Gatti 3 Argentinian 4 Advanced
   5 Canada

3.19 CD2 Track 11

1 A Oh no. I can't find my cell phone!
  B Well, you had it when we were in the cafe. You
    were texting your friend.
  A Yes, that's right. Maybe I left it in there.
  B Do you want to go back and see?
  A But can you call me first? Then if my cell's in the
    cafe, maybe someone will answer it.
  B OK. Hey, I can hear it. It must be in your bag
    somewhere.
  A No, it's in my jacket pocket.
2 A I'm starving. What time did you ask them to
    come?
  B I said to come at eight o'clock for drinks, and then
    dinner at 8:30.

  A Well, it's 8:15 now.
  B Yes, they should be here any minute. They're
    usually very punctual.
  A Ah – that must be them… Who was it?
  B Somebody collecting money for charity. Honestly,
    I think people should call when they're going to be
    late. It's very inconsiderate. It's almost twenty after
    now.
3 A No! Is that you? It doesn't look anything like you! I
    didn't know you used to have long hair!
  B Well, this passport is nearly ten years old. Which
    reminds me, I'm going to have to renew it soon.
  A Well, you definitely need a new photo. This one
    looks really awful.
  B OK, let's see yours then.
  A No, no, you can't see it. I hate showing people my
    passport photo.
  B Come on! You've seen mine. Oh, that's not bad. It's
    a lot better than mine. In fact, I think I prefer your
    hair as it was then.
4 A So where did you meet him?
  B At work. He's one of the designers.
  A And what's he like?
  B He's funny, intelligent…
  A Yes, but what does he look like?
  B Just like Orlando Bloom, tall, dark, and handsome
    – no, I'm joking. He has short dark hair and he's
    not very tall. But I think he's really good-looking.
5 A What happened? How did it go?
  B No comment.
  A Not again. What did you do this time?
  B Nothing. I mean, nothing wrong. It was really
    unfair. Just because I was going a little bit too fast
    down Main Street.
  A Oh well. You'll just have to take it again. Third
    time is the charm.

3.20 CD2 Track 12

A Hello, sit down. I'm the secretary and you are…?
B Daniel.
A And your last name is…?
B Gatti. G–A–T–T–I.
A Are you from Italy?
B No, my grandparents were Italian, but I'm
  Argentinian. But people always think I must be
  Italian because of my name.
A Oh, sorry. And what course were you thinking of
  taking?
B I'd like to take the advanced course. I took an upper-
  intermediate course in Buenos Aires last year, so I
  think I'll be able to handle an advanced course here.
A Well, you'll have to take a level test first. You might
  find the advanced course pretty difficult. Is this your
  first time in the US?
B Yes, but I've been to Canada last year.
A I *went* to Canada last year, you mean. You see, maybe
  you're not ready for the advanced after all. Now, the
  level test takes one hour.

4

A

G first conditional and future time clauses + *when, until,* etc.
V education
P /ʌ/ or /yu/?

Back to school, age 35

File 4 overview

This File reviews and extends three structures that SS should have previously seen and were in *American English File 2.* However, second conditionals (**4B**) and *used to* (**4C**) are structures that SS are unlikely to be able to use accurately and confidently, and need to be thoroughly presented again in order for SS to now incorporate them into their active grammar. Lesson **4A** reviews first conditional sentences and introduces future tense clauses with *when, until,* etc. In **4B** second conditional sentences are presented again and contrasted with first conditionals. In **4C** *used to* to describe past states and habits is presented again and extended, and SS are reminded how to talk about present habits. The main lexical areas in this File are education, houses, and friendship.

Lesson plan

This lesson is about education and provides two different angles on the topic. An adapted text from a newspaper looks at the experience of a 35-year-old journalist who spent a week, as a student, at a high school to see if school today is easier than it used to be. In the second half of the lesson, SS hear about the results of another experiment (this time a TV program) when some students from a modern day school spent a month in a 1953-style boarding school. The grammar focus reviews first conditional sentences and looks at the use of the present tense in other time clauses after *when, as soon as, until,* etc. In vocabulary, SS learn high-frequency words and phrases related to education, and then practice pronouncing some of these in the pronunciation section, which focuses on the letter *u.*

Optional lead-in (books closed)

Put SS in pairs. Write **SCHOOL SUBJECTS** on the board and give pairs three or four minutes to think of as many subjects as they can, e.g., *history.* When the time is up, write SS' ideas on the board.

1 VOCABULARY education

a ● Books open. Focus on the eight questions and give SS a time limit to answer them. Check answers.

1 1945	5 Albert Einstein
2 Bogotá	6 22 1/2 (or 22.5)
3 Cervantes	7 six
4 1,024	8 hydrogen and oxygen

b ● Now give SS a little more time to match questions 1–8 with the school subjects by writing the correct number in each box. Check answers and model and drill pronunciation, especially *geography* /dʒiˈɑgrəfi/ and *literature* /ˈlɪtərətʃər/.

chemistry 8	literature 3
geography 2	math 6
history 1	physics 5
information technology 4	biology 7

c ● Tell SS to go to **Vocabulary Bank** *Education* on page 150. Give them time to do section **1 Verbs** individually or in pairs. Check answers and elicit and drill pronunciation.

2 review	7 start, leave
3 learn	8 pass, fail
4 do	9 behave
5 cheat	10 graduate /ˈɡrædʒueɪt/
6 take	

● Now SS do section **2 Places and people**. Check answers and elicit and drill pronunciation of difficult items. Elicit / explain and the phrase *has a degree* in definition 10 (= has finished college and passed all the exams). Point out the different pronunciations of *graduate* as verb and noun.

1 public school	6 college
2 private school	7 principal
3 preschool	8 professor
4 elementary school	9 student
5 secondary school	10 graduate /ˈɡrædʒuət/

● Finally, have SS to do section **3 School life** matching sentences and pictures. Check answers.

1 B
2 A
3 E
4 C
5 D

● Focus on the final instruction "Can you remember the words on this page? Test yourself or a partner."

Testing yourself

For **Verbs** SS can cover the list and the **Verb** column. They look at sentences 1–10 and try to remember the verbs. For **Places and people** have SS cover the list and words 1–10. They read the definitions and try to remember the words, uncovering one by one to check. For **School life** have SS cover the words and look at the pictures and try to remember the phrases.

Testing a partner

See **Testing a partner** on page 15.

Study Link SS can find more practice of these words on the MultiROM and on the *American English File 3* Website.

● Tell SS to go back to the main lesson on page 52.

2 PRONUNCIATION & SPEAKING /ʌ/ or /yu/?

Pronunciation notes

The letter *u* has several different pronunciations, but between consonants, or at the beginning of a word, it is usually (but not <u>always</u>) /ʌ/, e.g., *sun, luck, summer* or /yu/, e.g., *music, cute, utility*.

SS often don't realize that there is a kind of "hidden sound" – /y/ – in words like *music* and *cute* and tend to pronounce them /muzɪk/ or /kut/.

Students are also reminded here about the rule governing the use of the indefinite article *a* or *an* before words beginning with *u*. If the *u* is pronounced /ʌ/ (i.e., a vowel sound), then *an* is used, e.g., **an umbrella, an uncle**, but if *u* is pronounced /yu/ (i.e., a consonant sound), then *a* is used, e.g., **a uniform, a university, a useful book**.

- Focus on the ⚠ box and point out the two common pronunciations of the letter *u*.
- You may want to point out here that *u* is also sometimes (but much less commonly) pronounced /ʊ/, e.g., *put* and *full*.

a • Focus on the task and make sure SS understand how the two sounds are pronounced. Give SS a few moments in pairs to put the words in the right column.

b • **4.1** Play the recording once for SS to check their answers. Then play it again, pausing after each word for SS to repeat.

4.1	CD2 Track 13
/ʌ/	/yu/
lunch	computer
fun	usually
result	uniform
study	university
subject	

- Finally, focus on the question about *a* / *an* before words beginning with *u* and elicit answers. (See **Pronunciation notes**.)

We use *a* when *u* is pronounced /yu/ and *an* when *u* is pronounced /ʌ/.

c • **4.2** Now SS practice saying sentences containing the two sounds. First, in pairs, have them practice saying the sentences to each other. Then play the recording for them to check their pronunciation (you could do this sentence by sentence). Then have individual students say the sentences.

4.2	CD2 Track 14
1 What subjects did you study in high school?	
2 Do students at that school wear uniforms?	
3 Most students have lunch in the cafeteria.	
4 We usually have fun in our music class.	

Study Link SS can practice more English sounds on the MultiROM and also on the *American English File 3* Website.

d • Education vocabulary is now put into practice in a free-speaking activity. SS interview their partner asking the questions in the questionnaire.
- Focus on the question prompts. Remind SS that if they are currently in high school, they should use the present tense (i.e., add *do* or *is* / *are* to the prompts). If they have finished school, they should use the past tense (i.e., add *did* or *was* / *were* to the prompts).

Extra support

Elicit the questions in the questionnaire before you start the activity.

- SS take turns interviewing each other. Remind the student who is interviewing to react to the interviewee's answers and ask for more information where possible (*Really?* / *That's interesting, etc.* / *Why didn't you like it?*, etc.).
- Get responses from the whole class at the end and find out, e.g., how many people liked / didn't like their school and what their best / worst subjects were.

3 READING

a • Focus on the photo on the left and elicit answers to the question.

One of the students is an adult.

b • Now have SS read the introduction and find out the answers to the two questions. Check answers.

He's a journalist. He wanted to see if it was true that school is getting easier. He went to a large, public high school.

c • Give SS a time limit to read the text, e.g., five minutes, and focus on the question. The first time they read, SS should just try to get a general understanding of the text. Tell them not to worry about the blanks. Check answers.

He finds school very different today because teaching methods have changed. He found it difficult to say if classes are more difficult or easier than when he went to school, but he found being a student in today's school very hard work.

d • SS now read the text again and try to complete the blanks with phrases A–H. Focus on the phrases first and make sure SS understand, e.g., *crowd* (= a big group of people), *be involved* (= take part, be engaged in something), and any other words from the phrases (i.e., not from the text, because they'll do these later) you think they may not know.
- Set a time limit again, e.g., five minutes, and then have SS compare their answers in pairs before checking answers.

2 D   3 H   4 C   5 G   6 B   7 E   8 A

e • In pairs, SS focus on the highlighted words and phrases. Set a time limit. If SS don't have dictionaries, they should ask another pair to help with the meaning of unknown words *before* they ask you. Move around the class helping SS, but then have a feedback stage at the end where you try to explain or translate any words or phrases SS aren't sure of.

> **interrogating** = asking questions in an aggressive way
> **in return** = in exchange
> **cafeteria** = a communal dining room, e.g., in a school or factory
> **spreadsheets** = a computer program used for financial planning
> **hand in** = give something to somebody in authority, e.g., a teacher
> **slightly dazed** = (a little bit) unable to think clearly
> **bell** = a metal object shaped like a cup that makes a ringing noise when you move it or hit it

f • Focus on the task. Demonstrate the activity by talking about your own high school. Then SS work in pairs while you move around listening and helping. If there's time, get a few SS to report to the class.

Extra idea

Instead of **e** and **f** you could now read each paragraph aloud, eliciting the meaning of the highlighted words and any others that cause problems. Then ask the whole class after each paragraph in what way their experiences in each subject were different.

4 GRAMMAR first conditional and future time clauses

a • Focus on the task and have SS, in pairs, answer the questions. Get some responses from the class, and tell them how you feel or felt about tests.

b • **4.3** & **4.4** SS now listen to two interviews with people who have just taken important tests. In the interviews the speakers use several examples of time clauses with *if, when, as soon as*, etc.

• Focus on the photos of the two students. Explain that SATs (Scholastic Aptitude Tests) are tests that US high school students take in their final year of school. Acceptance to a college depends on the scores they get. Explain that the TOEFL® is a test of English for foreigners. Foreign students who want to go to college in the US usually need to have a good score on this test.

• Tell SS that they are going to listen to Carla first. Focus on the questions and play the recording once for SS to try to answer them. Play the recording again for SS to complete their answers. You could have them compare their answers in pairs. Now check answers.

> **Carla**
> 1 Some parts were.
> 2 She will get her results next week online.
> 3 She doesn't want to plan any celebrations.
> 4 She will apply to schools that don't require such high scores.

4.3 CD2 Track 15

(audioscript in Student Book on page 125)
R = reporter, C = Carla
R So, you just took the Scholastic Aptitude Test, the SAT. What parts did you take?
C Well, I took the main parts of the test. Those include critical reading, math, and writing.
R Was it difficult?
C Well, yeah, some parts were and I need to get a pretty high score.
R Why?
C Because I want to be a doctor, and I want to get into a pre-med program at one of the big universities, like maybe the University of California. They probably won't admit me unless I get 650 or higher.
R Do you think you'll get it?
C I don't know. I think I did OK, but I'm a little worried about the math.
R When will you get the results?
C They'll go online next week. Believe me, as soon as they're online, I'll look up my scores.
R And how will you celebrate if you get high scores?
C I don't want to plan any celebrations until I get the results.
R And what will you do if you don't get the scores you need?
C I don't want to think about it. If I don't get into college, my parents will kill me. No, I'm joking. I suppose I could apply to some schools that don't require such high scores.
R Well, good luck!
C Thanks.

Extra challenge

You could ask SS a few more questions, e.g., *Which parts did Carla take?* (Critical reading, math, and writing.), *What does Carla want to study at the University of California?*, etc.

• **4.3** Now repeat the process for Ruben.

> **Ruben**
> 1 Not really.
> 2 In six or seven weeks, by mail.
> 3 He will have a pizza with other people in his class.
> 4 He will take the test again in June.

4.4 CD2 Track 16

(audioscript in Student Book on page 125)
RE = reporter, RU = Ruben
RE What test did you take?
RU The TOEFL. That's the Test of English as a Foreign Language.
RE Was it difficult?
RU Well, not really, but I need at least 550 to get into a college. One of the schools I've applied to requires 640! But I'm optimistic. I think I did pretty well.
RE When will you get the results?
RU When they score the tests, they'll mail the results. It takes about six or seven weeks!
RE And how will you celebrate if you get a high score?
RU I'll go out for pizza with the other people in my class – well, with the people who did well on the test.
RE Will you keep on studying English?
RU Probably not – at least formally. I mean, if I'm taking college classes, I'll be learning a lot every day anyway.
RE And if you don't get a high enough score?
RU I'll take the test again in June.

c • **4.5** Focus on the five sentences from the interviews and elicit who said them (Carla said 1–4, and Ruben said 5). Then play the recording, pausing for SS to complete the sentences. Check answers.

Extra challenge

Have SS try and complete the sentences before they listen.

> 1 They probably won't admit me **unless** I get 650 or higher.
> 2 **As soon as** they're online, I'll look up my scores.
> 3 I don't want to plan any celebrations **until** I get the results.
> 4 **If** I don't get into college, my parents will kill me.
> 5 **When** they score the tests, they'll mail the results.

4.5 CD2 Track 17

1 They probably won't admit me unless I get 650 or higher.
2 As soon as they're online, I'll look up my scores!
3 I don't want to plan any celebrations until I get the results.
4 If I don't get into college, my parents will kill me.
5 When they score the tests, they'll mail the results.

• Elicit / explain the meaning of *unless* (= if not) and *as soon as* (= the moment when). Then ask SS what tense the verbs are after the bold words (simple present) and if they refer to the present or to the future (the future).

d • Tell SS to go to **Grammar Bank 4A** on page 136. Go through the examples and read the rules with the class.

Grammar notes

First conditionals and future time clauses

• SS should be familiar with basic first conditional sentences (*if* + present, future (*will*)) from their low-intermediate course. Here they also learn to use *unless* (instead of *if…not*) in conditional sentences, and that other future time clauses (i.e., beginning with *when, as soon as, unless,* etc.) work in the same way as *if*-clauses, i.e., they are followed by a present tense, although they actually refer to the future. This may be new for your students.

• Emphasize that in the other (main) clause the verb form is usually *will* + base form but it can also be an imperative, or *going to.*

• A typical mistake: using a future form after *when, unless,* etc., e.g., ~~I'll call you when I'll arrive.~~

• Focus on the exercises for **4A** on page 137. Have SS do the exercises individually or in pairs. Check answers either after each exercise or when they have done both by having SS read the sentences aloud. Tell them to use contractions where possible.

> **a** 1 before 2 until 3 as soon as 4 if
>   5 when / as soon as 6 unless 7 when 8 until
>   9 before 10 Unless
> **b** 1 leave 2 finishes 3 won't get 4 'll tell
>   5 arrive 6 get 7 'll go 8 doesn't like 9 tell
>   10 'll be

• Tell SS to go back to the main lesson on page 54.

e • Put SS in pairs and focus on the task. Demonstrate yourself by making one or two true sentences.

• Give SS two or three minutes to choose their five sentences and complete them. Then SS take turns telling each other their sentences. Get a few SS to report to the class.

Extra challenge

Have SS do **e** orally without writing the sentences down.

f • **4.6** Tell SS they are going to hear Carla and Ruben being interviewed again after getting their results. Focus on the task and then play the recording twice. Have SS compare what they heard and then check answers.

> Carla's grades weren't as good as she hoped. (She got a 700 on critical reading, but only 620 on the math.) She's going to wait to see if one of the universities she wants will still accept her. If not, she will look into other schools.
> Ruben passed with a 650. He's going to celebrate with his friends (pizza and dancing).

4.6 CD2 Track 18

(audioscript in Student Book on page 125)
RE = reporter, C = Carla, RU = Ruben
RE Carla – I can see from your face that the results, uh, weren't exactly what you wanted. Am I right?
C Yeah. I got a 700 on critical reading but only 620 on math.
RE So what are you going to do now?
C Well, my reading score was pretty good, so I'm going to wait and see if one of the universities I want will still accept me. If not, I'll try to find other schools that will take me.
RE Were your parents angry?
C No, they've been really nice about it. They know how disappointed I am. Besides, it's not that my scores were really bad.
RE Well, Ruben, did you get a good score on the TOEFL?
RU Yes, I got a 650! I'm very happy. I didn't think I'd get such a high score.
RE And your friends?
RU They all did well, too, except one. But he didn't expect to do very well. He didn't do any work.
RE So are you going out to celebrate?
RU Oh yes. We're going out for pizza tonight and then we're going dancing.

Extra support

Pause after Carla, and repeat if necessary. Then play Ruben twice.

5 LISTENING

a ● Focus on the photo and the extract from the TV guide and have SS read it. Then focus on the questions and elicit answers from the whole class, but don't say if they are right or not at this stage.

Extra challenge

Have SS discuss questions 1–4 in pairs, and then get feedback from the whole class.

b ● **4.7** Tell SS they are going to listen to a TV critic talking about the program *That'll Teach 'Em* (from exercise **a**). SS should listen and find the answers to questions 1–4 in **a**.

● Play the recording once. Then tell SS in pairs to make notes alongside the questions and to circle the thing(s) that the teenagers hated most.

● Check answers.

> 1 The idea was to compare education today with education in the 1950s.
> 2 The food and taking cold showers.
> 3 Very strict. If the teenagers misbehaved, they had to go to the principal and were hit on the hand or made to stay after school and do extra work.
> 4 They did badly. Only one student passed all the exams.

Extra support

Play the recording in sections, pausing after each question is answered and playing again if necessary. Elicit the answers from the whole class.

c ● SS listen again and this time they mark sentences 1–10 T or F. Have them compare answers with a partner. Play the recording again if necessary. Check answers, and have SS say why the F ones are false.

> 1 F (Thirty teenagers took part.)
> 2 F (They had to live at the school.)
> 3 T
> 4 T
> 5 T
> 6 F (The kids didn't mind.)
> 7 F (They found most of the classes interesting.)
> 8 F (The students failed because the exams were different.)
> 9 F (He thinks school is different, but not necessarily easier.)
> 10 T

Extra support

If there's time, you could have SS listen to the recording with the audioscript on page 126 so they can see exactly what they understood / didn't understand. Translate / explain any new words or phrases.

4.7 CD2 Track 19

(audioscript in Student Book on page 126)

P = presenter, M = Michael

P Hello and welcome to our review of international TV programs. With me today is the television critic Michael Stein... So, Michael, what interesting foreign TV shows have you seen recently?

M I saw a British series called *That'll Teach 'Em*. I must say I found the whole series absolutely fascinating. They took a group of 30 16-year-old students and sent them – as an experiment – to a boarding school for one month. But it wasn't a modern boarding school; it was a 1950s boarding school. They recreated exactly the same conditions as in the 1950s – the same food, the same discipline, the same exams. The idea was to compare education today with education in the 1950s.

P I bet it was a shock for today's teenagers.

M Well, it was, of course. It wasn't just the classes – it was the whole atmosphere – I mean, they had to wear the uniform from the 50s – horrible uncomfortable clothes – they hated them and they weren't allowed to leave the school once for the whole month, or watch TV, or use cell phones. And they had to take cold showers every morning and go for cross-country runs!

P Well, what was the worst thing for them?

M The food, definitely! Most of them hated it. They said it was cold and tasteless. And the girls didn't like the cold showers much either...

P What about the classes?

M Well, of course the biggest difference for the kids was the discipline. It was silence all the time during classes – only the teacher spoke. And anyone who misbehaved had to go to the principal and was either hit on the hand or made to stay after school and do extra work. And of course they couldn't use computers or calculators, but strangely enough the kids didn't really mind that, and in fact most of them found the classes interesting. Some of them said they were more interesting than their normal classes. They had to work very hard, though.

P So what happened in the end? Did they pass the 1950s exams?

M No, most of them failed – although they were all really bright kids. There was only one student who actually passed all the subjects.

P So, do you think that school subjects really used to be harder in the 1950s?

M No, I think that the kids failed because the exams in the 1950s were very different. The students in the program will probably do very well in their own exams. On the other hand, 1950s students would probably find today's subjects very difficult.

P How did the kids themselves feel about the experiment?

M They were really positive. In general, they had a good time and they all felt they learned a lot. I think it made them appreciate their own lifestyle more. Some of them actually said it was the best month of their lives. It was an interesting experiment and the program was really well made. I really enjoyed watching it.

d ● Focus on the question and have a brief open class discussion.

6 SPEAKING

a ● Put SS in small groups (of three or four). Go through the discussion topics on the list, making sure SS understand them.

  ● Give SS time in their groups to each choose a different topic from the list. Then give them time (e.g., five minutes) to think of three reasons why they agree or disagree with the sentence. Help SS with any vocabulary they may need.

b ● Now focus SS' attention on the **Useful language**. SS in each group should now take turns saying whether they agree or disagree with the sentence they have chosen and why. The other SS should listen and say if they agree or disagree, and why.

  ● If there's time, you could have a brief open class discussion on each topic.

Extra photocopiable activities

Grammar
future time clauses: *if*, *when*, etc. page 149
Communicative
Sentence halves page 180 (instructions page 165)

HOMEWORK

Study Link **Workbook** pages 34–36

4

B

G second conditional
V houses
P sentence stress

In an ideal world...

Lesson plan

This lesson reviews second conditional sentences with *if* and introduces SS to conditional sentences without *if*. In the **Grammar Bank** the second conditional is contrasted with the first. The initial context is provided by a questionnaire from a newspaper where two famous people are asked hypothetical *What would you do / wear...?* type questions. In the second part of the lesson, SS learn house vocabulary and listen to people describe their dream houses. The theme of houses is continued with a reading about a very personal house, that of the painter Frida Kahlo in Mexico City. The pronunciation focus in this lesson is on sentence stress in conditional sentences.

Optional lead-in (books closed)

Tell SS to imagine that they could live in another country. Ask them what country they would choose and why. Find out which country is the most popular and why. Tell SS that they are going to read a questionnaire from a newspaper where famous people are asked similar questions.

1 GRAMMAR second conditional

a ● Books open. Focus on the two photos and have SS describe the people. Find out if they know anything about them. If they don't, use the notes below to tell SS about them.

> **Joaquín Cortés**
> Joaquín Cortés is Spanish and is a very well-known flamenco dancer. He began his career in the Spanish National Ballet at the age of 15. He formed his own dance company in 1992 and became famous all over the world after the success of his show *Gypsy Passion*.
>
> **Isabella Rossellini**
> Isabella Rossellini is an actress and has appeared in several movies, including *Blue Velvet* (1986). She also modeled (for Lancôme Cosmetics) and has her own cosmetics company.

b ● Focus on the questionnaire and explain that this is a weekly feature in a newspaper in which famous people are asked the same hypothetical questions. Go through the questions making sure that SS understand them. SS should realize that the first four questions are second conditionals, but you could check this by asking them.

● Now focus on the answers that have been removed from the questionnaire. Go through the answers making sure that SS understand them. Use the pictures to help deal with any difficult vocabulary, e.g., *fly, corset.*

● Remind SS that *I'd = I would* and that the answers are in the conditional, too.

● Focus on the task and have SS match two answers to each question. Then they should try and guess who each answer belongs to. Check answers.

> **1 B** (JC) and **J** (IR)
> **2 A** (IR) and **H** (JC)
> **3 D** (IR) and **F** (JC)
> **4 C** (JC) and **G** (IR)
> **5 E** (JC) and **I** (IR)

Extra idea

If you think they would enjoy it, you could now have SS answer these questions themselves in pairs.

c ● Focus on questions 1–4 and do this task as a whole class activity. Check answers.

> **1** The past tense.
> **2** The conditional form (*would* + base form).
> **3** There is no *if*-clause.
> **4** Imaginary situations.

d ● Tell SS to go to **Grammar Bank 4B** on page 136. Go through the examples and read the rules with the class.

Grammar notes

Second conditional sentences

● SS who previously used *American English File 2* or a similar level course will have already been introduced to second conditional sentences (*if* + past, conditional (*would / wouldn't*)).

● What should be new here is the use of the conditional tense without *if* in sentences like *I would never buy an apartment next to a bar or restaurant.* This use should not be too problematic as SS may have a conditional form of the verb in their L1, and they have also already met this use of the conditional in the phrase *I would like...*

● After *I / he / she / it* use *were* not *was*, e.g., *If I were younger, I'd have another child., If he were here, I'd ask him.*

● Typical mistakes include:
  – Using *would* in both clauses, e.g., ~~If I would have more time, I would learn another language.~~
  – Mixing up the form of first and second conditionals, e.g., ~~If I knew her cell phone number, I'll call her.~~
  – Using a first conditional where a second would be more appropriate or vice versa, e.g., ~~If I am shorter, I can wear those shoes.~~
  – ~~If I was you,...~~

● Now have SS do the exercises on page 137 individually or in pairs. Check answers either after each exercise or when they have finished both. Have SS read the whole sentences aloud and encourage them to use contractions. In exercise **b** you could ask SS after each sentence if it is a first or second conditional.

a 1 It would be better for me if we met tomorrow.
2 She wouldn't treat him like that if she really loved him.
3 If I could live anywhere in the world, I'd / I would live in New Zealand.
4 The kitchen would look bigger if we painted it white.
5 I wouldn't buy that house if I were you.
6 He'd / would be more attractive if he wore nicer clothes.
7 If we didn't have children, we'd / we would travel more.
8 What would you do in this situation if you were me?

b 1 take
2 'd / would feel
3 lost
4 'll cook
5 didn't live
6 doesn't get lost
7 gets
8 'd / would enjoy

e • Sit SS in pairs, **A** and **B**, preferably face to face. Tell them to go to **Communication** *What would you do if...?* **A** on page 117, **B** on page 120.
• Go through the instructions and make sure SS understand what they have to do.

Extra idea

You could have an **A** and a **B** student each choose a question to ask you first, before they start asking each other.

• Tell SS to go back to the main lesson on page 57.

2 PRONUNCIATION & SPEAKING sentence stress

Pronunciation notes

SS continue work on sentence stress and are given more practice in pronouncing the words in a sentence that convey important information, (e.g., nouns, verbs, adjectives, and adverbs).
Other, shorter words (e.g., articles and pronouns) should be pronounced less strongly. Getting this balance right will help SS pronounce English with correct rhythm.

a • Focus on the task and give SS a minute or two to match the sentence halves. Have them compare their answers in pairs.

b • **4.8** Play the recording for SS to check their answers

1 F   2 D   3 E   4 C   5 A   6 B

4.8   CD2 Track 20

1 I wouldn't wear that hat if I were you.
2 If you exercised more, you'd feel much better.
3 If it weren't so expensive, I'd buy it.
4 I'd get married tomorrow if I could find the right person.
5 She'd play better if she practiced more.
6 If you talked to her, I'm sure she'd understand you.

---

c • Ask SS why some words are underlined. (Because they are the words that carry important information and so they are stressed.) Play the recording for SS to listen and repeat, and encourage them to try to copy the rhythm by saying the underlined words more strongly and the unstressed words as lightly and quickly as possible.

d • Focus on the task and give SS time to choose and complete their three sentences. Go around making sure that SS are writing correct sentences.

Extra idea

Before SS start writing you could focus on the pictures and ask SS what job, country, etc., the artist has illustrated (to China, a Mini Cooper, cycling, an astronomer, to play the piano, a chalet in Switzerland).

• Put SS in pairs and they take turns telling their partners their true sentences and giving reasons. Monitor and encourage them to get the correct sentence rhythm.

3 VOCABULARY houses

a • Focus SS' attention on the cover of the magazine and explain that it is an American magazine that gives people ideas about how to decorate and furnish their houses. Focus on the two questions and elicit answers.

It's a living room. You can see a coffee table, a sofa, cushions, a carpet, an armchair, a fireplace, a bookcase.

b • Tell SS to go to **Vocabulary Bank** *Houses* on page 151. Focus on section **1 Types of houses**. SS do the exercise individually or in pairs. Check answers.

1 apartment building
2 townhouse
3 house
4 cottage

• Now focus on section **2 Where people live**, and give SS time to match the sentences. Check answers.

1 g   2 d   3 e   4 b   5 a   6 c   7 f

• Point out that *suburbs* does not have a negative connotation in English (it can cause some difficulty in some languages); in fact, American suburbs are often expensive areas.
• Now have SS match the words and pictures in section **3 Parts of a house**. Check answers.

1 balcony
2 roof
3 chimney
4 yard
5 porch
6 garden
7 steps
8 garage
9 fence
10 gate
11 patio

● Finally, get SS to do section **4 Furniture**. Check answers after **a**.

bathroom	kitchen	living room	bedroom
toilet	stove	coffee table	bedside table
shower	dishwasher	armchair	dresser

Make sure SS know exactly what the words in **4a** mean by describing or drawing on the board each piece of furniture.

● Now do **4b**. Give SS time to add words. Elicit words from SS and drill pronunciation.

Extra idea

When you check answers to **4**, copy the chart on the board. When you have checked **4a**, elicit SS' extra words (**b**) and write them on the board in the chart for other SS to copy down any new words.

● Finally, focus on the instruction "Can you remember the words on this page? Test yourself or a partner."

Testing yourself

For **Types of houses** and **Parts of a house** SS can cover the words and look at the pictures and try to remember the words. For **Where people live** SS can cover sentences 1–7 and look at sentences a–g and try to remember the words and phrases. For **Furniture** SS can cover the chart and try to remember the words in each column.

Testing a partner

See **Testing a partner** on page 15.

Study Link SS can find more practice of these words on the MultiROM and on the *American English File 3* Website.

● Tell SS to go back to the main lesson on page 58.

c ● Put SS in pairs, **A** and **B**. Give **A**s a few minutes to interview **B**s with the five questions before changing roles.

4 LISTENING & SPEAKING

a ● **4.9** Focus on the task and play the recording for SS to match the four speakers with their "dream house" by writing numbers 1–4 in the appropriate box.

● Check answers. Elicit that *a penthouse apartment* (4) is the top floor apartment of a building.

> 1 B   2 D   3 C   4 A

b ● Now SS listen for more detail. Play the recording again for SS to match the speakers to what they said by writing numbers 1–4 in the appropriate box. Check answers.

> **would not like to have other people living nearby** 2
> **would like to live somewhere that was partly old and partly modern** 3
> **would not spend much time inside their dream house** 1
> **doesn't think they will ever get their dream house** 4

Extra support

For **b**, play each speaker's words again and pause. Check which SS think is the corresponding sentence, and then ask SS a few more questions, e.g., for 1 *Where exactly would she like her house to be? What would the house be like? What view would she have?*, etc.

If there's time, you could have SS listen to the recording with the audioscript on page 126 so they can see exactly what they understood / didn't understand. Translate / explain any new words or phrases.

> **4.9**   CD2 Track 21
>
> (audioscript in Student Book on page 126)
>
> 1 When I retire, if I can afford it, I'd love to have a cottage down at the lake where we could go for the summer. I'd like to have a garden there. I've never been able to have one, as we live in an apartment in the city. Not too big, though. I'd like to grow vegetables and flowers and some fruit trees. I'd spend all my time either in the garden or sitting by the lake.
>
> 2 My dream house would be in the mountains, high up on the hillside with a beautiful view. It'd be modern and quite simple, with wooden floors and big windows, and from every window you'd be able to see the mountains and the forest. It'd be quite isolated, with no neighbors for miles and miles. Can you imagine? Just the sound of the wind in the trees.
>
> 3 I'd love to have a big old townhouse, maybe one of those beautiful houses with big rooms, high ceilings, and a lovely staircase going down to the hall. But the bathrooms and kitchen would have to be modern, because old ones are cold and impractical. I'd need some help looking after it, though...
>
> 4 If I won the lottery, which of course I won't, I'd buy a big penthouse apartment near the river with a great view, a really hi-tech place, you know, with one of those intelligent refrigerators that orders food from the supermarket all by itself when you're running out. And a huge TV and music system – but all very stylish and minimalist.

---

c ● Focus on the speaking task and give SS a few minutes to think about what they are going to say. Go around the class helping SS with any vocabulary they might need that isn't in **Vocabulary Bank** *Houses*.

d ● Put SS into small groups of three to five. They should take turns describing their dream house. They must also say which of the other houses they like best (not counting theirs). When the activity has finished, you could get a report from each group to find out which house was the most popular.

5 READING

a ● Ask the whole class the questions and elicit answers. Be ready to make suggestions if SS are slow to volunteer anything.

b ● Focus on the photos on page 59. Elicit or tell the class who the woman is (Frida Kahlo) and where she was from (Mexico).

● Focus on the task. Tell SS to read the article to find out which part of the house these things are connected to and why they are mentioned.

● Set a time limit and when it is up, elicit answers from the class.

Extra idea

You could read the text aloud to SS, as they follow along with you and look at the photos. After each paragraph, stop and get a reaction from the class, e.g., after the first paragraph, ask SS if they have seen the movie *Frida*, if they like her paintings, etc.; after paragraph two, ask what SS know about the various people mentioned. Deal with vocabulary as it comes up. When you get to the end, SS could do task **b** from memory, and then do **c**.

> Two giant statues – **the entrance**: they guard it, and are nearly 7 meters tall.
> Leon Trotsky – **the living room**. He was a political leader who was a friend of Frida Kahlo's and who visited the house.
> A yellow floor – **the kitchen** has a yellow floor to stop insects from coming in.
> A monkey and a parrot – **the kitchen**, where they used to have their meals. The monkey and parrot were Frida's pets. The parrot used to do tricks at the table in return for butter.
> A pair of shoes – **Diego's bedroom**. They can be seen there today. They are enormous because Diego had very big feet.
> A cupboard with a glass door – **upstairs in a bedroom**. It contains a colorful Mexican dress that Frida loved wearing.
> July 7, 1910 – this date is written **above the cupboard with the glass door**. It says that Frida was born on this day, but she wasn't. She was born three years earlier.
> 1929-1954 – These dates are written on the walls of **the patio**. It says that Frida and Diego lived in the house for those years. In fact they lived separately for some of that time.

c ● Focus on the task and have SS work individually and then compare their answers with a partner. Check answers.

> 1 china cabinet 3 entrance 5 upstairs 7 shutters
> 2 glass 4 gallery 6 airy 8 patio

d ● Focus on the two questions and get some feedback from the whole class.

6 4.10 ♪ **SONG** *Our house*

● This song was made famous by the British group Madness in 1982. If you want to sing the song in class, use the photocopiable activity on page 207.

4.10 CD2 Track 22
Our house
Father wears his Sunday best
Mother's tired she needs a rest
The kids are playing up downstairs
Sister's sighing in her sleep
Brother's got a date to keep
He can't hang around

Our house, in the middle of our street
Our house, in the middle of our...

Our house it has a crowd
There's always something happening
And it's usually quite loud
Our mom she's so house-proud
Nothing ever slows her down
And a mess is not allowed

Our house, in the middle of our street, etc.
Something tells you that you've got to move away from it

Father gets up late for work
Mother has to iron his shirt
Then she sends the kids to school
Sees them off with a small kiss
She's the one they're going to miss
In lots of ways

Our house, in the middle of our street, etc.

I remember way back then when everything was true and when
We would have such a very good time such a fine time
Such a happy time
And I remember how we'd play, simply waste the day away
Then we'd say nothing would come between us two dreamers

Father wears his…, etc.

Our house, in the middle of our street
Our house, in the middle of our...
Our house, in the middle of our street
Our house, in the middle of our...

Extra photocopiable activities

Grammar
second conditional page 150
Communicative
If you had to choose… page 181 (instructions page 165)
Song
Our house page 207 (instructions page 203)

HOMEWORK

Study Link **Workbook** pages 37–39

G *usually* and *used to*
V friendship
P /s/ or /z/?

Still friends?

Lesson plan

Friends and friendship provides the main theme for this lesson, which reviews and consolidates *used to* to talk about habitual actions in the past and states and actions that are no longer true.

The vocabulary focus of the lesson is words and phrases related to friendship. Pronunciation focuses on the contrast between /s/ and /z/. The main context is the true stories (although the real names and places have been changed) of two people who contacted the *Friends Reunited* website to try and get back in touch with old friends from their past. In the second half of the lesson, SS read a provocative text that encourages us to "edit" our friends, leading SS to discuss various aspects of friendship.

Optional lead-in (books closed)

- Ask the class to think about how many of their friends from elementary school they are still in touch with.
- Find out who has the most old friends from those years and how often they meet. If you are teaching adults, you could ask the same question about high school as well.

1 VOCABULARY & SPEAKING friendship

a • Books open. Focus attention on the photo of the two women and then on the task. Then give SS a few minutes to complete the text and to compare their answers with a partner's. Check answers.

1 known	5 have a lot in common
2 met	6 lost touch
3 coworker	7 keep in touch
4 get along very well	8 argue

b • Focus on the task and give SS a couple of minutes to think about a close friend and how they will answer the questions.
  • Put SS in pairs. They should take turns interviewing each other about their close friend. While they are doing this, go around monitoring and helping if necessary.

2 GRAMMAR *usually* and *used to*

a • Ask SS the questions and elicit any experiences SS have had.

b • Have SS read the information about *Friends Reunited* and answer the two questions.

It's for finding out what old friends are doing, and getting back in touch with them.
You find the web page for your old school or workplace and add your name to the list. You can also put a photo and some information. If you want to send a message to someone on the list, you do this via *Friends Reunited*, not personal e-mails.

- You could explain that *Friends Reunited* has been very successful in reuniting many old friends over the last few years. The inventors of the website have become millionaires.

c • Focus on the photos on page 61 and tell SS that these are two people who got back in touch with old friends through *Friends Reunited*. They are true stories although the names and places have been changed. Tell SS to read both texts and to answer the two questions. Check answers.

Carol wanted to meet Robert, an old boyfriend. She lost touch with him when they broke up.
Alex wanted to meet his old school friends. He thought they might help him recover his memory, which he lost after a motorcycle accident.

d • Focus on the *used to* phrases on the list and tell SS to read the texts again about Carol and Alex and to fill each blank with one of the phrases. SS can compare with a partner before you check answers.

1 We used to go out	4 used to come
2 he used to go to	5 I used to know
3 I used to live	

e • Focus on the task and the two questions. Do this as an open class activity. Elicit answers.

We use *used to* to talk about habitual actions or states in the past. We make negative sentences and questions with *did / didn't*, e.g., *Did you use to go to boarding school? I didn't use to have short hair.*

f • Tell SS to go to **Grammar Bank 4C** on page 136. Go through the examples and the rules with the class and drill the pronunciation of *used to*.

Grammar notes

usually and *used to*

- *Used to* is a grammar point that was presented in *American English File 2* and is reviewed and consolidated here. This is a "late assimilation" structure, as SS can express more or less the same idea by using the past tense + a time expression. Compare: *I used to go to that elementary school* and *I went to that elementary school (when I was a child)*. In that sense *used to* is a sophisticated structure and its correct use helps to give the impression of having a good level of English. In this lesson *used to* is contrasted with the use of the simple present with *usually* to talk about present habits.

- SS may have problems with *used to* as their L1 may either use a tense that doesn't exist in English for past habits, or may have a verb that can be used both for present and past habits, unlike *used to*, which can only be used in the past.

- Emphasize that we often don't repeat the main verb but just use the auxiliary verb with *anymore / any longer* when we contrast the past and present habits, e.g., *I used to like cartoons but I don't anymore*.

- Typical mistakes include:
  – Using *use to* instead of *usually* for present habits and states, e.g., ~~I use to go to bed at 11.00 every night~~.
  – Making mistakes of spelling, e.g., ~~We didn't used to wear a uniform at my school~~.
  – Confusing *used to* + base form with *be / get used to (doing something)*.

- Now have SS do the exercises on page 137 individually or in pairs. Check answers either after each exercise or after both.

> **a 1** I **used** to get up
> **2** Did she always **use** to...?
> **3** Do you **usually** have breakfast...?
> **4** They didn't **use** to have
> **5** he **usually** drinks tea
> **6** He used **to** be a teacher
> **7** Do **you usually** wear...?
> **8** we **went** to
> **9** **Did** she use to live...?
> **10** we **didn't** use to wear
> **b 1** used to live
> **2** Did ... use to have
> **3** didn't use to like
> **4** used to be
> **5** did ... use to work
> **6** used to play
> **7** used to have
> **8** Did ... use to argue
> **9** didn't use to be

- Tell SS to go back to the main lesson on page 61.

3 LISTENING

Tell SS that they are going to listen to what happened when Carol and Alex went to their reunions.

If this is a different lesson from when SS did exercise **2 GRAMMAR**, it would be a good idea to get them to read the texts again. Alternatively, you could read the texts aloud slowly to the class while they follow with books closed.

a ● **4.11** Focus on the task. Play the recording once, and tell SS they just have to listen to hear if the meeting was a success or not. Elicit the answer.

> Carol's reunion was not a success. They didn't have anything in common anymore.

b ● Now SS listen again for a more detailed understanding. Before SS listen, quickly go through questions 1–5 or give SS time to read them.

- Play the recording once all the way through. Then give SS time to discuss and answer the questions in pairs. Then play the recording once more if necessary, pausing to give SS time to complete their answers. Check answers.

> **Carol's story**
> **1** He always said that he would hate to be a teacher.
> **2** She thought "he always used to be late."
> **3** People say she looks five years younger than she is. He looked like an old man. He was bald (and was wearing a hideous jacket).
> **4** That they didn't have anything in common anymore.
> **5** He wasn't a rebel anymore, he was boring and conventional.

c **4.12** Now do the same for Alex.

> Alex's reunion was successful. He is now in touch regularly with the people he met and is going out with one of them.

d Now SS listen for the answers to questions 6–10.

> **Alex's story**
> **6** No, he didn't recognize anyone.
> **7** He felt nervous.
> **8** All the things he used to do when he was at school (e.g,. play on the basketball team, etc.).
> **9** He remembered that he used to wear glasses.
> **10** Anna is a girl who used to go to his school. They are now going out together.

> **4.11**   CD2 Track 23
> (audioscript in Student Book on page 126)
> **Carol**
> When Robert answered my e-mail, I got really excited. He didn't say very much about himself. He just told me that he was now a teacher, which surprised me because he always used to say that he would hate to teach. He also told me that he'd been married but was now divorced.
> Anyway, I answered his e-mail and we agreed to meet for lunch at a restaurant I like – a place where I often go on weekends.
> When I got there, I looked around to see if I could see him, but I couldn't, and I thought, "Typical! Same old Robert," because he always used to be late. So I sat down and ordered a drink. I was just sipping my drink when a man came over to my table and said, "Carol, how are you?" I could hardly believe it – I mean, I know neither of us is young anymore, but I think I look pretty good for my age. People usually say I look five years younger than I am. But Robert looked like an old man. His lovely long hair was all gone – in fact he was bald, with a few strands of hair sort of combed over his head – and he was wearing the most hideous jacket. Well, I know you shouldn't judge by appearances, so I smiled at him and we started talking – and well, I enjoyed the lunch and we talked a lot about the past – but I knew as soon as I saw him that we didn't have anything in common anymore. And I was right. Instead of the rebel he used to be, he was now, well, much more conventional than me. In fact, he seemed just like the sort of teachers we used to hate when we were young.

4.12   CD2 Track 24

(audioscript in Student Book on page 126)
Alex
I got to the restaurant late because I couldn't find it, but
when I walked in I saw a whole group of young people at
a table. I thought that must be them, though I didn't
really recognize anybody. So I went up and they all said
hello. They all recognized me, which was great, though it
felt a little strange. I must admit I was feeling really
nervous. Anyway, I sat down and we started talking. They
told me lots of things that I used to do when I was at
school, like play on the school basketball team – they said
I used to be really good – and they told me about all sorts
of other things: places we used to go to, things like that.
Some of my friends had even brought photos, and we
looked at them. I'd completely forgotten that I used to
wear these really awful big glasses – and I sort of relaxed
and I felt that I was getting to know them again, and
getting to know more about myself and my past. Anyway,
since we met that evening, we've all been e-mailing each
other and I've started going out with Anna – one of the
girls who was at the restaurant that night. She says she
used to like me a lot at school, but that I didn't use to take
any notice of her then! I can't remember any of that, but I
know I like her a lot now!

4 PRONUNCIATION & SPEAKING /s/ or /z/?

Pronunciation notes

Many learners tend to pronounce the letters *se* as the
unvoiced sound /s/ as in *bus*. In fact *se* is more often
pronounced as a voiced sound /z/, e.g., *lose*, *close*, etc.

a • **4.13** Focus on the two pronunciation pictures and
elicit the two example words: *snake* and *zebra* and the
/s/ and /z/ sounds. Focus on the task and point out
that SS need to be careful with *se* because the
pronunciation may be /s/ or /z/.

• Focus on the first two sentences, and before playing
the recording, ask SS how *used* is pronounced in each
one. (It is pronounced with /s/ in 1 and /z/ in 2.)

• Play the recording for SS to write *s* or *z* in the box after
each sentence. Have them compare their answers in
pairs and then play the recording again. Check
answers, and elicit that the most common
pronunciation of *se* is /z/.

1 /s/   2 /z/   3 /z/   4 /z/   5 /z/   6 /s/   7 /z/

4.13   CD2 Track 25

1 I used to live in New York.
2 I used my credit card to pay.
3 Excuse me. Can you help me?
4 We won't win, we'll lose.
5 They advertise on TV.
6 They promised to keep in touch.
7 Could you close the window?

b • Have SS work in pairs to practice saying the sentences
and then ask individual SS to say them. You could also
get SS to listen and repeat after the recording before
practicing in pairs.

Extra challenge

You could also tell SS that in the same way that *used* is
pronounced differently depending on its meaning, *close*
also is /z/ when it's a verb but /s/ when it's an adjective.
(As in a *close friend*.)

c • Put SS in pairs, **A** and **B**. Focus on the task and give SS
a few minutes to choose their three topics and plan
what they are going to say.

• **A**s start and tell **B**s about their first topic, giving as
much information as they can. **B**s can ask for more
information, too. Then **B**s tell **A**s about their first
topic, etc.

Extra support

Choose one of the topics and tell SS a little about it. This
way you both demonstrate what you want SS to do and
give them extra listening practice.

• As SS are talking, move around monitoring and
helping.

Study Link SS can find more practice of English
sounds on the MultiROM and also on the *American
English File 3* Website.

5 READING

a • Ask the whole class the three questions one by one and
elicit some answers from individual SS.

Extra idea

Before doing **a**, you could write on the board A FRIEND,
A COWORKER, A CLASSMATE and ask SS what the
difference is.

a friend = someone who you know and like
a coworker = someone who you work with in a job
a classmate = someone who is in the same class as you

b • Focus on the task and the title of the article. Give SS a
time limit to read the article once and find out what
exactly "editing your friends" means.

edit your friends = decide which of your friends are
important, and stop seeing / spending time with the
rest

c • Focus on the task. SS should now read the article for
more detail and choose the best summary for each
paragraph. Have them compare their answers with a
partner before checking answers.

1 c   2 b   3 a   4 c

d • Focus on the task and give SS three or four minutes to
do this. Give information about some of the words
and phrases they have chosen.

e • Ask the whole class these questions and elicit some
responses.

HOW WORDS WORK...

1 Focus on the instructions and give SS a few minutes, in pairs or individually, to match the *get* phrases that have come up during the lesson with definitions A–G. Check answers and make sure SS are sure what each *get* phrase means. Point out that the verb *get* has several different meanings and is one of the most common verbs in English. SS may already know or will come across other meanings, e.g., *I didn't get the joke* (here *get* = understand).

> 1 F 2 B 3 D 4 G 5 A 6 E 7 C

2 Focus on the task and give SS a minute or so to do it. Check answers and then get SS to quickly ask each other the questions in pairs.

> 1 get along with 2 get to know 3 get
> 4 get in touch 5 get rid of

6 LISTENING & SPEAKING

a ● **4.14** Focus on the instructions and go through sentences A–F. Don't get your SS' opinions at this stage.

● Play the recording and pause after the first speaker. Let SS discuss with a partner which sentence they think he is talking about. Check answers.

> Speaker 1 B   Speaker 2 A   Speaker 3 D

b ● Now play the recording again, also pausing after each speaker. This time SS listen to see if the speakers agree or disagree with the sentence and listen for the reasons and examples they give. Have SS compare what they understood with their partner before eliciting answers.

> 1 Disagrees. He thinks it's easier because you can text, e-mail, and chat online. He gives the example of several friends he met on vacation last year. He is still in touch with them.
> 2 Agrees. She thinks that men keep friends longer because their friendships are less intense (and less intimate) than women's – they don't talk about their personal lives much. As a result, they don't have arguments.
> 3 Agrees. He says that if you criticize your friend's boyfriend or girlfriend while they are still together (and in love), you will lose the friendship. You should wait until they break up. He gives the example of how he once criticized his friend's girlfriend and now they aren't friends anymore.

Extra support

If there's time, you could have SS listen to the recording with the audioscript on page 126 so they can see exactly what they understood / didn't understand. Translate / explain any new words or phrases.

4.14   CD2 Track 26

(audioscript in Student Book on page 126)

1 I don't agree at all. I think it's much easier. Today you can text, you can e-mail, you can chat online and things like that. I'm still in touch with some friends I met on vacation last year, even though they live miles away.

2 Actually, I think it's probably true. Because I know a lot of men who are still friends with people they went to elementary school with, but I don't know many women who are. For example, my brother has a friend named Tim who he's known since they were three years old. But I think the reason is that men's friendships are less intense, sort of less intimate than women's friendships. As men only ever talk about sports or superficial things, it doesn't matter if they've completely changed and don't have much in common anymore – they can still talk about baseball.

3 You definitely shouldn't. I mean, that's the quickest way to lose a friendship. If you don't like a friend's boyfriend or girlfriend, you should just keep quiet. You have to wait until they break up, and of course then you can say how awful you thought the person was and your friend will agree and think you're being supportive. But if you say anything bad while they're still madly in love, it's a disaster. I know because it happened to me once with a friend of mine. I said something negative about his girlfriend. And now we're not friends anymore.

c ● Focus on the task and have SS put a check or an x next to the sentences according to their own opinions. Give SS a few minutes to think about their reasons. They can write notes if they want.

d ● Put SS in groups and go through the expressions in **Useful language**. Then tell SS to take turns discussing each sentence and giving their opinion. Have a few SS report their opinions to the whole class.

Study Link SS can find a dictation and a Grammar quiz on all the grammar from File 4 on the MultiROM and more grammar activities on the *American English File 3* Website.

Extra photocopiable activities

Grammar
used to page 151
Communicative
Am I telling the truth? page 182 (instructions page 165)
Vocabulary
What's the difference? page 198 (instructions page 193)

HOMEWORK

Study Link Workbook pages 40–42

Function Making suggestions
Language *Let's..., Why don't we..?*, etc.

Lesson plan

In the first part of the lesson SS learn and practice ways of making suggestions. Allie and Mark discuss how they are going to entertain Scarlett, a "difficult" young pop star who is in Paris for a concert that evening. In the second half of the lesson (**Social English**), they take Scarlett to an expensive restaurant, but Scarlett is not impressed.

Study Link These lessons are on the *American English File 3 Video*, which can be used instead of the Class Audio CD with these lessons (see Introduction page 9). The main functional section of each episode is also on the MultiROM with additional activities.

Optional lead-in (books closed)

- Review what happened in the previous episode by eliciting the story from SS, e.g., *Where did Mark find an apartment? How did he go to see it? What happened when Mark was looking at the apartment? Did Mark decide to rent it?*

- Also try to elicit the phrases they learned, e.g., *How far is it? How long does it take?* (You could write these with blanks on the board to help SS remember.)

  If you are using the Video, you could play the previous episode again, leaving out the "Listen and Repeat" sections.

MAKING SUGGESTIONS

a • **4.15** Focus on the photo and questions, and tell SS to cover the conversation with their hand or a piece of paper. Alternatively, write the questions on the board and get SS to close their books.

- Play the recording once all the way through. Then play it again, pausing if necessary. Check answers.

The problem is that Jacques is delayed in Rome, so he can't take care of Scarlett Scarpino, a young pop singer who will be in Paris that day. Jacques was going to take care of her, but now Allie and Mark will have to. They decide to take her on a boat trip, then to the Eiffel Tower, and finally to lunch at La Renaissance (Jacques's favorite restaurant).

b • Now have SS look at the conversation. In pairs, they read it and see if they can guess or remember the missing words. Emphasize that they shouldn't write the words in the conversation, but pencil in alongside or on a separate sheet of paper.

c • Play the recording again, pausing if necessary for SS to check or write answers. Then go through the conversation line by line and check answers. Find out if SS had guessed the words correctly. Where they had not guessed correctly, see if their alternative also fits.

4.15 CD2 Track 27

A = Allie, J = Jacques, B = Ben, M = Mark

A I got a message this morning. It's from Jacques.
J *Allie, it's Jacques. I'm in Rome. My return flight's been canceled. There's a small problem. Scarlett Scarpino is in Paris for her concert this evening. I was going to look after her today. Could you possibly take care of her? Thank you. And see you later.*
A You've met Scarlett Scarpino, haven't you, Ben?
B The punk princess? Yeah, I met her in London last year.
A What's she like?
B Let's say she's a bit… difficult.
A What are we going to **do** with her?
M Why **don't** you show her around Paris?
A I have a **better** idea. Why don't *you* show her around Paris?
M What, me? I'm new here!
A You can't leave me to do this on my own.
M OK, why **don't** we take her to Notre Dame? I mean, it's her first time in Paris, isn't it?
B I don't think churches are really her thing.
M How **about** taking her on a boat trip?
A Brilliant!
M And then we could go up the Eiffel Tower.
A **That's** a good idea. I'm sure she'll love the view.
B And she might fall off!
M Thanks for your help, Ben. Shall we have lunch after that?
A **Let's** go somewhere really nice. Do you have any recommendations, Ben?
B **What** about La Renaissance? It's Jacques's favorite.
A That sounds perfect. Uh, Ben, do you want to come, too?
B Sorry, Allie. I'm really busy. But I'm sure you'll have an unforgettable meal.

---

d • **4.16** Now focus on the key phrases highlighted in the conversation. Play the recording, pausing after each sentence for SS to repeat. Encourage them to copy the rhythm and intonation.

4.16 CD2 Track 28

A = Allie, M = Mark, B = Ben

A What are we going to do with her?
M Why don't you show her around Paris?
A I have a better idea.
M Why don't we take her to Notre Dame?
M How about taking her on a boat trip?
A That's a good idea.
A Let's go somewhere really nice.
B What about La Renaissance?

---

e • Focus on the task. Give SS a few moments to try to memorize the highlighted phrases in the conversation. Then get them to cover the converation and try to complete the blank sentences. Have them compare their answers in pairs before checking answers.

Why don't we take her to Notre Dame?
How about taking her on a boat trip?
Let's go somewhere really nice.
What about La Renaissance?

- Point out that:
  - you can use either *What about..?* or *How about…?* in the second and fifth sentences. If you use a verb after *What / How about*, it must be in the *-ing* form.
  - *Let's...* is an abbreviation of *Let us...* and is a kind of imperative used to make a strong suggestion, i.e., when you have a clear idea of what you think is the best thing to do.
  - the other ways of making suggestions are less strong, i.e., you use them to ask someone their opinion about what the best thing to do is.
  - The use of *shall* for suggestions is more common in British English. It sounds more formal in American English. *Should* is more common in American English.

f • Put SS in groups of three. Focus on the task and then give them a few minutes to plan their evening. Encourage them to use the language of making suggestions that they have just learned.
- Alternatively, you could do this as a whole class activity.

SOCIAL ENGLISH An unforgettable meal

a • **4.17** Focus on the photo and the task. Before they listen, ask SS to predict if they think Scarlett likes the restaurant.
- Play the recording once. Ask SS if Scarlett liked the restaurant (she didn't until the end) and elicit what food she finally ate.

> A pizza margherita.

b • Focus on sentences 1–7 and go through them quickly. Then play the recording for SS to mark them T or F. Play the recording again if necessary. Check answers and have SS correct the false sentences.

> 1 F (She's hungry but thinks that the food in the restaurant is "horrible".)
> 2 T
> 3 F (She's allergic to mushrooms, strawberries, and nuts.)
> 4 T (She was "seasick".)
> 5 F (Scarlett didn't want to because she can't stand heights.)
> 6 T (She thinks she's spoiled.)
> 7 T

4.17 CD2 Track 29

(audioscript in Student Book on page 126)
M = Mark, S = Scarlett, A = Allie, W = waiter
M So… Scarlett. What would you like?
S Nothing.
M Aren't you hungry?
S Sure. But this food's really horrible.
A This is one of the finest restaurants in Paris.
S Well, I can't eat this stuff. I never touch meat…
A The seafood looks good…
S Hey, fish have feelings, too.
M What about the mushroom risotto?
S Mushrooms? No way! Didn't they tell you guys about my allergies? I'm allergic to mushrooms, strawberries, nuts…

M Shall we go someplace else?
S Whatever. I'm going to the restroom.
A Well, that was a disastrous morning. The boat trip made her feel sick and she wouldn't go up the Eiffel Tower. "I can't stand heights."
M It's a pity we didn't just take her shopping.
A She's so spoiled.
M Oh, come on, she's just a kid really.
A So, what are we going to do about lunch? Shall we leave now?
M No, hang on. I have an idea. Let me talk to the waiter.
W Monsieur?
M Do you think you could possibly do me a favor?
W Yes, of course, sir. What would you like?
M Well, I think this place is great. More wine, Allie?
A No, thanks.
W Mademoiselle…
S What's this?
M It's your lunch, Scarlett.
S But I didn't order anything.
W Voilà!
S Hey, pizza margherita! Cool!

Extra support
Let SS listen one more time with the audioscript on page 126. Help them with any vocabulary or expressions they didn't understand.

c • **4.18** Now focus on the USEFUL PHRASES. Give SS a moment to try to complete them, and then play the recording to check.

4.18 CD2 Track 30

M = Mark, A = Allie, S = Scarlett
A What **would** you like?
M Aren't you **hungry**?
A The seafood **looks** good.
S I'm **allergic** to mushrooms, strawberries, nuts…
M No, **hang** on. I have an idea.
M Do you think you could **possibly** do me a favor?

Extra idea
Ask SS if they can remember who said each phrase (and in what context), e.g., Mark asks Scarlett *Aren't you hungry?* (Because she says she doesn't want anything to eat.)

d • Play the recording again, pausing for SS to repeat. In a monolingual class elicit the equivalent expressions in SS' L1.

HOMEWORK

Study Link Workbook page 43

4 WRITING: DESCRIBING A HOUSE OR AN APARTMENT

Lesson plan

This fourth writing task focuses on describing a house or apartment and recycles the vocabulary of **File 4**.

There is also a focus on using more expressive descriptive adjectives such as *magnificent*, *superb*, etc.

We suggest that you do exercises **a–c** in class, but assign the actual writing (the last activity) for homework. If there's time, you may also want to do the planning in class.

a • Focus on the descriptions of the house and apartment, which are from ads on a property rental website. Tell SS to quickly read both ads once and then to decide which of the two properties they would prefer to rent for a two-week vacation.

b • Focus on the task and set a time limit. Tell SS to read only the first ad again and to highlight the adjectives that help to "sell" the house. Check answers, and make sure SS understand all the adjectives.

> **Suggested answers**
> spacious, large, breathtaking, ideal, quiet, safe, warm, friendly, excellent, amazing, perfect

c • Focus on the task and the second ad. Explain that the adjective *nice* is not a very expressive word, so it is not a very good adjective to use in an ad when you are trying to persuade people to rent your place.

• Focus on the example and point out that *superb* is a much more positive adjective than *nice*. Ask SS if they could use any other of the adjectives from the list here, and elicit that, e.g., *magnificent* would also be possible.

• Now have SS continue in pairs, and then check answers.

nice 150-square- meter apartment	spacious / magnificent 150- square-meter apartment
nice living room	magnificent / spacious living room
nice view	breathtaking / magnificent view
nice for people who…	perfect / ideal
nice for couples	perfect / ideal

• Focus on the **Useful language** box and make sure SS understand all the phrases.

WRITE a description of a house / apartment

Go through the instructions. Then either have SS plan and write their description in class (set a time limit of 20 minutes) or have them plan their description in class and write at home, or assign both the planning and writing for homework.

Before SS hand in their descriptions, have them exchange them with another student to read and check for mistakes.

Extra idea

You could display SS' descriptions around the class and have SS move around reading them and choosing one to rent.

4 REVIEW & CHECK

For instructions on how to use these pages, see page 30.

GRAMMAR

a 1	will / 'll take	**4**	would / 'd ban
2	drank	**5**	arrives
3	are		
b 1	c	**4**	a
2	b	**5**	c
3	c		

VOCABULARY

a 1 village (It's a place. The others are kinds of houses.)
  2 shower (It's in the bathroom. The others are all in the kitchen.)
  3 uniform (It's a noun. The others are all adjectives describing schools.)
  4 exam (It's a noun. The others are all verbs related to exams.)
  5 friendship (It's a concept. The others all describe people you spend time with.)
b 1 subjects **2** semesters **3** private **4** professor
  5 suburbs **6** chimney **7** roof **8** gate
c 1 about **2** in, with **3** in **4** along **5** at **6** in

PRONUNCIATION

a 1	student (It's /u/.)	**4**	cottage (It's /ɪ/.)
2	punish (It's /ʌ/.)	**5**	homework (It's /oʊ/.)
3	country (It's /ʌ/.)		

b <u>u</u>niform, <u>ex</u>am, <u>se</u>condary, resi<u>den</u>tial, <u>co</u>worker

CAN YOU UNDERSTAND THIS TEXT?

a 1 T **2** F **3** DS **4** T **5** F **6** F **7** T **8** DS **9** F
b court = the place where a judge or jury decide if someone has broken the law
royalties = money, e.g., a musician earns from the sales of a record, or when a song he / she wrote or performed is played on the radio
chorus = the part of a song that is repeated several times
kids = an informal word for *children*
banned = prohibited / didn't allow
regret = feel sorry for something (you did or didn't do)
degree = a university qualification

CAN YOU UNDERSTAND THESE PEOPLE?

a 1 b **2** a **3** c **4** c **5** a		
b 1 18	**4**	beginning of July
2 700	**5**	Parking
3 gas and electricity		

4.19   CD2 Track 31

1 A Good evening. I'm Mrs. Connors... John
   Connors's mother.
 B Oh, hello. Nice to meet you. Please, sit down.
 A So, what's the problem with John? He's pretty lazy,
   isn't he?
 B Yes, but that isn't what I wanted to talk to you
   about.
 A Did he fail his math exam again?
 B Yes.
 A What did he get?
 B He got 90%.
 A But that's good, isn't it?
 B It would be excellent, except that he copied all the
   answers from the girl sitting in front of him. That's
   what we need to talk about.
 A That John! Just wait till I get home!
2 A Do you see that woman over there? She used to go
   to my school.
 B Which one? The tall one with long, dark hair?
 A No, the one next to her with short, blond hair.
   What was her name? Janet. That's right. She's
   changed a lot. She's really thin now. She used to be
   kind of overweight. But it's definitely her.
3 A So, what have you decided about these two houses?
 B Well, we both loved the house with the big yard
   around it… That would be ideal…
 A But…?
 B The kitchen's tiny.
 A And the townhouse?
 B Could we see that one again?
 A Certainly. How about tomorrow morning?
4 A And our next caller is…
 B Dennis.
 A Go ahead, Dennis. We're listening.
 B Thank you. I used to go to a high school in a
   suburb of New York and I'm trying to find an old
   friend of mine, named Eddie. We lost touch with
   each other after we left school.
 A And when was that, Dennis?
 B Let me think. I started there when I was 11, so
   that's 1981, and I graduated six, no, seven years
   later.
 A So if you're listening, Eddie, your old friend
   Dennis wants to get in touch with you. If you hear
   this message, you can call the show or send us an
   e-mail. The phone number is…
5 A Hi, this is Sophie.
 B Oh, hi, Sophie. Haven't heard from you in a long
   time.
 A Sorry. I've just been so busy.
 B Me too. We never have time to see each other these
   days.
 A That's why I'm calling. What about lunch next
   week?
 B Great! What day?
 A Monday?
 B Can't. I have a business lunch. Tuesday?
 A I have my yoga class at 1:00. Best day for me would
   be Thursday.
 B Let me see. I have a meeting at 12:30, but I should
   be finished by 2:00 at the latest. How about a late
   lunch?
 A Fine. I'll come to you and meet you in the coffee
   shop downstairs.
 B Perfect. I'll see you then.
 A Bye!

4.20   CD2 Track 32

 A Hello. Is this Jake?
 B Yes, it is.
 A Oh, I'm calling about the apartment share.
 B Oh, yes. Well, it's a three-bedroom apartment,
   kitchen, living room, bathroom. And it's on the
   first floor, so there's a small yard.
 A Where is it exactly?
 B It's on Elm Street, number 18. Do you know
   this area?
 A Yeah. I know where that is. How much is the rent?
 B It's 700 hundred a month plus gas and electricity.
 A OK. So how many other people will be living in
   the apartment?
 B Me and one other guy. We're both students at the
   university. Are you a student?
 A Yes. I'm in my second year. Engineering. If I'm
   interested, when could I move in?
 B Well, the guy who's leaving will stay till the end of
   this month, so the room's free from the beginning
   of July.
 A Fine. Uh, I've got a car. What's the parking
   situation like?
 B Uh… that's a bit of a problem. You'll have to get a
   permit if you want to park on Elm Street. It costs
   about $60 a year.
 A OK. Well, thanks for all that. I'll think about it and
   I'll call you back. Is this a good time to call?
 B Yeah, between six and eight there's usually
   someone here.
 A OK. Bye then.

G quantifiers
V noun formation
P *-ough* and *-augh*

5A Slow down, you move too fast

File 5 overview

Each lesson in this File either extends or brings together language points previously taught separately. **5A** focuses on quantifiers, **5B** on the use of articles, and **5C** on gerund and infinitive. The File also looks at forming nouns from verbs and adjectives, the use of prepositions after certain verbs and adjectives, and vocabulary related to work.

Lesson plan

This lesson presents again and extends SS' knowledge of quantifiers, e.g., *a lot of, plenty of, too much, not enough*, etc. through the topic of modern lifestyles. The grammar is presented through the topic of people's work–life balance and how they feel about it. They also hear an expert giving tips on how we can slow down in our daily lives. In the second half of the lesson SS read and talk about the "Slow Movement." This movement, which began in Italy but has since spread all over the world, aims to promote a slower, healthier world where people eat "slow food" and live in "slow cities." The vocabulary focus is on word building, this time focusing on noun formation. Pronunciation focuses on the frequently problematic combinations *-ough* and *-augh*.

Optional lead-in (books closed)

- Write on the board:
  15 MINUTES   60 MINUTES   150 MINUTES
  30 MINUTES   90 MINUTES
- Ask SS *How can you say these times in another way?* and give them a couple of minutes in pairs to write the answers. Elicit and check answers. Remind SS of the silent *l* in *half* /hæf/ and the silent *h* in *hour* /ˈaʊər/.

a quarter of an hour	an hour and a half
half an hour	two and a half hours
an hour	

1 GRAMMAR quantifiers

a ● Books open. Focus on the instructions, and have SS write down approximate times, and then compare.

Extra idea

You could start by having SS ask you the questions.

- Get responses from the class. You could find out, e.g., who works / studies the most / least, etc.

b ● Focus on the article and instructions and elicit / explain the meaning of *work–life balance* (= the amount of time you spend working compared to the amount of free time you have). Give SS a time limit to read the article and get an idea of the difference between the three people. Tell SS not to choose the correct grammatical form at this stage. Then ask the whole class *Which of the three situations is most typical in your country?*

c ● Focus on the task and have SS, either individually or in pairs, read the texts again and underline the correct phrases. Check answers.

2 long enough	8 a lot of
3 a lot of	9 Lots of
4 enough time	10 too hard
5 much time	11 too much
6 too many	12 a few
7 plenty of	

d ● Tell SS to go to **Grammar Bank 5A** on page 138. Go through the rules and examples with the class. Drill pronunciation where necessary, e.g., *enough* /ɪnʌf/.

Extra idea

In a monolingual class, you could have SS translate the example sentences and compare the expressions they would use in their L1.

Grammar notes

Quantifiers
- SS should have seen most or all of these forms previously, but here they are brought together.

Large quantities
- *Lots of* is a colloquial equivalent of *a lot of*. Be careful SS don't say *a lots of*.

Small quantities
- *A little* and *very little* are quite different in meaning (the second is more negative). The same applies to *a few* and *very few*.

Zero quantities
- *not … any* is the most common way to talk about zero quantities, e.g., *I don't have any money*; *there isn't any milk*.
  However, you can also use *no* + noun after *there is* and *have*, e.g., *There's no milk*.
- *None* is a pronoun, so it is used on its own, e.g., *Is there any milk? No, I'm afraid there's none left*.

More / less than you need
- Typical mistakes are:
  – using *too much* + an adjective, e.g., ~~I'm too much busy~~.
  – the position of *enough*, e.g., ~~I'm not enough tall to open the cupboard~~.
  – mispronouncing *enough*.
  – some nationalities confuse *plenty of* and *full of* because of L1 interference.

- Focus on the exercises on page 139 and have SS do them individually or in pairs. Check answers.

a 1 too many **2** very few **3** ✓	
4 enough parking lots **5** ✓	
6 a lot **7** a little **8** any time	
b 1 plenty of time	**5** ✓
2 too much work	**6** ✓
3 ✓	**7** None
4 old enough	**8** a lot of / lots of

- Tell SS to go back to the main lesson on page 68.

e • Focus on the instructions and give SS a few minutes to talk in pairs or small groups. Monitor and correct any mistakes with quantifiers. Ask a few SS to report their discussion to the whole class.

2 PRONUNCIATION -ough and -augh

Pronunciation notes

The aim of these exercises is to help SS remember the pronunciation of a group of high-frequency words that contain -ough / -augh – a combination of letters that has a rather irregular spelling–pronunciation relationship.

a • Focus on the information box. Then focus on the five columns and elicit the sound word for each, e.g., *up*.

- Now have SS put the words in the right column. They could do this in pairs. Encourage them to say the words out loud and to use their instinct to help them decide.

b • **5.1** Play the recording once for SS to check. Check answers.

5.1				CD2 Track 33
up /ʌ/	saw /ɔ/	phone /oʊ/	cat /æ/	boot /u/
enough	bought	although	laugh	through
tough	brought			
	caught			
	daughter			
	thought			

- Now check answers to the two questions. Elicit that:
  - /ɔ/ is the most common pronunciation (especially when there is a *t* after -ough or -augh). This includes the past tense / participle forms (*bought, brought, caught, taught,* and *thought*).
  - *Enough, tough,* and *laugh* finish with the /f/ sound.
- Emphasize that this is a small group of very common (but slightly irregular) words and it is worthwhile for SS to memorize their pronunciation.
- Finally, play the recording again for SS to listen and repeat the words in the chart.

c • **5.2** Focus on the sentences, which all contain the target sounds. Give SS time to practice saying the sentences in pairs. Then play the recording for them to check, and let them say them again.

Extra support

Play the recording first, pausing for SS to repeat. Then let SS practice saying them again.

5.2	CD2 Track 34
1 I bought some steak, but it was very tough.	
2 Although it was dark, we walked through the tunnel.	
3 I thought I'd brought enough money with me.	
4 I laughed when my daughter caught the ball.	

Extra idea

Remember to test SS on the pronunciation of -ough / -augh words at the start of the next class and later in the course.

Study Link SS can find more practice of English sounds on the MultiROM and also on the *American English File 3* Website.

3 LISTENING

a • **5.3** Focus on the instructions and give SS a moment to read the five tips.

- Now play the recording once all the way through. Play again if necessary. Check answers.

1 sitting down	4 in silence
2 gym, yoga	5 bath, shower
3 long walk	

5.3	CD2 Track 35

(audioscript in Student Book on page 127)

Tip number 1. Eat breakfast sitting down. Most people stay in bed until the last minute and then have a cup of coffee and a piece of toast standing up. This is really bad for you because it means that you start the day in a hurry. Your body and mind are already moving too fast. So do yourself a favor. Get up ten minutes earlier every day and have breakfast – nice and slowly.

Tip number 2. Forget the gym, and do yoga instead. Many people go to the gym after work to exercise because they think that this relaxes them, but it doesn't, believe me. I really think that a gym is a very stressful place. Exercising hard, for example, doing aerobics, makes your heart beat more quickly, so it doesn't relax your body at all. In fact, it does the opposite. So, forget the gym and try doing yoga. Yoga will not only help you get fit, but it will also slow your body down and help you think more clearly.

Tip number 3. Go for a long walk. Walking is the most traditional form of exercise, but many people have just forgotten how to do it. These days we all just get into our cars. The great thing about walking is that you can't walk very fast, so walking actually slows you down. And when we walk, we look around us at the birds, the trees, the stores, other people. It reminds us of the world we live in and it helps us stop, and think, and relax.

Tip number 4. Spend 10 minutes each day in silence. Meditation isn't new. People have been doing it for thousands of years and now it is becoming really popular again. In the United States you can find meditation rooms in companies, schools, airports, and even hospitals. Meditation is a fantastic way to teach your mind to slow down and to think more clearly. And spending time in silence every day will also benefit your general health.

And finally, tip number 5. Take a bath, not a shower. Taking a shower is very quick and convenient, but it is another part of our fast-living culture. When you come home from work, instead of taking a shower, take a bath and spend half an hour there. A bath is one of the most relaxing things you can do. And it will really help to slow you down at the end of a hard day.

b ● Play Tip 1 again. Then pause and give SS time to write down anything they understood about *why* you should do this. Have them compare with a partner and play the recording again if necessary. Check answers for Tip 1, and then do the same for Tip 2, etc.

> 1 Eat breakfast sitting down. If you eat it standing up, you start the day in a hurry.
> 2 Forget the gym. Do yoga. The gym is stressful. Aerobics, etc. makes your heart beat quickly. Yoga helps you slow down (and get in shape).
> 3 Go for a long walk. When we walk we can't do it fast. We have time to look at everything and everybody (birds, trees, stores, people, etc.). Helps us stop, think, and relax.
> 4 Spend ten minutes each day in silence. Meditation teaches your mind to slow down and think more clearly (good for your general health, too).
> 5 Take a bath, not a shower. A half an hour bath is relaxing and will slow you down at the end of a hard day.

Extra support

If there's time, you could have SS listen again with the audioscript on page 127 so they can see exactly what they understood / didn't understand. Translate / explain any new words or phrases.

c ● In pairs, have SS choose what they think are the two best tips and say if they do them. Then get responses from the class and find out which are the two most popular tips.

4 READING & VOCABULARY

a ● Focus on the leaflet and ask SS who they think wrote it. (A politician or political party.) Then focus on the instructions and have SS, in pairs, match the verbs to their dictionary definition. Check answers, and have SS underline the stressed syllable.

> | 1 en<u>cou</u>rage | 4 pro<u>mote</u> |
> |---|---|
> | 2 in<u>crease</u> | 5 re<u>duce</u> |
> | 3 ban | 6 pro<u>tect</u> |

b ● Now focus on the question and the introduction to the article *Slow down, you move too fast*. Have SS read it, or read it aloud yourself, and then elicit the answer from the whole class. Ask SS if they agree with the first paragraph.

> The counterrevolution is a movement whose aim is to slow life down (so that we live in a happier and healthier way).

c ● Put SS in pairs, **A** and **B**. Focus on the instructions and go through the questions. Make sure they understand the vocabulary in the questions, e.g., *aims* and *spread*. Set a time limit, e.g., four minutes, for **A** and **B** to read their part of the article and answer the questions. Tell SS not to write their answers, but just to underline the relevant parts of the article.

> **A 1** Carlo Petrini, an Italian journalist. Because he saw that a fast-food restaurant had opened in a beautiful square in Rome.
> **2** He thought it was tragic that people live too quickly to sit down to eat a proper meal and that they only eat mass-produced food.
> **3** To encourage people to stop during the day and eat slowly, use local shops and markets, eat out in small family restaurants, cook with traditional recipes.
> **4** It is now a global organization and has members in 100 countries.
> **B 1** It was inspired by the Slow Food movement. It was started by the mayor of Greve in Chianti, Italy.
> **2** Its aims are to make our towns places where people enjoy living and working and to protect things that make the town different. Slow cities have to reduce traffic and noise, increase the number of green areas, build pedestrian areas, and promote local businesses and traditions.
> **3** It has spread all over the world.
> **4** Most people are very happy ("delighted") because they think it increases their quality of life. Teenagers aren't so happy. They have to travel 25 km to the nearest city if they want excitement.

d ● Now have SS cover the text and tell each other their answers to the questions, giving as much detail as they can remember. Monitor and help.

● Then have SS read the part of the article they didn't read. Ask SS which words / phrases they had problems with and elicit / explain / translate the meaning.

e ● Ask the whole class this question. Find out how many people would like to eat "slow food" and live in a "slow city" and why (not).

5 VOCABULARY noun formation

a ● Focus on the information box and go through it with SS. Then, focus on the instructions and the words in the list and elicit word by word whether they are verbs or adjectives (*crazy*, *happy*, and *similar* are adjectives; the others are verbs).

● Give SS time, individually or in pairs, to form nouns and to write them in the correct column.

b ● **5.4** Play the recording once for SS to check their answers. Then play it again, pausing after each word for SS to underline the stressed syllable. Check answers.

● Elicit the answer to the question *Which ending has a stressed syllable?* (-*ation* is the only noun ending here that is stressed).

> | <u>gov</u>ernment | organi<u>za</u>tion | dis<u>cus</u>sion |
> |---|---|---|
> | <u>move</u>ment | relax<u>a</u>tion | re<u>ac</u>tion |
> | pro<u>pos</u>al | <u>cra</u>ziness | pos<u>si</u>bility |
> | sur<u>vi</u>val | <u>hap</u>piness | simi<u>lar</u>ity |

> | **5.4** | | CD2 Track 36 |
> |---|---|---|
> | government | discussion | craziness |
> | movement | reaction | happiness |
> | organization | proposal | possibility |
> | relaxation | survival | similarity |

6 SPEAKING

a ● Focus on the instructions and go through the proposals. Give SS a few moments individually to put a check or an x next to the proposals and think of a reason why they agree / disagree.

b ● Focus on the instructions and go through the **Useful language**. Have SS work in groups of three or four. They should discuss each proposal in turn, giving reasons for or against, and decide (by a vote) whether to support it or not.

● Monitor and help, encouraging them to use the **Useful language** expressions.

c ● Get responses from each group to find out which proposals they support. Write the proposals supported by each group on the board to find out which are the most popular.

Extra idea

Ask SS if they think any of these things are happening or will happen in the future in their town / city.

Extra photocopiable activities

Grammar
quantifiers page 152
Communicative
Lifestyle survey page 183 (instructions page 166)

HOMEWORK

Study Link **Workbook** pages 44–46

5 B

G articles: *a / an*, *the*, no article
V verbs and adjectives + prepositions
P sentence stress, *the*, /θ/ or /ð/?

Same planet, different worlds

Lesson plan

In this lesson, SS practice when (and when not) to use an article, and which article to use. The rules given are the most common ones, for example, the non-use of the definite article when generalizing. Other less common or more complex uses will be dealt with in subsequent levels of *American English File*. The topic of the lesson is a light-hearted look at men and women. In the first half of the lesson, the focus is on what men and women talk about, and in the second half their different attitudes to certain activities, e.g., visiting a spa. There is a focus on sentence stress, the sounds /ð/ and /θ/, and the two pronunciations of *the*. In vocabulary, SS learn common verb and adjective + preposition combinations.

Optional lead-in (books closed)

- Write the following sentences on the board:
  Where are my socks? I can't see them anywhere.
  You just relax. I'll organize our summer vacation this year.
  We need to talk.
  That wasn't a strike! The ball was definitely high.
- Then ask SS who they think would probably say these sentences, a man or a woman. Get them to say why.

1 GRAMMAR articles: *a / an*, *the*, no article

a • Books open. Focus on the instructions and give SS a couple of minutes to fill in the blanks. Have them compare with a partner before checking answers. Don't give any grammar explanations, as this will come in **b**.

1 (-) 2 (-), the 3 a, the, an 4 (-), (-), (-) 5 a, (-)

b • Tell SS to go to **Grammar Bank 5B** on page 138. Go through the examples and rules with the class. In a monolingual class, you could have SS compare what they use in their L1.

Grammar notes

Articles: *a, an, the,* no article

- SS have learned rules for using articles before, but here the main ones are brought together. Most nationalities will have some problems using articles correctly, but especially those who don't have articles in their language.
- In this lesson the main rules are covered. Others will be introduced in subsequent levels of *American English File*.
- Typical mistakes include:
  – omission of the article, e.g., ~~I saw old man with dog~~.
  – incorrect use of definite article when generalizing, e.g., ~~The~~ men usually love ~~the~~ football.

- Focus on the exercises on page 139 and have SS do them individually or in pairs. Check answers.

a 1 the door, the house
 2 a Russian, a lawyer
 3 the theater, a month
 4 a beautiful day, the patio
 5 classical music, Italian food
 6 the girl, the window
 7 home, work
 8 Men, women
 9 dinner, bed
 10 a lovely face, attractive eyes
b 1 the, (-), a   **4** a, an
 2 (-), (-), the   **5** the, the, (-)
 3 (-), an   **6** (-), a, the

- Tell SS to go back to the main lesson on page 72.

c • Focus on the instructions and on the sentences. Then have SS complete them in pairs.
- Check answers.

1 a, the **2** the **3** the, the **4** the **5** (-), the, the

2 PRONUNCIATION sentence stress, *the*, /θ/ or /ð/?

Pronunciation notes

This pronunciation section focuses first on the fact that articles typically have a weak pronunciation, e.g., *a* /ə/ and *the* /ðə/. Then the focus moves to the two different pronunciations of *the*, depending on whether the following noun begins with a vowel sound or not. Finally, there is a focus on the two possible pronunciations of *th*, /ð/ or /θ/. The actual difference between the two is small (the first is voiced, the second unvoiced), and the important thing is to make sure SS are not substituting another sound, e.g., /s/ or /d/.

a • **5.5** Focus on the instructions. Tell SS they are going to hear six sentences that all contain definite or indefinite articles. They will hear each sentence twice. The first time they should make sure they write down the key (stressed) words, and the second time the unstressed words.
- Play the recording, pausing after each sentence. Have SS compare, then elicit the sentences and write them on the board.

5.5   CD2 Track 37
1 Let's go for a walk in the park.
2 He's a doctor at the local hospital.
3 Is there a bookstore in the shopping mall?
4 I'd like a ticket for the game on Thursday, please.
5 They have a big house in the country.
6 We can have a break at the end of this exercise.

- Elicit that articles are <u>not</u> normally stressed.

b • **5.6** Now focus on the instructions and the phrases. Play the recording for SS to listen and repeat. Elicit that *the* is pronounced /ðə/ when the next word begins with a consonant sound (e.g., *the store, the sun, the world*), and /ði/ when the next word begins with a vowel sound (e.g., *the address, the owner, the engineer*).

5.6	CD2 Track 38
the store	
the address	
the owner	
the sun	
the engineer	
the world	

c • **5.7** Focus on the information box and remind SS of the two pronunciations of *th*. It can be pronounced /ð/ like *mother* or /θ/ like *thumb*.

• Emphasize that:
– /ð/ is a voiced sound (i.e., it is made using the voice box in the throat). SS should feel their throat vibrate when they say it.
– /θ/ is made in the mouth, not the throat (i.e., it's an unvoiced sound). SS should be able to feel air on their hand when they say it.
– there are no rules for how *th* is pronounced, but SS can use their dictionary to check the pronunciation of new words.

• Then play the recording, pausing after each sentence for SS to circle *th* if it is pronounced /ð/.

• Have them compare with a partner and then play the recording again. Check answers. (See audioscript below.)

5.7	CD2 Track 39
1 (Th)at man over (th)ere is very wealthy.	
2 June is (th)e sixth month of (th)e year.	
3 (Th)ere are three things you have to remember.	
4 I threw it away (th)e o(th)er day.	
5 We have math in (th)e third year.	
6 (Th)e athletes run through (th)at gate.	

• Play the recording again for SS to listen and repeat. Make sure SS don't pronounce *th* as /s/ or /d/.

• Then, have SS practice saying the sentences themselves before asking individual SS to say them.

Study Link SS can find more practice of English sounds on the MultiROM and also on the *American English File 3* Website.

3 READING & SPEAKING

a • Before starting you might want to pre-teach a few key words or phrases in the article that you think your SS might not be able to guess from context, e.g., *gossip* (= chat, often about other people and their personal lives).

• Put SS in pairs. Focus on the instructions and do the first two or three subjects with the whole class. Then give SS time to mark the words **M** or **W**. Then get answers from the class.

b • Now give SS a few minutes to read the first paragraph of the article. Check answers, and ask the class if they agree with the writer.

sports M	**movies** W
work M	**politics** W
clothes W	**cars** M
health W	**their house** W
family W	**the opposite sex** M and W

c • Focus on the task. Set a time limit for SS to read the whole article and to choose a, b, or c.

• Have SS compare their answers with a partner before you check answers. You could have SS point out the relevant part of the text that gave them the right answer.

1 c   2 b   3 b   4 a   5 a

d • This speaking task is meant to be a lighthearted response to the article, but will also provide practice of not using the definite article *the* when you generalize.

• Focus on the task. Put SS in pairs or groups of three. If you have a more or less equal number of men and women in your class, put them in mixed groups and have them time each other.

• Monitor and correct, especially if SS use the article incorrectly when speaking in general (e.g., *I think ~~the~~ baseball is very boring*).

• Find out which topic the men and women in your class found most difficult to talk about.

HOW WORDS WORK...

This exercise focuses on some common phrases that are often used to connect ideas in a text. SS should be familiar with *also* and *however*, but may not have met the other expressions before.

1 Give SS a few minutes in pairs to focus on the highlighted expressions and match them to their uses. Check answers, making sure SS are clear about the meaning of these expressions.

2 however, on the other hand
3 also   4 according to

• Point out that:
– *However* is usually used at the beginning of a sentence and is followed by a comma; *while* is usually in the middle of a sentence.
– *On the other hand* is usually used at the beginning of a sentence to introduce an opposite argument and is followed by a comma. You might like to point out that when two arguments are being put forward we sometimes introduce the first one with *On the one hand,...* and the second with *On the other hand,...*

2 Now have SS complete the sentences and check answers.

1 also
2 However / On the other hand
3 According to
4 while
5 On the other hand / However

4 LISTENING

a ● Focus on the photo and ask SS where they think the people are and elicit that they're in a spa, having some kind of skin treatment.

● You might want to tell your students that a *spa* traditionally means a place where mineral water comes out of the ground and where people go to drink and bathe in the water to treat a variety of health problems. Nowadays, the meaning of spa also covers places where you can receive various kinds of health and beauty treatments, e.g., massages, facials, manicures and pedicures, etc.

● Find out if anyone in the class has been to a spa and if they enjoyed it, etc.

b ● Focus on the instructions and give SS a few minutes to read the introduction (including the treatments) and answer the questions. Check answers to the first question (to find out if men enjoy spas as much as women) and then elicit ideas for which treatment Joanna and Stephen will like best, getting SS to say why. Explain / translate any vocabulary as necessary.

c ● **5.8** , **5.9** & **5.10** Focus on the chart and the instructions. Play the first part (5.8), and have SS complete the chart for Stephen and Joanna for the first treatment. Let SS compare answers and then play the recording again for them to check.

● Do the same thing with the next two parts (5.9 and 5.10).

● Check answers and find out if any SS had guessed right in **b**. Try not to focus at this point on the meaning of the words, which SS will listen for in **d** (below).

Stephen	Points / reasons
The body polish	0: Horrible, uncomfortable; fruit is for eating.
The facial	4: Boring, long, too many creams
The foot treatment	9: His feet look great!

Joanna	Points / reasons
The body polish	10: Smelled good, relaxing, etc.
The facial	9: Enjoyed it. Skin feels great / healthy
The foot treatment	9: A luxury, great nail color.

5.8 CD2 Track 40

(audioscript in Student Book on page 127)
V = voice-over, J = Joanna, S = Stephen
V 1 The body polish
J So? What did you think?
S It was just horrible! Horrible. Fruit's for eating, not putting on your body. It was hot and sticky and extremely uncomfortable. And I felt so stupid. I'd never do that again. I give it zero out of ten.
J Sticky? It was fruit, for goodness sake! I thought it was wonderful. It smelled so good and it was incredibly relaxing. I mean, how could anybody not like it? And the head massage was fantastic! That was one of my favorite spa treatments ever. Ten out of ten. OK, so now, the facial.
S Hmm. How long is this one?
J One hour 40 minutes.
S Oh, you're joking. That's too long.
J Too long? It'll be heaven. See you later.

5.9 CD2 Track 41

(audioscript in Student Book on page 127)
V = voice-over, J = Joanna, S = Stephen
V 2 The facial
S Oh, that was so boring. It went on forever.
J I loved it.
S Well, I must admit my face feels different – much smoother. But I'm not sure I really want a smooth face. And it was nearly two hours and she used about 12 different creams and things. It normally only takes me a minute to wash my face – and I just use soap and water. The therapist said I ought to buy *five* different products!
J Well, I enjoyed every second. My skin feels great – really healthy. I give it nine out of ten.
S Hmm… I give it four.
J Your problem was that you were hungry, so you couldn't relax. We could have a glass of fruit juice before the last treatment…
S Fruit juice? Oh, OK then, if you really want one.

5.10 CD2 Track 42

(audioscript in Student Book on page 127)
V = voice-over, J = Joanna, S = Stephen
V 3 The foot treatment
S Wow!
J Don't tell me, you liked it!
S It was wonderful!
J I must say, your feet look… well, better. Clean anyway.
S Well, I've never liked my feet much to be honest, but now they look and feel great. That was definitely worth the time and money. Nine out of ten. What do you think?
J Yes, it was great. A real luxury. And I love the color they painted my nails. I agree – nine out of ten. You see, I knew…

d ● **5.11** Focus on the instructions. Remind SS that just as they guess words from context when they read, they need to do the same when they listen.

● Play the recording once, pausing after each sentence for SS to try to write the missing word. Then play it again and have SS compare answers.

● Check answers by having individual SS guess how the missing words are spelled and what they mean.

1 sticky	2 fantastic	3 smoother	4 soap	5 nails

⚠ In a monolingual class, you can elicit a translation. In a multilingual class, use mime, drawings, or definitions.

5.11 CD2 Track 43

S = Stephen, J = Joanna
1 S It was just horrible! Horrible. Fruit's for eating, not putting on your body. It was hot and sticky and extremely uncomfortable.
2 J And the head massage was fantastic! That was one of my favorite spa treatments ever.
3 S Well, I must admit my face feels different – much smoother. But I'm not sure I really want a smooth face.
4 S It normally only takes me a minute to wash my face – and I just use soap and water.
5 S What do you think?
  J Yes, it was great. A real luxury. And I love the color they painted my nails.

e • You could have the class vote with a show of hands to see which of the treatments described in the introduction to the text is the most popular. If you have both men and women in the class, have the women vote first and then the men to see if they agree with Stephen and Joanna.

Extra support

If there's time, you could have SS listen again with the audioscript on page 127 so they can see exactly what they understood / didn't understand. Translate / explain any new words or phrases.

5 SPEAKING

- Put SS into groups of three or four. Focus on the task and quickly go through the ten activities.
- Now focus on the **Useful language** and have SS underline the stress in *generally / general* and <u>common</u>. Also focus on the advice in the ⚠ box.
- Monitor and check as they discuss, correcting any misuse of articles and encouraging them to use the expressions in **Useful language**.
- Get quick responses from a different group for each topic. Tell SS if you agree or not and why.

6 VOCABULARY verbs and adjectives + prepositions

a • Focus on the example sentences and remind SS that they have to remember which prepositions to use after certain verbs and adjectives, e.g., you talk *to* a person *about* something / someone.

- Focus on the instructions and remind SS to write the prepositions in the column on the right, <u>**not**</u> in the sentence. Give them time to complete the column individually or in pairs.
- Check answers.

1	to, about	6	from	11	as	16	of
2	about	7	to	12	for	17	in
3	for	8	to	13	at	18	about
4	with	9	for	14	at		
5	for	10	for	15	from		

- Then have SS quickly test their memory by covering the prepositions column with a book or piece of paper. SS should look at the sentences with blanks and try to remember the missing preposition. They can uncover the prepositions column sentence by sentence to check.

b • Focus on the instructions and put SS in pairs, **A** and **B**. Make sure they cover the prepositions column with a book or a piece of paper. They take turns asking and answering the questions, adding the correct prepositions from memory.

- Have SS change roles.

7 5.12 ♫ SONG Sk8ter Boi

- *Sk8er Boi* was originally recorded by Avril Lavigne in 2002 and was a worldwide hit. For copyright reasons this is a cover version. If you want to sing this song in class, use the photocopiable activity on page 208. The listening task helps to consolidate the grammar point in the lesson.

5.12   CD2 Track 44

Sk8er Boi
He was a boy, she was a girl
Can I make it any more obvious?
He was a punk, she did ballet
What more can I say?
He wanted her, she'd never tell
Secretly she wanted him as well
But all of her friends stuck up their nose
They had a problem with his baggy clothes

He was a skater boy
She said, "See you later boy"
He wasn't good enough for her
She had a pretty face
But her head was up in space
She needed to come back down to earth

Five years from now, she sits at home
Feeding the baby, she's all alone
She turns on TV. Guess who she sees?
Skater boy rocking up MTV.
She calls up her friends, they already know
And they've all got tickets to see his show
She tags along, but stands in the crowd
Looks up at the man that she turned down.

He was a skater boy
She said, "See you later boy"
He wasn't good enough for her
Now he's a superstar
Slamming on his guitar
Does your pretty face see what he's worth?

He was a skater boy
She said, "See you later boy"
He wasn't good enough for her
Now he's a superstar
Slamming on his guitar
Does your pretty face see what he's worth?

Sorry girl but you missed out
Well tough luck, that boy's mine now
We are more than just good friends
This is how the story ends.
Too bad that you couldn't see,
See the man that boy could be
There is more than meets the eye
I see the soul that is inside.

He's just a boy, and I'm just a girl
Can I make it any more obvious?
We are in love, haven't you heard
How we rock each other's world?

I'm with the skater boy, I said see ya later boy
I'll be back stage after the show,
I'll be at the studio
Singing the song we wrote
About a girl you used to know.

I'm with the skater boy, I said see ya later boy
I'll be back stage after the show,
I'll be at the studio
Singing the song we wrote
About a girl you used to know.

Extra photocopiable activities

Grammar
articles: *a*, *an*, *the*, no article page 153
Communicative
Generally speaking page 184 (instructions page 166)
Song
Sk8er Boi page 208 (instructions page 204)

HOMEWORK

Study Link **Workbook** pages 47–49

5C

G gerunds and infinitives
V work
P word stress

Job swap

Lesson plan

In this lesson, SS practice discriminating between gerunds (or -*ing* forms) and infinitives. The context is work, and SS look at two angles that hopefully will interest them whether or not they are working themselves. The first angle involves a questionnaire that helps people see what job would most suit their personality, and the second is a reality TV program where contestants have to learn to do a new job in a month and then try to fool a panel of judges into believing that they are professionals. The vocabulary focus is on words and expressions related to work, and the pronunciation focus is on getting the correct word stress in multisyllable words.

Optional lead-in (books closed)

- Jobs quiz. Put SS in pairs or small groups. Then read the following quiz questions aloud or write them on the board:
  Can you name…?
  – two jobs that people do in a restaurant
  – two jobs connected with transportation
  – two jobs that people do at home
  – two jobs where you spend a lot of time outside
- Check answers, making sure SS can spell and pronounce the words correctly.
  Some possible answers
  waiter, chef, etc.
  taxi driver, pilot, bus driver, etc.
  housewife, writer, etc.
  police officer, farmer, soccer player, etc.

1 VOCABULARY work

a • Books open. Focus on the pictures and sentences, and give SS, in pairs, a couple of minutes to match them.
  • Check answers and model and drill pronunciation of the bold words.

1 E	2 B	3 H	4 F	5 A	6 D	7 G	8 C

- Point out that:
  – we use *apply for* when we send a letter or a completed form to a company to ask for a job (usually in response to an advertisement).
  – A *résumé* is a document that shows your qualifications, experience, and interests (SS will learn to write one in **Writing 5**).
  – *overtime* = extra hours that you work over and above your normal working hours.
  – *fired* and *promoted* can be used with either *be* or *get*. If you are *fired*, you lose your job. If you are *promoted*, you are given a better job in the same company.

b • Now have SS cover the sentences and look at the pictures. Have them retell the story in pairs from memory, **A** testing **B** and then changing roles. Then elicit the story from the class by asking individual SS.

c • Now tell SS to go to **Vocabulary Bank** *Work* on page 152. Focus on section **1 Describing your job** and have SS do the exercises individually or in pairs. Check answers and drill pronunciation where necessary.

a A **1** is a librarian, B **2** is a plumber.
b 2 experience **7** quit
3 training course **8** temporary (permanent)
4 working hours **9** part-time (full-time)
5 self-employed **10** qualifications
6 retire

- Now focus on section **2 Saying what you do** and give SS a few moments to complete the **Prepositions** column. Remind SS **not** to write the prepositions in the sentences so later they can cover the **Prepositions** column and test their memory. Check answers.

1 for	**2** as	**3** in, of	**4** in	**5** for	**6** in	**7** in

- Now focus on section **3 People** and the typical endings for job words. In pairs, give SS time to add two more to each column.
- Write the column headings on the board and elicit the new words from different pairs. Write them on the board for the others to copy down. If you did the optional lead-in, SS could also add these words to the columns and drill pronunciation.

Some possible answers				
-er	**-or**	**-ist**	**-ian**	**other**
builder	doctor	receptionist	musician	housewife
teacher	author	journalist	politician	nurse

- Focus on the ⚠ box and drill the pronunciation of the two words.
- Finally, focus on the instruction "Can you remember the words on this page? Test yourself or a partner."

Testing yourself

For **Describing your job** SS can cover the words on the right, read definitions 1–10, and try to remember the words. For **Saying what you do** SS can cover the **Prepositions** column, read sentences 1–7, and try to remember the prepositions. For **People** SS can cover the chart except for the endings (-*er*, etc.) and try to remember the jobs.

Testing a partner

See **Testing a partner** on page 15.

Study Link SS can find more practice of these words on the MultiROM and on the *American English File 3* Website.

- Tell SS to go back to the main lesson on page 76.

2 PRONUNCIATION & SPEAKING
word stress

a • Focus on the words and phonetics and ask SS if they can remember how the phonetics show them where the stress falls (the syllable <u>after</u> the stress mark (ˈ) is the one that is stressed). Have them underline the stressed syllable in each word using the phonetics to help.

b • **5.13** Play the recording, pausing after each word to check answers. You could also ask SS to tell you how each word is pronounced just before you play it.

1 <u>apply</u>	6 <u>permanent</u>
2 <u>contract</u>	7 qualifi<u>cations</u>
3 employ<u>ee</u>	8 <u>quit</u>
4 ex<u>perience</u>	9 re<u>tire</u>
5 <u>overtime</u>	10 <u>temporary</u>

• Now give SS a few minutes to practice saying the words. You could have them practice saying them correctly by looking at the phonetics and also by repeating after the recording.

5.13	CD2 Track 45
1 apply	6 permanent
2 contract	7 qualifications
3 employee	8 quit
4 experience	9 retire
5 overtime	10 temporary

c • Put SS in pairs. Focus on the questions and give SS a few minutes to read them and think whether they have a family member or friend who fits any of the categories. They should try to think of someone for as many of the questions as possible.

• SS work in pairs, telling each other about people they know. Encourage them to give, and ask for, as many details as they can.

3 GRAMMAR gerunds and infinitives

a • Focus on the instructions and the questionnaire. Have SS complete it, individually or in pairs, and check answers. They should be able to do this reasonably well from what they already know and by instinct. If SS ask for a reason why a particular verb has to be in the gerund or infinitive, tell them that they will see all the rules in the **Grammar Bank**.

2 helping	7 to work	12 improvising
3 not earning	8 managing	13 Doing
4 to work	9 expressing	14 solving
5 making	10 to follow	15 to understand
6 Taking	11 to be	16 to calculate

b • Now tell SS to read each sentence in the questionnaire carefully, and check the sentences that they <u>strongly</u> agree with.

• When they have finished, have them compare their answers with another student, explaining why they have checked certain statements.

c • Focus on the instructions and have SS read the "answer" paragraph corresponding to the section where they have most checks. Some SS may have an equal number of checks in two sections, in which case they should read both answer sections.

• Ask a few SS for their results to find out what kind of job, according to the questionnaire, would suit them, and if this is the kind of job that they would actually like to do (or are actually doing).

d • Now focus on the rules and give SS a few minutes to complete them individually or in pairs. Check answers.

1 the gerund	4 the gerund
2 the infinitive	5 the gerund
3 the infinitive	

e • Tell SS to go to the **Grammar Bank 5C** on page 138. Go through the examples and rules, and have SS compare what form they use in their L1.

Grammar notes
Gerunds and infinitives

• SS have learned rules for using gerunds (or *-ing* forms) and the infinitive before, but separately. In this lesson they are brought together.

• SS will see in this lesson that there are three common verb forms in English: *go* (base form), *to go* (infinitive), and *going* (gerund or *-ing* form).

• Verbs that can take either the gerund or infinitive, but with a different meaning, will be focused on in more detail in the next level of *American English File*.

• Emphasize the importance of learning which verb form to use after a particular verb or construction, and give SS plenty of practice. In time they will develop an instinctive feel for whether a gerund or infinitive is required.

• Focus on the exercises on page 139 and have SS do them individually or in pairs. Check answers.

a 1 to rent	5 failing	8 to find
2 flying	6 dancing	9 learning
3 to reserve	7 Being	10 to be able to
4 not to make		
b 1 working	5 working	8 Working
2 to work	6 working	9 to work
3 work	7 to work	10 to work
4 work		

• Tell SS to go back to the main lesson on page 77.

f • Focus on the instructions. Give SS a few minutes to choose five topics and to think about what they are going to say. Demonstrate the activity by talking about a couple of the topics yourself.

• Put SS in pairs and tell them to talk to each other about the topics they have chosen. Monitor to check that SS are using the right forms of the verbs.

• Get responses from a few different SS.

4 READING

a • Focus on the instructions and on the title of the article and elicit some qualities from the class, e.g., *You need to be extroverted, self-confident*, etc.

b • Now focus on the photo of Jessica on page 78 and on the one on page 79 in which she is doing a TV interview, and ask SS if she looks very different.

• Now focus on the instructions and the headings. Check that SS understand *challenge* (= something difficult somebody has to do) and *contestant* (= person who takes part in a contest, e.g., a quiz show on TV).

• Read the first paragraph with the class, and check that they understand how the program works. Then give SS a couple of minutes to read the rest of the text fairly quickly and to match the other headings to the paragraphs. Check answers.

2 The contestant	4 The teachers
3 The challenge	5 The training

c • Focus on the definitions and have SS, in pairs, find the words in the text. Check answers and have SS underline the stressed syllables.

2 a panel	5 journalist
3 reporter	6 politician
4 judge	

d • Now set a time limit, e.g., four or five minutes, for SS to read the text again more carefully and tell them that they should try to remember the main facts. Help with any vocabulary problems.

• Then put them in pairs, **A** and **B**, and tell them to go to **Communication Test your memory**, **A** on page 117 and **B** on page 120.

• Go through the instructions. SS should ask each other alternate questions, with **A** going first.

• Ask SS to see who had the best memory.

e • Ask the whole class the question, and elicit ideas and reasons. Then tell them they are going to listen and find out what happened.

Extra idea

You could have SS underline or highlight five words or phrases they want to remember from the text. Have them compare their words / phrases with a partner and then get some responses from the class.

5 LISTENING

• **5.14**, **5.15**, **5.16** & **5.17** To create a bit of suspense it is best to do this activity section by section so that SS listen to one week at a time. Give SS a few minutes to look at questions 1–4 or read them aloud. Then play the recording for **Week one** and have SS answer the questions. Let them compare their answers in pairs, then play the recording again. Then repeat the procedure for **Weeks two**, **three**, and **four**. For dramatic effect you could pause the recording in 5.17 after Adam says, "The judges gave their verdict…" and ask the class if they think Jessica passed the final test; then let them hear the verdict.

Week one
1 They thought she was nice.
2 He thought she was too shy and nice, not aggressive enough. Also she didn't know anything about politics.
3 Watch political interviews on TV, learn to speak more clearly and confidently, and read the political sections of all newspapers.
4 She felt exhausted.
Week two
5 She had her hair cut and got new, more stylish clothes.
6 She learned how to interview someone (in front of the camera).
7 She had to ask the president a question.
8 No, the president didn't hear the question.
Week three
9 He thought Jessica was finally making some progress and was more relaxed.
10 She had to interview a politician from the Republican party.
11 She said "Democratic party" instead of "Republican party."
12 She had to learn to keep going and not lose her confidence.
Week four
13 She had to interview the secretary of education "live." She felt nervous, but well prepared.
14 Yes, she made him answer the question.
15 No. None of the three judges realized that Jessica wasn't the professional reporter. She passed the test!
16 No, because she's much happier working in the library.

5.14 CD2 Track 46
(audioscript in Student Book on page 127)
V = voice-over, J = Jessica, A = Adam
V Week one.
J When I got to the studio on the first day, I was really nervous. I met my teachers, Adam and Sally. They were very nice to me, but I could see that they thought it was going to be impossible to teach me to be a reporter in just a month.
A The problem with Jessica at the beginning was that she was too shy and too nice. Political reporters need to be hard – almost aggressive sometimes – and I've never met anyone less aggressive than Jessica. And also she knew nothing about politics – she knew who the president was but not much else!
J I spent the first week watching lots of political interviews on TV, and Adam and Sally taught me how to speak more clearly and more confidently. In the evenings they made me read the political sections of all the newspapers. It was very boring. At the end of the week, I was exhausted.

5.15 CD2 Track 47
(audioscript in Student Book on page 127)
V = voice-over, J = Jessica, A = Adam
V Week two.
J Adam and Sally said I had to change my image for TV, so I had my hair cut and colored, and I got new, more stylish clothes. I must say I liked my new look. I spent the week learning how to interview someone in front of a camera.

A Then came Jessica's first big challenge. The president was arriving home after a visit to Asia. They'd arranged an informal news conference at the airport and she had to wait with the other reporters and try to ask him a question.

J It was a disaster. I was so nervous I was shaking. There were a lot of other reporters pushing and shouting. They didn't let me get near the president. I tried to ask my question, but he didn't hear me. I felt really stupid.

5.16 CD2 Track 48

(audioscript in Student Book on page 127)
V = voice-over, J = Jessica, A = Adam
V Week three.
A Jessica was finally making some progress. She was more relaxed. This week she had to interview a politician from the Republican party in the studio.
J In the beginning it was fine. But then I made a stupid mistake.
J *So could you tell us what the Democratic party is going to do about… sorry, I mean, the Republican party…* I said the "Democratic party" instead of the "Republican party." And after that I was really nervous again.
A We all make mistakes sometimes. Jessica just has to learn to keep going and not to lose her confidence.

5.17 CD2 Track 49

(audioscript in Student Book on page 127)
V = voice-over, J = Jessica, A = Adam, S = secretary
V Week four.
J I spent the last week preparing for the test. It was going to be a live interview with the secretary of education. There would be three professional reporters and me all asking him questions. I'd done lots of research, so although I was nervous, I felt well prepared.
J *Secretary, many people think that the real reason there aren't enough teachers is that their salaries are so low. Are you proposing an increase in teachers' salaries?*
S *Well, let's not forget that salaries are much higher today than they were under the previous government.*
J *Yes, but you haven't answered my question. Are you going to increase them?*
M *Well, we're planning to spend a lot more money on education in the next two years.*
J *Is that a yes or a no?*
S *There are no immediate plans to increase teachers' salaries…*
J *So it's a no then. Thank you, Secretary.*
J When it was all over, came the worst part. I had to wait while the judges decided which of us they thought *wasn't* a professional reporter.
A The judges gave their verdict – and incredibly *none* of the three realized that Jessica wasn't a professional! She did very well. Who knows, maybe one day soon you'll be seeing her on TV… and this time she'll be a real reporter, not pretending!
J It was a great experience and I was pleased how I did, but actually I wouldn't like to change jobs. I'm much happier working in the library.

Extra support

If there's time, you could have SS listen again with the audioscript on page 127 so they can see exactly what they understood / didn't understand. Translate / explain any new words or phrases.

6 SPEAKING

- Focus on the instructions and the jobs, and make sure SS understand them (*stuntman* = the person who does dangerous things in a movie, e.g., car chases, instead of the main actors).
- Now focus on the **Useful language**. Demonstrate the activity by talking about the first job (soccer coach), using some of the phrases in **Useful language**. Then have SS talk, in pairs or small groups, about each of the jobs. Tell them that they must end up each choosing the one they would most and least like to learn to do.
- Ask for responses to see which jobs SS would most / least like to learn to do.

Extra idea

If you have a class where several SS are working, you could have the rest of the class interview them. Write their names and jobs on the board. Then have those who work prepare a few notes about the pros and cons of their job. Meanwhile, have the other SS prepare a couple of questions for each person. Then have the SS with jobs sit at the front of the class. Each should explain what he / she does and talk for a few minutes about the pros and cons of his / her job. Then the other SS ask their questions. This activity may take some time, but often provides real and motivating communication.

Study Link SS can find a dictation and Grammar quiz on all the grammar from File 5 on the MultiROM and more grammar activities on the *American English File* 3 Website.

Extra photocopiable activities

Grammar
gerunds and infinitives page 154
Communicative
Can you guess? page 185 (instructions page 166)
Vocabulary
Pick a card page 199 (instructions page 194)

HOMEWORK

Study Link **Workbook** pages 50–52

Function Giving opinions
Language *In my opinion…, Personally, I think…*

Lesson plan

In this lesson, SS practice asking for and giving opinions. The context is a meeting in the MTC office, where Allie, Mark, and Jacques discuss the best way to promote Scarlett's new CD. Mark and Jacques express their ideas and, to Mark's annoyance, both Allie and Scarlett agree with Jacques.

In **Social English** Mark and Allie go to the Louvre. At first, Mark is tense because of the meeting, but then he relaxes. They are enjoying themselves in the gallery when Mark suddenly sees Ben. Mark and Allie leave the gallery hoping that Ben hasn't seen them.

Study Link These lessons are on the *American English File 3* Video, which can be used instead of the Class Audio CD for these lessons (see Introduction page 9). The main functional section of each episode is also on the MultiROM with additional activities.

Optional lead-in (books closed)

- Review what happened in the previous episode by eliciting the story, e.g., *What did Mark and Allie have to do with Scarlett in the last episode? What happened when they took her to an expensive restaurant? What did Mark do to solve the problem?*, etc.
- Remind SS of the language that they learned in the last lesson (ways of making suggestions). You could write some of the key expressions on the board with blanks for SS to complete.
- If you are using the Video, you could play the previous episode again, leaving out the "Listen and Repeat" sections.

GIVING OPINIONS

a • **5.18** Tell SS to cover the conversation with their hand or a piece of paper. Focus on the photo and the questions. Alternatively, you could write the questions on the board and have SS listen with books closed.

- Play the recording once all the way through and check answers.

> Jacques has the best idea. His idea is that Scarlett should tour clubs and festivals.

b • Now have SS look at the conversation. Have them read it in pairs and see if they can guess or remember the missing words. Emphasize that they shouldn't write the words in the conversation, but pencil them in alongside or on a separate sheet of paper.

c • Play the recording again for them to check. Then go through the conversation line by line and check answers. Find out if SS had correctly guessed the actual words spoken. When they had not guessed correctly, see if their alternative also fits.

- Deal with any vocabulary problems. Point out that *actually* (line 10) = in fact. It doesn't mean *now*.

5.18 CD2 Track 50

A = Allie, S = Scarlett, M = Mark, J = Jacques

A That was a great concert last night, Scarlett.
S Thanks.
A As we know, Scarlett's got a new CD coming out soon. So let's have a look at the best way we can promote it in France.
M OK, well, I think Scarlett **should** visit the major music stores. In my **opinion**, that's the best way to meet her fans.
A I'm not so **sure**. What do you **think**, Jacques?
J Actually, I don't **agree** with Mark. Scarlett isn't commercial in that way.
A Scarlett? Scarlett?
S I agree **with** Jacques. I don't have a commercial image. It isn't my style.
M OK, but Scarlett needs more publicity. What about a series of TV and radio interviews? **Don't** you agree?
A Yes, but that's what everybody does. What we want is something different.
J **Personally**, I think Scarlett should tour clubs and summer festivals. She can DJ, play her favorite music, play the new CD, and meet her fans, too.
A Yes, **absolutely**. That's a much better idea. Mark?
M OK, why not?
A Scarlett?
S I think that's a **great** idea. Thank you, Jacques.

d • **5.19** Now focus on the key phrases highlighted in the conversation. Play the recording, pausing after each sentence so SS can repeat. Encourage them to copy the rhythm and intonation.

5.19 CD2 Track 51

A = Allie, S = Scarlett, M = Mark, J = Jacques

M I think Scarlett should visit the major music stores.
M In my opinion, that's the best way to meet her fans.
A I'm not so sure.
A What do you think, Jacques?
J Actually, I don't agree with Mark.
S I agree with Jacques.
M Don't you agree?
J Personally, I think Scarlett should tour clubs and summer festivals.
A Yes, absolutely.
S I think that's a great idea.

e • Focus on the chart and show SS how the first phrase has been written in each column. Give them time working in pairs to write in the other phrases. Check answers.

Asking people what they think	Saying what *you* think	Agreeing / Disagreeing
What do you think?	I think…	I'm not so sure.
Don't you agree?	In my opinion,…	I don't agree with Mark.
	Personally, I think…	I agree with Jacques.
	I think that's a great idea.	Yes, absolutely.

Extra support

You can have SS read the conversation in pairs, further practicing the rhythm of the phrases.

f ● Put SS in pairs, **A** and **B**, and have them go to **Communication *What do you think?*, A** on page 117 and **B** on page 120. Go through the instructions. Here SS should take turns asking each other questions and giving opinions.

Extra support

Remind SS to say *Sorry, could you repeat that?* if they don't understand the questions the first time.

● Ask a few pairs for their responses to find the majority opinion for one or two of the questions.

SOCIAL ENGLISH Why is she smiling?

a ● ⬤ **5.20** Focus on the photo and ask *Where are they?* (In the Louvre.) *What's the painting?* (The *Mona Lisa*.) Play the recording once for SS to answer the question. Check answers.

> They see Ben.

b ● Focus on the questions. Then play the recording again. Have SS compare answers, and then play the recording again if necessary. Check answers, and elicit or explain the meaning of any words or expressions SS didn't understand, e.g., *self-portrait*.

> 1 No, it's his first time.
> 2 Because Allie agreed with Jacques's idea at the meeting.
> 3 That she had to do her job. / She really thought Jacques's idea was better.
> 4 That she was the wife of a banker. / That she's a self-portrait of Leonardo da Vinci, the painter.
> 5 That she's the director of a music company!
> 6 Because they don't want Ben to see them.

Extra support

If there's time, let SS listen one more time with the audioscript on page 127. Help them with any words or expressions they didn't understand.

5.20   CD2 Track 52

(audioscript in Student Book on page 127)
A = Allie, M = Mark
A It's great to be on our own again.
M Yeah.
A Is this the first time you've been to the Louvre?
M Uh huh.
A What's the matter? Is this about the meeting? Because I agreed with Jacques and not with you?
M Yeah, well, we knew it wouldn't be easy. Working together, I mean.
A It's difficult for me as well. But if I don't agree with you,…
M I know, I know, you're the boss.
A And I have to do my job. I really thought that Jacques's idea was better. And so did Scarlett.
M It's not a big deal, Allie. I'm fine, really. So who exactly was the Mona Lisa?
A I'm not sure. I think she was the wife of a banker…
M Is that why she's smiling? Because her husband has a good salary?
A I also read somewhere that she was a self-portrait of Leonardo.

M A self-portrait? You're kidding. Now, I don't know much about art, but Leonardo da Vinci was a man, right?
A Well, it's just a theory. Why do you think she's smiling?
M Well, in my opinion, she's the managing director of a music company.
A What?
M She lives in Paris, she's in love with her marketing director, and she has a lot of fun telling him what to do.
A That's really unfair!
M Hey, we're not in the office now – you can't tell me I'm wrong! Let's get a coffee.
A Good idea.
M Don't turn around!
A What is it?
M I've just seen Ben from the office.
A Where?
M I said don't look! I don't think he's seen us. Let's get out of here. Come on.

c ● ⬤ **5.21** Now focus on the **USEFUL PHRASES**. Give SS a minute to try to complete them, and then play the recording to check.

5.21   CD2 Track 53

A = Allie, M = Mark
A What's the **matter**?
M It's not a big **deal**.
M You're **kidding**.
M Now, I don't know much **about** art.
A That's really **unfair**!
M Don't **turn** around.
M Let's **get** out of here.

Extra idea

Ask SS if they can remember who said each phrase (and in what context), e.g., Allie says *What's the matter?* (Because Mark doesn't seem happy.)

d ● Play the recording again, pausing for SS to repeat. In a monolingual class, elicit the equivalent expressions in SS' L1.

HOMEWORK

Study Link **Workbook** page 53

Lesson plan

In this fifth writing lesson SS practice writing a résumé and a formal "cover" letter, i.e., the letter you include with your résumé when you send it to a company or organization in response to a job advertisement. The style applies both to letters and e-mails.

a • Focus on the instructions. Give SS a minute to read the advertisement, and elicit answers. Deal with any vocabulary problems.

b • Focus on the résumé and go through the headings. Then give SS a few minutes to match the headings. Check answers.

1 Work experience	3 Languages
2 Education	4 Computer skills

Extra idea

Have SS cover the résumé and ask a few comprehension questions, e.g., *Where is he from? Where does he work?*, etc.

c • Now focus on the cover letter. Explain that a cover letter is a letter you send when you also enclose something else, e.g., a résumé or form, where you explain what you are sending and why. Remind SS that the letter is formal, and that they should circle the expression that they think is more formal from each pair. SS can do this individually or in pairs.

• Check answers.

1 I am writing
2 I have been working
3 I speak German fluently
4 I enclose
5 I look forward to hearing from you
6 Yours truly

d • Finally, focus on the **Useful language** box and have SS complete it. Check answers.

You don't know the person's name: finish *Yours truly*
You know the person's last name: finish *Sincerely*

• Go through the rules, using the letter as an example, and remind SS that this format can also be used for a formal e-mail.

WRITE your résumé and a cover letter

Go through the instructions. SS could write the résumé in class and the letter for homework, or write both for homework. If SS have not had any work experience, tell them to invent the details.

Before SS hand in their work, have them exchange their résumés and letters with another student to read and check for mistakes.

For instructions on how to use these pages, see page 30.

GRAMMAR

a 1 c 2 c 3 a 4 b 5 c
b 1 without locking 2 a few 3 getting up 4 to rent
5 big enough

VOCABULARY

a 1 government 2 reaction 3 happiness
4 possibility 5 qualifications
b 1 for 2 about 3 with 4 at 5 at 6 as
c 1 overtime 2 off 3 fired 4 promoted
5 salary 6 contract 7 apply 8 self-employed
9 quit

PRONUNCIATION

a 1 movement (It's /u/.)   4 short (It's /ɔr/.)
2 afraid (It's /eɪ/.)   5 résumé /(It's /z/.)
3 prefer (It's /ɪ/.)
b emp<u>loy</u>ee unem<u>ploy</u>ed res<u>pon</u>sible <u>tem</u>porary
ex<u>per</u>ience

CAN YOU UNDERSTAND THIS TEXT?

a 1 F 2 T 3 T 4 DS 5 F 6 T 7 DS 8 T 9 F
b **a very advanced age** = be very old
single-handedly = by himself, without any help
centenarians = people who are a hundred years old or more
in the shade = in the area that isn't in direct sunlight and is darker and cooler
use up = use completely, expend (energy)
multiplying = increasing

CAN YOU UNDERSTAND THESE PEOPLE?

a 1 b 2 a 3 c 4 b 5 a
b 1 T 2 F 3 F 4 F 5 T

5.22   CD2 Track 54

1 **A** Excuse me, is there a bookstore near here?
B Uh, sorry, I don't think so. Uh, what are you looking for?
A I'm looking for a guidebook. Is there anywhere around here where I might be able to get one?
B Actually, there aren't very many bookstores in this town at all. I think there's one downtown, but that's all. But you might be able to get a guidebook at a newsstand. There's one on the corner on the right, and another one a little farther along on this street.
A Oh good, thanks for your help.

2 A Where should we have lunch?
   B What do you think, Albert? You know the restaurants here.
   C Well, you could go to Garibaldi's. The food's wonderful – home cooking. You need time, though – they're a little slow.
   B We're sort of in a hurry because we're meeting Anna at 2:30.
   C Well, there's Trattoria Marco – they do good pasta, and Roberto's. Their fish is very good.
   A I had pasta last night.
   B Me too. Let's go to the fish place then. Where is it exactly?

3 A There's nothing on TV tonight. Why don't you go out and rent a DVD?
   B Why don't you go?
   A OK, but if I go, I choose the movie.
   B No way. I don't want to see another horror movie for the rest of my life.
   A Well, you go then.
   B We could both go and then get takeout for dinner.
   A Good idea!

4 A Come in, sit down.
   B Thank you.
   A It's, uh, James Baker, isn't it?
   B That's right.
   A Tell me a little about the last hotel where you worked. You were front desk manager, is that right?
   B Yes, I was a front desk clerk for two years and then I got promoted to front desk manager.
   A But you do realize that this hotel's much bigger than where you were before and the vacant position here is for a front desk clerk.
   B Yes, yes, I know.
   A Why did you decide to get a job straight out of school? I mean, why did you decide not to go on with your education?
   B To be honest, I wanted to earn some money. But I'd like to get an associate's degree in hospitality, maybe studying part-time.

5 A Have you applied for college next year?
   B Yes. I've been accepted at the University of California. I'm going to major in biology.
   A That's great! Are you going to be pre-med?
   B Well, actually, I've changed my mind about that. I don't really want to work as a doctor, but I'd like to do medical research.

5.23   CD2 Track 55

   A So what do you think?
   B I think I like the SUV the best. It's so comfortable. And I love the color. It's a really nice shade of blue.
   A Don't think about the color. That's a ridiculous reason for buying a car. The question is, is a sedan big enough?
   B There's not much space for luggage – the trunk's much smaller than the one in the SUV.
   A Yes, but think about it – we only go on vacation once a year. The rest of the time we only use the trunk for shopping. And the sedan would be much easier to park – that's the advantage of a smaller car. You know parking's not your strong point.
   B I can park perfectly, thank you very much.

   A Come on! What about last week when you hit the mirror?
   B That wasn't parking. It was when I was driving down Main Street. Anyway, large cars are safer than small cars on the road – everybody says so.
   A The SUV's much more expensive, you know. If we bought it, we'd have to get a bank loan.
   B How much more expensive is it?
   A About 20 percent more. We wouldn't be able to go to California this summer.
   B Hmm... what about that one? Over there. It's cheaper than the sedan or the SUV. And what a great color! I've always wanted a yellow car.
   A Look, we've been here more than an hour and I thought we'd agreed we were going to buy either the sedan or the SUV.
   B Yes, but now I'm not sure.

G reported speech: statements, questions, and commands
V shopping
P consonant sounds: /g/, /dʒ/, /k/, /ʃ/, /tʃ/

6A

Love in the supermarket

File overview

This File has three different grammatical and lexical areas. **6A** focuses on reported speech: statements, questions, and commands. **6B** reviews and extends SS' knowledge of the passive. **6C** focuses on defining and non-defining relative clauses. Lexical areas covered in the File are shopping, the movies, and adjective formation.

Lesson plan

Shopping and complaining are the main themes for this lesson, which reviews and extends SS' knowledge of reported speech. The first half of the lesson focuses on reported statements and questions, which may be review for some SS (it was covered in the last unit of *American English File 2*). SS learn vocabulary related to shopping, which they put into practice in a questionnaire. In the second half of the lesson, reported commands are introduced through the context of complaining about things you've bought or bad service in a restaurant or hotel. The pronunciation focus in this lesson is common consonant sounds.

Optional lead-in (books closed)

● Write these questions on the board:
Do you ever go to a supermarket? Which one?
How often do you go there?
Why do you go to that supermarket?
What do you like or not like about it?
Do you ever talk to other people who are shopping there?

● Put SS in pairs and get them to answer the questions. Get some responses from the class.

1 GRAMMAR reported speech: statements and questions

a ● Books open. Focus on the short story and the pictures. Tell SS to read the story and try to guess the missing last word (they can use the pictures to help them). Elicit ideas and then give them the right answer. The missing word is *over* (i.e., their relationship was finished).

b ● Focus on the task and give SS time to complete the speech bubbles in the pictures with the lines of conversation A–K. Get them to compare answers with their partners.

c ● **6.1** Play the recording for SS to check answers. Make sure SS finish with the speech bubbles correctly filled with the lines of conversation.

> **1** F, H **2** I, D **3** J **4** A, C **5** G, K **6** E, B

> **6.1**   CD3 Track 2
>
> **Man**   Do you need any help?
> **Woman**   Thanks. My name's Olga.
> **Woman**   I'm a student. What do you do?
> **Man**   I work in advertising.
> **Man**   Olga, I'm falling in love with you.
> **Man**   Will you marry me?
> **Woman**   Yes, I will.
> **Man**   Do you know how many calories there are in a
>   bar of chocolate?
> **Woman**   Are you saying I'm fat?
> **Woman**   I don't think you're really my type.
> **Man**   I'll see you around. Bye.

d ● Remind SS what "reported speech" is by asking them what a "reporter" does. (He / She works for a newspaper or TV company and interviews people and writes down what they say.) "Reported speech" is when we say or write what another person said.

● Focus on the task and have SS find and compare the two lines of "direct speech" (the actual words that the man spoke) and how they are "reported" (written down) in the story. Give them a few moments to complete the sentences then check answers.

> He told her (that) he was falling in love with her.
> He asked her if she would marry him.

● Ask SS what differences they can see between "direct" and "reported" speech:

> **sentence:** the verb *tell* is used + person + *that, is* changes to *was, I* changes to *he, you* changes to *her*
> **question:** the verb *ask* is used, *will* changes to *would, if* has been added, *you* changes to *she, me* changes to *him*

e ● Tell SS to go to **Grammar Bank 6A** on page 140. Read the examples and go through the rules for **reported speech: statements and questions** with the class.

Grammar notes

Reported speech: statements and questions

● This is a structure that may be new for some students and not for others (it was introduced in *American English File 2*). The basic principle of reported speech is fairly straightforward – when you report what someone else said you move the tenses "backwards", i.e., present to past, *will* to *would*, etc. Making the link between a "reporter" who reports (i.e., tells other people what someone has said) and "reported speech" may help SS understand both the grammatical term and concept.

● Point out that the use of *that* after *say* and *tell* is optional.

● You should point out that when direct speech is reported at a later time or in a different place from that in which it was originally said, some time / place words may change as well, e.g., *tomorrow* may change to *the next day, this* to *that*, etc.

! In conversation people often do not change the past to the past perfect.

- Typical mistakes are:
  - SS sometimes confuse *tell* and *say*, e.g., ~~He said me that he was ill.~~
  - they forget to change the tenses, e.g., ~~The waiter said he will call the manager.~~
  - they forget to change the word order in reported questions, e.g., ~~She asked him what was his name.~~

- Have SS do exercise **a** (**not b**) on page 141 in pairs or individually. Check answers.

> **a 1** The waiter said (that) he would call the manager.
> **2** Jack said (that) he had passed all his exams.
> **3** They said that we should get to the airport early.
> **4** Jack said (that) he might be late.
> **5** Mary said (that) she hadn't told anybody.
> **6** She asked us if we could help her.
> **7** He asked me if I wanted to dance.
> **8** I asked her if she had been there before.
> **9** She asked me what music I liked.
> **10** I asked her where the nearest bank was.

- Tell SS to go back to the main lesson on page 84.

- **f** ● Focus on pictures 1–6 and choose individual SS to change the direct speech in each speech bubble to reported speech. Remind SS that they should use *He / She said...* or *He / She told him / her...* but NOT ~~He / She said him / her.~~

- Then have SS retell the story in pairs in reported speech. Elicit each sentence back from individual students.

> He asked her if she needed any help. She said thank you and (told him) said that her name was Olga. She said (told him) that she was a student and she asked him what he did. He said (told her) that he worked in advertising. He said (told her) that he was falling in love with her and he asked her if she would marry him. She said that she would. Then he asked her if she knew how many calories there were in a bar of chocolate. She asked him if he was saying she was fat. She said (told him) that she didn't think he was really her type. He said (told her) that he would see her around and he said good-bye.

Extra support

Simply elicit the story around the class rather than in pairs.

2 VOCABULARY shopping

a ● Focus on the task. Give SS a few minutes to talk in pairs and then check answers.

> A **supermarket** is a large store that sells food, drink, and cleaning materials for the house, etc. They are often owned by big companies.
> A **market** is a place, often outside, where people can buy and sell things. There are usually a lot of individually owned "stalls."
> A **drugstore** and a **pharmacy** are the same thing: a store that sells medicine, etc.

> A **shopping mall** is a place where there are many stores together under one roof (sometimes outside a town).
> A **department store** is a large store divided into departments that sell a lot of different things.
> A **library** is a place where you can borrow (but not buy) books to read.
> A **bookstore** is a store where you can buy books.

b ● Have SS answer the questions with a partner, and then elicit answers from individual SS.

c ● Tell SS to go to **Vocabulary Bank** *Shopping* on page 153. Have them do section **1 Places** individually or in pairs. Check answers and model and drill pronunciation where necessary.

> **a 1** department store   **2** supermarket
>   **3** shopping mall   **4** farmers' market
> **b 5** stationery store   **6** newsstand   **7** drugstore
>   **8** bakery   **9** bookstore   **10** shoe store
>   **11** flower shop   **12** travel agency

- Now have SS do section **2 In the store**. Check answers and model and drill pronunciation if necessary.

> **1** sale   **7** shopping cart
> **2** bargain   **8** refund
> **3** store window   **9** basket
> **4** receipt   **10** customer
> **5** discount   **11** manager
> **6** salesperson   **12** cash register

- Now have SS do section **3 Verbs and phrases**. Check answers and model and drill pronunciation, e.g., *online* /ɑnˈlaɪn/.

> **1** c   **2** g   **3** d   **4** h   **5** a   **6** e   **7** b   **8** f

- Finally, focus on the final instruction "Can you remember the words on this page? Test yourself or a partner."

Testing yourself

For **Places** SS can cover the words and look at the pictures and try to remember the words. For **In the store** they can cover the list and words 1–12. They read the definitions and try to remember the words. For **Verbs and phrases** they cover sentences 1–8 and read sentences a–h and try to remember the verbs and phrases.

Testing a partner

See **Testing a partner** on page 15.

Study Link SS can find more practice of these words on the MultiROM and on the *American English File 3* Website.

- Tell SS to go back to the main lesson on page 85.

3 PRONUNCIATION consonant sounds:
/g/, /dʒ/, /k/, /ʃ/, /tʃ/

Pronunciation notes

The problems your SS have with these sounds will depend on whether similar sounds exist in their own language. You could go through these rules when SS go to the **Sound Bank** in **c**.
Remind SS that:
/g/ – The letter *g* is usually pronounced /g/, e.g., *goal*, with the exceptions below in /dʒ/.
/dʒ/ – The letters *j* and *dge* are always pronounced /dʒ/, e.g., *jacket*, *bridge*, and *g* before *i* or *e* is often /dʒ/ too, e.g., *manager*, *German*.
/k/ – The letters *ck* and *k* are always /k/ and the letter *c* is often /k/, e.g., *come*, *across*.
/ʃ/ – This sound occurs in *sh*, e.g., *wash* and in words with *ti-*, and *ci-*, e.g., *patient*, *information*, *delicious*, *special*.
/tʃ/ – This sound occurs in words with *ch*, *tch*, and in the ending *-ture*, e.g., *future*.

a ● **6.2** Focus on the five sound pictures and elicit the words and sounds: *girl* /g/, *jazz* /dʒ/, *key* /k/, *shower* /ʃ/, *chess* /tʃ/.
  ● Now play the recording for SS to try to cross out the word with a different sound.
  ● Play the recording again and check answers. Have SS tell you how the highlighted letter in the different word is pronounced.

> **1** travel **agent** – the *g* sound is /dʒ/.
> **2** **gift** shop – the *g* sound is /g/.
> **3** re**c**eipt – the *c* sound is /s/.
> **4** **c**ereal – the *c* sound is /s/.
> **5** **sch**edule – the *ch* sound is /k/.

6.2			CD3 Track 3
1 girl	/g/	bargain travel agent argument drugstore	
2 jazz	/dʒ/	vegetables manager change gift shop	
3 key	/k/	discount bakery quit receipt	
4 shower	/ʃ/	shoe store stationery store cereal cash	
5 chess	/tʃ/	lunch schedule cheese choose	

Extra support

Play the recording again for SS to repeat the sounds. Then have them practice individually or in pairs.

b ● **6.3** Focus on the task and play the recording for SS to repeat. Then have them practice saying them individually or in pairs.

6.3	CD3 Track 4
1 You can't choose your own schedule!	
2 I had an argument with the manager of the gift shop.	
3 The bakery gave us a discount.	
4 Could you give me the receipt for the shoes, please?	
5 My new green jacket was a bargain.	

c ● Tell SS to go to the **Sound Bank** on page 159 and go through the possible spellings for these sounds. (See **pronunciation notes**.)

Study Link SS can find more practice of English sounds on the MultiROM and also on the *American English File 3* Website.
  ● Now tell SS to go back to the main lesson on page 85.

4 SPEAKING

  ● Focus on the questionnaire and quickly go through the questions with the whole class.
  ● Put SS in pairs, preferably face to face. **A** (book open) asks **B** (book closed) the questions in the questionnaire. When they change roles, tell **B** to ask the questions in a different order.
  ● Monitor and help SS with any more vocabulary they may need. When they have finished, get some responses from individual SS.

Extra idea

Have the class interview you first with some or all of the questionnaire.

5 READING

a ● Ask the whole class this question and elicit some opinions / experiences. Tell SS what you usually do.

b ● Focus on the article and task. Give SS a time limit to read it and number the paragraphs. Check answers.

> **2** A **3** G **4** B **5** D **6** F **7** C

c ● Focus on the task. SS now read the article again with the paragraphs in the right order and complete the chart. Have SS compare their answers with a partner's and then check answers. You could write the answers on the board.

	Mr. Jones	Mr. Olsen
1 What did he complain about?	His laptop computer.	A DVD player/ recorder.
2 What was the problem?	It was getting slower.	They didn't have one in stock.
3 How did he try to solve it?	He took it to a local repairman and then to a computer store.	He went back to the store and called many times.
4 Why wasn't he successful?	It was too expensive to repair.	Because the machine never arrived.
5 Who did he write to?	The computer company.	The managing director of the store.
6 What happened as a result?	The company picked up the laptop, repaired it, and returned it free of charge.	He got his DVD player/ recorder + ten recordable DVDs.

d ● Focus on the task and give SS a few minutes to do this. Check answers and drill pronunciation of new words, e.g., *staff* /stæf/ and *guarantee* /gærənˈti/.

1 branch	**5** services
2 staff	**6** compensation
3 goods	**7** guarantee
4 in stock	

Extra support

Go through the text (reading it aloud) paragraph by paragraph with the class, making sure SS understand it. If necessary, use SS' L1 to clarify.

e ● Focus on the last part of the article "Top tips for complaining" and on the five phrases (*Be reasonable*, etc.). Make sure SS understand what they mean. Have SS read the text and complete it with the phrases. Have them compare their answers with a partner's and then check answers. Deal with any vocabulary problems SS may have.

● Finally, have SS vote on which two tips they think are most important and why.

1 Act quickly
2 Always go to the top
3 Keep a record
4 Don't lose your temper
5 Be reasonable

6 GRAMMAR reported speech: commands

a ● Focus on the two sentences from the article in **5 READING**, and ask SS to imagine the actual words used by the salesperson. You could refer SS to the cartoon in the text for the first one.

Possible answers
1 "(If you want my advice,) buy a new one." / "If I were you, I'd buy a new one." / "I think you should buy a new one."
2 "Come back in a week, sir." / "Could you come back next week?"

● Emphasize that when the salespersons words were "reported", i.e., turned into "reported speech", the construction was *They told him* + the infinitive.

b ● Focus on the instructions, and the four cartoons and speech bubbles. Tell SS to complete the four sentences using the affirmative or negative infinitive of a verb. Put SS in pairs and set them a time limit. Check answers.

1 She asked the salesperson to give her a refund.
2 He told the people at the next table not to make so much noise.
3 She asked the clerk to give her a bigger room.
4 He told the taxi driver not to go so fast.

c ● Tell SS to go to **Grammar Bank 6A** on page 140. Read the examples and go through the rules for **reported speech: commands**.

Grammar notes

Reported speech: commands

● This structure is not difficult, but can be a problem for SS who use, for example, a subjunctive in their L1.

● Some typical mistakes are:
 – not using an infinitive, e.g., ~~He told me I not worry / that I don't worry~~.
 – forgetting to use the *to*, e.g., ~~He told me not worry~~.

● Have SS do exercise **b** on page 141 either individually or in pairs. Check answers.

b	
1	to be quiet
2	not to smoke
3	to open my mouth
4	not to tell anyone
5	to show him my driver's license
6	to turn off our cell phones
7	not to eat with her mouth open
8	to bring him the check
9	to get off at the next stop
10	not to wait

● Tell SS to go back to the main lesson on page 87.

7 LISTENING & SPEAKING

a ● **6.4** Focus on the questions and go through them. Then play the recording and pause after the first story (the taxi). Give SS time to answer the questions in pairs. Then play this story again if necessary. Check answers, and ask a few more comprehension questions, e.g., *Where were they? Where was the speaker going?*, etc. Then repeat the process for the other two stories.

The taxi
1 Because the taxi driver said that all American people were loud and pushy.
2 He asked him to stop the taxi.
3 He got out and he didn't pay anything.
The hotel
4 It wasn't clean. It was a mess. The bed hadn't been made, there were dirty towels on the floor, and the bathroom was filthy.
5 He said that she would have to wait for half an hour while they cleaned her room.
6 She told him to give her another room. He did this.
The restaurant
7 Because there was a long, black hair in it.
8 Because they had charged him for the soup. He thought they shouldn't charge for it.
9 He complained, and they didn't have to pay for the soup.

6.4 CD3 Track 5

(audioscript in Student Book on page 128)

1 I was in a taxi in Greece, in Athens, and I was going downtown to do some shopping, and the taxi driver started talking to me. He asked me where I was from. When I said I was American, he started getting really aggressive. He said that he didn't like Americans and that all Americans were loud and pushy. He went on and on – he just wouldn't stop. I got really annoyed. I mean, I thought, "Why do I have to listen to all of this?" So I asked him to stop the taxi and let me get out. Luckily, he stopped and I got out – and of course, I didn't pay him anything.

2 This happened to me recently when I was traveling around on business. I was really tired because I'd been working and traveling all day. Anyway, when I got to the hotel in Philadelphia – it was the evening – I checked in and the front desk clerk gave me the key to my room. So I went up to my room and opened the door, but it was a complete mess! The bed wasn't made, there were dirty towels on the floor and the bathroom was *filthy*. I went downstairs and told the clerk, and he said that I would have to wait for half an hour while they prepared the room. But I was exhausted and needed to rest, so I told him to give me another room right away. Luckily, he did.

3 This happened to me last week. I went to a restaurant in San Francisco with my family to celebrate my dad's birthday. Anyway, my dad ordered soup and when the soup arrived, he saw that it had a long, black hair in it. So he asked the waitress to take it back and bring him another bowl. She brought him another bowl of soup and it was fine, and we finished our meal. But when my dad asked for the check, he saw that they had charged us for the soup. He didn't think that was right. He thought the soup should be free because he had found a hair in it. So he asked the waitress to take it off the check. She went away and spoke to the manager, and he came out and apologized and he took the soup off the check.

Extra support

If there's time, you could have SS listen to the recording with the audioscript on page 128 so they can see exactly what they understood / didn't understand. Translate / explain any new words or phrases.

b • Put SS in pairs and focus on the task. Have SS discuss questions 1 and 2 for a few minutes. Then get responses from the class.

Extra idea

Have SS ask you the questions first and tell them about any experiences you have had.

c • Put SS in pairs, **A** and **B**, preferably face to face. Tell them to go to **Communication *I want to speak to the manager*, A** on page 118 and **B** on page 121. Go through the instructions for the first roleplay situation. Remind SS that in the first situation student **A** is the customer and **B** is the salesperson. Tell **A** to start first saying *Excuse me, I bought…*

• When they have finished role-playing the first situation, tell them to read the instructions for the second situation. This time **A** is the restaurant manager and **B** is the customer. **B** starts *Good evening. Are you the manager?*

• Find out whether different "customers" achieved their objectives or not.

Extra photocopiable activities

Grammar
reported speech page 155
Communicative
Who asked what? page 186 (instructions page 166)

HOMEWORK

Study Link **Workbook** pages 54–56

6 B

G passive: *be* + past participle
V movies
P sentence stress

See the movie... get on a plane

Lesson plan

The topic of this lesson is the movies. In the first half of the lesson there is an article about exotic film locations, that have inspired people to visit them. This provides the context for review and extension of the passive form. In the second half of the lesson, movie vocabulary is presented and then put into practice in a questionnaire where SS talk about their own preferences and experiences. Finally, SS listen to the true story of a young student who met, and then worked for, a world famous movie director.

Optional lead-in (books closed)

- Put SS in pairs or groups of three.
- Write on the board the names of some famous movies you think your SS will know that are set in a different country from where your SS are studying.
- Then teach SS the question *Where is the movie set?* (= In which country does the action take place?)
- Set a time limit, e.g., three minutes. Tell each pair or group to write down the <u>country</u> in which each movie is set.
  Some possible movies:
  Casablanca (Morocco), *Zorro* (Mexico), *Harry Potter* (England), *Braveheart* (Scotland), *Independence Day* (US), *Memoirs of a Geisha* (Japan), *The Da Vinci Code* (France and Britain)

1 READING

a • Books open. Focus on the question and elicit answers from the class.

b • Ask SS to read the article once and try to guess the name of each movie and where it was filmed. Tell SS to write the name of the movie next to the numbered blank and the name of the country in which it was filmed in the blank in the texts. Set a time limit, e.g., five minutes. Check answers.

> 1 *The Beach*, Thailand
> 2 *Out of Africa*, Kenya
> 3 *The Lord of the Rings*, New Zealand

c • Focus on the questions and make sure SS understand everything, especially:
were based on a book = when a movie is made using a story or novel (e.g., the Harry Potter books)
was set at the beginning of the 20th century / was set in a place where... = the movie was situated at a particular time and in a particular place. Point out that *set* is an irregular verb (*set-set-set*).

- Set a time limit for SS to read the article again and answer the questions with the name of the movie. Sometimes they need to answer with more than one movie. Have SS compare their answers with a partner and then check answers.

> 1 *The Lord of the Rings*
> 2 All three movies
> 3 *Out of Africa*
> 4 *The Beach*
> 5 *Out of Africa*
> 6 *The Beach*
> 7 *Out of Africa*
> 8 *The Lord of the Rings*

Extra support

You could now go through the whole article, dealing with any vocabulary problems.

d • Do this as a whole class activity. Ask the class about each movie and find out how many people have seen it and how many liked it. Then, with a show of hands, find out which of the three countries they would most like to visit.

Extra idea

You could have SS underline or highlight five words or phrases they want to remember from the text. Have them compare their words / phrases with a partner and then get some responses from the class.

2 GRAMMAR passive: *be* + past participle

a • Focus on the instructions. Ask SS which is the first example of a passive in *The Beach* (*is set*). Then, give SS a few minutes to underline more examples. Check answers by eliciting and writing the sentences (or parts of sentences) on the board. Elicit the rule for making the passive.

> **Possible answers**
> **Present passive:** It is based on a best-selling book.
> **Past passive:** It was directed by Danny Boyle. / The movie was shot on the island of Phi Phi Leh. / Most of the hotels were destroyed in 2004 by the tsunami.
> **Present perfect passive:** ... they have now been rebuilt.
>
> The passive is formed with the verb *be* (in the appropriate tense) and the past participle.

Extra challenge

You could have SS underline more examples of the passive in the other two texts.

b • Focus on the chart and have SS underline the verbs in the Active column and tell you the tense of the verb.

> **inspire**: simple present
> **directed**: simple past
> **are making**: present continuous
> **will release**: future
> **have visited**: present perfect

- Put SS in pairs and have them complete the chart with passive verbs. Emphasize that they have to use the verb *to be* first (in the correct tense) and then a past participle. Check answers by writing the passive verbs on the board.

> **Passive**
> The movie **is being made** on location.
> The movie **will be released** next year.
> The country **has been visited** by thousands of fans.

c • Tell SS to go to **Grammar Bank 6B** on page 140. Read the examples and go through the rules with the class.

Grammar notes

The passive: *be* + past participle

- If your SS previously used *American English File 2*, they will already have had an introduction to the passive, although only in the present and past tenses.
- The form of the passive (*be* + participle) is fairly straightforward, and the easiest way to approach this grammar point is to emphasize that there are two ways of saying the same thing (active and passive) but sometimes with a change of emphasis or focus.
  Active: *Peter Jackson directed* The Lord of the Rings. (The focus is on Jackson.)
  Passive: The Lord of the Rings *was directed by Peter Jackson*. (The focus is on the movie.)
- Depending on your SS' L1 it may be worth pointing out that we often use the passive in sentences like *It's made in…*, and *They're grown in…*, where some languages use an impersonal subject. Some contrasting with their L1 may help SS to see when to use the passive.
- Typical mistakes include:
  – using the active instead of the passive, e.g., ~~The tickets sell at a newsstand~~.
  – SS thinking they always have to use *by (somebody)* when they make a passive sentence.
  – problems of form, e.g., leaving out the verb *be* or not using the participle correctly.

- Now have SS do the exercises on page 141 in pairs or individually. Check answers either after each exercise or when SS have finished both.

> **a 1** is being built
> **2** was / is based on
> **3** was watched by
> **4** was stolen
> **5** were written by
> **6** my computer was being repaired
> **7** You will be taken
> **8** has been canceled
> **9** is spoken
> **10** must be worn
> **b 1** are subtitled
> **2** were thrown away by mistake
> **3** is being painted
> **4** have been sold
> **5** will be played tomorrow
> **6** must be paid tomorrow

- Tell SS to go back to the main lesson on page 89.

3 PRONUNCIATION sentence stress

Pronunciation notes

> Remind SS that information words are the ones which are usually stressed. These are the words which you hear more clearly when somebody speaks to you. The unstressed words are heard much less clearly.

a • **6.5** Focus on the task and tell SS that they are going to hear six passive sentences that they have to try to write down.
- Play the recording, pausing after each sentence to give SS time to write down the sentences.
- Play the recording again for SS to check their answers. Check answers by writing the correct sentences on the board. (See audioscript below.) Leave the sentences on the board for the next exercise.

b • Play the recording again and have SS tell you which words to underline in the sentences. Point out that it is the words that carry the most important information (usually nouns, adjectives, and verbs) that are stressed more strongly. Finally, play the recording again, pausing for SS to repeat and copy the rhythm.

> | **6.5** | CD3 Track 6 |
> |---|---|
>
> 1 How is <u>this</u> <u>word</u> <u>pronounced</u>?
> 2 <u>My</u> <u>car's</u> been <u>stolen</u>.
> 3 <u>When</u> was this <u>house</u> <u>built</u>?
> 4 Our <u>television's</u> <u>being</u> <u>repaired</u>.
> 5 I've been <u>offered</u> the <u>job</u>.
> 6 <u>When</u> will the <u>new</u> <u>airport</u> be <u>finished</u>?

c • Focus on the task. Play the recording, pausing after each sentence for SS to repeat. Encourage them to use the correct rhythm by stressing the underlined words more strongly.

4 VOCABULARY movies

a • Focus on the task and give SS a couple of minutes to see if they can remember (without turning back to the previous page) the words from the article related to movies.

b • Have SS compare with a partner before telling them to look back at text 2 on page 88 to check their answers. Then elicit and write the answers on the board.

> | | |
> |---|---|
> | **1** the soundtrack | **4** the crew |
> | **2** the director | **5** on location |
> | **3** the cast | **6** the screen |

c • Tell SS to go to **Vocabulary Bank *Movies*** on page 154 and do section **1 Kinds of movies** either individually or in pairs. Check answers and drill pronunciation of any difficult words. You could elicit famous movies of each type from your SS.

> | | |
> |---|---|
> | **1** western | **5** thriller |
> | **2** action movie | **6** comedy |
> | **3** musical | **7** science fiction |
> | **4** horror movie | |

6 B

Extra challenge

Elicit other kinds of movies, e.g., war movie (e.g., *Apocalypse Now* / *Platoon* / *Jarhead*), romantic comedy (e.g., *Love Actually*), musicals (e.g., *Chicago*), etc.

- Have SS do section **2 People and things** and then check answers. Elicit and drill the pronunciation of any difficult words (e.g., words where the phonetics are given).

1 cast	5 plot	9 special effects
2 star	6 scene	10 script
3 director	7 audience	11 extra
4 soundtrack	8 sequel	12 subtitles

- Finally, have SS do section **3 Verbs and phrases** and then check answers. Elicit and drill the pronunciation of any difficult words.

1 b	2 e	3 f	4 a	5 c	6 d

- Now, focus on the final instruction "Can you remember the words on this page? Test yourself or a partner."

Testing yourself

For **Kinds of movies** SS can cover the words and look at the pictures and try to remember the movie types. For **People and things** they can cover the list and words 1–12. They look at the definitions and remember the words, uncovering one by one to check. For **Verbs and phrases** they can cover the phrases 1–6 and look at the definitions a–f and try to remember the phrases.

Testing a partner

See **Testing a partner** on page 15.

Study Link SS can find more practice of these words on the MultiROM and on the *American English File 3* Website.

- Tell SS to go back to the main lesson on page 90.

5 SPEAKING

a ● Focus on the movie questionnaire and quickly go through the questions. Give SS two or three minutes to think about their answers.

b ● Put SS in pairs. They should take turns interviewing each other to find out if they have similar tastes.

Extra idea

If there's time, you could have the class interview you.

6 LISTENING

This interview is with a Polish woman, Dagmara, who became Steven Spielberg's interpreter in the movie *Schindler's List*.
Schindler's List was partly shot in Krakow, where Dagmara lives, and is based on the true story of Oskar Schindler, a German who saved the lives of many Jews during the Second World War by employing them in his factory in Poland. The movie stars Liam Neeson and Ben Kingsley and won nine Oscars in 1993.

a ● Focus SS' attention on the photograph and the task. Have SS quickly discuss the four questions. Don't check answers at this stage. You may want to tell your students that the word *film* is also used in American English, especially for art movies and in expressions like *foreign film*, *film festival*, etc. *Movie* is more common, though.

b ● **6.6** Play the recording for SS to check their answers. Elicit answers from the class.

> The man is Steven Spielberg and the woman is Dagmara, a Polish student.
> They are on a movie set.
> The movie is *Schindler's List*.
> They are talking to the Polish "extras". Dagmara is interpreting for Spielberg, i.e., he is speaking in English and Dagmara will then give his instructions in Polish.

c ● Focus on the questions and go through them quickly. Tell SS not to try to write answers while they listen but to wait until the end. Play the recording again. Then let them discuss the answers in pairs.
- Play the recording again if necessary, pausing after each of Dagmara's answers, and then check answers.

> 1 In Krakow in Poland.
> 2 She was working in the movie company's office, translating documents and parts of the script.
> 3 No, she was a student at the time.
> 4 At a party, just before the shooting started.
> 5 She had to translate Spielberg's speech because the person who was going to do it didn't come.
> 6 She was very nervous and she made some mistakes, but she got to the end.
> 7 Spielberg thanked her and asked her to be his interpreter for the movie.

6.6 CD3 Track 7

(audioscript in Student Book on page 128)
I = interviewer, D = Dagmara
I So how did you get involved in the film, Dagmara?
D Well, as you probably know, a lot of the film *Schindler's List* was shot in Krakow, in Poland, which is where I live. And before the actual shooting of the film started, the film company had an office in Krakow and I got a job there translating documents and parts of the script – things like that – I was a university student at the time.
I But how did you get the job as Spielberg's interpreter in the film?
D It's a funny story. I didn't think I would ever get to meet Spielberg or any of the actors. But then, just before the shooting started, there was a big party in one of the hotels in Krakow and I was invited. At first, I wasn't going to go – I was tired after working all day, and I didn't think I had anything suitable to wear. But in the end, I borrowed a jacket from a friend and I went. But when I arrived at the party, the producer – who was Polish – came up to me and said, "Dagmara, you're going to interpret for Steven Spielberg. You have to translate his opening speech because the girl who was going to do it couldn't come."

I How did you feel about that?

D I couldn't believe it! I was just a student – I had no experience of interpreting – and now I was going to have to speak in front of hundreds of people. But when I started speaking, I was so nervous that I confused the dates of the Second World War – but luckily I managed to get to the end without making any more mistakes.
And afterwards, during the party, Spielberg came up to speak to me to say thank you – he was really nice to me and said he was impressed by the way I had interpreted. And then he said, "I'd like you to be my interpreter for the whole film." I couldn't believe it. I had to pinch myself to believe that this was happening to me.

d ● **6.7** Focus on the task and go through the headings under which SS have to take notes. Tell them just to listen and to make notes <u>after</u> they have heard the recording. Play the recording.

e ● Have SS compare their notes and then play the recording again for them to check or complete their notes. Play again if necessary, pausing after each section. Elicit answers and write them on the board.

> **The most difficult thing about the job**
> When they had to shoot a scene many times. She thought it was her fault – maybe she hadn't translated correctly.
> **The worst moment**
> Once when they repeated a scene many times Spielberg got angry and shouted at her. Later he apologized.
> **What it was like to work with Spielberg**
> He was demanding but he treated her well – like a daughter, e.g., he made sure she was warm enough. It was hard work but she enjoyed it.
> **Her opinion of the movie**
> She thinks it's great, a masterpiece. The actors were brilliant. She likes the way it was mainly shot in black and white.
> **How she feels when she watches the movie**
> She can't be objective. She remembers where she was in each scene.

● Finally, ask SS if they have seen *Schindler's List* and what they thought of it – if they agree with Dagmara. You could also ask them if they would like to have done Dagmara's job, or which director they would like to interpret for.

Extra support

If there's time, have SS listen to the whole interview with Dagmara with the audioscript on page 128 so they can see exactly what they understood / didn't understand. Translate / explain any new words or phrases.

6.7 CD3 Track 8

(audioscript in Student Book on page 128)
I = interviewer, D = Dagmara

I So what exactly did you have to do?

D I had to go to the film set every day. A car came every day to pick me up from my house – I felt really important! And then what I had to do was to translate Spielberg's instructions to the Polish actors, as well as the extras. I had to make them understand what he wanted. It was really exciting – sometimes I felt as if I was a director myself.

I Was it a difficult job?

D Sometimes it was really difficult. The worst thing was when we kept having to shoot a scene again and again because Spielberg thought it wasn't exactly right. Some scenes were repeated as many as 16 times – and then sometimes I would think that maybe it was my fault – that I hadn't translated properly what he wanted, so I'd get really nervous. I remember one scene where we just couldn't get it right and Spielberg started shouting at me because he was stressed. But in the end, we got it right and then he apologized, and I cried a little, because I was also very stressed – and after that, it was all right again.

I So, was Spielberg difficult to work with?

D Not at all. I mean he was very demanding – I had to do my best every day – but he was really nice to me. I felt he treated me like a daughter. For instance, he was always making sure that I wasn't cold – it was freezing on the set most of the time – and he would make sure I had a warm coat and gloves and things. It was hard work but it was fascinating – an amazing experience.

I What did you think of the finished film?

D I believe that *Schindler's List* is truly a great movie, a masterpiece. I think the actors were brilliant, especially Liam Neeson and Ben Kingsley – and I love the way it was shot in black and white, with color in just one scene.
But, as you can imagine, I can't be very objective about it – I mean, I lived through nearly every scene. And when I watch it – and I've seen it a lot of times – I always remember exactly where I was at that moment. I can't help thinking, "Oh, there I am, hiding under the bed, or standing behind that door."

Extra photocopiable activities

Grammar
passive: *be* + past participle page 156
Communicative
Movie quiz page 187 (instructions page 167)

HOMEWORK

Study Link Workbook pages 57–59

G relative clauses: defining and non-defining
V what people do
P word stress

I need a hero

Lesson plan

The theme of this lesson is heroes and icons. The first half of the lesson focuses on one of the most iconic figures of the 20th century: the revolutionary Che Guevara (whose face has adorned many students' walls and T-shirts). This context is used to review and extend SS' knowledge of relative clauses. They should be familiar with defining clauses, but probably won't be familiar with non-defining ones. The second half of the lesson focuses on people who *Time* magazine consider to be heroes and icons of the 21st century. The lexical and pronunciation focus is on nouns describing what people do. At the end of the lesson, SS talk about people (dead or alive) who they admire.

Optional lead-in (books closed)

- Put SS in pairs. Tell SS to imagine that they are going to sell T-shirts to raise money for the school. The T-shirts will have on them the face of a famous person. Each pair has to choose whose face they want to have on their T-shirt and be ready to explain why.
- Give SS a few minutes to do this and then ask each pair who they have chosen and why.

1 GRAMMAR relative clauses

a ● **6.8** Books open. Focus on the picture and the quiz and put SS in pairs. Set a time limit and then play the recording for students to check answers.

| 1 c | 2 b | 3 c | 4 a | 5 b | 6 b | 7 b |

6.8   CD3 Track 9

Che Guevara was born in the city of Rosario, Argentina, on June 14, 1928. His first name was really Ernesto. He was the oldest of five children in his family. At the university, he studied medicine and had plans to be a doctor. He spent many vacations traveling around Latin America by motorcycle. The poverty he saw convinced him that revolution was the answer to Latin America's problems. In 1956, he met Fidel Castro in Mexico and joined him in the Cuban Revolution. In 1966, Guevara went to Bolivia to lead a revolution in that country. On October 8, 1967, he was captured by the Bolivian army and shot.

b ● Tell SS to cover texts A–E on page 93. Focus on the photos on pages 92 and 93 and tell SS to try to guess what the connection is between the photos and Che Guevara. Elicit ideas from SS (e.g., *I think the motorcycle is the one that Che Guevara rode in the movie "The Motorcycle Diaries"*, etc.) but don't tell them if they are right or wrong yet.

c ● Have SS read texts A–E to find out the connection between the photos and Che Guevara. Elicit answers. Go through the texts (you could read them aloud). Translate / explain any words or phrases that caused problems.

d ● Tell SS to cover the texts and look at sentences 1–6 (which are all taken from the texts). They should complete the blanks with a relative pronoun. Check answers.

| 1 whose, that/which | 2 that/which, that/which |
| 3 who/that | 4 where | 5 which |
| 6 who/that, who/that |

e ● Now focus on the instructions and have SS compare sentences 1 and 2 with the almost identical sentences in text **A** and find two differences. Elicit the answer from the class.

The text says "…*the motorcycle journey Che made with his friend Alberto across South America*" (the relative pronoun **that/which** is omitted), "…*it was the poverty he saw on this trip…*" (the relative pronoun **that/which** is omitted.)

- Tell SS that they will learn the rules for when they can leave out the relative pronoun and when they can't use *that* instead of *who* or *which* in the **Grammar Bank**.

f ● Tell SS to go to **Grammar Bank 6C** on page 140. Read the examples and go through the rules with the class.

Grammar notes

Relative clauses

- SS who used *American English File 2* will have already had an introduction to defining relative clauses but not to non-defining ones. In writing it is always clear which is which because of the comma(s) that always separate off the extra information in a non-defining clause.
- Although *that* is a common alternative to *who* / *which* in defining relative clauses, it cannot be used in non-defining clauses.
- *Whom* is also sometimes used as a relative pronoun instead of *who* to refer to the object of the verb in the relative clause, or after prepositions, e.g., *She's the woman whom I met yesterday. He's the man to whom I spoke yesterday*. It is much less common and more formal than *who*. You may wish to point out its use to SS.
- Typical mistakes include:
  - using a personal pronoun, e.g., ~~He is the man who he works with my father.~~
  - using *that* in non-defining relative clauses, e.g., ~~This movie, that won an Oscar in 1999, will be shown on TV tonight for the first time.~~

- Have SS do exercise **a** on page 141, in pairs or individually. Check answers.

1 where	4 that/which	7 whose	10 that/which
2 who/that	5 that/which	8 who/that	
3 whose	6 where	9 that/which	

- Now have SS do exercise **b** in pairs or individually. Check answers. Point out that this exercise is based on defining clauses.

The following sentences should be checked: 5 and 10

- Now have SS do exercise **c** in pairs or individually. This exercise is based on both defining and non-defining clauses. Check answers.

> 1 ✓
> 2 ✗ **who** you met...
> 3 ✓
> 4 ✗ **which** is...
> 5 ✗ **whose** yard...
> 6 ✓
> 7 ✓
> 8 ✗ who ~~they~~ come from...

- Tell SS to go back to the main lesson on page 92.

g • Now have SS cover the text and look only at the photos. Ask them if they can remember what the connection was between each photo and Che Guevara. SS will probably use a relative clause in some of their answers, e.g., *It's the town where Che Guevara was born. / It's the motorcycle that was used in the movie.*

2 LISTENING & SPEAKING

a • 6.9 Focus on the task and explain the meaning of *icon* (= a famous person that people see as a symbol of a particular idea, way of life, etc.). Put SS in pairs and explain that they are going to hear a quiz program with a series of clues to identify eight famous people. Point out that the presenter always gives the first letter of each person's first and last names as an extra clue. So, for example if the person was Nelson Mandela, the letters would be N and M. Emphasize that SS **must not call out answers** but that they should write them down on a piece of paper.

- Play the recording once all the way through, and then again. Alternatively, you could pause the recording after each question and give SS time to discuss with a partner who they think the person is.

- Then ask how many pairs think they have correctly identified all eight people. If there are several, check answers. If nobody seems to have gotten all of them, play the recording again before checking answers.

> 1 Bill Gates   5 Jackie Onassis
> 2 Nelson Mandela   6 Martina Navratilova
> 3 Madonna   7 George Clooney
> 4 Giorgio Armani   8 Maria Callas

Extra support

If there's time, you could have SS listen to the recording again with the audioscript on page 128 so they can see exactly what they understood / didn't understand. Translate / explain any new words or phrases.

6.9   CD3 Track 10

(audioscript in Student Book on page 128)
It's 12:00 noon and so it's time for today's contest. Today the topic is "Heroes and Icons." As usual, the rules are very simple. I'm going to give you eight clues and you

have to identify the people. If you know all the answers, e-mail them to me right away. The first person who sends me the correct answers wins a prize. Today's prize is two plane tickets to… the Big Apple, New York City!

OK, so lets get started with those clues. I'll say each one twice only. And remember, I always give you the first letter or letters of the word I'm looking for. Today they are all people's names.

Let's start with an easy one. Two letters, B and G. It's a man who's probably the richest man in the world, the founder of Microsoft. That's BG, the man who started Microsoft.

Number 2. Two letters again, N and M. He's a man whose courage and humanity made him an icon for millions of people all over the world. He spent many years in prison in South Africa because of his fight against apartheid, but he eventually became president of that country.

Number 3 begins with M, just one word. It's the name of a woman who's had a lot of different jobs. She's been an actress, she's even written children's books, but she's most famous as a singer. One word beginning with M.

And number 4. This time it's a man, and the letters are G and A, though many people just know him by his last name. He's an Italian designer whose clothes are considered among the most elegant in the world, and whose name is also on perfume bottles everywhere. G and A, for an Italian fashion designer.

On to number 5. Two letters, J and O. It's the name of a famous American woman, whose first husband was president of the United States and whose second husband was a Greek millionaire. Although she died in 1994, she is still admired for her style all over the world. Two letters, J and O.

And number 6. It's a woman again and the letters are M and N. She's the woman who changed the shape of women's tennis, and is possibly the greatest female player of all time. She was born in Prague but later became a US citizen. M and N for the greatest ever woman tennis player.

Number 7 is an American actor. He was born in Kentucky in 1961, and he is often called the most attractive male actor in Hollywood today. He first became famous in a TV hospital drama in which he played the part of a doctor. His first name begins with G and his last name with C. So that's a Hollywood actor, G and C.

Finally, number 8. Two letters. M and C. She was born in Greece and died in Paris, and she is the woman whose voice is familiar to lovers of opera all over the world. Nicknamed "La Divina" her life was tragic, but her voice will never be forgotten. MC, "La Divina."

So if you think you have the eight correct answers, e-mail them to me now at this address, Guessthenames@hitmail.com. That's Guessthenames@hitmail.com. And the first person with the correct answers will win those two tickets to New York.

Time for some music.

b • Put SS in pairs, **A** and **B**, preferably face to face. Tell SS to go to **Communication** *Relatives quiz*, **A** on page 118 and **B** on page 121.

- Go through their instructions and make sure SS understand what they have to do. You could demonstrate the activity by doing number 1 (for **A** and **B**) with the whole class, before getting them to write their questions. Monitor to make sure SS are writing sensible questions.

- SS then take turns asking their partners the questions.

Extra Challenge

You could encourage SS to make their clues a bit cryptic, so that they are more difficult to get, e.g., if the word were *generous*, instead of defining it as *a person who likes giving presents*, they could define it as, e.g., *a person who is always the first to take out his wallet in a restaurant when the waiter brings the check.*

- Tell SS to go back to the main lesson on page 94.

3 READING

a • Focus on the task and have SS try to match the photos and people. Check answers, and for each person ask the class what he / she is famous for. Elicit ideas but don't tell them if they are right or wrong.

> Wangari Maathai 5
> Bono 1
> Thierry Henry 2
> Bernard Kouchner 3
> Queen Rania of Jordan 4

b • Have SS read the article and match the five names with the texts. Check answers.

> **A** Thierry Henry
> **B** Queen Rania of Jordan
> **C** Bono
> **D** Wangari Maathai
> **E** Bernard Kouchner

Extra idea

Alternatively, you could read each paragraph aloud to the class and elicit who the person is, and also the meaning of any new words or phrases.

c • Set a time limit, e.g., six or seven minutes, and have SS read the article again and answer the questions. Check answers.

> 1 Bono. He couldn't take the child with him.
> 2 Queen Rania of Jordan, by getting children vaccinated.
> 3 Wangari Maathai, by planting more than 20 million trees in Kenya.
> 4 Bernard Kouchner. He participated actively himself in aid work.
> 5 Bono and Thierry Henry. Bono is trying to free Africa of hunger and poverty, and Henry is trying to eradicate racism from sports.

d • Focus on the task and have SS read the article again to find the nouns. Check answers, and have SS underline the stressed syllable.

> 2 mo<u>der</u>nity   5 defore<u>sta</u>tion
> 3 <u>hun</u>ger   6 ope<u>ra</u>tion
> 4 <u>pov</u>erty   7 sale

e • In pairs, tell SS to cover the article and try to remember as much as they can about each person.

Extra support

Do this as a whole class activity.

4 VOCABULARY & PRONUNCIATION what people do, word stress

Focus on the information box and remind SS that these are the common endings for words that tell us what someone's profession or occupation is.

a • Now focus on the chart and the four examples. SS do the exercise in pairs or individually and then compare with a partner.
- Check answers.

-er	-or	-ian	-ist
composer	*actor*	*musician*	*cyclist*
de<u>sign</u>er	con<u>duc</u>tor	politician	gui<u>tar</u>ist
<u>lead</u>er	di<u>rec</u>tor		<u>phys</u>icist
<u>paint</u>er	in<u>ven</u>tor		<u>sci</u>entist
pho<u>tog</u>rapher	<u>sculp</u>tor		vio<u>lin</u>ist
<u>play</u>er			
pre<u>sen</u>ter			

b • **6.10** Play the recording for SS to underline the stressed syllable in each word. Check answers, and have SS practice saying the words. Remind them that endings added to words are usually not stressed.

Extra challenge

You could have SS underline the stressed syllable first and then listen to check.

6.10			CD3 Track 11
composer	actor	musician	cyclist
designer	conductor	politician	guitarist
leader	director		physicist
painter	inventor		scientist
photographer	sculptor		violinist
player			
presenter			

5 SPEAKING

a • This is a free-speaking activity that gives SS a chance to talk about their own heroes.
- Give SS time to write a name in three of the categories and give them a few minutes to prepare to talk about them (who they are, what they have done, and why they admire them). Monitor and help SS with any vocabulary they may need.

b • Put SS into groups of three (or if this is impractical, in pairs).
- SS take turns talking about the people they admire (i.e., each student talks about one person, then the next student speaks about one of their heroes, etc.).
- If there's time, get some responses from the whole class on which people SS chose.

Extra idea

Begin by telling SS about a couple of people that you admire and explain why.

6 6.11 ♫ **SONG** *Holding out for a hero*

- This song originally recorded by Bonnie Tyler in 1982 was used as the theme song in the movie *Shrek* 2 (2004). For copyright reasons this is a cover version. If you want to do this song in class, use the photocopiable activity on page 209.

6.11   CD3 Track 12

Holding out for a hero

Where have all the good men gone and where are all the gods?
Where's the streetwise Hercules to fight the rising odds?
Isn't there a white knight upon a fiery steed?
Late at night I toss and I turn and I dream of what I need

I need a hero
I'm holding out for a hero till the end of the night
He's gotta be strong and he's gotta be fast
And he's gotta be fresh from the fight
I need a hero
I'm holding out for a hero till the morning light
He's gotta be sure and it's gotta be soon
And he's gotta be larger than life
Larger than life

Somewhere after midnight
In my wildest fantasy
Somewhere just beyond my reach
There's someone reaching back for me
Racing on the thunder and rising with the heat
It's gonna take a Superman to sweep me off my feet

I need a hero
I'm holding out for a hero till the end of the night
He's gotta be strong and he's gotta be fast
And he's gotta be fresh from the fight
I need a hero
I'm holding out for a hero till the morning light
He's gotta be sure and it's gotta be soon
And he's gotta be larger than life

I need a hero
I'm holding out for a hero till the end of the night

Up where the mountains meet the heavens above
Out where the lightning splits the sea
I could swear there is someone somewhere watching me
Through the wind and the chill and the rain
And the storm and the flood
I can feel his approach like a fire in the blood

I need a hero
I'm holding out for a hero till the end of the night
He's gotta be strong and he's gotta be fast
And he's gotta be fresh from the fight
I need a hero
I'm holding out for a hero till the morning light
He's gotta be sure and it's gotta be soon
And he's gotta be larger than life

Study Link SS can find a dictation and a Grammar quiz on all the grammar from File 6 on the MultiROM and more grammar activities on the *American English File* 3 Website.

Extra photocopiable activities

Grammar
relative clauses page 157
Communicative
Which definition is right? page 188 (instructions page 167)
Vocabulary
Alphabet race page 200 (instructions page 194)
Song
Holding out for a hero page 209 (instructions page 204)

HOMEWORK

Study Link **Workbook** pages 60–62

Function Giving and reacting to news
Language *You'll never guess what's happened! You're joking! Are you serious?*, etc.

Lesson plan

In the first part of the lesson, SS learn and practice ways of giving and reacting to news. Ben tells the other people in the office that he saw Mark and Allie together in the Louvre, and they express their surprise and disbelief. In the second part of the lesson (**Social English**), Mark arrives at work and Ben questions him about his weekend. Then Allie, by mistake, sends a personal e-mail to everyone in the office.

Study Link These lessons are on the *American English File 3* Video, which can be used instead of the Class Audio CD for these lessons (see Introduction page 9). The main functional section of each episode is also on the MultiROM with additional activities.

Optional lead-in (books closed)

- Review what happened in the previous episode by eliciting the story from SS, e.g., *Why did they have a meeting with Scarlett? Who did Allie agree with, Mark or Jacques? Where did Mark and Allie go in Paris on the weekend? Why did they have to leave the museum quickly?*, etc.
  If you are using the Video, you could play the previous episode again, leaving out the "Listen and Repeat" sections.

- You could also try to elicit from the SS the phrases they reviewed / learned in the previous episode for giving opinion, e.g., *Personally, I think Scarlett should..., I agree with Jacques*, etc. (You could write the phrases with blanks on the board to help SS remember.)

GIVING AND REACTING TO NEWS

a ● **6.12** Tell SS to cover the conversation with their hand or a piece of paper. Focus on the photo and the two questions. Alternatively, write the two questions on the board and have SS close their books.

- Play the recording all the way through. Check answers.

> Ben's news is that he saw Allie and Mark together in the Louvre, holding hands.
> Jacques is more surprised than Nicole, who already suspected that Mark and Allie were going out together.

b ● Now have SS look at the conversation. In pairs, they read it and see if they can guess or remember the missing words. Emphasize that they shouldn't write the words in the conversation but pencil them in alongside or on a separate sheet of paper.

c ● Play the recording again for them to check. Then go through the conversation line by line and check answers. Find out if SS had guessed the words correctly. Where they had not guessed correctly, see if their alternative also fits.

6.12   CD3 Track 13

B = Ben, N = Nicole, J = Jacques, M = Mark
B   Hi.
N / J   Hi. / Hello.
N   Did you have a nice weekend?
B   Oh yeah. You'll never **guess** who I saw on Saturday.
N   Who?
B   Allie… and Mark. In the Louvre… together.
N   **Really**?
J   You're **joking**.
B   It was definitely them. And they looked really close. I think they were holding hands.
J   No! I don't **believe** it.
B   It's true, I'm **telling** you! And I think they saw me because they turned and left really quickly.
J   Are you **serious**?
N   You know, I'm not surprised. I think they've been seeing each other ever since Mark arrived. Or maybe even before.
J   That's **incredible**. What makes you say that?
N   When I went to look at Mark's new apartment, I'm sure Allie called him on his mobile. And I've seen her looking at him in a certain way…
B   Hey, quiet everyone. It's Mark.
M   Hi.
B   Hi.
J / N   Good morning.

---

d ● **6.13** Now focus on the key phrases highlighted in the conversation. Play the recording, pausing after each sentence for SS to repeat. Encourage them to copy the rhythm and intonation.

6.13   CD3 Track 14

B = Ben, N = Nicole, J = Jacques
B   You'll never guess who I saw on Saturday.
N   Really?
J   You're joking.
J   No! I don't believe it.
B   It's true, I'm telling you!
J   Are you serious?
J   That's incredible.

---

e ● Have SS cover the conversation and try to remember five ways of reacting to news with surprise or interest. You could have SS work with a partner or do it as a whole class activity.

> Really?
> You're joking.
> I don't believe it.
> Are you serious?
> That's incredible.

Extra support

You could write the first letter of each phrase on the board to help SS.

f ● Focus on the instructions and demonstrate the activity by inventing a piece of news to tell the class, e.g., about a local celebrity. Encourage SS to react with surprise, and ask for details to which you should invent answers. (Don't forget to tell SS after that your news isn't really true!)

- Then put SS in pairs and give them a few minutes to invent their piece of news. You could remind them that we often use the present perfect to give news, e.g., *The president has resigned / X and Y have broken up*, etc.
- They then take turns telling the class their news. The class should react using the expressions from **e**. If they are enjoying the activity, let them continue inventing more news for a few minutes.

SOCIAL ENGLISH For your eyes only

a ● 6.14 Focus on the e-mail and the question. Play the recording, replaying the relevant line if necessary. Check the answer.

> Thank you for the information. And thank you, darling, for a wonderful weekend.

b ● Now focus on sentences 1–5 and go through them quickly. Then play the recording for SS to mark the sentences T or F. Play the recording again as necessary. Check answers. Have SS correct the wrong sentences.

> 1 F (He said it was "very quiet".)
> 2 F (He says "one evening".)
> 3 F (He says he went on his own.)
> 4 F (He says he didn't see Mark.)
> 5 T

> 6.14   CD3 Track 15
>
> (audioscript in Student Book on page 129)
> **M = Mark, B = Ben, J = Jacques, N = Nicole**
> M Dear all,
>   Please find attached a copy of the latest sales report from the USA. Mark.
> M So, did you guys have a good weekend?
> B Yes, fine.
> J Not bad. Very quiet.
> B What about you, Mark?
> M Oh, I spent most of the time at home… just being domestic, you know. The apartment's looking pretty nice now. You must come round for a meal one evening.
> J That would be very nice.
> B So didn't you go out at all?
> M Oh sure. I went to the Louvre on Saturday. I felt like getting a bit of culture.
> J On your own?
> M Yeah. I kind of prefer going to museums and galleries on my own. You can look at everything at your own pace.
> B That's funny. I went to the Louvre on Saturday, too.
> M Really? I didn't see you.
> B Well, it's a big place. I didn't see you either.
> N I've just had an e-mail from Allie.
> J So have I.
> M Me, too...
> N Dear Mark,
>   Thank you for the information. And thank you, darling, for a wonderful weekend.
>   Allie.

Extra support

Let SS listen one more time with the audioscript on page 129. Help them with any vocabulary or expressions they didn't understand.

- Finally, ask SS what they think Mark and Allie will do now.

c ● 6.15 Now focus on the **USEFUL PHRASES**. Give SS a moment to try to complete them, and then play the recording to check.

> 6.15   CD3 Track 16
>
> **M = Mark, B = Ben, J = Jacques**
> J That **would** be very nice.
> B So didn't you go out at **all**?
> M I felt **like** getting a bit of culture.
> B That's **funny**. I went to the Louvre on Saturday, too.
> B I didn't see you **either**.

Extra idea

Ask SS if they can remember who said each phrase.

d ● Play the recording again, pausing for SS to repeat. In a monolingual class, elicit the equivalent expressions in SS' L1.

HOMEWORK

Study Link **Workbook** page 63

Lesson plan

This writing task focuses on writing a movie review. The task recycles both the grammar and vocabulary from **File 6**. There is also a "mini focus" on using prepositions correctly. We suggest that you do exercises **a–c** in class, but assign the actual writing (the last activity) for homework. If there's time, you may also want to do the planning in class.

a ● Focus on the title of the movie and the photos, and ask SS if anyone has seen it and if they liked it.

b ● Now focus on the task and tell SS to first read the review through once without worrying about the blanks. Ask SS if the review makes them want to see the movie. Then, give them a few minutes to complete the task. Have them compare in pairs before checking answers.

Paragraph 1	The name of the movie, the director, etc.
Paragraph 2	Where and when it was set
Paragraph 3	The plot
Paragraph 4	Why you recommend this movie

c ● Have SS read the text again and complete the blanks with prepositions from the list. Check answers.

2 for **3** about **4** At **5** back **6** In **7** about **8** as **9** to **10** in

⚠ For number 4 you may need to explain the difference between *in the beginning* and *at the beginning*. We say *in the beginning* when it is a phrase on its own (= At first), followed by a comma, e.g., *In the beginning, nobody understood what was going on.* We say *at the beginning* when it is followed by *of* sth, e.g., *At the beginning of the book / program / class*, etc.

d ● Focus on the question and elicit that we normally use the present tense to tell the plot of a movie or book.
● Finally, focus on the **Useful language** box and make sure SS understand all the phrases. Tell them to imagine they are writing, e.g., about *The Lord of the Rings* and elicit the sentences from them, e.g., *It was directed by Peter Jackson.*

Extra idea

If there's time, you could have SS practice the **Useful language** phrases by using them to tell a partner about the movie they are going to write about.

WRITE a movie review

Go through the instructions. Then, either have SS plan and write their movie review in class (set a time limit of 20 minutes) or have them plan their review in class and write at home, or assign both the planning and writing for homework.

Before students hand in their work, have them exchange their movie reviews with another student to read and check for mistakes.

For instructions on how to use these pages, see page 30.

GRAMMAR

1	I wanted	6	was made
2	she would	7	being built
3	he was	8	been bought
4	to open	9	whose son
5	not to	10	that/which cuts

VOCABULARY

a 1 store window (The others are types of stores.)
2 sale (It's a noun. The others are verbs related to shopping.)
3 special effects (The others are all people who are involved in making a movie.)
4 sequel (It's a movie made as a continuation of an earlier one. The others are all specific kinds of movies.)
5 plot (It's a noun. The others are participles related to the movie.)
b 1 bakery 2 receipt 3 cash register 4 cart 5 subtitles 6 soundtrack 7 audience 8 bargain
c 1 on 2 by 3 about 4 back 5 on 6 by 7 in

PRONUNCIATION

a 1 special (It's /ʃ/.)   4 drugstore (It's /ɔr/.)
2 compare (It's /ɛr/.)   5 schedule (It's /k/.)
3 scene (It's /s/.)
b <u>s</u>ubtitles, com<u>pl</u>ain, re<u>ceip</u>t, <u>sound</u>track, <u>cu</u>stomer

CAN YOU UNDERSTAND THIS TEXT?

a 1 c 2 c 3 b 4 a 5 b
b **manipulative tactics** = ways of controlling or influencing people
trust their own tastes = believe in their own opinions and judgement about what to wear
have a good eye = spot problems and details
to take risks = do something that you know might fail or be dangerous
exorbitant prices = much more expensive than they should be

CAN YOU UNDERSTAND THESE PEOPLE?

a 1 c 2 c 3 b 4 c 5 b
b 1 1835 2 died 3 newspaper 4 happily 5 boy 6 75

1 A Did you go to that new restaurant last night?
  B Yeah, but I wouldn't recommend it.
  A Why not?
  B Well, our soup was cold and then I asked for my steak well-done, but it was burned. So I asked the waiter to take it back, and then I had to wait 20 minutes for another one. By that time my husband's meal was cold.

2 A What did you think of it, then?
  B I was a little disappointed, to be honest.
  A Yeah? I loved it. What didn't you like?
  B Well, I thought Scarlett Johansson was good and the one who played her husband…
  A Orlando Bloom.
  B Yeah, he was good, too. But the story was just ridiculous. I mean the part when he went to see his ex-wife. A man would never do that.
  A Oh I don't agree. I thought it was completely believable. I loved the soundtrack, too.
  B Yeah, that was all right.

3 A Oh, I like your sweater. Is it new?
  B Yeah. I bought it on sale.
  A How much?
  B What do you think?
  A $80, $100?
  B No. It was originally $90 but then it had a 25 percent discount.
  A $70?
  B Less! $67. It was a real bargain.

4 A You were an extra in a movie once, weren't you?
  B Yeah. It was when I was living in Santo Domingo, and they were making *The Godfather II* there, you know, with Al Pacino.
  A Oh yeah. I remember.
  B Anyway, I saw an advertisement in the paper saying that they were looking for extras. So I went and I was put in a scene in a big conference room – the one where the "Godfather" gives Batista a gold telephone.
  A What did you have to do?
  B Well. I didn't have to say anything, but I was sitting right next to Al Pacino. I had to pass him the gold telephone. When I saw the movie in the theater, I waited and waited for my scene and suddenly there I was, on the screen right next to Al Pacino!
  A Wow! What a thrill!
  B Yeah, it was pretty exciting.
  A So did you ever get another job as an extra?
  B Nope, that was the end of my "movie career."

5 A I saw a fascinating program on TV last night.
  B What was it about?
  A It was about Brunel. Did you see it?
  B No. Who's Brunel? Isn't he that boxer?
  A A boxer? No, that was Frank Bruno.
  B Oh yeah.
  C Brunel was a famous architect, wasn't he?
  A Well, you're a little closer than Susan. He built lots of famous bridges.
  C Oh, that's right – he was an engineer, wasn't he?
  A Yes. Not exactly a boxer.

This is Mark Twain's house. He built it and lived here with his family from 1874 to 1891. However, Twain was not from Connecticut, and in fact Mark Twain was not his real name. He was born in the state of Missouri on November 30th, 1835, and named Samuel Clemens. The sixth of seven children, he grew up in Hannibal, Missouri, a town on the Mississippi River. Now, when Sam was 11 years old, his father died. Then Sam left school and started to work as a printer for a local newspaper. When Clemens was older, he started writing for newspapers and later he began writing his wonderful novels. Probably his most famous novels are *Tom Sawyer* and *Huckleberry Finn*, which are based on his life as a boy near the Mississippi. Clemens was very happily married to Olivia Langdon, and they had four children. Sadly, three of his children died young. Only his daughter Clara was alive when Clemens, or Mark Twain, died in 1910, at the age of 75. Now, if you follow me through here, we can see the library…

7A

G third conditional
V making adjectives and adverbs
P sentence stress

Can we make our own luck?

File 7 overview

In **7A** SS practice using the third conditional, which they may or may not have studied in their previous course. In lesson **7B** SS look at some new ways of asking questions (using tag questions and indirect questions). This will probably be new to most SS. In the final lesson of the course, the focus is on phrasal verbs, which SS should already be familiar with. Here SS learn more high-frequency verbs and review and extend their knowledge of separable and non-separable verbs.

Lesson plan

This lesson presents the third conditional in the context of two true, good and bad luck stories. This conditional has the most complex form of the three conditionals, but the concept (speculating hypothetically about a past situation) is usually not difficult to put across to SS.

In pronunciation SS focus on the rhythm of third conditional sentences. The vocabulary focus is on word building and SS learn to use suffixes and prefixes to form adjectives and adverbs. The topic of luck is further developed through a text that argues that we are not born lucky or unlucky, but that we can make ourselves lucky.

Optional lead-in (books closed)

- Draw a horseshoe on the board with the open part at the top. Ask SS what it is, and tell them that in the US people believe that if you find a horseshoe, it will bring you good luck. Ask if it also means good luck in SS' country.
- Then put SS in pairs and ask them to think of things that in their country are believed to bring either good luck or bad luck.
- Get SS' responses and write them in two columns – GOOD LUCK / BAD LUCK – on the board. Then ask SS if they really believe in this.

1 READING & LISTENING

a ● Books open. Focus on the article and photos. Tell SS that the man and woman in the first story had very bad luck, and the woman in the second had very good luck.

- Now focus on **Bad luck?** and set a time limit (e.g., three minutes) for SS to read it. Then elicit ideas about what happened next, but don't tell them the answers and try to build suspense. Deal with any vocabulary problems.

Extra idea

Alternatively, you could read the text aloud, asking SS the meaning of words / phrases as you go along.

b ● ⬭ **7.1** Focus on the instructions and tell SS they are going to hear how the story ended. Play the recording once. Have SS compare what they understood and see whether they had guessed right.

c ● Play the recording again. Put SS in pairs to write a couple of sentences to explain what happened. Check answers. Ask a few more comprehension questions, e.g., *Who was Eddie? What happened in Singapore? What was Ian's "special reason" for going to England?*, etc.

> Amy had traveled to Sydney to surprise Ian at exactly the same time he was traveling to the UK to surprise her. When they spoke on the phone, Ian asked her to marry him and she said yes.

⬭ 7.1   CD3 Track 19

(audioscript in Student Book on page 129)
N = narrator, I = Ian, A = Amy

N Ian thought Amy had gone out for the evening and sat down to wait for her to come back. Tired after his long journey, he fell asleep. When he woke up, the phone was ringing. Ian answered the phone. It was Amy.

I I said, "Where are you?" She said, "Ian, I'm sitting in your flat in Australia." At first, I didn't believe her, but then she gave the phone to Eddie, who lives in my flat in Sydney, and he told me it was true. I was so shocked I couldn't speak.

N Amy had had the same idea as Ian. She had flown from London to Sydney via Singapore at exactly the same time Ian was flying in the opposite direction. Incredibly, both their planes stopped in Singapore at the same time. Ian and Amy were sitting in the same airport lounge, but they didn't see each other.

A I had saved all my money to buy a ticket to Sydney. I wanted it to be a fantastic surprise for Ian. I couldn't wait to see his face when I arrived. You can't imagine how I felt when I arrived at his flat and his friend Eddie told me he had gone to England! I just couldn't believe it! When I spoke to Ian on the phone, he told me that he had flown back to England for a special reason and then he asked me to marry him. I didn't know whether to laugh or cry but I said, "Yes."

I It was just bad luck. If one of us had stayed at home, we would have met. It's as simple as that.

---

d ● ⬭ **7.2** Now follow the same procedure for the second story, **Good luck?** For dramatic effect you could briefly pause the recording after "…but they didn't." Comprehension questions could include *Where was the medical conference? Where did the plane land? What happened when Mrs Fletcher got back to England?*, etc.

⚠ When SS read the article make sure they understand what a *call button* is in the last line (= the button a passenger presses on a plane if he/she wants, e.g., a glass of water, or needs help).

> There were 15 cardiologists from different countries on the plane, all going to a conference. They gave her emergency treatment and managed to save her life, so she was able to go to her daughter's wedding.

7.2   CD3 Track 20

(audioscript in Student Book on page 129)

N = narrator, MF = Mrs. Fletcher

N The cabin crew put out a desperate call to the passengers: "If there's a doctor on the plane, could you please press your call button..."
The cabin crew were hoping to hear this [*bell on airplane*], but they didn't. They heard this [*lots of bells*]. Incredibly, there were *fifteen* doctors on the plane, and *all* of them were cardiologists. They were from different countries and they were traveling to Florida for a medical conference.
Four of the doctors rushed to give emergency treatment to Mrs. Fletcher. At one point, they thought she had died, but finally they managed to save her life. The plane made an emergency landing in North Carolina, and Mrs. Fletcher was taken to a hospital. After being in the hospital for four days, she was able to go to her daughter's wedding.

MF I was very lucky. If those doctors hadn't been on the plane, I would have died. I can't thank them enough.

N But now that she's back in England, Mrs. Fletcher has been less lucky with the British hospitals.

MF I had *fifteen* heart specialists on that plane, but I'll have to wait three months until I can see *one* in this country!

Extra support

If there's time, you could have SS listen again with the audioscript on page 129 so they can see exactly what they understood / didn't understand. Translate / explain any new words or phrases.

2 GRAMMAR third conditional

a ● Focus on the two sentences and put SS in pairs to complete them. They probably won't find this easy.

Extra support

You could write *have*, *would*, *hadn't*, and *stayed* on the board and have SS put them in the right place in the sentences.

b ● **7.3** Play the recording for SS to check. Check answers.

1 stayed, would   2 hadn't, have

7.3   CD3 Track 21

Ian If one of us had stayed at home, we would have met.

Mrs. Fletcher If those doctors hadn't been on the plane, I would have died.

c ● Focus on the questions and have SS answer orally in pairs. Check answers and elicit / explain that in both sentences they are imagining how something in the past could have been different.

1 No. No.   2 Yes. No.
3 Something that didn't happen.

d ● Tell SS to go to **Grammar Bank 7A** on page 142. Go through the examples and the rules with the class. Model and drill the example sentences.

Extra idea

In a monolingual class, you could have SS translate the example sentences and compare the tenses they would use in their L1.

Grammar notes

The third conditional

● If SS have a similar tense in their own language, they may not have too many problems with the concept. However, most SS will have problems with the "mechanics" of the structure, i.e., remembering which verb form goes in each part of the sentence, and also in understanding and producing contracted forms.

● Typical mistakes are:
  – using *would have* in the *if*-clause, e.g., *If I would have known, I would have done something about it*.
  – using the past perfect in both clauses, e.g., *If I had known, I had done something about it*.

● Focus on the exercises on page 143 and have SS do them, individually or in pairs. Check answers either after each exercise or when they have done both.

a 2 G 3 H 4 K 5 C 6 J 7 A 8 E
    9 D 10 B 11 F
c 1 would have won, hadn't been
  2 'd known / had known, wouldn't have gone out
  3 would have lent, 'd asked / had asked
  4 'd had / had had, would have spent
  5 would have been able, 'd told / had told
  6 'd asked / had asked, would have changed
  7 would have enjoyed, 'd come / had come

● Tell SS to go back to the main lesson on page 101.

3 PRONUNCIATION sentence stress

Pronunciation notes

The main focus here is on getting SS to say third conditional sentences with good rhythm, by stressing the information words. You may also want to encourage your SS to produce the weak forms of *would*, *have*, *been*, and *had* in these kinds of sentences. These forms are commonly used by native speakers, but SS at this level will find these tricky to imitate and produce.

a ● **7.4** Focus on the instructions and give SS a moment to read the sentences.
● Play the recording once for SS to listen. Then play it again, pausing after each sentence for SS to repeat.

7.4   CD3 Track 22

1 If you'd <u>told</u> me <u>earlier</u>, I would have <u>gone too</u>.
2 If the <u>weather</u> had been <u>better</u>, we would have <u>stayed longer</u>.
3 If I <u>hadn't stopped</u> for <u>gas</u>, I would have <u>arrived before</u> he <u>left</u>.
4 We would have been <u>late</u> if we <u>hadn't taken</u> a <u>taxi</u>.
5 She <u>wouldn't</u> have <u>come</u> if she'd <u>known</u> he was <u>here</u>.
6 It would have been <u>cheaper</u> if we'd <u>gone last month</u>.

- Remind SS that:
  - the stressed words in the sentence are the information words.
  - negative auxiliaries, e.g., *wouldn't* and *hadn't* are always stressed.
  - *would, have been,* and the contracted form of *had* (*'d*) have a weak pronunciation.

b • Put SS in pairs, **A** and **B**, and tell them to go to **Communication** *Guess the conditional*, **A** on page 118 and **B** on page 121.
  - Demonstrate the activity. Write on a piece of paper *If I had known it was your birthday, I would have bought you a present.* Don't show the sentence to your SS.
  - Then write on the board *If I had known it was your birthday, I _____* (+). Tell SS that you have this sentence completed on a piece of paper, and they have to try to guess what it is.
  - Elicit possible completions with an affirmative (+) verb phrase (e.g. *would have said happy birthday / sent you a card*). Say "try again" if they say something different, until someone says the phrase *I would have bought you a present.* Then say, "That's right."
  - Now go through the instructions. Emphasize that SS should write their ideas next to the sentence but not in the blank, and only complete the blank when their partner says, "That's right."
  - SS continue in pairs. Monitor and help.

4 SPEAKING

a • Point out that this questionnaire was created by a real psychologist. (See article on page 102.)
  - Focus on the questionnaire and go through the statements. Help SS with new vocabulary like *anxious, instinct,* and *the bright side of life.*
  - Then give SS a few minutes to mark their answers. Stress that they shouldn't read the interpretation yet.

b • Have SS compare and explain their answers. Demonstrate by saying what you would put for 1 and why, e.g., *I put 1 because I'm a little shy and I'm not very good at talking to people I don't know. I certainly don't enjoy it.*

c • SS now check their scores, compare with a partner, and say if they agree or not. Get responses to find out how many people agree with their score and how many fall into each category.

5 READING

a • Focus on the title. Then ask SS if they think people are born lucky, or if they make their own luck. Don't expect SS to be able to explain why exactly, just find out whether they agree or not.
  - Read the first two paragraphs aloud with SS, and establish that Dr. Wiseman thinks that people who <u>think</u> they are lucky create good luck for themselves.

b • Now tell SS that they are going to learn how to become luckier! Explain that there are four pieces of advice about how to become luckier and four "exercises" that you can do to put the advice into practice. The exercises A–D have been separated from the pieces of advice 1–4.

- Focus on the task and give SS two minutes to read tip 1 and to match it to its exercise. Elicit the answer.

> **1** B

- Now set a time limit (e.g., five minutes) for SS to read tips 2–4 and to match them to the other three exercises. Have SS compare their answers with a partner before you check answers.

> **2** D   **3** A   **4** C

c • Focus on the instructions and give SS a minute to read the article again (not the exercises). Then have them complete the expressions with the missing verb. Check answers and model and drill pronunciation. Then have SS test themselves by covering the left-hand column.

> **1** seem   **2** achieve   **3** vary   **4** bump into
> **5** make an effort   **6** convince   **7** realize

d • Now put SS in pairs to read exercises A–D again and choose which one they think is the best. Get responses from the class to find out which one is the most popular.

HOW WORDS WORK...

- Focus on the examples and then explain the difference between *what* and *that* as relative pronouns. Emphasize that *what* is generally used after a verb or preposition, whereas *that* is used after a noun or noun phrase. If you know your SS' L1, point out what they would use in their language.
- Now give SS a few minutes to do the exercise and check answers.

> **1** what   **2** that   **3** that   **4** what   **5** that   **6** what

6 VOCABULARY making adjectives and adverbs

a • Focus on the sentence from the text, and elicit that *lucky* is an adjective, and *luck* is a noun.
  - Now focus on the chart. Then put SS in pairs to complete it. Check answers.

> careful, careless, carefully, carelessly
> comfortable, uncomfortable, comfortably, uncomfortably
> patient, impatient, patiently, impatiently
> fortunate, unfortunate, fortunately, unfortunately

- Point out that:
  - the suffixes *-y* and *-able* are both typical adjective endings.
  - the prefixes *un-* and *im-* are common to make an adjective negative, but adjectives formed with the suffix *-ful*, e.g., *careful*, normally make the opposite adjective with *-less*, e.g., *useful, useless.*
  - the suffix *-ful* = *full of* or *with.*
  - the suffix *-less* = *without.*
  - sometimes there are spelling changes, e.g., the final *le* is dropped before an *-ly* suffix in *comfortably*, and the *y* changes to *i* in *luckily.*

b ● Focus on the three two-syllable nouns, *comfort*, *patience*, and *fortune*, and elicit that they are all stressed on the first syllable. Now ask SS how this will help them stress the adjectives and adverbs correctly.

> The stressed syllable doesn't change, even when you add a prefix (e.g., *un-*) or a suffix (e.g., *-ly*).

● Now give SS a few moments in pairs to practice saying the words with the right stress.

Extra support

Have SS underline the stressed syllable in all the words in the chart.

c ● Focus on the instructions. Tell SS to first decide if they need an adjective or an adverb, and then if it should be positive or negative. You could do the first one or two with the whole class.

● Either have SS do the exercise in pairs or individually and then compare with a partner. Check answers and drill pronunciation.

1 un<u>for</u>tunately	6 <u>luck</u>ily
2 <u>com</u>fortable	7 <u>pa</u>tiently
3 <u>care</u>less	8 <u>care</u>ful
4 un<u>luck</u>y	9 <u>for</u>tunately
5 im<u>pa</u>tient	10 <u>com</u>fortably

7 [7.5] ♫ SONG *Ironic*

● *Ironic* was originally recorded by the Canadian singer Alanis Morissette in 1995. For copyright reasons this is a cover version. If you want to sing this song in class, use the photocopiable activity on page 212.

7.5   CD3 Track 23

Ironic

An old man turned ninety-eight
He won the lottery and died the next day
It's a black fly in your Chardonnay
It's a death row pardon two minutes too late
And isn't it ironic... don't you think?

It's like rain on your wedding day
It's a free ride when you've already paid
It's the good advice that you just didn't take
And who would've thought...? It figures.

Mr. Play-It-Safe was afraid to fly
He packed his suitcase and kissed his kids good-bye
He waited his whole damn life to take that flight
And as the plane crashed down he thought
"Well isn't this nice..."
And isn't it ironic... don't you think?

It's like rain on your wedding day
It's a free ride when you've already paid
It's the good advice that you just didn't take
And who would've thought...? It figures.

Well life has a funny way of sneaking up on you when
You think everything's OK and everything's going right
And life has a funny way of helping you out when
You think everything's gone wrong and everything blows up
In your face.

A traffic jam when you're already late
A no-smoking sign on your cigarette break
It's like ten thousand spoons when all you need is a knife
It's meeting the man of my dreams
And then meeting his beautiful wife
And isn't it ironic... don't you think?
A little too ironic... yeah, I really do think.

It's like rain on your wedding day
It's a free ride when you've already paid
It's the good advice that you just didn't take
And who would've thought...? It figures.

Well life has a funny way of sneaking up on you
And life has a funny, funny way of helping you out, helping you out.

Extra photocopiable activities

Grammar
third conditional page 158
Communicative
Third conditional game page 189 (instructions page 167)
Song
Ironic page 210 (instructions page 204)

HOMEWORK

Study Link Workbook pages 64–66

[Handwritten notes:]

① adverb - modifies verbs

when, where, how, in what manner, to what extent an action is performed.

when! He ran yesterday,
where - he ran here
how - he ran quickly.
In what manner - He ran barefeet / way
To what extent He ran the fastest

many end in ly not all do
fverey well very, most, least, more, less

② adjective - modifies noun, grey elephant, happy elephant, big elephant

7
B

G tag questions, indirect questions
V compound nouns
P intonation in tag questions

Murder mysteries

Lesson plan

In this lesson, SS learn two new ways of making questions, using tag questions and indirect questions. They will probably have seen both types before, but won't have focused on how they are formed and used. The context is murder mysteries; first the true story of Jack the Ripper and a detective novelist's theory as to who he was, and then an extract from a detective novel by Donna Leon. The vocabulary focus is on compound nouns, and SS also review other compound nouns that have come up in previous Files.

Optional lead-in (books closed)

- Write the word **MURDER** on the board and elicit what it means and how it's pronounced /mərdər/. Then give SS, in pairs, three minutes to brainstorm ten words connected with murder. Write their suggestions on the board.
  Possible words include
  murderer, kill, victim, detective, knife, gun, police, police station, body, blood, suspect, crime, witness, etc.

- Finally, ask SS if they can think of a famous British murderer from the past. Give clues if necessary to elicit Jack the Ripper.

1 READING & LISTENING

a ● Books open. Focus on the instructions and set a time limit (e.g., five minutes) for SS to read the article and answer the questions. They could either answer them orally in pairs, or in writing.
  ● Check answers. Deal with any vocabulary problems.

> 1 In London in the fall of 1888.
> 2 He sent the police letters signed "Jack the Ripper."
> 3 Seven.
> 4 For three months.
> 5 A doctor, a businessman, a painter, and a member of the royal family.
> 6 She's a crime writer.
> 7 By analyzing DNA samples.

Extra idea

You could read the article paragraph by paragraph together with SS, asking them to guess the meaning of new words as you go, and explain / translate the meaning of any that they can't guess.

Alternatively, you could have SS underline or highlight five words or phrases they want to remember from the text. Have them compare with a partner and then get some feedback from the class.

b ● **7.6** Focus on the three photos of the suspects, and the task. Then play the recording once all the way through. Have SS compare with a partner and play the recording again, pausing after each person if necessary. Check answers.

> Prince Albert, Queen Victoria's **grandson**
> **James** Maybrick, a cotton merchant
> Walter Sickert, an **artist** ✓

> **7.6**   CD3 Track 24
>
> (audioscript in Student Book on page 129)
> **I = interviewer, K = Ken**
> I Good morning and thank you for coming, Mr. Morton – or should it be Inspector Morton – you were a detective with Scotland Yard, weren't you?
> K Yes, that's right. For twenty-five years. I retired last year.
> I People today are still fascinated by the identity of Jack the Ripper, more than a hundred years after the crimes were committed. It's incredible, isn't it?
> K Well, it's not really that surprising. People are always interested in unsolved murders – and Jack the Ripper has become a sort of cult horror figure.
> I Who are the main suspects?
> K Well, there are a lot of them. But probably the best known are Prince Albert, Queen Victoria's grandson, the artist Walter Sickert, and a Liverpool cotton merchant named James Maybrick.
> I Patricia Cornwell in her book *Jack the Ripper – case closed* says that she has identified the murderer. Who does she think he was?
> K Well, she's convinced that Jack the Ripper was Walter Sickert, the painter.

c ● **7.7** Focus on the instructions and give SS time to read the sentences first. Make sure they understand *evidence, confess,* and *serial killer.* Then play the recording a couple of times. Have SS compare their answers with a partner, explaining why they think they are true or false.

- Check answers, getting SS to say why the F ones are false.

> 1 T
> 2 F (From a painting)
> 3 T
> 4 T
> 5 F (A diary)
> 6 F (He thinks it's a ridiculous theory.)
> 7 F (He doesn't know.)
> 8 F (He thinks it will be solved someday.)

> **7.7**   CD3 Track 25
>
> (audioscript in Student Book on page 129)
> **I = interviewer, K = Ken**
> I What evidence did she discover?
> K Well, she mainly used DNA analysis. She actually bought a painting by Sickert at great expense and she cut it up to get the DNA from it – people in the art world were furious.
> I I can imagine.

K And then she compared the DNA from the painting with DNA taken from the letters that Jack the Ripper sent to the police. Patricia Cornwell says that she's 99 percent certain that Walter Sickert was Jack the Ripper.

I But you don't think she's right, do you?

K No, I don't. I don't think her scientific evidence is completely reliable and there's a lot of evidence which says that Sickert was in France, not London, when some of the women were killed.

I There's been another recent theory, hasn't there? About James Maybrick? Do you think he was the murderer?

K Well, somebody found a diary, which is supposed to be his, where he admits to being Jack the Ripper. But nobody has been able to prove that the diary is genuine and, personally, I don't think he was the murderer.

I And Prince Albert, the queen's grandson?

K This for me is the most ridiculous theory. I can't seriously believe that a member of the royal family could be a serial murderer. In any case, Prince Albert was in Scotland when at least two of the murders were committed.

I So, who do *you* think the murderer was?

K I can't tell you because I don't know.

I So you don't think we'll ever solve the mystery?

K No, I wouldn't say that. I think that someday the mystery *will* be solved. Some new evidence will appear and we'll be able to say that the case of Jack the Ripper is finally closed. But at the moment it's still a mystery, and people like a good mystery.

Extra support

If there's time, you could have SS listen again with the audioscript on page 129 so they can see exactly what they understood / didn't understand. Translate / explain any new words or phrases.

2 GRAMMAR tag questions

a ● **7.8** Focus on the instructions and questions 1–4. Play the recording, pausing to give SS time to write. Check answers.

> 1 weren't you 2 isn't it 3 do you 4 hasn't there

Extra challenge

You could elicit ideas first for what the two missing words are.

> **7.8** CD3 Track 26
> 1 You were a detective with Scotland Yard, weren't you?
> 2 It's incredible, isn't it?
> 3 But you don't think she's right, do you?
> 4 There's been another recent theory, hasn't there?

b ● Ask the whole class the questions, and elicit that the interviewer thinks she knows what the inspector is going to answer and is just checking what she knows to be true. This is probably because she has already discussed Patricia Cornwell's theory with the inspector *before* the interview.

c ● Tell SS to go to **Grammar Bank 7B** on page 142. Read the examples and rules for tag questions, and have SS compare what they use in their L1.

Grammar notes

Tag questions

● Tag questions are difficult for SS to use with any fluency because they need to use the correct auxiliary each time, depending on the tense or modal verb they are using. Getting the right intonation can also be tricky. This lesson provides SS with a gentle introduction and focuses on their most common use, which is to check information.

● Focus on exercise **a** only on page 143 and have SS do it individually or in pairs. Check answers.

> **a** 1 do you   6 wasn't she
> 2 aren't they   7 haven't we
> 3 can he   8 did you
> 4 doesn't she   9 wouldn't you
> 5 will you   10 isn't it

● Tell SS to go back to the main lesson on page 105.

3 PRONUNCIATION & SPEAKING
intonation in tag questions

Pronunciation notes

The normal intonation for a tag question when we say something that we think is right or true, and that we expect the other person to agree with, is a falling tone. Examples would include: *It's hot today, isn't it? You're Mexican, aren't you?* (I'm sure you're Mexican).

⚠ Tag questions can sometimes be used as real questions with rising intonation, normally to express surprise, or to check information that we are not very sure about. This use is not focused on here.

a ● **7.9** Focus on the conversation between a policeman and a suspect.

● Point out that the policeman probably already has the information and is just checking. Play the recording once for SS to listen. Then give them a few minutes to complete the tag questions, and then play the recording again for them to check. Check answers.

> **7.9** CD3 Track 27
> P = policeman, S = suspect
> P Your last name's Jones, **isn't it**?
> S Yes, it is.
> P And you're 27, **aren't you**?
> S Yes, that's right.
> P You weren't at home last night at 8:00, **were you**?
> S No, I wasn't. I went for a walk.
> P But you don't have any witnesses, **do you**?
> S Yes, I do. My brother was with me.
> P Your brother wasn't with you, **was he**?
> S How do you know?
> P Because he was at the police station. We arrested him last night.

b ● **7.10** Play the recording, pausing for SS to repeat the policeman's questions.

7 B

7.10 CD3 Track 28

1 Your last name's Jones, isn't it?
2 And you're 27, aren't you?
3 You weren't at home last night at 8:00, were you?
4 But you don't have any witnesses, do you?
5 Your brother wasn't with you, was he?

Extra support

Give SS extra practice by having them read the conversation in pairs.

c ● Put SS in pairs, **A** and **B**, preferably face to face. Tell them to go to **Communication** *Just checking*, **A** on page 118 and **B** on page 121. If there is an odd number of SS, you should take part in the activity yourself. Go through the instructions. Make sure SS are clear that first **A** (as the police officer) will ask **B** some questions and try to remember the answers, and then he / she will check them with tag questions. Then they change roles. Demonstrate the activity by taking **A**'s role and asking one student the questions and then checking.
  ● Monitor and help SS form the tag questions correctly. When both have done their interviews, get responses to find out which "police officers" had the best memory.
  ● Tell SS to go back to the main lesson on page 106.

4 GRAMMAR indirect questions

a ● Ask the whole class the questions, and tell them about yourself and your tastes. Focus on the book cover and ask SS if any of them have read any Donna Leon books. (They are translated into many languages.)

b ● **7.11** Focus on the instructions. Then play the recording. Have SS listen and read, and underline the detective's questions as they read. Check answers.

> Could you tell me how long you and your husband were married?
> How many children do you have?
> Are they in school in Venice?
> Would you say yours was a happy marriage?
> Could you tell me if your husband had any particularly close friends or business associates?
> Other friends?

7.11 CD3 Track 29

"I'd like to ask you some questions about your personal life, signora."
"Our personal life?" she repeated, as though she had never heard of such a thing. When he didn't answer this, she nodded, signaling him to begin.
"Could you tell me how long you and your husband were married?"
"Nineteen years."
"How many children do you have, signora?"
"Two. Claudio is seventeen and Francesca is fifteen."
"Are they in school in Venice, signora?"
She looked up at him sharply when he asked this.
"Why do you want to know that?"
"My own daughter, Chiara, is fourteen, so perhaps they know each another," he answered, and smiled to show what an innocent question it had been.

"Claudio is in school in Switzerland, but Francesca is here. With us. I mean," she corrected, rubbing a hand across her forehead, "with me."
"Would you say yours was a happy marriage, signora?"
"Yes," she answered immediately, far faster than Brunetti would have answered the same question, though he would have given the same response. She did not, however, elaborate.
"Could you tell me if your husband had any particularly close friends or business associates?"
She looked up at this question, then as quickly down again at her hands. "Our closest friends are the Nogares, Mirto and Graziella. He's an architect who lives in Campo Sant'Angelo. They're Francesca's godparents. I don't know about business associates: you'll have to ask Ubaldo."
"Other friends, signora?"
"Why do you need to know all this?" she said, voice rising sharply.
"I'd like to learn more about your husband, signora."
"Why?" The question leaped from her, almost as if beyond her volition.
"Until I understand what sort of man he was, I can't understand why this has happened."
"A robbery?" she asked, voice just short of sarcasm.
"It wasn't robbery. Whoever killed him intended to do it."

c ● Ask SS if they think Brunetti is aggressive or polite when he interviews Signora Trevisan, and elicit that he is very polite and that Signora Trevisan is nervous and worried. Then ask SS if they think she murdered her husband and elicit ideas. (She didn't murder him herself, but is involved in the murder.)
  ● Now go through the text quickly with SS and help SS with any words or phrases they find difficult.

Extra idea

You could then play the recording again with books closed so that SS can just listen and try to enjoy it.

d ● Focus on the four questions and ask SS which two they think are more polite (the two beginning *Could you tell me…*).
  ● Then write on the board:
  How long were you and your husband married?
  Did your husband have any particularly close friends…?
  ● Have SS compare the two direct questions with the indirect ones. Elicit that after "*Could you tell me…*", the word order is normal – subject + verb – not inverted as in a normal question, and there is no auxiliary verb.

e ● Tell SS to go back to **Grammar Bank 7B** on page 142. Go through the examples and rules for **Indirect Questions**.

Grammar notes

Indirect questions

● In many ways, indirect questions are the same as reported questions, which SS have worked on recently, the only difference being that the tense of the verb doesn't change.
● SS mainly have problems remembering not to invert the subject and verb, typical mistakes being, e.g., ~~Could you tell me where is the station?~~

- Focus on exercise **b** on page 143 and have SS do it individually or in pairs. Check answers.

> **b 1** where they live ~subject~
> **2** if there's a bank near here ~verb, verb phrase~
> **3** where I can buy some stamps
> **4** if this bus goes downtown
> **5** what time the stores open
> **6** where the restrooms are
> **7** if Susan's (is) at work today
> **8** if the Mets won last night
> **9** where we parked the car
> **10** what time it is

- Tell SS to go back to the main lesson on page 107.

f ● (7.12) SS now practice transformations from direct questions they hear. Demonstrate by giving them a couple more questions to transform, e.g.,

> **T:** Where's the bus stop?
> **SS:** Could you tell me where the bus stop is?
> **T:** Is this the town hall?
> **SS:** Could you tell me if / whether this is the town hall?, etc.

- Now play the recording, pausing after each direct question for SS to complete the indirect question. Check answers.

> **7.12** CD3 Track 30
> **1** How much does it cost? (*beep*)
> Could you tell me **how much it costs**?
> **2** Is there a bank near here? (*beep*)
> Do you know if **there's a bank near here**?
> **3** What time does the next train leave? (*beep*)
> Could you tell me **what time the next train leaves**?
> **4** Is the museum open on Saturdays? (*beep*)
> Can you tell me if **the museum is open on Saturdays**?
> **5** Where's the bus station? (*beep*)
> Can you tell me **where the bus station is**?
> **6** Does this bus go to the beach? (*beep*)
> Do you know if **this bus goes to the beach**?

Extra challenge

You could do this again with books closed or covered so that SS do the tranformations orally.

g ● Focus on the situation. If you were interviewing someone in the street, it would be natural to use a polite question form.

- Elicit the first question from the class. (*Could you tell me what your name is?*) Now SS practice in pairs. One student should ask all the questions, and then they change roles.

5 VOCABULARY compound nouns

a ● SS have already been introduced to compound nouns (in lesson **2C**). Remind them that these phrases are two nouns but the first noun (always singular) describes the second one, i.e., it functions as an adjective. Usually they are written as two words, but occasionally with a hyphen or as one word (e.g., *sunglasses*).

- Focus on the instructions and the example (detective novel). Give SS time to match the words in the two squares to make five other compound nouns.

b ● (7.13) Play the recording for SS to check answers, and ask them which word is normally stressed more (the first one).

> **7.13** CD3 Track 31
> detective novel
> murder mystery
> horror movie
> crime writer
> police station
> police inspector

c ● This activity reviews compound nouns that have come up during the course. Focus on the race and set a time limit, e.g., two minutes. SS can do it individually or in pairs / groups. When the time is up, check answers. Encourage SS to use articles and prepositions as in the key.

> **1** A credit card.
> **2** At a train station.
> **3** He's a movie director.
> **4** The rush hour.
> **5** Your seat belt.
> **6** A department store.
> **7** On a tennis court.
> **8** A boarding pass.
> **9** A public school.
> **10** At a gas station.
> **11** The ring tone.
> **12** A traffic jam.

Extra photocopiable activities

Grammar
tag questions, indirect questions page 159
Communicative
The scariest places in London page 190 (instructions page 168)

HOMEWORK

Study Link **Workbook** pages 67–69

7C

G phrasal verbs
V television, phrasal verbs
P review of sounds, linking

Turn it off

Lesson plan

Television is the context for reviewing and extending SS' knowledge of phrasal verbs. First, SS talk about their TV watching habits and then the grammar is presented through three amusing newspaper stories, which all feature TV in some way. In the second part of the lesson, SS read about a couple who lived for 37 years without electricity and say which modern electrical devices they would not want to live without. Pronunciation focuses on TV words and common phrasal verbs and reviews some common sounds and sound linking.

Optional lead-in (books closed)

- In a monolingual class, you could ask SS what they think is the best TV program in their country at the moment. Write the suggestions on the board and then have a class vote. Then repeat the process for the worst program on TV at the moment.
- In a multilingual class, ask SS to evaluate from 1–10 (10 = fantastic) the quality of TV programs in their country. Get feedback to find out which country's TV is rated the best.

1 VOCABULARY & SPEAKING television

a • Books open. Focus on the TV survey and go through the questions, making sure SS understand them. Focus especially on the meaning and pronunciation of the bold words.
- Clarify meaning, e.g., by asking SS to name some of the channels in their country. Use the photos to help you with the meaning of the different types of TV program and ask SS to give you examples.
⚠ *Soap operas* (often called *soaps*) = a weekly or daily drama series usually about everyday life in different families. Point out that they were originally called *soap operas* because when this kind of program was invented they were used to advertise soap (the advertisements were shown in program breaks).

b • Give SS a few moments to think about their answers to the questions. Have them write L, H, or DM in the boxes next to the kinds of programs.
- Put SS in pairs and have them interview each other using the questionnaire. They could either take turns asking the questions (**A** book open, **B** book closed) or they could look at and answer the questions together.

Extra idea

Have the class ask you the questions first.

- Discuss the last question with the whole class, eliciting examples.

2 GRAMMAR phrasal verbs

a • Focus on the task and give SS one clear example of a phrasal verb (= verb + particle) related to TV, e.g., *turn on*.

> **Some possible answers**
> turn on / off
> turn up / down
> plug in (opposite *unplug*)

b • Focus on the task and the list of verbs A–G. Then tell SS that they should first read each true story on page 109 before they fill in the blanks. Set a time limit, e.g., five minutes.
- Have SS compare with a partner before checking answers. *Pass away* is a polite / formal way of saying *die. Look out* = be careful. You can also use *watch out*.
- Deal with any other vocabulary problems SS may have.

> 1 E looking forward to
> 2 D turn off
> 3 B sold out
> 4 F find out
> 5 G passed away
> 6 C picked ... up
> 7 A Look out

c • Focus on the task and have SS read the texts again trying to memorize the main details.
- Put SS in pairs and tell them to cover the texts and look at the pictures. Then together they try to remember the stories. Finally, elicit the three stories from the class.

Extra support

Instead of putting SS in pairs, simply have them close their books and elicit the stories from the whole class by asking questions, e.g., *Who was Mitch Altman? Where did he go with his friends? What happened?*, etc.

d • Remind SS that with some phrasal verbs there are two possible word orders, e.g., *turn off the TV* or *turn the TV off*.
- Focus on the task and the dictionary extract and elicit answers.

> When the abbreviation *sth* (= something) goes between the verb and the particle (*off, on*, etc.), the verb and particle <u>can</u> be separated.

- Point out too that *sth* and *sb* are used in dictionaries as abbreviated forms of *something* and *somebody*, respectively.

e • Tell SS to go to **Grammar Bank 7C** on page 142. Go through the examples and the rules with the class. Model and drill the example sentences.

Grammar notes

Phrasal verbs

- Phrasal verbs (a verb + particle, i.e., a preposition or adverb) are a feature of English and it is important that SS can recognize and use a limited number of high-frequency verbs like *turn on*, *find out*, but it is also important not to make them seem like an obstacle for SS.

- Although we have pointed out for reference the three most common grammatical groups, SS will probably already "have a feel" for when they can separate the particle from the verb.

- Some useful points to emphasize:
  - Phrasal verbs often have a more formal (often Latin-based) synonym, e.g., *fill out* (this form) can be replaced by *complete* (this form), *come back* has the same meaning as the more formal *return*.
  - Other phrasal verbs have no easy equivalent, *e.g., I get along* (with my boss) would require a long phrase to paraphrase it, e.g., *I have good, friendly relations* (with my boss). These are the phrasal verbs that are essential for SS to learn and be able to use.
  - The same phrasal verb sometimes has more than one meaning, e.g., *take off your coat / the plane took off*. A dictionary will give these different meanings.
  - Sometimes the particle (*up*, *on*, etc.) has a clear, literal meaning, e.g., *go away* and sometimes it doesn't, e.g., *take up* (= start doing something regularly).
  - Phrasal verbs are an area of English that SS will pick up little by little. They should aim at slowly increasing their knowledge and not worry about "learning them all."
  - When phrasal verbs are non-separable (groups 1 and 2) they cannot be separated by an adverb either, e.g., you can't say ~~I go often out with my friends~~.

- Typical mistakes include:
  - confusing the particle, e.g., *It's hot.* ~~Take away your coat.~~
  - problems of word order, e.g., ~~Turn off it. We came early back.~~

- Now have SS do the exercises on page 143 either individually or in pairs. Check answers after each exercise or after SS have done both.

> **a 1** up **2** back **3** up **4** over **5** out **6** out
>   **7** up **8** up **9** up **10** out
> **b 1** Take them off.
>   **2** Could you fill it out?
>   **3** Do you get along with her?
>   **4** Turn them off.
>   **5** I'm looking for them.
>   **6** Please pick it up.
>   **7** Turn it down!
>   **8** I'm really looking forward to it.
>   **9** Can I try it on?
>   **10** Don't throw it away!

- Tell SS to go back to the main lesson on page 110.

3 PRONUNCIATION revision of sounds, linking

Pronunciation notes

> In the first exercise, SS review some common sounds and try to remember how these sounds are transcribed using phonetic symbols found in dictionaries. Once again emphasize the importance of being able to use this system to check pronunciation. It is well worth the investment of time to learn the sound words and symbols in the **Sound Bank** on pages 157–9.
>
> In the second exercise, SS practice understanding and saying short phrases spoken fairly fast, where some of the words become joined or linked together (a common characteristic of spoken language).

a • To demonstrate the activity focus on the pink letters in the first sentence and the examples.

  • Put SS in pairs and have them try and complete the chart. SS may not remember all the symbols, but tell them not to check in the back of the book until you tell them.

b • Now tell SS to go to the **Sound Bank** on page 157 to check their answers, before returning to the main lesson on page 110.

  • Elicit answers from the class and write the completed chart on the board.

Sound word	Symbol
2 bike	/aɪ/
3 horse	/ɔr/
4 up	/ʌ/
5 chess	/tʃ/
6 flower	/f/
7 bull	/ʊ/
8 mother	/ð/

c • **7.14** Play the recording for SS to listen and repeat the sentences. Play again for extra practice.

> **7.14**   CD3 Track 32
> 1 We can't go. It's sold out.
> 2 I'd like to find out about train times.
> 3 I'm looking forward to Saturday morning.
> 4 I was talking to my mother but we were cut off.
> 5 In the future, remember to turn off the kitchen lights.
> 6 Philip's not old enough to take care of a five-year-old.
> 7 We put on our seat belts before the flight took off.
> 8 They don't get along with each other.

Extra support

Have SS practice saying each sentence in pairs. They take turns saying the sentences.

Study Link SS can find more practice of English sounds on the MultiROM and also on the *American English File 3* Website.

d • **7.15** Focus on the task and quickly run through the six sentences. Tell SS that they are going to hear each sentence plus another three-word phrase (which contains a phrasal verb). They have to write the second phrase. Explain that the first phrase will help them by giving the context and that the phrases will be said fairly quickly so that most of the words will be linked together (making the phrase more difficult to understand).

- Play the recording once all the way through and let SS just listen to the six sentences without writing anything.
- Now play the recording again, preferably pausing after each sentence, for SS to write them down.
- Play again if necessary. Check answers and write the six phrases on the board.

7.15   CD3 Track 33

1 There's a towel on the floor. **Pick it up**.
2 I hate this music. **Turn it off**.
3 Your jacket's on the chair. **Put it away**.
4 You don't need a coat. **Take it off**.
5 I can't hear the TV. **Turn it up**.
6 Coffee is bad for you. **Give it up**.

- Finally, play the recording again, pausing after each sentence for SS to repeat.

4 VOCABULARY & SPEAKING

a • Tell SS to go to the **Vocabulary Bank** *Phrasal verbs* on page 155. Focus on the instructions in **a** and demonstrate the activity by doing sentence 1 with the whole class.

- SS uncover the first sentence to check their answer. They then continue, looking at each sentence with the particle covered and testing themselves to see if they can remember it.
- Finally, focus on the ⚠ box below and go through the information and examples.
- Now, focus on the instruction "Can you remember the words on this page? Test yourself or a partner." Tell SS to test themselves regularly on these verbs.

Testing yourself

SS can cover the **Particle** column and look at sentences 1–40 and try to remember the particle (*for*, *out*, *up*, etc.). They can uncover, one by one, to check.

Testing a partner

See **Testing a partner** on page 15.

Study Link SS can find more practice of these words on the MultiROM and on the *American English File 3* Website.

- Tell SS to go back to the main lesson on page 110.

b • Focus on the task and give SS time to choose their six questions. Deal with any vocabulary problems.

c • Put SS in pairs and focus on the task, emphasizing that they should try to keep the conversation going when possible by asking more questions and giving more information.

Extra support

Demonstrate by having SS choose some questions to ask you, and elicit follow-up questions to keep the conversation going.

- Have SS ask and answer their questions in pairs. If there's time, get some responses from the class.

5 READING

a • Focus on the task and tell SS to choose two things. Elicit ideas from the class but don't give answers at this stage.

b • Focus on the article and set a time limit, e.g., three or four minutes, for SS to read the article once to check their answers to **a**. Find out if anybody guessed the two things.

An iron and a vacuum cleaner.
No, they don't.

---

c • Give SS a few minutes to read the article again more carefully. Then tell SS to cover the article and see if they can remember what the numbers in the list refer to. Make sure they don't look at the numbers while they are reading the text for the second time. Elicit answers from the class.

---

37 - The number of years they lived without electricity.
74 and 72 - The ages of the couple.
19,000 - It will cost £19,000 to install electricity.
200 - The house is 200 years old.
3 - The house has three bedrooms.
9 - The couple has nine children.
24 - The couple has 24 grandchildren.
8 - They have eight great-grandchildren.

---

d • Focus on the questions and give SS a few minutes to answer them. Then have them compare their answers with a partner. Check answers.

---

1 Yes, one.
2 She's happy ("looking forward to it") but she doesn't think they missed anything by not having electricity in the past.
3 No. (They "got by".)
4 From the land (their garden).
5 Because they played together, made up games, or read stories.
6 It was a very healthy way of life. They were never seriously ill.

---

e • Focus on the task and give SS, in pairs, a few minutes to complete the chart. Remind them that if *sth / sb* are in the middle of the blank, it means that the verb is separable. If it's at the end, it means that the verb is non-separable. Check answers.

Phrasal verbs
1 grow up   5 make sth up
2 get by   6 live off sb / sth
3 put sth in   7 bring sb up
4 move back

- Point out the difference between *bring up*, which is what parents do to their children (i.e., take care of them, feed them, teach them things) and *grow up*, which is what the children do (i.e., get older, bigger until they are an adult).

6 LISTENING

a ● **7.16** Focus on the task and play the recording once all the way through for SS to find out the two things the people would miss the most. Check answers.

Cindy:	1 refrigerator	2 laptop (computer)
Andy:	1 cell phone	2 MP3 player
Julia:	1 dishwasher	2 iron
Tyler:	1 cell phone	2 lights

b ● Play the recording again, pausing after each speaker for SS to write why they would miss these things. Have them compare in pairs before checking answers.

Cindy
(refrigerator) She would miss cold drinks and would have to go shopping every day.
(laptop) She wouldn't be able to work.
Andy
(cell phone) He needs his cell phone to keep in touch with people.
(MP3 player) He needs his music.
Julia
(dishwasher) She has a family and lots of dishes.
(iron) Everybody in the family would look terrible without one.
Tyler
(cell phone) There are some numbers he only has in his cell phone.
(lights) It's often dark early in the morning and in the afternoon at this time of year.

Extra support

If there's time, you could have SS listen again with the audioscript on page 129 so they can see exactly what they understood / didn't understand. Translate / explain any new words or phrases.

7.16 CD3 Track 34

(audioscript in Student Book on page 129)
Cindy
Well, it wouldn't be electric light because I love candles. And I could live without a washing machine for a week – I often do when I'm on vacation. I think I would miss the refrigerator, though – I'd hate not having cold drinks, and it would mean having to go shopping every day for food or it would go bad. So a refrigerator would be one thing, and then probably my laptop. It has a battery, but I could only use it for three hours or so without charging it. So I wouldn't be able to do much work.
Andy
Uh, well, it depends. I'd really miss the TV, but I suppose I could live without it for a week if I had to. And, uh, what else – oh no, my cell phone. I wouldn't be able to charge it. I couldn't *live* without my cell. I mean, that's how I keep in touch with all my friends. And my MP3 player. I need my music. Yes, definitely those two.
Julia
I think for me it would have to be first and foremost the dishwasher. Because with a family and so many dishes to do, I would just be at the sink forever. It would be a nightmare for me to have no dishwasher because I've gotten so used to it. So that would be the first thing. And the second thing, probably again because of having

a family, a young family, would be an iron, because there's so much ironing. If I had to go without that, everyone would look terrible. Nobody would look very neat. So those would be my two things.
Tyler
Well, I suppose the first thing I'd miss most would be my cell phone, because I couldn't charge it, so I couldn't use it, and I'd get very upset about that. There are some people's numbers that are only stored in the phone. I don't have them written down, and I wouldn't be able to get in touch with those people. So cell phone. And the other thing I'd miss would be the lights. At this time of year especially, when the days are short, the mornings are dark, late afternoon's dark too, I'd miss lights. So cell phone and lights.

c ● Focus on the task. Give SS a minute to talk about what they would miss and then elicit some answers from the whole class. You could also tell SS what you would miss most.

Study Link SS can find a dictation and a Grammar quiz on all the grammar from File 7 on the MultiROM and more grammar activities on the *American English File* 3 Website.

Extra photocopiable activities

Grammar
phrasal verbs page 160
Communicative
Phrasal verbs race page 191 (instructions page 168)
Vocabulary
Split crossword puzzle page 201 (instructions page 194)

HOMEWORK

Study Link **Workbook** page 70–72

Function Apologizing, giving excuses
Language *I'm really sorry. I did it without thinking*, etc.

Lesson plan

This is the last **Practical English** lesson. In the first part of the lesson SS learn and practice ways of apologizing and giving excuses. Mark tells Allie that she has mistakenly sent a personal e-mail intended for his eyes only to everyone in the office. Allie then apologizes to everyone in the office for not being completely honest about her relationship with Mark.

In the second part of the lesson (**Social English**), Mark and Allie go for a walk by the river Seine and discuss how the people in the office discovered their secret. Then Mark asks Allie to marry him.

Study Link These lessons are on the *American English File 3* Video, which can be used instead of the Class Audio CD for these lessons (see Introduction page 9). The main functional section of each episode is also on the MultiROM with additional activities.

Optional lead-in (books closed)

- Review what happened in the previous episode by eliciting the story from SS, e.g., *What did Ben tell Jacques and Nicole about his weekend? Who didn't believe him at first? Why did Nicole believe him?*, etc.
- If you are using the Video, you could play the previous episode again, leaving out the "Listen and Repeat" sections.
- You could also try to elicit from the SS the phrases they reviewed / learned in the previous episode for expressing surprise and interest, e.g., *Really? You must be joking. I don't believe you.* (You could write the phrases with blanks on the board to help SS remember.)

APOLOGIZING, GIVING EXCUSES

a ● **7.17** Tell SS to cover the conversation with their hand or a piece of paper. Focus on the photo and the two questions, or write the questions on the board and do the first listening with books closed.

- Play the recording once all the way through. Then play it again, pausing after each question to give SS time to answer. Check answers.

> To Mark. Because she sent a personal e-mail to everyone in the office. (She pressed "Reply to all" by mistake.)

b ● Now have SS look at the conversation. In pairs, they should read it and see if they can guess or remember the missing words. Emphasize that they shouldn't write the words in the conversation but pencil them in, alongside or on a separate sheet of paper.

c ● Play the recording again for them to check. Then go through the conversation line by line and check answers. Find out if SS had guessed the words correctly. Where they had not guessed correctly, see if their alternative also fits.

7.17 CD3 Track 35

M = Mark, A = Allie, N = Nicole
M Mark Ryder.
A Mark, can you come in?
M Sure.
A Thanks for the sales report.
M I think there's something more important to talk about right now.
A What do you mean?
M That message you sent me. You hit "reply to all." You sent it to everyone in the office.
A Oh no. You're joking. Oh, Mark. I'm **so** sorry. I did it without **thinking**.
M It's **all right**, Allie. It's an easy mistake to make.
A How could I be so **stupid**? I just wasn't **concentrating**.
M Allie…
A I'm **really** sorry.
M Don't **worry** about it. It doesn't **matter**. But I think we should talk to the others.
A Yes, you're right. I'll do it. It was my **fault**. Listen, everybody. I just want to say that I'm **terribly** sorry. I haven't been honest with you. Uh, we… Mark and I…
N That's OK, Allie. We had already guessed. It wasn't really a surprise.

d ● **7.18** Now focus on the key phrases highlighted in the conversation. Play the recording, pausing after each sentence for SS to repeat. Encourage them to copy the rhythm and intonation.

7.18 CD3 Track 36

A = Allie, M = Mark
A I'm so sorry.
A I did it without thinking.
M It's all right, Allie.
A How could I be so stupid?
A I just wasn't concentrating.
A I'm really sorry.
M Don't worry about it.
M It doesn't matter.
A It was my fault.
A I'm terribly sorry.

e ● Have SS look at the highlighted phrases in the conversation and use them to complete the chart. Check answers.

Apologizing	Admitting… / Explaining	Responding to an apology
I'm so sorry.	I did it without thinking.	It's all right. (It's an easy mistake to make.)
I'm really sorry.	How could I be so stupid?	Don't worry about it.
I'm terribly sorry.	I just wasn't concentrating. It was my fault.	It doesn't matter.

- Point out that:
  - I'm *so / really / terribly sorry* are stronger forms of apology than *I'm sorry*.
  - As well as *It's OK* and *That's OK*, you can also use *It's all right* and *That's all right*.

f ● Put SS in pairs, **A** and **B**, preferably face to face. Tell SS to go to **Communication** *I'm so sorry!* **A** on page 118 and **B** on page 121. Give SS a minute or so to read their instructions. Then demonstrate the activity by taking the part of first student **A** then **B**, and do the first situation for both. Try to elicit a reasonable sounding excuse, and then accept it with, e.g., *That's OK.*

● Now have SS work together in pairs and complete the task.

SOCIAL ENGLISH A walk by the Seine

a ● (7.19) Focus on the photo and the question. Play the recording once for SS to answer the question. Elicit the answer.

Mark asks Allie to marry him. She says yes.

b ● Focus on questions 1–5 and go through them quickly. Then play the recording. Play the recording again if necessary. Check answers.

1 She thinks Mark said something to the people in the office. (He's bad at keeping secrets.)
2 No. He thinks they guessed. (Because the French are experts on love affairs.)
3 No, because now they don't have to pretend anymore.
4 Because a boat on the river makes a noise (a boat horn).
5 He asks her to send him her answer in an e-mail. (He's joking.)

7.19   CD3 Track 37

A = Allie, M = Mark
A I still can't work out how they knew about us. I was always really careful not to treat you differently.
M You were really hard on me.
A Mark, I wasn't.
M Oh, you were just being fair and very British.
A So if it wasn't me, it must have been you.
M What?
A I've got my own office. You're with them all the time. You must have said something. You're hopeless at keeping secrets!
M Don't blame me. This wasn't my fault. They probably just guessed.
A How?
M You know the French, they're experts on love affairs.
A Maybe.
M Actually, I think it's great that everyone knows. Now we don't have to pretend anymore.
A Yeah. That's true.
M Allie, there's something I've been wanting to ask you for a long time… I just haven't said anything. But… it's now or never. Allie, will you marry me?
A Sorry, Mark. I didn't hear a word you said.
M I said…Will you marry me?
A Yes, I will.
M Was that a "yes?"
A Yes!
M Can you confirm that in an e-mail for me? Just don't send it to everyone in the office this time.

---

c ● (7.20) Now focus on the **USEFUL PHRASES**. Give SS a moment to try to complete them, and then play the recording to check. Elicit / explain that *hopeless at =* very bad at.

7.20   CD3 Track 38

A = Allie, M = Mark
A So if it **wasn't** me, it must have been you.
A You're **hopeless** at keeping secrets!
M Don't **blame** me.
M But it's now or **never**.
A I didn't hear a **word** you said.
M Can you **confirm** that in an e-mail?

Extra idea

Ask SS if they can remember who said each phrase and what they were talking about.

d ● Play the recording again, pausing for SS to repeat. In a monolingual class, elicit the equivalent expressions in SS' L1.

HOMEWORK

Study Link **Workbook** page 73

WRITING: AN ARTICLE FOR A MAGAZINE

Lesson plan

This final writing task focuses on writing a "for and against" article for a magazine. This is the kind of writing task SS are often asked to do if they take official exams. The task focuses on the organization of ideas and on the use of connecting phrases like *First,… On the other hand,… In conclusion,…*.

There is also a mini-focus on using error correction.

We suggest that you do exercises **a–d** in class, but assign the actual writing (the last activity) for homework. If there's time, you may also want to do the planning in class.

a ● Focus on the article and on the task. Give SS five or six minutes to read the article and correct the ten mistakes. Check answers.

1 has	6 programs
2 talking	7 documentaries
3 better shape	8 what's (or what is)
4 different	9 although
5 their	10 off

b ● Focus on the task and put SS in pairs. Tell them to read the article again and then cover it and answer the questions together from memory. Then check answers.

1 Families spend more time talking to each other. They do more creative things like reading. They are usually in better shape.
2 Children who don't have a TV may feel different from their friends. They might know less about what is happening in the world.
3 The writer is for having a TV but thinks we should only watch good programs.

c ● Focus on the task and put SS in pairs. Give them a few minutes to make a list of advantages and disadvantages.

Some possible answers
advantages: very convenient – you always have a phone to use wherever you are / people can always contact you wherever you are / very useful in a crisis – you can call for help / very useful when you are trying to meet someone, e.g., in a crowded place, etc.
disadvantages: more expensive than normal phones / people can call you at inconvenient times, e.g., when you are driving or having a meal in a restaurant / it can be annoying when people talk loudly on their phone in a public place or answer their phone when they are talking to you, etc.

d ● Focus on the task and have SS number their advantages and disadvantages 1–3.
   ● Now focus on the **Useful language** box and make sure SS understand all the phrases.

WRITE an article

Go through the instructions. Then either have SS plan and write their article in class (set a time limit of 20 minutes) or have them plan their article in class and write it at home, or assign both the planning and writing for homework.

Before SS hand in their work, have them exchange their article with another student to read and check for mistakes.

For instructions on how to use these pages, see page 30.

GRAMMAR

a 1 c 2 b 3 c 4 a 5 b
b 1 hadn't gotten 2 you arrived 3 if ... stops
  4 doesn't it 5 forward to

VOCABULARY

a 1 unfortunately 2 impatient 3 comfortable
  4 lucky 5 carelessly
b 1 station 2 horror 3 apartment 4 ticket 5 soap
c 1 Look 2 up 3 back 4 up 5 take 6 Slow
  7 get 8 on 9 up 10 broke

PRONUNCIATION

a 1 put (It's /ʊ/.)   4 careful (It's /ɛr/.)
  2 patient (It's /eɪ/.)   5 machine (It's /ʃ/.)
  3 down (It's /aʊ/.)
b impatient, comfortable, documentary, cartoons,
  detective

CAN YOU UNDERSTAND THIS TEXT?

a 1 F 2 T 3 F 4 DS 5 T 6 T 7 T 8 DS
b give up = stop
  kept on = continued, didn't stop
  picked out = chose
  going back = returning to
  turn up = arrive, appear

CAN YOU UNDERSTAND THESE PEOPLE?

a 1 a 2 c 3 a 4 b 5 c
b 1 spiders 2 Detective 3 9:30 4 PBS
  5 *Out of Africa*

7.21   CD3 Track 39

1 A So then I spoke to the manager... Hey, my
    computer's not working.
  B The electricity's just gone off. It'll come back on in
    a minute.
  A Oh no. I don't know if I've saved the article I was
    writing.
  B Doesn't it save automatically?
  A Yes, but only every half hour. Oh – it's back on
    again. Now we'll see. Yes, thank goodness, it's all
    there. If I hadn't saved it, I would have had to look
    up all that information again.
  B You were lucky. So tell me what the manager said...

2 A Why do you always wear that yellow T-shirt when
    you play?
  B It's my lucky shirt. I put it on under my uniform
    shirt.
  A Do you really believe it brings you luck?
  B Well, I suppose it's just superstition really. But the
    one time I wasn't wearing it, we lost.
  A Why weren't you wearing it?
  B Because I'd left it out the night before on my chair,
    but my wife thought it looked dirty and put it in
    the washing machine.

3 A What are you reading?
  B *The Minotaur* by Barbara Vine.
  A She's a detective writer, isn't she?
  B Yes, she's fantastic.
  A You're always reading detective novels. Don't you
    ever read anything else?
  B Of course I do. I read lots of classics, and science
    fiction too. It's just that when I'm on a train or a
    bus, I need something light. And anything's better
    than reading the sports papers like you do.
    Anyway, be quiet now and let me read. I'm just
    about to find out who the murderer is.

4 A OK, now I'm going to ask you a few questions.
    And just so that you know, this interview will be
    recorded. This is detective inspector Carlos Moya
    interviewing Jonathan Carter on Thursday, May
    the 20th. OK, let's start with what you were doing
    last night.
  B I was at home.
  A Any witnesses?
  B My mother. She was there. You can ask her if you
    like.
  A So you didn't go out at all?
  B No, I stayed in and watched TV. Well, I went to the
    corner store to get some milk. But that was just
    five minutes.
  A Did you watch anything in particular? On TV?
  B Yeah, the basketball game. Knicks and Nets.
    Terrible game.
  A So you weren't anywhere near the cafe? Goud's
    Cafe?
  B The cafe? Me? No way.
  A So you'd be surprised to hear that three people saw
    you there.
  B They're lying. And I'm not going to answer any
    more questions without a lawyer.

5 A Could you turn off the TV, please?
  B But, Mom, it hasn't finished yet.
  A What hasn't finished?
  C The movie. It's *Star Wars. The Return of the Jedi.*
  A But you've seen it before. I know you have.
  B Yes, but it's so good. And it's nearly finished, I
    promise. Just five more minutes.
  A I don't care. It's 10 o'clock and it's time to go to
    bed. It's already half an hour past your normal
    bedtime.
  C But yesterday you said we could watch it if we'd
    finished our homework.
  A Yes, but I didn't know it was on so late. It's
    bedtime and that's that.

7.22 CD3 Track 40

And finally, *Tonight's TV* – a word about what's on television tonight. At 8:00 p.m. on PBS you can see *Eight-legged Wonders*, a documentary about those fascinating insects – well, arachnids I should say – spiders. It's a must for anyone who's interested in nature and wildlife.

However, if you suffer from arachnophobia, you'd be better off watching ABC, as at the same time as *Eight-legged Wonders*, you can see the first episode of a new crime series called *The Silent Detective*, starring Amanda Hobbs. Then after that on ABC, at 9:30, there's this week's edition of *Who wants to be a millionaire?* Note that the time has changed for this quiz show, as it used to be on at 9:00.

On PBS a little later, at 10:00, the film in the *Great Films* series is the wonderful Ingmar Bergman film *Fanny and Alexander*. So if you're a fan of foreign films, don't miss it.

And finally, a change of program on ABC. Instead of tonight's episode of *Hospital Life*, at 10:30, as a tribute to Sydney Pollack, ABC will be showing his Oscar winning film, *Out of Africa*. So if you're waiting to find out what's going to happen to Doctor Hammond and Nurse Marshall, you'll have to wait till next week. And now…

Extra photocopiable activities

Grammar
review and check page 161
Communicative
Review page 192 (instructions page 168)
Vocabulary
Review page 202 (instructions page 194)

CONTENTS

Photocopiable material

- There is a **Grammar activity** for each main (A, B, and C) lesson of the Student Book.
- There is a **Communicative activity** for each main (A, B, and C) lesson of the Student Book.
- There is a **Vocabulary activity** for each File of the Student Book.
- There are six **Song activities**. These can be used as part of the main lesson in the Student Book or in a later lesson. The recording of the song can be found in the main lesson on the Class Audio CD.

Using extra activities in mixed-ability classes

Some teachers have classes with a very wide range of abilities, and where some students finish Student Book activities much more quickly than others. You could give these students a photocopiable activity (either Communicative or Grammar) while you help the slower students. Alternatively, some teachers might want to give faster students extra oral practice with a communicative activity while slower students consolidate their knowledge with an extra grammar activity.

Tips for using Grammar activities

The Grammar activities are designed to give students extra practice in the main grammar point from each lesson. How you use these activities depends on the needs and abilities of your students and time you have available. They can be used in the lesson if you think all of your class would benefit from the extra practice, or you could assign them as homework for some or all of your students.

- All of the activities start with a writing stage. If you use the activities in class, have students work individually or in pairs. Allow students to compare before checking the answers.
- Many of the activities have a final section that has students cover the sentences and test their memory. If you are using the activities in class, students can work in pairs and test their partner. If you assign them for homework, encourage students to use this stage to test themselves.
- If students are having trouble with any of the activities, make sure they refer to the relevant Grammar Bank in the Student Book.
- Make sure that students keep their copies of the activities and that they review any difficult areas regularly. Encourage them to go back to activities and cover and test themselves. This will help with their review.

Tips for using Communicative activities

- We have suggested the ideal number of copies for each activity. However, you can often manage with fewer, e.g., one copy per pair instead of one per student.
- When SS are working in pairs, if possible, have them sit face to face. This will encourage them to really talk to each other and also means they can't see each other's sheets.
- For pairwork, if your class has an odd number of SS, take part yourself, have two SS share one role, or have one student monitor, help, and correct.
- If some SS finish early, they can change roles and do the activity again, or you could have them write some of the sentences from the activity.

introduction a

2 a   3 b   4 c   5 c   6 a   7 b   8 c   9 a   10 a   11 a
12 b   13 a   14 b   15 a   16 c   17 c   18 b   19 b   20 a

introduction b

3 I have / 've lived   4 My **husband's** name's Pedro
5 We don't have **any** children   6 ✓   7 we'd like **to have**
8 We are looking **for an apartment**   9 ✓   10 Pedro is **an**
engineer   11 work very **hard**   12 we don't have **to do**
13 ✓   14 **much** free time   15 ✓   16 ✓
17 I don't have **enough time**   18 I want **to be**   19 ✓
20 I **often make** mistakes   21 ✓   22 to take

1A   present tenses: simple and continuous

a   2 I'm majoring   3 do you come   4 do you have
5 It depends   6 Are you going   7 Do you mean
8 I need   9 I'm moving   10 are you living
11 I'm staying   12 are you doing   13 want
14 I'm meeting

b   2 'm visiting   3 don't mind   4 are you staying
5 'm going   6 do you like   7 Do you know   8 comes
9 are you doing   10 're waiting   11 do you live
12 aren't doing   13 Are you carrying   14 have
15 Do you want   16 says

1B   past tenses

2 hadn't studied   3 was raining   4 arrived
5 had already started   6 couldn't   7 had ever given
8 was sitting   9 was writing   10 looked
11 was standing   12 wasn't looking   13 threw
14 had already finished   15 called   16 was holding
17 had / 'd both failed   18 had / 'd written

1C   future forms

2 c   3 b and c   4 b and c   5 a   6 a   7 c
8 a and c   9 a and c   10 a   11 c   12 b and c

2A   present perfect and simple past

a   2 I've been   3 did you go   4 finished
5 I've already been   6 did you go   7 went

b   2 taught   3 came back   4 have you been   5 was
6 started   7 haven't finished   8 have you been   9 had
10 did you meet   11 went   12 've known
13 got   14 were you   15 met

2B   present perfect continuous

2 A How long has it been raining?
   B It's been raining since yesterday morning.
3 A How long have you had that jacket?
   B I've had it for ten years.
4 A How long has he been working / worked here?
   B He's been working / worked here since he graduated.
5 A How long have they been married?
   B They've been married for 60 years.
6 A How long have you been studying Chinese?
   B I've been studying Chinese for three years.

b   2 Have you been waiting   3 have you been doing
4 I've been shopping   5 've been playing
6 've been watching

2C   comparatives and superlatives

2 **more nervous** than   3 ✓   4 ✓   5 **nicer** than
6 the **worst** one   7 ✓   8 ✓   9 ✓   10 **lazier** than
11 the highest divorce rate **in** the world   12 **more slowly**
13 the **best** chocolate cake   14 ✓   15 as cold **as**
16 **the** most affectionate   17 **hotter** than   18 ✓
19 same school **as**   20 ✓

3A   must, have to, should

a   2 must not   3 ✓   4 had to   5 ✓   6 don't have to

b   2 don't have to   3 must / have to   4 should
5 must not / shouldn't   6 must / have to   7 shouldn't
8 don't have to

3B   must, may, might, can't

a   2 might   3 must   4 can't   5 may

b   1 must   2 might not / may not, must
3 might / may, can't, must   4 might / may, can't, must

3C   can, could, be able to

a   2 ✓   3 be able to   4 be able to   5 ✓   6 will be able to
7 ✓   8 ✓   9 being able to   10 ✓

b   2 be able to   3 can't   4 been able to   5 could
6 be able to   7 being able to   8 can   9 couldn't
10 could   11 be able to

4A   future time clauses: if, when, etc.

2 finish   3 'll text   4 finishes   5 Come   6 can
7 don't call   8 get   9 're / are   10 are
11 won't be able to   12 pass   13 meet   14 don't study
15 won't have

4B   second conditional

a   2 had, could   3 would be, didn't go out
4 shared, would get along   5 went, wouldn't be
6 painted, wouldn't look   7 would feel, went
8 wouldn't argue, didn't borrow   9 didn't have to, could
10 did, would improve

b   2 could   3 don't reduce   4 see   5 were   6 doesn't take
7 had   8 wouldn't drive   9 won't eat   10 would look

4C   used to

2 don't live   3 used to dream   4 used to be
5 didn't use to worry   6 used to share   7 don't go
8 didn't use to like   9 don't ride   10 used to ride
11 spend   12 didn't use to be   13 didn't use to eat
14 used to have

5A   quantifiers

2 too much   3 a lot of   4 little   5 How many   6 None
7 a lot of   8 enough time   9 any   10 plenty   11 A few
12 little   13 too   14 few   15 too much   16 enough
17 no

5B   articles: a, an, the, no article

a   2 a   3 a   4 The   5 the   6 a   7 The   8 a   9 a   10 (−)
11 (−)   12 the   13 The   14 (−)

b   1 (−)   2 (−)   3 a   4 a   5 a   6 the   7 a   8 a   9 the

c   1 (−)   2 (−)   3 The   4 (−)   5 a   6 (−)   7 a   8 a
9 (−)   10 the   11 a   12 (−)   13 (−)   14 the

5C gerunds and infinitives

a 2 spending   3 to talk   4 to be able   5 to explain
6 going   7 to spend   8 to know   9 to ask   10 to read
11 guessing   12 to do

b 2 to do   3 Getting   4 losing   5 to wait   6 being / to be
7 thinking   8 to ask   9 to go   10 to make

c 2 to go   3 to go   4 go   5 go   6 to go   7 go

6A reported speech

a 2 would have to   3 were going to   4 this could
5 'd / had just come   6 'd / had agreed   7 hoped
8 would agree   9 had to

b 1 who he thought would be the next president of the UN
2 if more countries would be present at the next meeting
3 if he had discussed that with the US president
4 what the rich countries should do to eliminate world
   poverty

c 1 asked us to put our seat belts on
2 told her boyfriend not to worry   3 told us not to cheat
4 asked his friend to slow down   5 asked me not to tell

6B passive: *be* + past participle

a 2 were used   3 will be seen   4 have been made
5 was nominated   6 was paid   7 was being made, was asked
8 had been murdered   9 were used   10 are being made

b 2 was directed   3 is set   4 is sent   5 takes   6 speaks
7 falls   8 is rescued   9 learns   10 was written
11 have been sold

6C relative clauses

a 2 that   3 that   4 that   5 who / that   6 that   7 where
8 who / that   9 whose

b 2, 3, 4, 6

c 3, 6

d 2 whose best-known painting is *Guernica*
3 which is the capital of Australia
4 where I used to work
5 whose daughter is the local doctor
6 who died in 2005
7 which was the worst for over 75 years
8 who is a clothes designer

7A third conditional

a 2 I wouldn't have won this Oscar if it hadn't been for my
   wonderful director.
3 If you had listened to me, you wouldn't have married
   him.
4 I would have passed my test if I hadn't driven through a
   red light.
5 If I had known that the letter was important, I wouldn't
   have thrown it away.
6 He wouldn't have forgotten their anniversary if he
   had written it in his calendar.

b 2 would have / 've arrived, hadn't got
3 had / 'd known, would have / 've taken
4 would have / 've done, hadn't been
5 hadn't taken, would have / 've gotten
6 hadn't sat, would never have met

7B tag questions, indirect questions

a 2 are you   3 aren't you   4 are you   5 have you
6 wouldn't you   7 don't you   8 didn't I   9 can't you
10 isn't it   11 didn't you

b 2 what time the bank opens   3 if this train goes
4 how this photocopier works   5 if there's a hotel near
here

7C phrasal verbs

a 2 out   3 in   4 on   5 up   6 out   7 down   8 off

b 2 going   3 growing   4 get   5 calm   6 set   7 go

c 2 ✗ write **them down**   3 ✓   4 ✗ is looking **for a new job**
5 ✓   6 ✗ I pick **you up**   7 ✓   8 ✓   9 ✓
10 ✗ Give **it back**

review and check

1 finishes
2 studying
3 hadn't locked
4 was raining
5 have you been studying
6 won't be able to
7 did
8 see
9 've / have had
10 need
11 didn't watch
12 'll
13 be
14 to go
15 not to tell
16 works
17 would have seen
18 will win / is going to win
19 's / is being repaired
20 've / have been working

● Circle the correct answer, a, b, or c.

1 My brother _____ a job at the moment.
   a hasn't   b don't have   c doesn't have

2 _____ Mr. Roberts live here?
   a Does   b Is   c Do

3 My dad _____ at the university.
   a teachs   b teaches   c teach

4 I _____ to the movies with Katie tonight. I've bought the tickets.
   a go   b will go   c 'm going

5 I _____ back from New York this morning.
   a flied   b flown   c flew

6 He didn't _____ the vacation very much.
   a like   b liked   c likes

7 What _____ you do if there were a snake in your room?
   a will   b would   c did

8 A I'm thirsty.

   B _____ get you a drink.
   a Will I   b I going to   c I'll

9 A I have a new cell phone.
   B I'm sure you _____ it, just like your last one.
   a 'll lose   b 're losing   c lose

10 A Would you like something to eat?
   B No, thanks, _____ lunch.
   a I've already had   b I already have had
   c I've had already

11 Have you ever _____ to Paris?
   a been   b go   c went

12 The traffic is _____ than it used to be.
   a badder   b worse   c more bad

13 Cycling isn't as dangerous _____ skiing.
   a as   b than   c that

14 I _____ a shower when the water stopped working.
   a took   b was taking   c were taking

15 I'll come to your party if I _____ work early enough.
   a finish   b will finish   c finished

16 You drive much _____ than me.
   a slowly   b slowlier   c more slowly

17 If I _____ you, I'd look for a new job.
   a was   b am   c were

18 My bike _____ last week.
   a is stolen   b was stolen   c stole

19 We were too late. When we arrived at the station, the train _____.
   a already left   b had already left
   c has already left

20 "I love you." He said he _____ her.
   a loved   b love   c is loving

ⓐ Read about Fernanda. Then look at the **bold** phrases. Put a check (✓) next to the phrases that are right and correct the wrong ones.

My name's Fernanda. **I'm 26** and I'm from Brazil.

I am born in Recife and **I live** there all my life.

I'm married. **My husband name's Pedro**. He's from Recife, too.

We don't have some children. We live with Pedro's parents in

their apartment, **and I get along with them** very well, but

we'd like having our own place. **We are looking an apartment for** at

the moment. **I work for** a bank and **Pedro is engineer**.

We both **work very hardly**, but **we don't have do** the housework.

Pedro's parents are retired, so they **help us to take** care of the house.

I don't have **many free time**, but when I have the chance

I enjoy listening to music. **I used to play** the piano,

but now **I don't have time enough**. I'm learning English because

I need it for my job. My speaking is OK, but **I want be**

better at writing. **I have to write** letters and e-mails in English

and **I make often mistakes**.

Next summer **I'm going to go to** the US **for take** an economics course.

1	✓		
2	*I was born*	3	
4			
5			
6			
7		8	
9		10	
11		12	
13			
14			
15		16	
17			
18			
19			
20			
21		22	

ⓑ Write a similar paragraph about yourself, where you live, your work and / or studies, your hobbies, and why you are learning English.

139

American English File 3 Teacher's Book
Photocopiable © Oxford University Press 2008

a Circle the correct form of the verbs.

LAURA ¹What **do you study /** are you studying ?
VICTOR Political science.
LAURA ²**I major / I'm majoring** in social anthropology. Where ³**do you come / are you coming** from?
VICTOR I'm from Lima, in Peru.
LAURA How many hours of classes ⁴**do you have / are you having** a day?
VICTOR ⁵**It depends / It's depending** on the day, but usually four. ⁶**Do you go / Are you going** to the party tonight?
LAURA ⁷**Do you mean / Are you meaning** the one for new students? I can't, because ⁸**I need / I'm needing** to get organized tonight. ⁹**I move / I'm moving** to a rented apartment tomorrow.
VICTOR Where ¹⁰**do you live / are you living** right now?
LAURA ¹¹**I stay / I'm staying** with friends.
VICTOR What ¹²**do you do / are you doing** on Sunday afternoon? If you ¹³**want / are wanting**, we could meet and look around the city.
LAURA ¹⁴**I meet / I'm meeting** some friends in the afternoon. What about Sunday morning?
VICTOR Fine. Where should we meet?

b Complete the dialogues with the correct form of the verbs in parentheses: simple present or present continuous.

DRIVER So, What ¹ _are you doing_ (do) here in Chicago, sir?
MAN I ² _____ (visit) some clients.
DRIVER Where are you from? You ³ _____ (not mind) my asking, do you?
MAN Not at all. From Inchon, in Korea.
DRIVER Good place to be! Me, I'm from Kansas. How long ⁴ _____ (stay) here?
MAN Three days. I ⁵ _____ (go) home on Saturday.
DRIVER OK. Hey, ⁶ _____ (like) steak? ⁷ _____ (know) where the best steak in all of America ⁸ _____ (come) from? That's right – Kansas!

POLICEMAN What ⁹ _____ (do) here?
JOSH Nothing. Why?
POLICEMAN We ask the questions here.
JOSH We ¹⁰ _____ (wait) for someone.
POLICEMAN Where ¹¹ _____ (live)?
JOSH 151 Penn Street.
POLICEMAN What are your names?
JOSH I'm Josh and he's my brother, Wayne. We ¹² _____ (not do) anything illegal, are we?
POLICEMAN ¹³ _____ (carry) any form of identification?
JOSH Yes. I ¹⁴ _____ (have) my driver's license. ¹⁵ _____ (want) to see it? Here!
POLICEMAN It ¹⁶ _____ (say) John Allen on this license.
JOSH Does it? Oh yes, it's my dad's.

American English File 3 Teacher's Book
Photocopiable © Oxford University Press 2008

a Complete the text with the correct form of the verbs in parentheses: simple past, past continuous, or past perfect.

My test **nightmare**

I ¹ _woke up_ (wake up) on the morning of the math test with a horrible feeling in my stomach. I knew that I ² _____ (not study) enough the night before and that I was going to fail.

When I left home it ³ _____ (rain) and there was a lot of traffic. I ⁴ _____ (arrive) five minutes late and the test ⁵ _____ (already / start). I sat down quickly and looked at the questions. I ⁶ _____ (not can) answer any of them! It was the most difficult test the teacher ⁷ _____ (ever / give) us.

I ⁸ _____ (sit) next to one of my friends, Sophie, and I could see that she ⁹ _____ (write) very quickly. She was great at math. Suddenly I had an idea. I ¹⁰ _____ (look) at the teacher, Mr. Everitt. He ¹¹ _____ (stand) by the window and he ¹² _____ (not look) at us. I wrote a message on a piece of paper and ¹³ _____ (throw) it to Sophie. It said "I need help." Sophie ¹⁴ _____ (already / finish) the test. She copied the answers on a piece of paper and quickly passed it to me.

The following day Mr. Everitt ¹⁵ _____ (call) us both to his room. We saw that he ¹⁶ _____ (hold) my test, and Sophie's, too. He told us that we ¹⁷ _____ (both / fail) the test. We ¹⁸ _____ (write) exactly the same answers for every question, including several wrong answers.

b Cover the text and try to remember the story.

● Circle the best answer. Sometimes two answers are possible.

1 A _____?

   B Tomorrow. My flight is in the morning.

   a When will you leave

   (b) When are you leaving

   (c) When are you going to leave

2 A You must bring the money tomorrow.

   B Don't worry, _____.

   a I'm not forgetting

   b I'm not going to forget

   c I won't forget

3 A Do you have any plans for tonight?

   B Yes, _____.

   a I'll meet some friends

   b I'm going to meet some friends

   c I'm meeting some friends

4 A The interviews for the new manager were yesterday.

   B I think _____.

   a Bob is getting the job

   b Bob is going to get the job

   c Bob will get the job

5 A This suitcase is too heavy for me.

   B _____.

   a I'll carry it for you

   b I'm carrying it for you

   c I'm going to carry it for you

6 A What would you like to drink?

   B _____.

   a I'll have a cappuccino, please

   b I'm going to have a cappuccino, please

   c I'm having a cappuccino, please

7 A Here's my e-mail address.

   B Thanks. _____ tomorrow.

   a I'm going to send you the photos

   b I'm sending you the photos

   c I'll send you the photos

8 A _____ this weekend?

   B No, I have to work on Saturday.

   a Are you going to go away

   b Will you go away

   c Are you going away

9 A Miami is playing Dallas tomorrow.

   B I'm sure _____.

   a they'll lose

   b they're losing

   c they're going to lose

10 A My train arrives at 2:15.

   B OK, _____ by the information desk.

   a I'll meet you

   b I'm going to meet you

   c I'm meeting you

11 A What time does the movie start?

   B I don't know. _____ call the movie theater and check.

   a Will I

   b Am I going to

   c I'll

12 A Do I need to bring an umbrella?

   B No, I don't think _____.

   a it rains

   b it'll rain

   c it's going to rain

11–12 **Excellent.** You can use different future forms very well.

7–10 **Good,** but check the rules in the Grammar Bank (Student Book page 130) for any questions that you got wrong.

0–6 **This is difficult for you.** Read the rules in the Grammar Bank (Student Book page 130). Then ask your teacher for another photocopy and do the exercise again at home.

a Circle the correct verbs.

STEVE   So, where should we go for our honeymoon?

NATALIE   I don't know. [1]Have you ever (been)/ went to Thailand?

STEVE   Yes, [2]**I've been / I've went** there twice.

NATALIE   I didn't know that. When [3]**have you been / did you go** there?

STEVE   The year after I [4]**have finished / finished** college.

NATALIE   What about Vietnam?

STEVE   [5]**I've already been / I already gone** there, too.

NATALIE   Yes? Who [6]**have you been / did you go** with?

STEVE   With an ex-girlfriend. But we only [7]**have been / went** to Hanoi. Let's go there.

NATALIE   No, let's go somewhere else.

b Complete the dialogues with the correct form of the verbs in parentheses: simple past or present perfect.

A   [1] _Have you taught_ (you / teach) English abroad before, Mr. Cooper?

B   Yes, I [2]_____ (teach) from 2001 to 2003 in Taiwan, and I [3]_____ (come back) from a six-month job in Japan yesterday.

A   How long [4]_____ (you / be) a language teacher?

B   For eight years. Before that I [5]_____ (be) a public school teacher for two years.

A   Do you have a graduate degree?

B   I [6]_____ (start) a part-time MA at City University two years ago, but I [7]_____ (not finish) it yet.

A   How long [8]_____ (you / be) married, Dave?

B   Ten years. Anna and I [9]_____ (have) our anniversary last month.

A   Where [10]_____ (you / meet) Anna? At work?

B   No, we [11]_____ (go) to the same school as kids. We [12]_____ (know) each other since we were five years old. What about you?

A   I'm divorced. I [13]_____ (get) divorced last year.

B   How long [14]_____ (you / be) married?

A   Only three years.

B   So you're on your own now?

A   Yes, but I [15]_____ (meet) someone new last week. We're going out this weekend.

143

a Complete the questions and answers with the present perfect continuous **or** present perfect simple and *for* or *since*.

1 **A** How long *have they been playing together*? (they / play together)

  B They *'ve been playing together since* 1985.

2 **A** How long _____? (it / rain)

  B It _____ yesterday morning.

3 **A** How long _____? (you / have that jacket)

  B Let me think. I _____ ten years.

4 **A** How long _____? (he / work here)

  B He _____ he graduated.

5 **A** How long _____? (they / be married)

  B They _____ 60 years.

6 **A** How long _____? (you / study Chinese)

  B I _____ three years.

b Look at the pictures. What have they been doing? Complete with a verb in the present perfect continu⟨ous⟩

1 He 's ___*been cooking*___ .

2 Sorry I'm late. _____ for a long time?

3 You're filthy. What _____?

4 I'm exhausted. _____ all morning.

5 They _____ for an hour.

6 They _____ a sad movie.

c Cover the sentences. Look at the pictures and remember the sentences.

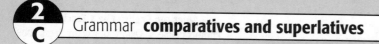
● Put a check (✓) next to the sentences that are right and correct the wrong ones.

1 This painting looks ~~the same than~~ *the same as* the other one.

2 Coffee makes you **nervouser than** tea.

3 This is **the most beautiful country** I've ever been to.

4 He doesn't speak English **as well as** his wife.

5 Are those jeans new? They're **more nice than** your other ones.

6 Her last novel was **the worse** one she has written.

7 Do football players earn **less money than** soccer players?

8 This club is very expensive. Should we go somewhere **a little cheaper**?

9 Do you think Americans **work harder than** Japanese people?

10 Meredith is **more lazy than** her sister.

11 The US has **the highest divorce rate of the world**.

12 Can you speak **slowlier** please? I can't understand you.

13 That was delicious. It's **the better chocolate cake** I've ever eaten.

14 Which athlete has won **the most Olympic medals**?

15 I hope this winter isn't **as cold than** the last one!

16 Ben is **most affectionate** of all my nieces and nephews.

17 July is usually **hoter than** June here.

18 Do girls learn languages **more easily than** boys?

19 I go to **the same school that** your sister.

20 Driving is **much more dangerous than** flying.

18–20	**Excellent.** You can use comparatives and superlatives very well.
13–17	**Good**, but check the rules in the Grammar Bank (Student Book page 132) for any questions that you got wrong.
0–12	**This is difficult for you**. Read the rules in the Grammar Bank (Student Book page 132). Then ask your teacher for another photocopy and do the exercise again at home.

a Circle the correct verb. Put a check (✓) next to the sentence if both are possible.

1 A Did you see that movie last night?
  B Yes, it was wonderful. You **must / should** go and see it. ✓

2 When you open the photocopier, you **must not / don't have to** touch this part here; it's very hot.

3 You **should / have to** get a visa if you want to go to Russia.

4 In the early 1960s, in the US, young men **must / had to** do military service.

5 You **must not / shouldn't** be late. Once the concert has started, you can't go in.

6 When you drive across many European Union borders, you **must not / don't have to** show your passport.

b Complete the sentences with *must, must not, have to, don't have to, should,* or *shouldn't*.

1 You ___have to___ pay for food and drink separately.
2 You _____ leave a tip in this restaurant.
3 You _____ fasten your seat belt now.
4 You _____ drink this wine at 14 to 16°C.
5 Hotel staff _____ go into this room.
6 If you're in transit, you _____ go to the American Airways desk.
7 You _____ eat this after March 4th.
8 You _____ have any experience to work here.

❶ Please pay for food and drink separately
❷ Service included. Tip optional
❸ Fasten seat belt
❹ Chilean red wine: ideal temperature 14–16°C
❺ Do not disturb
❻ Transit passengers please report to American Airways desk
❼ Best consumed before March 4th
❽ Salespeople required. No experience necessary

146

a Circle the correct verbs.

A Isn't that Grant Duncan, over there?

B No, it ¹(can't)/ must be. He lives in New York now.

A I'm sure it's Grant.

B Well, I suppose it ²can't / might be him. But his hair is very gray. Grant doesn't have gray hair.

A But it ³must / can't be three years since we last saw him. A man's hair can go gray in three years.

B Who's the woman he's with? She ⁴can't / might not be his wife, can she?

A No, I'm sure it isn't his wife. I think it ⁵may / can't be his daughter. She looks just like him. Should we go and say hello?

b Complete the dialogues with *must, might, might not,* or *can't.*

1 A This pizza ____can't____ be for me. It looks like a margherita and I ordered a pepperoni.

B It _____ be mine, then. I ordered a margherita.

2 A What time is Jane coming?

B She wasn't sure. She's working late. She said she _____ be here until 8:30 or 9:00.

A She _____ be very busy, then.

3 A Which city is this?

B I'm not sure. It _____ be Rome.

A No, it _____ be Italy. The street sign is in French.

B It _____ be Paris, then. That's the only place I've been to in France.

4 A Can you help me finish this crossword puzzle? I can't do eight across.

B Let's see. An animal found in Australia. It _____ be *kangaroo* or maybe *crocodile.*

B It _____ be *kangaroo*. It ends in a *y*. I know! It _____ be *wallaby.*

A That's right. Well done!

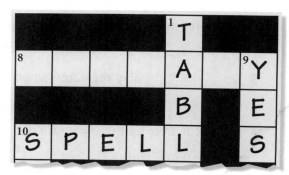

a Circle the correct verbs. Put a check (✓) if both are possible.

Tango dancing

I decided to try to learn tango about six months ago. I've never ¹(**been able to**) / **could** dance well, though both my parents are good dancers. I thought: well, if they ²**could** / **were able to** do it, I should ³**can** / **be able to** learn, too. But the tango's not an easy dance to learn, because the steps aren't fixed, and every eight steps the man has to decide what move he's going to make, and he has to ⁴**can** / **be able to** transmit that to his partner. My first partner and I ⁵**weren't able to** / **couldn't** understand each other at all, so she changed partners. I think my new partner understands me better, so I hope we ⁶**will can** / **will be able to** dance well soon.

Irish

As my grandparents are Irish, I thought I should learn to speak the language. I found a school and started going to classes, but the first problem was that I ⁷**couldn't** / **wasn't able to** go to class every week, and the second was that it's a very difficult language. Also, I ⁸**wasn't able to** / **couldn't** find the time to do much homework, and trying to learn a language without ⁹**can** / **being able to** study between classes is almost impossible. If ¹⁰**I can** / **I'm able to** find time to go to Ireland in the summer, I'll definitely try again.

Céad mille failte!

b Complete the sentences where possible with *can* / *can't* or *could* / *couldn't*. If neither is possible, complete with a form of *be able to*.

1 I started reading *War and Peace*, but I ___couldn't___ finish it. It was too long.

2 I've invited Mark to the party, but I don't think he'll _____ come.

3 You _____ park there. There's not enough room.

4 I want to buy a new car next year, but I haven't _____ save much money yet.

5 He _____ play the piano when he was only four years old.

6 If that car were a little cheaper, I'd _____ buy it.

7 I like _____ do what I want when I'm on vacation.

8 We don't have to buy the tickets now – we _____ get them on the train.

9 I didn't enjoy the movie because I _____ understand what was going on.

10 Excuse me, do you think you _____ help me with my bags?

11 We won't _____ meet tonight, I'm working.

American English File 3 Teacher's Book
Photocopiable © Oxford University Press 2008

● Complete the e-mails with the verbs in the correct form: simple present, imperative, or *will* + base form.

Time: 11:05
Sender: Corinne
Subject: Final exams!

Hi Elena,

How's it going? I'm studying hard, but I need a break. We could meet tomorrow night for dinner. I [1]____*'ll call*____ (call) you when I [2]_____ (finish) class tomorrow, OK?

Love, Corinne

Time: 11:07
Sender: Elena
Subject: RE: Final exams!

Hi Corinne,

I'm studying too. My first exam is tomorrow afternoon. I'm really worried about it. OK for tomorrow night, but not too early. I [3]_____ (text) you when the exam [4]_____ (finish).

Love, Elena

Time: 11:08
Sender: Corinne
Subject: RE: Final exams!

OK. [5]_____ (come) to my place as soon as you [6]_____ (can). We can order a take-out pizza or something.

Time: 11:09
Sender: Elena
Subject: RE: Final exams!

OK, but [7]_____ (not call) until I [8]_____ (get) there. I might be late. I've been thinking, if you [9]_____ (be) free when all our exams [10]_____ (be) over in June, why don't we go away for a few days?

Time: 11:10
Sender: Corinne
Subject: RE: Final exams!

Great idea! But I [11]_____ (not be able to) go away unless I [12]_____ (pass) all the exams! We can talk about it when we [13]_____ (meet) here tomorrow night.

Time: 11:11
Sender: Elena
Subject: RE: Final exams!

OK. Time to go back to work. If I [14]_____ (not study) a little more tonight, I [15]_____ (not have) any chance of passing biology tomorrow. See you tomorrow, and wish me luck!

a Complete the sentences with the correct form of the verbs in parentheses to make second conditional sentences.

1 I _wouldn't be_ (not be) so broke if I ____spent____ (spend) a little less on going out.

2 If I _____ (have) more money, I _____ (can) travel next summer.

3 My parents _____ (be) happier if I _____ (not go out) so much.

4 Maybe if I _____ (share) an apartment with friends, I _____ (get along) better with my parents.

5 If I _____ (go) to bed earlier, I _____ (not be) so tired all the time.

6 If I _____ (paint) my room white, maybe it _____ (not look) so depressing.

7 I _____ (feel) a lot better if I _____ (go) to the gym more.

8 I _____ (not argue) with my brother if he _____ (not borrow) my things all the time.

9 If my girlfriend _____ (not have to) work so hard, we _____ (can) see each other more often.

10 If I _____ (do) something with my life instead of just thinking about it, maybe things _____ (improve).

b First or second conditional? Complete the sentences with a verb from the list in the correct form.

can   be   ~~catch~~   not drive   not eat   not take   look   have   not reduce   see

1 If we hurry, _we 'll catch_ the earlier train. It leaves in three minutes.

2 If it weren't so windy, we _____ have lunch outside.

3 They'll never sell their house if they _____ the price.

4 If you _____ James, tell him to call me. I need to speak to him urgently.

5 If I _____ you, I'd buy the black dress. It's much more "you."

6 He won't pass his driving test if he _____ a few more lessons.

7 If I _____ more time, I'd do it myself.

8 I _____ to work if public transportation were better in this town.

9 Gavin _____ that soup if it has meat in it. He's a strict vegetarian.

10 Your sister _____ much better if she cut her hair a little shorter.

Pablo and Luciana as students

Pablo and Luciana today

● Look at the table and complete the sentences with a correct form of *used to* or the simple present.

	then	now
Occupation	university students	Pablo: journalist, Luciana: psychologist
Residence	Buenos Aires, Argentina	Barcelona, Spain
Hopes and dreams	go into politics	that their son is happy and successful
Personality	relaxed, almost lazy	very worried about work; hardworking
House	shared an apartment with other students	own apartment, with 18-year-old son
Vacations	hitchhiking	go to small apartment on the Costa Brava
Musical tastes	pop and rock; Luciana: disco	jazz, classical, tango
Vehicle	bikes; Pablo: an old scooter	cars; son has motorcycle
Clothes	informal	similar, but more expensive taste
Body type	slim	getting a little overweight
Food	vegetarians	omnivores
Friends	lots of friends	just a few close friends

1 Pablo _____*works*_____ as a journalist. **work**

2 They _____ in Argentina anymore. **not live**

3 They _____ of going into politics. **dream**

4 They _____ a little lazy. **be**

5 They _____ about work. **not worry**

6 They _____ an apartment with other students. **share**

7 They _____ hitchhiking anymore. **not go**

8 Luciana _____ listening to jazz. **not like**

9 They _____ bikes anymore. **not ride**

10 Pablo _____ an old scooter. **ride**

11 They _____ more on clothes than before. **spend**

12 Luciana _____ overweight. **not be**

13 They _____ meat, but they do now. **eat**

14 They _____ lots of friends. **have**

American English File 3 Teacher's Book
Photocopiable © Oxford University Press 2008

Two presidential candidates are having a debate on live TV.

ⓐ Circle the correct answer for each blank.

A After four years in government, what have you done? Look at the state of the country: there isn't ▢▢▢ money for Social Security, there's ▢▢▢ unemployment, and ▢▢▢ children are failing in school.

B Our problem is that we have had very ▢▢▢ time to repair the damage that your government did before us. ▢▢▢ people were happy with the education system when you were in government? ▢▢▢!

A Nonsense! You don't know what you're doing! And ▢▢▢ people in your own party are now saying that, too. You say you haven't had ▢▢▢? I say you don't have ▢▢▢ ideas!

B We have ▢▢▢ of ideas, and they're working! ▢▢▢ years ago our economy was getting worse; not anymore. We have very ▢▢▢ unemployment now, compared to when you were in office. The people of this country are ▢▢▢ intelligent to believe your ideas again.

A Really? Well, I think very ▢▢▢ of them will be convinced by your arguments.

B The problem is that your party spends ▢▢▢ time insulting the government, and not ▢▢▢ time thinking of new ideas.

C Thank you very much, gentlemen. I'm afraid we have ▢▢▢ more time today...

1 no / (enough)
2 too many / too much
3 a lot of / a lot
4 few / little

5 How much / How many
6 Any / None

7 much / a lot of
8 enough time / time enough
9 any / no
10 plenty / many
11 A few / A little
12 few / little

13 enough / too
14 few / little

15 too much / too
16 many / enough

17 any / no

ⓑ Now cover the words and look at the conversation. Try to remember the missing words.

American English File 3 Teacher's Book
Photocopiable © Oxford University Press 2008

● Complete the texts with *a, an, the,* or – (no article).

a

Apartment for rent

Located close to Gaudí's masterpiece, ¹ _the_ Sagrada
Familia, this apartment was built in 1993 and is ideal for
three people.
There are two bedrooms, one with ²_____ double bed
and one with ³_____ single bed. ⁴_____ windows of
⁵_____ large bedroom look onto ⁶_____ small balcony.
⁷_____ living room also has ⁸_____ balcony, with ⁹_____
table and ¹⁰_____ chairs so you can have ¹¹_____
breakfast in ¹²_____ sun.
¹³_____ apartment has ¹⁴_____ air-conditioning and
central heating.

b

Move your account to 24/7

24/7 is ¹_____ one of the country's leading 24-hour personal banks. You can take care of all
your banking needs by ²_____ telephone or online, at ³_____ time and place that is convenient
for you, 24 hours ⁴_____ day, 365 days ⁵_____ year. We haven't closed since ⁶_____ day we
opened in 2004. Our friendly and professional staff is always here to help you. You can call or
just click to check your account, pay ⁷_____ bill, or arrange ⁸_____ personal loan.

24/7

Why not do it today? Just complete ⁹_____ application form below
and e-mail it to us.

c

Hi Meg,
Hope all is well. Here ¹_____ life is a little hectic. Jim and I are really busy at ²_____ work – we hardly
ever have time to talk to each other. ³_____ children are all busy, too. Mark has his driving test ⁴_____
next Thursday. He should pass, because he has lessons three times ⁵_____ week. Tom is working hard
at ⁶_____ school – he has suddenly decided he wants to be ⁷_____ doctor! What ⁸_____ surprise!
Anna is fine – she just finished ⁹_____ elementary school. I must say she is definitely ¹⁰_____ easiest
of the three. I suppose that's because she's ¹¹_____ girl. There's no question that ¹²_____ girls are less
work than ¹³_____ boys.
Can't write more just now, I have to go to ¹⁴_____ store before it closes.
Love, Sue

a Circle the correct form.

JENNY So how's it going with Luke?

EMILY Well, not bad. He's quit ¹**smoking**/ **to smoke**, so that's good.

JENNY What about his friends?

EMILY They're OK. I don't mind ²**to spend / spending** time with them. They're nice.

JENNY But?

EMILY The thing is, although he says I'm easy ³**to talk / talking** to, we don't seem ⁴**to be able / being able** to communicate very well.

JENNY For example?

EMILY Well, it's difficult ⁵**to explain / explaining**. But for example, when I suggested ⁶**to go / going** away together, he was very enthusiastic, but when my family invited us ⁷**spending / to spend** a week in Arizona with them, he said "no," but he didn't say why. I need ⁸**knowing / to know** where this relationship is going.

JENNY Well, you need ⁹**to ask / asking** him. Don't expect him ¹⁰**to read / reading** your mind. Men aren't very good at ¹¹**to guess / guessing** what other people are thinking.

EMILY Well, I tried ¹²**to do / doing** that last Saturday… oh, there's my phone. Oh, it's him. Hi, Luke…

b Complete the conversation with the verbs in the gerund or infinitive.

ALEX So, have you decided ¹ ___to ask___ (**ask**) her, Luke?

LUKE Well, I was planning ² _____ (**do**) it yesterday, but then I didn't. What if she says "no?" ³ _____ (**get**) engaged is such a big step. She might think it's too soon. I'm worried about ⁴ _____ (**lose**) her.

ALEX You can't afford ⁵ _____ (**wait**) forever. You love her, don't you?

LUKE Uh, yes, of course. And I love ⁶ _____ (**be**) with her, I can't stop ⁷ _____ (**think**) about her.

ALEX Then do it. Call her now. Invite her out for dinner, somewhere really romantic.

LUKE You're right. I'll call her now. … Hi, Emily. I just called ⁸ _____ (**ask**) you if you're doing anything on Friday night. Would you like ⁹ _____ (**go**) out to dinner? … At Café du Marché… OK. Great. I'll pick you up at 8:00. … No, I won't forget ¹⁰ _____ (**make**) a reservation…

c Complete with *to go* or *go*.

1 I really should ___go___ now. It's getting late.

2 I have _____ to the bank before it closes.

3 When I was a child I used _____ to the beach every summer.

4 Should I _____ to the supermarket, or will you?

5 My dad won't let me _____ to the Halloween party tonight.

6 Will you be able _____ to the party next weekend?

7 My parents always made me _____ to bed early.

a Read the journalist's interview. Then complete her report with the **bold** verbs in the correct tense.

JOURNALIST Dr. Makele, you said recently in New York that big changes are necessary if we want to avoid a global catastrophe. What changes were you thinking of?

DR. MAKELE Well, first, we ¹**cannot** continue to use up the world's natural resources at the present rate. Second, the richer countries ²**will have to** allow developing countries to export more. And third, we ³**are going to** have to devote more resources to fighting serious diseases.

JOURNALIST And how ⁴**can this** be done, Dr. Makele?

DR. MAKELE Well, ⁵I **just came** from a top-level meeting in Mexico City, and there we ⁶**agreed** on a series of proposals to take to next month's G8 meeting. I ⁷**hope** the richer nations ⁸**will agree** to help eliminate poverty in the next 20 years. At the same time, we ⁹**must** promote responsible government in the developing world.

Dr. Paul Makele of the United Nations told me that we ¹ _could not_ continue to use up the world's natural resources. He said that rich countries ² _____ allow developing countries to export more. He added that we ³ _____ have to devote more resources to fighting serious diseases. When I asked him how ⁴ _____ be done, he said that he ⁵ _____ from a top-level meeting in Mexico City where they ⁶ _____ on a series of proposals to take to next month's G8 summit. Dr. Makele said that he ⁷ _____ the richer nations ⁸ _____ to help eliminate poverty in the next 20 years. He said that we ⁹ _____ promote responsible government in the developing world.

b Write some other questions journalists asked Dr. Makele in reported speech.

1 Who do you think will be the next president of the UN?

1 Journalist 1 asked Dr. Makele _____.

2 Will more countries be present at the next meeting?

2 Journalist 2 asked him _____.

3 Have you discussed this with the US president?

3 Journalist 3 asked him _____.

4 What should the rich countries do to eliminate world poverty?

4 Journalist 4 asked him _____.

c Complete the reported imperatives / requests using *asked* or *told*.

Can you put your seat belts on, please?

1 The pilot _____ us _____.

Don't worry, Toni. Alex is only a friend.

2 She _____ her boyfriend _____ because Alex was only a friend.

Don't cheat!

3 The teacher _____ us _____.

Can you slow down, please?

4 He _____ his friend _____.

Please don't tell anybody.

5 My friend _____ me _____ anybody.

a Complete the sentences by putting the verbs into the correct passive tense.

DID YOU KNOW...?

1 The country with the smallest movie industry is Iceland, where only three movies ___*are made*___ every year. (**make**)

2 More than 26,000 costumes _____ in the 1963 movie *Cleopatra*. (**use**)

3 In the near future more movies _____ on computers than at the movie theater. (**see**)

4 The most filmed character is Sherlock Holmes. Until now, more than 200 different movies _____ about him. (**make**)

5 Spielberg's movie *The Color Purple* _____ for 11 Oscars in 1985, but didn't win any. (**nominate**)

6 Macaulay Culkin _____ $4.5 million dollars for his role in *Home Alone* in 1990. (**pay**) This was a record for a child at the time.

7 The director Stanley Kubrick died while his movie *Artificial Intelligence* _____ (**make**). Spielberg _____ to finish the movie. (**ask**)

8 When the actress Marilyn Monroe died of a drug overdose in 1962, many people believed that she _____ by the CIA. (**murder**)

9 Over 300,000 extras _____ for the crowd scenes in the movie *Gandhi* in 1982. (**use**)

10 At this very moment, thousands of movies _____ all over the world. (**make**)

b Active or passive? Circle the correct form.

Movies to collect on DVD: *The Piano*

The Piano [1](won)/ **was won** the Palme d'Or at the Cannes Film Festival in 1993. It [2]**directed / was directed** by Jane Campion, and it starred Holly Hunter and Harvey Keitel. It [3]**set / is set** in New Zealand in the 19th century, and is about a Scottish woman, Ada, who [4]**sends / is sent** there by her parents to marry a local man. She only [5]**takes / is taken** two things with her: her daughter and her piano. Ada never [6]**speaks / is spoken**, and has a very unhappy time with her new husband, who is a violent man. Ada [7]**falls / is fallen** in love with a neighbor and finally she [8]**rescues / is rescued** by him from her husband, and in her new life she [9]**learns / is learned** to speak again. The unforgettable soundtrack [10]**wrote / was written** by Michael Nyman, and millions of copies of the CD [11]**have sold / have been sold** all over the world.

a Complete the text with *who*, *that*, *where*, or *whose*.

A place? A song? A number? An object? A person? An animal? A store? A photo?

We ask readers to tell us about things that have a special meaning for them. This week, the TV actor Gavin Jones.

"Well, I've chosen Paris because it's the place ¹___*where*___ I lived for the first ten years of my life. A song? Well, that has to be Eurythmics singing *Sweet Dreams Are Made of This* because it was the song ²_____ was playing in the background in the cafe at the exact moment when I met my girlfriend. My number is 13. It's a number ³_____ some people think is unlucky, but it's my date of birth and it's lucky for me. For the object in my house, I have chosen an antique camera ⁴_____ was a present from my parents. The person is Kenneth Branagh. He's the actor ⁵_____ inspired me when I was a student. My animal is a cat, because they are the animals ⁶_____ I like most in the world. A store? That was easy – one called The Strand, in New York, because it's the place ⁷_____ I worked for a year after finishing college. And the last thing is a photo, a photo of someone ⁸_____ is very important in my life but ⁹_____ name I'm not going to tell you."

b In which sentences could you also use *which*?

c In which sentences could you leave out *who* or *that*?

d Combine the two sentences using a non-defining relative clause.

1 Our neighbors are both pharmacists. They work for the same pharmaceutical company.
   Our neighbors, __*who are both pharmacists*__, work for the same pharmaceutical company.

2 Pablo Picasso's best-known painting is *Guernica*. He was born in Málaga in 1881.
   Pablo Picasso, _____, was born in Málaga in 1881.

3 Canberra is the capital of Australia. It's smaller than Sydney and Melbourne.
   Canberra, _____, is smaller than Sydney and Melbourne.

4 Our local post office is closed. I used to work there.
   Our local post office, _____, is closed.

5 Mrs. Bradbury is my mother's best friend. Her daughter is the local doctor.
   Mrs. Bradbury, _____, is my mother's best friend.

6 George Best was possibly the most talented British soccer player of his generation. He died in 2005.
   George Best, _____, was possibly the most talented British soccer player of his generation.

7 The hurricane caused millions of dollars' worth of damage. It was the worst for over 75 years.
   The hurricane, _____, caused millions of dollars' worth of damage.

8 My sister is a clothes designer. She's opening her own company next month.
   My sister, _____, is opening her own company next month.

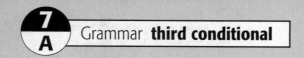

American English File 3 Teacher's Book
Photocopiable © Oxford University Press 2008

a Put the words in the correct order to make third conditional sentences.

1 would / ~~he~~ / scored / ~~if~~ / had / the / they / have / won / game

If he ___*had scored, they would have won the game*___ .

2 have / my / it / wonderful / won / hadn't / this / director / if / ~~I~~ / been / for / wouldn't / Oscar

I _____ .

3 married / ~~you~~ / you / him / wouldn't / ~~if~~ / listened / me / have / had / to

If you _____ .

4 test / driven / passed / red / ~~I~~ / light / would / I / have / my / if / a / hadn't / through

I _____ .

5 known / that / I / thrown / ~~if~~ / was / important / ~~I~~ / had / wouldn't / it / away / have / the letter

If I _____ .

6 in / had / their / ~~he~~ / calendar / if / his / forgotten / written / it / he / wouldn't / anniversary / have

He _____ .

b Put the verbs in parentheses in the correct tense to make third conditional sentences.

1 I _*would have enjoyed*_ (enjoy) college more if I _*had chosen*_ (chose) a different subject.

2 We _____ (arrive) half an hour earlier if we _____ (not get) lost.

3 If I _____ (know) how cold it was going to be in Boston, I _____ (take) a warmer coat.

4 Andrea _____ (do) much better on the test if she _____ (not be) so nervous.

5 It was raining a lot. If we _____ (not take) a taxi, we _____ (get) completely wet.

6 If we _____ (not sit) next to each other on the plane, we _____ (never / meet).

a Complete the dialogues with the correct tag questions.

MOTHER What is it, Paula? What's wrong?

PAULA Nothing.

MOTHER It's not school, [1] _is it_ ?

PAULA No, it's not school. School's OK.

MOTHER You aren't having problems with the other kids, [2]_____?

PAULA No, I'm not. Everything's fine, Mom.

MOTHER And you're enjoying school, [3]_____?

PAULA Enjoying school? I don't know; it's OK.

MOTHER You're not feeling sick, [4]_____?

PAULA I feel fine, Mom.

MOTHER You haven't had an argument with one of your friends, [5]_____?

PAULA Of course not. We never argue.

MOTHER Paula, you would tell me if something were wrong, [6]_____?

PAULA Yes, Mom. Now, will you please leave me alone?

FATHER You know how to print digital photos from the computer, [7]_____?

EMILY Yes, Dad, I told you how to do it last week, [8]_____?

FATHER But you can tell me how to do it again, [9]_____? I've done everything you said, but nothing's happening.

EMILY OK. The computer's turned on, [10]_____?

FATHER Of course it is. I'm not stupid.

EMILY And the printer?

FATHER What?

EMILY Oh, Dad, you forgot to turn the printer on again, [11]_____? Parents! They never learn.

b Complete the indirect questions that these people ask strangers.

1 Excuse me, could tell me _what this says_ ?

2 Excuse me, could you tell us _____ ?

3 Excuse me, could you tell us _____ to Boston?

4 Excuse me, do you know _____ ?

5 Excuse me, could you tell us _____ ?

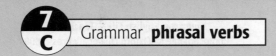

7C Grammar phrasal verbs

a Complete the text with the correct particles from the list.

on ~~back~~ down off in out (x2) up

"Hello, Dave? I tried calling earlier and you told me to call you
¹ ___back___ . Yes, I bought this computer yesterday and it doesn't work. And neither do the speakers or the webcam. Can you help me figure it ² _____? What? Of course I've plugged it ³ _____! And yes, I've turned it ⁴ _____, too. I tried to read the instructions, but I gave ⁵ _____. They don't make any sense. I can't find ⁶ _____ how to start it up. Dave, I can't hear you, can you turn ⁷ _____ the music, please?… What? You want me to turn it ⁸ _____ and start all over again? OK. Here we go…"

b Complete the text with the correct verbs from the list.

calm get go going growing ~~looking~~ set

"Oh yes, leaving the city and coming to live here was the best thing we've ever done. I have to tell you, I wasn't ¹ ___looking___ forward to it at all. I thought that I'd miss ² _____ out in the evenings, the movies, the theaters, and all the things you can do in a city. But we love it here. The kids are ³ _____ up in a clean, healthy environment, and they ⁴ _____ along very well with the other kids in the local school, so that's good. And we don't have to rush everywhere anymore, I've managed to ⁵ _____ down, which is exactly what my doctor told me to do. And Tom, that's my husband, has been able to ⁶ _____ up his own business and work from home. I wouldn't want to ⁷ _____ back to the city now."

c Are the **bold** phrases right (✓) or wrong (✗)? Correct the wrong ones.

1 I'm broke. **Can you pay me back** the money I lent you? ✓

2 These words are all new, so please **write down them**.

3 Your room's a mess. Please **put your clothes away**.

4 My sister is **looking a new job for**.

5 The game **will soon be over**.

6 Should **I pick up you** at the airport.

7 Can I **take my jacket off?** It's too hot in here.

8 Are you going **to try that dress on**? I think it'll look great on you.

9 **Could you fill this form out**, please, before the plane lands.

10 That's my book! **Give back it**!

● Put the verbs in parentheses in the correct form.

1 Do you know what time the movie _____? (**finish**)

2 Are you going to keep on _____ Korean next year? (**study**)

3 Five minutes after we left, I remembered that I_____ the back door. (**not lock**)

4 When I woke up this morning, I could hear that it _____ very hard. (**rain**)

5 **A** How long _____you _____ English? (**study**)

   B Since October.

6 I'm sorry, but I _____ come to the meeting on Wednesday. I'm away until Friday. (**be able to**)

7 He asked me what I _____ and I told him I was a lawyer. (**do**)

8 I'll tell him as soon as I _____ him. (**see**)

9 I _____ this computer for at least six years. I need a new one. (**have**)

10 I'm really tired at the moment. I _____ a vacation! (**need**)

11 If you _____ so much TV every night, you would have more time for reading. (**not watch**)

12 **A** I'm really hungry.

   B I _____ you a sandwich. (**make**)

13 You've been traveling all day. You must _____ exhausted. (**be**)

14 We can't afford _____ to that restaurant. It's too expensive. (**go**)

15 I told Jane _____ anybody, but of course she told everyone. (**not tell**)

16 He won't pass his final exams unless he _____ a lot harder. (**work**)

17 You _____ them if you'd arrived five minutes earlier. They just left. (**see**)

18 Who do you think _____ the game tomorrow? (**win**)

19 We can't use the elevator because it _____ at the moment. (**repair**)

20 **A** You look exhausted!

   B I am. I _____ in the garden all morning. (**work**)

18–20 **Excellent**. You can use the verb tenses from *American English File 3* very well.

13–17 **Good**, but check the rules in the Grammar Bank (Student Book pages 130–142) for any questions that you got wrong.

0–12 **This is difficult for you.** Read the rules in the Grammar Bank (Student Book pages 130–142). Then ask your teacher for another photocopy and do the exercise again at home.

Getting to know you

A pairwork activity

This photocopiable "getting to know you" activity can be used together with the Grammar activities on pages 138 and 139 as a first-day class, especially if your SS do not yet have the Student Book.

SS write information about themselves. They then exchange with a partner and ask each other to explain the information.

Copy one page of questions and spaces (**A** or **B**) per student.

> **LANGUAGE** General review of *American English File 2* grammar and vocabulary

- Put SS in pairs and give each student a chart and a sheet of instructions (**A** or **B**).
- Give SS five minutes to write answers in the appropriate spaces. When they have finished, take back the instruction sheet or tell them to turn it over.
- Now have SS exchange charts. Demonstrate the activity by taking a chart from a student and asking him / her *Why did you write…?* Ask follow-up questions to continue the conversation.
- SS now do the activity in pairs. Make it clear to them that they had different instructions, and stress that they can ask about the information in any order. Monitor and help where necessary. Stop the activity when most SS have asked about all their partner's information.

A time for everything

A pairwork information gap activity

SS read different parts of a text about chronobiology (the best time of day to do certain activities), and then share the information with their partner to establish the "ideal" daily routine. Copy one sheet per person.

> **LANGUAGE** Simple present
> Daily routine: *What time do you usually have lunch?*

- Put SS in pairs and give out the sheets.
- Focus on **a** and the chart. Point out that we are talking about when it is best for your body to do these activities, not when it suits you best. Elicit ideas for the first one (*have a big meal*) and tell SS to complete the chart with what they think.
- Set a time limit, e.g., five minutes, for SS to talk and complete the **We think** column.
- Now focus on the text, and read the introduction aloud with SS. Then have **A** read the first part of the article, and **B** the second part. **Tell SS not to read each other's text**. Monitor and help with any unknown vocabulary.
- Now in pairs, SS look at the chart and help each other complete the **Expert opinion** column with an exact time

(e.g., 7–8 a.m.), i.e. they must tell each other what is the best time (and why) to do the things they read about in *their* text.

- Check answers. Then have SS compare the answers with what they had predicted.

1	12–2 p.m.	**7**	8–10 p.m.
2	10–11 p.m.	**8**	7–9 a.m.
3	4–6 p.m.	**9**	6–8 p.m.
4	9–10 a.m.	**10**	3–5 p.m.
5	11 p.m.–7 a.m.	**11**	7–9 a.m.
6	10 a.m.–12		

Extra support SS could now exchange and read the other part of the article that they didn't read.

d Now ask SS how many of them have their big meal between 12 and 2, and find out what time the others have it and why. SS continue in pairs, saying when they do each thing.

- Finally get responses to find out which SS do most things at the "best" time.

Extra idea As a final activity you could tell the class about yourself and when you do some of these things and why.

What a cheater!

A pairwork activity

SS complete different texts about cheating in sports with verbs in the right tense (simple past, past continuous, or past perfect) and then memorize and tell each other their story. Copy one sheet per pair and cut into **A** and **B**.

> **LANGUAGE** Past tenses
> Sports vocabulary

- Put SS into pairs and have them sit face to face if possible. Give out the sheets. Explain that they each have a different true story about cheating in sports.
- Focus on **a**. Give SS a few minutes to read the story and then complete the numbered spaces with the verbs in the box.
- Check answers by copying the key on the board.

Rosie Ruiz	Ben Johnson
1 came	**1** was competing
2 won	**2** were waiting
3 became	**3** noticed
4 noticed	**4** began
5 wasn't sweating	**5** had won
6 investigated	**6** had beaten
7 had seen	**7** said
8 said	**8** lasted
9 had seen / saw	**9** had taken / took
10 took	**10** took
11 had finished / finished	**11** gave
12 had cheated / cheated	**12** discovered

Extra support You could have two **A**s and two **B**s work together to complete their stories.

- Focus on **b**. Explain that SS are now going to tell each other their stories, and ask their partner a final question about the story.

- Give SS time to reread and memorize the story.

- Now have **A** tell **B** from memory about Rosie Ruiz, and then ask **B** the final question (instruction **c**). They should try to tell the story from memory, but can use their texts as prompts where necessary.

- **B** then does the same for Ben Johnson and asks the final question **c**.

- Ask SS who they think was the worse cheater and why.

1 Future questions
C A group activity

SS pick questions about the future to ask other people in their group. Copy and cut up one set of cards per 3 or 4 SS.

LANGUAGE	Future forms (*going to*, *will*, and present continuous)

- Put SS in groups of 3 or 4 and give each group a set of cards face down.

- SS take turns picking a card and asking the other people in the group the question. Remind them to use *What about you?* when they repeat the question to the second or third student.

- Demonstrate by picking a card yourself and asking one group. Ask extra questions for more information, to encourage SS to do the same.

- SS then continue. Monitor and correct any mistakes with future forms.

- Stop the activity when one group has asked all the questions, or when you think it has gone on long enough.

Non-cut alternative Copy one sheet per pair of SS, and cut in half. Put SS in pairs (preferably sitting face to face) and give them one half each. **A** asks **B** his / her first question. **B** answers, and then returns the question by saying *What about you?* Then **B** asks **A** his / her first question.

2 Numbers quiz
A A pairwork activity

SS practice saying large numbers, percentages, etc. Copy one sheet per pair and cut into **A** and **B**.

LANGUAGE	Numbers, fractions, percentages, etc.

- Focus on **a**. Put SS into pairs and give out the sheets. Explain that they should circle what they think is the right answer to each question.

- Quickly go through all the questions to make sure SS understand everything, e.g., *bones, snail, senator, cheetah*. Refer SS to the pictures.

Extra support You could put SS in groups of four and have two **A**s and two **B**s.

- Focus on **b**. **A** now checks his / her answers saying to **B**, e.g., *I think the population of London is three million five hundred thousand.* **B** has to decide if **A** has said the number correctly. **A** gets one point for choosing the right number, and one point for saying the number correctly, so there is a possible total of 16 points for the whole quiz.

- Now **B** checks his/her answers in the same way.

- Get responses to see if any SS got 16 points!

Extra idea You could divide the whole class in two and do this as a team game.

2 How long have you been doing it?
B A whole-class mingling activity

SS have a question which they use to survey the rest of the class. Copy and cut up one sheet per 12 SS.

LANGUAGE	Present perfect simple and continuous: *How long have you been driving? For ten years.*

- If you have more than 12 SS, divide the class into two groups and make them move to different sides of the class. Give each student a different question card. Tell SS to figure out what the second question is (they must use either the present perfect simple or continuous), but not write it. Elicit and check the questions before SS start the activity.

> Driving: How long have you been driving?
> Glasses: How long have you been wearing them?
> Close friend: How long have you known him / her?
> Exercise: How long have you been going there?
> Home: How long have you lived / have you been living there?
> Languages: How long have you been studying it?
> This school: How long have you been coming here?
> Musical instrument: How long have you been playing it?
> Sport: How long have you been playing it?
> Restaurant: How long have you been going there?
> Book: How long have you been reading it?
> Car: How long have you had it?

Extra support You could let SS write down their second question on the card.

- Now tell SS they have to ask all the other SS in the class or group their question and make a note of the answers.

- SS stand up and mingle, asking their questions. If you have two groups, get them to mingle in different halves of the classroom. Take part yourself and monitor.

- When SS have asked everyone their questions, have them sit down.

- Get responses for each card to find out who has been doing each activity the longest.

Non-cut alternative Copy one sheet per pair of SS, and cut in half. Put SS in pairs (preferably sitting face to face) and give them one half each. **A** asks **B** his / her first question. **B** answers, and then returns it, saying *What about you?* Then **B** asks **A** his / her first question. They find out between the two of them who has been doing each thing the longest.

2 Questionnaire

C — A pairwork questionnaire

SS review comparatives and superlatives by completing a questionnaire with comparatives or superlatives and then asking and answering the questions. Copy one sheet per pair and cut into **A** and **B**.

> **LANGUAGE** Comparatives and superlatives

- Put SS into pairs and give out the questionnaires.
- Focus on the adjectives / adverbs and tell SS to complete each question with a comparative or superlative of the adjective / adverb.
- ⚠ Tell SS that there may be two comparatives or two superlatives – it is not always one of each.
- Check answers. You could copy the key on the board, so that SS don't actually hear each other's questions yet.

A	B
more active	harder
the most unhealthy	more healthily
more often	more enjoyable
the farthest	the worst
the most useful	the most difficult
easier	higher
the most relaxing	the most often
the best	the best
more safely	closer
the most talkative	the laziest

- Now focus on **b**. Have SS (sitting face to face if possible) ask and answer the questions. They can either ask alternate questions, or **A** can interview **B** and they then change roles. If there's time, they could also return the questions asking *What about you?*

3 Are they true?

A — A pairwork activity

SS read about laws and customs from around the world. Together they have to discuss and then decide whether they are true or not. Copy one sheet per pair.

> **LANGUAGE** *You have to… You don't have to…*
> *You should… You shouldn't…*
> *You must… You must not…*

- Put SS into pairs and give out the sheets. Focus on **a**. Point out that five of the laws and customs are false.
- Give SS a few minutes to read all the laws and customs. Then set a time limit, e.g., ten minutes, for pairs to discuss each law and custom one by one and to decide if it is true or false.
- Check answers and see if any pair correctly identified the five false laws. The false ones are 3, 5, 11, 16 and 19. The othes are all true (as far as we know!).
- Focus on **b**. Tell SS to go through each law / custom and decide which three laws they would like to have in their country.
- Get responses to decide which three are the most popular.

3 Spot the difference

B — A pairwork information gap activity

SS describe their pictures and find ten differences between them. Copy one sheet per pair and cut into **A** and **B**.

> **LANGUAGE** Appearance:
> *He's short and a little overweight.*

- Pre-teach any words that you think SS may have forgotten for clothes or appearance, and remind SS that to refer to each person they will need to say, e.g., *the first / second man on the left / right*, etc.
- Put SS in pairs, ideally face to face, and give out the sheets. **Make sure SS can't see each other's sheets.**
- Explain that they both have the same picture, but it has been changed so that there are ten differences.
- Have **A** start by describing the first person on the left e.g., *She's a little short. She has shoulder-length hair…* **B** should listen, and ask questions if necessary, to see if there are any differences. Then **B** describes the next person.
- SS continue in pairs. When they have found the differences, they can show each other the pictures to make sure they have identified the differences correctly.
- Check the differences orally with the class.

1 In picture **A** the woman on the left has **shoulder-length hair**. In **B** she has **long straight hair**.
2 In picture **A** the woman **isn't carrying a bag**. In **B** she **is**.
3 In picture **A** the man on the left has **a beard and a mustache**. In **B** he only has **a mustache**.
4 In picture **A** the woman in the middle has **short, curly hair**. In **B** she has a **ponytail and bangs**.
5 In picture **A** the woman in the middle is wearing **pants**. In **B** she is wearing a **skirt**.
6 In picture **A** the man in the middle is **fairly tall**. In **B** he is **short**.
7 In picture **A** the man in the middle has **short dark hair**. In **B** he is **bald**.
8 In picture **A** the tall woman on the right **isn't wearing glasses**. In **B** she **is**.
9 In picture **A** the man on the right is **slim**. In **B** he is **well-built**.
10 In picture **A** the man on the right is **wearing a watch**. In **B** he **isn't**.

3 Find someone who…

C — A whole-class mingling activity

SS ask each other questions to complete a survey. Copy one sheet per student.

> **LANGUAGE** *can, could,* and *be able to*:
> *Would you like to be able to travel more?*

- Elicit the questions 1–10.

1 Would you like to be able to travel more?
2 Will you be able to come to the next class?
3 Could you swim before you were four years old?
4 Have you been able to speak English outside class this week?
5 Can you park in very small spaces?

6 Would you like to be able to speak another language?
7 Can you make good cake?
8 Have you been able to do all the homework this week?
9 Can you ski? (Would you like to be able to?)
10 Do you need to be able to speak English in your job (or in a job you'd like to do)?

⚠ Make sure SS don't try and ask negative questions for questions 2, 5, 8, and 9.

- Focus on the **More information** column and elicit follow-up questions for questions 1 and 2 to help SS get the idea, e.g., *Where to? Why can't you travel now?*

- Demonstrate the activity. Ask a student the first question: "*Would you like to be able to travel more?*" Elicit "Yes, I would." or "No, I wouldn't." If the student answers "Yes," write their name in the column on your sheet, then ask a follow-up question, and write the answer under **More information**. If the student answers "No," then say "Thank you" and ask another student until somebody answers "Yes."

- Tell SS to try to find and write the name of a different student for each question. SS mingle, asking each other the questions, follow-up questions, and writing in names and more information.

- Get responses to find out who in the class would like to be able to travel more, etc. You may need to teach *nobody*.

④Ⓐ Sentence halves

A whole-class mingling activity

SS mingle and try to match their sentence halves to others. Copy and cut up one sheet per 18 SS. Each student should have one beginning and one end of a sentence. If you have more than 18 SS, give the same cards to two students, or invent some more. If you have a very small class, give more cards to each student.

⚠ Make sure that all beginnings and ends are given out. If you have an odd number of SS, you could take some cards yourself.

LANGUAGE	First conditionals and future time clauses:
	As soon as I know anything, I'll call you.
	We won't get a cheap flight unless we book early.

- Give out two cards to each student, one beginning and one ending of a sentence. The endings are all on shaded cards. Explain or demonstrate the activity. SS must move around the class saying their sentence beginnings to each other, and seeing if it matches an ending. When they think they have found a match, the student who has the ending of the sentence should give it to the student who has the beginning.

- The activity finishes when everyone has found their matching ending and has one complete sentence (or more if you have given each student more than one beginning).

- Have SS sit down, and check by getting each student to read out his / her sentences.

As soon as I know anything, I'll call you.
We can't go out until it stops raining.
Hannah will be really angry when she finds out.
You'll feel better if you take an aspirin.
I'll never finish this today unless you help me.
Write that down before you forget it.
He would like to retire when he's 55.

I'm not going to start the class until everyone stops talking.
I'll go to the bank as soon as it opens.
Jack won't leave home until he gets a job.
I can't buy the food until I know how many people are coming to lunch.
We won't get a cheap flight unless we make reservations early.
If you make any noise, you'll wake the baby up.
Unless we run, we won't catch the bus.
Turn off all the lights and lock the door before you go to bed.
We won't catch the 6 o'clock train unless we take a taxi to the station.
You can go home as soon as you finish the exercises.
When I graduate from high school I want to go to college.

Non-cut alternative Copy one sheet per student (or pair of SS). In pairs, SS have to match the sentence halves (by writing "1" next to the first beginning and then "1" next to its ending, etc.). When they have finished, check answers. Then **B** puts his / her sheet face down, and **A** reads the first nine beginnings to see if **B** can remember the endings. Then **B** does the same with the last nine.

④Ⓑ If you had to choose…

A pair or groupwork activity

SS ask and answer questions about preferences, either with a partner or in small groups. SS have to say which alternative they would prefer and why. Copy one sheet per pair or small group. You can personalize the activity if you want by inventing more alternatives yourself.

LANGUAGE	Second conditionals:
	I would prefer to live in a small suburb, because it would be quieter and healthier.

- Put SS in pairs or small groups and give out the sheets.

- Demonstrate the activity by having a student ask you one of the questions. Answer in as much detail as possible. SS then continue either asking their partner the question or asking all the people in the group. Tell the other student(s) to return the question using *What about you?*

- While SS are talking, go around and monitor, correcting any mistakes with conditionals.

- When the activity finishes, get responses from a few pairs.

④Ⓒ Am I telling the truth?

A pairwork activity

SS talk about their childhood, sometimes inventing information and sometimes telling the truth. Their partner asks questions to find out if their partner is telling the truth or inventing their answers. Copy one sheet per pair and cut into **A** and **B**.

LANGUAGE	*used to*:
	I used to love playing "Monopoly."
	Who did you use to play with?

- Put SS in pairs, ideally face to face, and hand out the sheets. Focus on instruction **a**. Give SS a few minutes to complete the circles with real or invented information.

- Focus on **b** and **c** and have SS read the instructions. Then demonstrate the activity. Get one student to tell you about his / her first circle. Then ask several questions, and finally say *I think you're telling the truth* (or *I don't think you are telling the truth*). You could also choose one circle and tell SS your own answer, and get them to ask you questions.

- SS continue in pairs, each speaking about one circle alternately.
- Get responses from some of the pairs to find out if they were good at spotting when their partner wasn't telling the truth.

5 A Lifestyle survey

A pairwork activity

SS compare information about their diet, lifestyle, etc. and practice using quantifiers. Copy one sheet per pair and cut into **A** and **B**.

> LANGUAGE Quantifiers:
> *How much free time do you have? Not enough.*

- Put SS into pairs and give out the sheets. Focus on **a,** and give SS a few minutes to read all their question prompts. Then focus on **b** and on the expressions SS should use in their answers.

Extra support Drill all the questions with the whole class.

- Demonstrate the activity by having an **A** and a **B** ask you their first question. Answer with an expression from the box, and then explain it, and elicit follow-up questions.
- SS ask and answer in pairs. Have them ask alternate questions, and, if there's time, to return the questions with *What about you?*
- Get some responses from the class.

5 B Generally speaking

A group discussion

SS practice generalizing by discussing topics in small groups. Copy one sheet per group of 3 or 4 and cut into cards.

> LANGUAGE Not using *the* for generalizing:
> *I think dogs make the best pets because…*

- Put SS in groups of 3 or 4. Give out one set of cards to each group and put face down.
- Pick up the top card from one group and read it out. Say whether you agree or disagree, and give a reason.
- SS continue in groups. One student picks a card and reads it out, says whether he / she agrees or not, giving reasons, and the others then say what they think. Monitor and correct any misuse of the definite article.
- Get some responses to see whether, generally speaking, SS agree or disagree with the sentences.

Extra support You could write some useful expressions on the board for SS to use, e.g., *I agree / don't agree, (Personally,) I think…, In my opinion,…, For example,….* Remind SS not to use the definite article *the* when they generalize.

Non-cut alternative Give one sheet to each pair or group and get them to discuss the statements one by one.

5 C Can you guess?

A pairwork activity

SS complete sentences by guessing real information about their partner. Copy one sheet per pair and cut into **A** and **B**.

> LANGUAGE Gerunds, infinitives, and base forms:
> *(I think) you would like to learn to ski.*

- Demonstrate the activity by writing on the board: *When you're on your own, you enjoy…* . Elicit that you need to continue with a gerund. Then tell SS to guess what *you* enjoy doing when you're on your own. Elicit answers and then tell the class what you *really* enjoy doing.
- Sit SS in pairs, ideally face to face, and give out the sheets. **They must not look at what their partner writes.** Tell them to complete the sentences, trying to guess how their partner would complete each sentence. Monitor and check that they are using gerunds and infinitives correctly.
- Now SS take turns reading their completed sentences to their partner, who tells them if they have guessed correctly or not. Encourage them to react by contradicting what their partner has said, and then giving the real answer if the guess is wrong, e.g., *No, I don't. I don't enjoy reading! But I love walking,* etc.
- Get responses from several pairs and find out who, in the pair, had more correct guesses.

Extra challenge If you want to give more practice, have SS repeat the activity but changing roles **A** and **B**.

6 A Who asked what?

A class survey

SS survey each other with one question each. Then the rest of the class has to remember which question each person asked, and the person reports the answers. Copy and cut up one set of cards per 20 SS. If you have a bigger class, invent a few more questions or give one question card to two SS.

> LANGUAGE Reported speech:
> *Ken asked me if I had a pet.*

- Give each student a card with a question, and tell them to memorize it. Then tell them they have to survey the rest of the class by asking everyone the question. They should quickly and briefly note down everyone's answers.
- SS mingle, asking all other SS their question and making a note of the answers.
- When all SS have asked everyone, tell them to sit down.
- Now put SS in pairs, and have them try to remember which question each person asked, and then write it in reported speech (see LANGUAGE box). Set a time limit.
- Check answers. Point to one SS, and then ask somebody else in the class *What did (Ken) ask you?*

Extra idea If there's time, you could get each student to briefly give the result of his / her survey. They should just give the most significant fact, e.g., *Ten people in the class have never changed a tire on a car. Eight people said that oranges were their favorite fruit.* It will help to give the class a couple of examples.

Non-cut alternative Copy one sheet per pair and cut in half. SS ask and answer the questions. Then take away the sheets and give SS five minutes to try to write down in reported speech the ten questions they were asked.

Movie quiz
B A pair or group quiz

SS answer questions about movies. Copy one sheet per pair or group.

LANGUAGE	The passive
	movie vocabulary

- Divide the class into pairs, small groups, or teams. If you think your SS know a lot about the movies, they could do the quiz in pairs. If not, groups of 4 or even teams may work better.
- Give out one quiz to each pair or group, and place it face down. Big teams may need more than one copy.
- When you say "Go" SS turn over the sheet. Set a time limit for them to choose the right answers.
- Check answers, where possible making SS give you the whole sentence (not just saying **a**, **b**, or **c**).

Movies
1 b 2 c 3 a
Places
1 Paris c, Tokyo a, London b   2 b   3 a
Music
1 b 2 a 3 b
People
1 c 2 a 3 b (Quentin Tarantino)
Famous lines
1 e 2 b 3 d 4 c 5 a
Movie titles
1 Close Encounters of the Third Kind
2 The Chronicles of Narnia: The Lion, the Witch and the Wardrobe
3 Dead Poets' Society
4 Crocodile Dundee
5 Four Weddings and a Funeral
6 The Godfather
7 A Hundred and One Dalmatians
8 Kill Bill
9 Mission Impossible
10 Silence of the Lambs

6 Which definition is right?
C A group card game

SS play a definitions game in groups of 4 or 6. Copy and cut up one set of cards per 12–18 SS (see below). You will need at least two cards per group.

LANGUAGE	relative clauses:
	a thing that… a person who…

- Put SS into small groups of 4–6. The group then divides into two teams, **A** and **B** (two or three SS in each).
- Demonstrate the activity. Write the following word and phonetics on the board: **A broom** /brum/.
- Explain that you are going to give three possible definitions

of the word. SS have to listen and decide which they think is correct. Now read out the following definitions:
1 It's a small room that is both a bedroom and a living room, which students often rent.
2 It's a thing made of wood or plastic that people use to clean the floor.
3 It's the thing in a car that you press to make the car go faster.

- Repeat the definitions, and then have SS vote by a show of hands as to which they think is the correct one (2).
 If any SS actually know what the word means, ask them not to tell the others.
- Now give each team a card. Tell them they have three words on the card. Each word has a correct definition (checked) and a false definition. The team has to write one more false definition for each word. Give them at least five minutes to do this.
- When they are ready, each **A** team reads their first word and the three definitions to the **B** team, who have to choose the right one. Then the **B** team reads their first word and definitions. The team that guesses most words right wins.
- If you have time, give each team another card (there are enough for each team to have three different cards).

7 Third conditional game
A A group board game

SS review third conditionals by moving around a board and completing sentences. Copy one sheet per group of 3 or 4.

LANGUAGE	Third conditional:
	If I had known it was your birthday, I would have bought you a present.

- Put SS in groups of 3 or 4 and give each group a copy of the board game. They will also need counters (or pieces of paper) and a coin.
- Explain the rules of the game. SS throw the coin and move one square for heads and two for tails. When they land on a square, they must finish the sentence so that it is grammatically correct and makes sense. Encourage them to use contracted forms. The rest of the group are "judges," but they should ask the teacher in case of dispute. If the sentence is correct, they can stay on the square they have landed on. If not, they have to go back to where they came from.
- The youngest student in each group starts. If a student lands on the same square where another student has been on previously, he / she must complete the sentence in a different way, e.g., if A lands on square 1 and makes the sentence *If it hadn't been subtitled, I wouldn't have understood it*, and then B also lands on square 1, he / she can say, e.g., *If it hadn't been subtitled, I wouldn't have gone to see it* or *I would have been very bored*, etc.
- SS play the game in groups. The game finishes when someone reaches the last square.

Example sentence endings
1 …wouldn't have understood anything.
2 …would have won.
3 …hadn't taken a taxi.
4 …wouldn't have left him.

5 ...had taken a map.
6 ...had worked harder.
7 ...hadn't been so expensive.
8 ...had told us you were coming.
9 ...would have bought you a present.
10 ...had studied more.
11 ...had loved me.
12 ...hadn't driven so fast.
13 ...would have studied history.
14 ...hadn't had two cups of coffee.
15 ...had called earlier.
16 ...would have gone to the zoo.
17 ...hadn't missed the bus.
18 ...had been a little taller.

7 B The scariest places in London

A pairwork information gap activity

SS role-play being tourists and use indirect questions to find out about four "scary" tourist attractions in London. Copy one sheet per pair and cut into **A** and **B**.

| LANGUAGE | Indirect questions: *Could you tell me what time the museum closes?* |

- Put SS into pairs, ideally face to face and give out the sheets. **Make sure SS can't see each other's sheets.** Go through the instructions.
- First, give SS time to think about their questions, and read their information.

Sherlock Holmes Museum
Could you tell me if the museum opens / is open on Saturdays?
Could you tell me what time it closes?
Could you tell me where it is?
Could you tell me how much an adult's ticket costs / an adult's ticket is?

The Bloody Tower
Could you tell me if the Bloody Tower opens / is open on Sundays?
Could you tell me what time it opens?
Could you tell me what the nearest subway station is?
Could you tell me how much a child's ticket costs / a child's ticket is?

Chamber of Horrors
Could you tell me if the Chamber of Horrors opens / is open on Saturdays?
Could you tell me what time it closes?
Could you tell me what the nearest subway station is?
Could you tell me how much an adult's ticket costs / an adult's ticket is?

The London Dungeon
Could you tell me where the London Dungeon is?
Could you tell me if it opens / is open every day?
Could you tell what time it closes?
Could you tell me how much a child's ticket costs / a child's ticket is?

- **A** plays the role of the tourist first, and asks **B** politely for his / her missing information. Then they change roles.
- When they have both finished, focus on **c**, and give them a few minutes to decide which place they want to visit. Get feedback to see which place is the most popular.

7 C Phrasal verbs race

A brainstorm activity

SS race to think of answers to questions using phrasal verbs. Copy one sheet per student or per group of 3 or 4.

| LANGUAGE | Phrasal verbs (*ask for, break up, check in,* etc.) |

- Put SS in pairs or groups of 3 or 4. Give each pair or group a sheet face down.
- Explain that the activity is a race. Each group should have a "secretary" who writes down the answers. The winner is the pair or group who can find the most correct answers in the time limit. They only have to write one answer to each question unless it specifies more, and if they are stuck with one question, they should move on to the next.
- Set a time limit, e.g., five minutes, and tell SS to start. Give more time if you can see that SS need it.
- When the time limit is up, check answers, encouraging SS to use full sentences, e.g., *When you get to a restaurant the first thing you usually ask for is a table (or a menu).*

Suggested answers (but others are possible)
1 a table, a menu
2 (use a recent example)
3 before you catch a plane, when you arrive at a hotel
4 take a shower, have breakfast
5 by looking on the Internet, calling the movie theater, etc.
6 sugar, bread, potatoes, etc.
7 soccer player, actress, etc.
8 Bye.
9 the summer vacation, national holidays, etc.
10 (use recent examples)
11 Bill Gates.
12 when they are driving (or talking) too fast
13 definition of words, pronunciation of words
14 the lights, the TV, etc.
15 jogging, tennis, etc.
16 the receipt
17 your seat belt
18 a form
19 before they play a game or before they train
20 TV, DVD player, etc.

7 Review

Questions to review vocabulary and verb forms and tenses

SS ask each other questions about key vocabulary areas using a range of tenses and verb forms from files 1–7. This could either be used as a final "pre-test" review or as an oral exam. Copy and cut up one set of cards per pair.

| LANGUAGE | Grammar and vocabulary of the book |

- SS work in pairs. Give each pair a set of cards. Set a time limit, e.g., ten minutes. SS take turns taking a card and talking to their partner about the topic on the card, using the prompts. Encourage SS to ask follow-up questions. Monitor, help, and correct.

Non-cut alternative Make one copy per pair. Give SS a few moments to read through the cards. Then **A** chooses a number for **B** to talk about what's on the card for that number. They continue taking turns choosing a topic for their partner to talk about.

A

a Read your instructions and write your answers in the correct place.

In the star, write your first name and last name.
In circle 1, write the year when you started studying English.
In square 2, write two things you like doing on weekends.
In circle 3, write the number of the month when you were born (e.g., July = 7).
In square 4, write the name of a famous person you admire.
In circle 5, write the name of the last movie you saw in the movie theater.
In square 6, write the name of the most beautiful city you've ever visited.
In circle 7, write the name of two sports you think are really exciting to watch.
In square 8, write the name of the person you get along with best in your family.
In circle 9, write the name of a famous group or singer you really like (or don't like).
In square 10, write the name of a TV program you usually watch.

b Change charts with **B**. Ask **B** to explain the information in his /her chart. Ask for more information.

c Explain your answers to **B**.

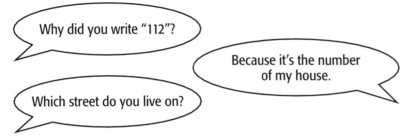

Why did you write "112"?

Because it's the number of my house.

Which street do you live on?

A

B

a Read your instructions and write your answers in the correct place.

In the star, write your first name and last name.
In circle 1, write the number of brothers and sisters you have.
In square 2, write two things you don't like doing on weekends.
In circle 3, write the number of the house or apartment where you live.
In square 4, write the name of a really good friend.
In circle 5, write the name of the place where you spent your last vacation.
In square 6, write the name of a magazine or newspaper you usually read.
In circle 7, write the name of a subject you really hate(d) at school.
In square 8, write the name of two kinds of music you really like.
In circle 9, write an animal you have or would like to have as a pet.
In square 10, write the name of a TV personality you really like (or don't like).

b Change charts with **A**. Explain your answers.

c Ask **A** to explain the information in his / her chart. Ask for more information.

Why did you write "watching TV and going out with my friends?"

Because they're two things I like doing on weekends.

What kind of programs do you watch?

B

American English File 3 Teacher's Book
Photocopiable © Oxford University Press 2008

a Answer the questions in pairs. Complete the **"We think"** column with *morning, noon, afternoon, evening,* or *night.*

b Now **A** read part 1 of the article on body rhythms, **B** read part 2.

c In pairs, complete the **Expert opinion** column with the exact times. Tell each other why it's the best time of day.

d In pairs say at what time of day you do these things. Who has the "best" daily routine?

What do you think is the best time of day (for your body) to...?	We think	Expert opinion
1 have a big meal	_____	_____
2 take a bath	_____	_____
3 do your math homework	_____	_____
4 get a shot	_____	_____
5 sleep	_____	_____
6 be creative	_____	_____
7 call friends	_____	_____
8 take vitamins	_____	_____
9 put on face cream	_____	_____
10 play sports or exercise	_____	_____
11 eat without putting on weight	_____	_____

A time for everything

The new science of chronobiology tells us the best time of day to do everything, from writing a poem to taking pills.
By following your body's natural daily rhythms, you can get more out of every day.

Part 1

7 a.m.–9 a.m.	Have a good breakfast. The metabolism is at its most active in the morning, and everything you eat at this time gives you energy, but doesn't make you put on weight. It's also the best time of day to take vitamins. If you take them in the afternoon or evening, some vitamins can cause indigestion or keep you awake.
9 a.m.–10 a.m.	Go to the doctor or dentist. Shots are least painful at this time of day.
10 a.m.–12	Work, study, paint a picture or write a poem. The brain is at its most creative at this time of day.
12–2 p.m.	Eat. This is the best time of the day to have lunch. The digestive system works very efficiently at this time. You should have your big meal of the day now, and not in the evening.
2 p.m.–3 p.m.	Take a nap. After lunch the body temperature goes down and the brain works more slowly. There are a lot of road accidents at this time of day because drivers fall asleep at the wheel.

Part 2

3 p.m.–5 p.m.	Go to the gym. Physically our body is at its peak now. Most Olympic records are broken at this time of day.
4 p.m.–6 p.m.	Do homework, especially math. Research shows that children are better at arithmetic at this time of day.
6 p.m.–8 p.m.	Eat and drink (in moderation) and enjoy yourself. Our sense of smell and taste are at their best at this time, so now is the moment for a light but delicious dinner. It is also the time when the skin absorbs cream best, so before dinner is the time to put on face or body cream.
8 p.m.–10 p.m.	Call your friends. This is the time of day when people most often feel lonely (and it's also cheaper to make a phone call in many parts of the world).
10 p.m.–11 p.m.	Get ready for bed. One of the best ways to make sure you sleep well is to take a hot bath, which will relax your mind and body.
11 p.m.–7 a.m.	Sleep. After 11 o'clock, the metabolism slows down, preparing us for sleep. If we stay awake after midnight, our attention drops dramatically, and this is the time of day when people find it most difficult to concentrate if they are studying or working.

1B Communicative **What a cheater!**

A

a Put the verbs from the list into the story in the simple past, past perfect, or past continuous.

1 come   2 win   3 become   4 notice   5 not sweat   6 investigate   7 see   8 say   9 see   10 take
11 finish   12 cheat

ROSIE RUIZ

ON APRIL 21 1980, 23-year-old Rosie Ruiz 1 _____ in first in the Boston Marathon. She 2 _____ the race in the third-fastest time ever recorded for a female runner (2 hours, 31 minutes, 56 seconds).

However, the organizers 3 _____ suspicious because they 4 _____ that when she crossed the finishing line she 5 _____ at all.

When they 6 _____ they found out that none of the course officials 7 _____ her passing checkpoints. Other competitors didn't remember seeing her at all.

Then a few spectators 8 _____ that they 9 _____ Ruiz join the race just for the final kilometer. She had simply sprinted from there to the finish line.

The marathon organizers 10 _____ away Ruiz's medal and gave it to Jacqueline Gareau, who 11 _____ second in the race.

Later they also found out that Ruiz 12 _____ in the New York Marathon, the race she used to qualify for the Boston event, earlier in the same year but in a different way…

b Read the story again and remember it. Tell **B** about Rosie Ruiz.

c Ask **B** *How do you think she cheated in the New York Marathon?* (Answer: She took the subway!)

B

a Put the verbs from the list into the story in the simple past, past perfect, or past continuous.

1 compete   2 wait   3 notice   4 begin   5 win   6 beat   7 say   8 last   9 take   10 take
11 give   12 discover

Ben Johnson

In the Seoul Olympics in 1988, the Canadian runner Ben Johnson was running in the 100 meters final. People called it "the race of the century" because Johnson 1 _____ against his greatest rival – the American sprinter Carl Lewis.

When the runners 2 _____ to start the race, some people 3 _____ that Johnson's eyes were yellow.

The race 4 _____ and moments later Johnson was the Olympic champion. His time of 9.72 seconds was a new world record. Johnson was euphoric, because he 5 _____ the gold medal and 6 _____ his American rival, Carl Lewis. After the race, Johnson 7 _____ : "My name is Benjamin Sinclair Johnson Jr. and this world record will last 50 years, maybe 100 years."

But he was wrong. His world record 8 _____ only a few hours. That evening, drug tests showed that Johnson 9 _____ steroids before the race.

The Olympic committee 10 _____ away his gold medal and 11 _____ it to Carl Lewis. Johnson was also banned from athletics for two years.

But 15 years later people 12 _____ some amazing news about Carl Lewis…

b Read the story again and remember it. Tell **A** about Ben Johnson.

c Ask **A** *What do you think people discovered about Carl Lewis?* (Answer: He had also tested positive for drugs in 1988, just before the Seoul Olympics, but the American Olympic committee didn't ban him.)

Where are you going after class?	What are you doing this weekend?	Is anyone in your family getting married soon?	Are you meeting anyone after class?
Are you going out on Friday night?	Where are you having lunch tomorrow?	Are you going away for the weekend soon?	Are you coming to the next English class?
What are you going to do next summer?	Are you going to watch TV tonight? Which programs?	What's the next thing you're going to buy for yourself?	What's the next movie you're going to see?
Are you going to use the Internet tonight? Why?	Are you going to cook tonight?	Who do you think is going to get the best grades in the next English test?	What time are you going to get up tomorrow?
Do you think women's sports will ever be as popular as men's sports?	Do you think people will work more or less in the future?	Do you think you will pass the final English test?	Do you think you will ever go and live abroad?
Do you think you will ever speak "perfect" English?	Do you think you will have the same job all your life?	Do you think you will have more than two children?	Do you think you will live to be more than 80?

American English File 3 Teacher's Book
Photocopiable © Oxford University Press 2008

A

a Choose what you think is the right answer to each question.

1	What was the approximate population of London in 2006?	3,500,000	5,750,000	7,500,000
2	How far is it from New York to Los Angeles?	3,932 km	6,851 km	8,592 km
3	How many countries are there in the United Nations?	124	192	208
4	How far away is the nearest star (not including the Sun)? (one light year = about six billion miles)	1.5 light years away 2.75 light years away 4.3 light years away		
5	What is $1/2$ divided by $1/3$?	$1/4$	$1/5$	$1/6$
6	How many bones are there in the human body?	206	258	291
7	How far can the fastest land snail travel in an hour?	20 meters	38.6 meters	48.3 meters
8	How many words does the average woman say a day?	1,400	3,700	8,800

b Tell **B** your answers. He / She will tell you if you are right.

c Use the information below to correct **B**'s answers.

1 The population of Mexico City (metropolitan area) was approximately 19,500,000 in 2006.
2 It is 6,430 km from Moscow to Vladivostok.
3 202 countries took part in the 2004 Athens Olympics.
4 The Moon is 384,000 km from the Earth.
5 Three quarters of the body is made up of water.
6 Sixteen percent of senators in the US in 2006 were women.
7 A cheetah can run at 100 km/h.
8 The average man says 6,000 words a day.

> *I think the population of London was three million, five hundred thousand in 2006.*

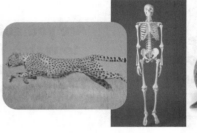

B

a Choose what you think is the right answer to each question.

1	What was the approximate population of Mexico City in 2006?	15,500,000	19,500,000	25,000,000
2	How far is it from Moscow to Vladivostok? (route of the Trans-Siberian railway)	6,430 km	9,302 km	11,794 km
3	How many countries took part in the 2004 Athens Olympics?	151	202	296
4	How far away is the Moon from the Earth?	38,400 km	384,000 km	3,840,000 km
5	What proportion of the body is made up of water?	$3/4$	$1/2$	$1/3$
6	What percentage of senators in the US were women in 2006?	3.5%	16%	48%
7	At what speed can a cheetah (the fastest mammal) run?	100 km/h	150 km/h	200 km/h
8	How many words does the average man say a day?	1,200	2,400	6,000

b Use the information below to correct **A**'s answers.

1 The population of London (metropolitan area) was approximately 7,500,000 in 2006.
2 It is 3,932 km from New York to Los Angeles.
3 There are 192 countries in the United Nations.
4 The nearest star is 4.3 light years from Earth.
5 $1/2$ divided by $1/3$ is $1/6$.
6 There are 206 bones in the human body.
7 The fastest land snail can travel 20 meters in an hour.
8 The average woman says 8,800 words a day.

c Tell **A** your answers. He / She will tell you if you are right.

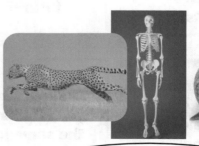

> *I think the population of Mexico City was twenty-five million.*

DRIVING

Do you have a driver's license?
How long / drive?

THIS SCHOOL

Do you like this school?
How long / come here?

GLASSES

Do you wear glasses or contact lenses?
How long / wear / them?

MUSICAL INSTRUMENT

Can you play a musical instrument?
How long / play it?

CLOSE FRIEND

Do you have a close friend? Male or female?
How long / know him (or her)?

SPORTS

Do you play any sports?
How long / play it?

EXERCISE

Do you go to a gym?
How long / go there?

RESTAURANT

Do you have a favorite restaurant?
How long / go there?

HOME

Where do you live?
How long / live there?

BOOKS

What book are you reading at the moment?
How long / read / it?

LANGUAGES

Are you studying another language? Which?
How long / study it?

CAR

Do you have a car or motorcycle?
How long / have it?

A

a Complete the questions with a comparative or superlative.

b Ask **B** your questions. Ask for more information.

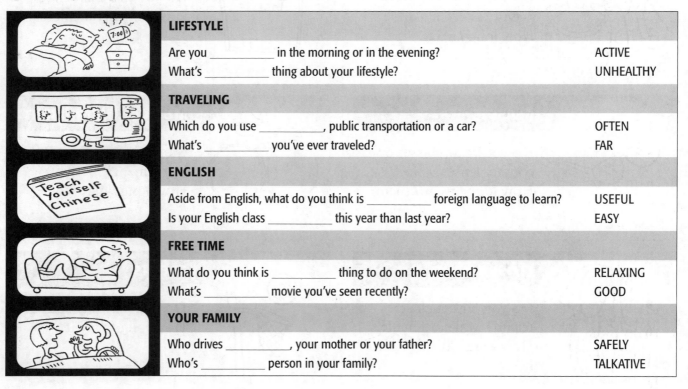

	LIFESTYLE	
	Are you _____ in the morning or in the evening?	ACTIVE
	What's _____ thing about your lifestyle?	UNHEALTHY
	TRAVELING	
	Which do you use _____, public transportation or a car?	OFTEN
	What's _____ you've ever traveled?	FAR
	ENGLISH	
	Aside from English, what do you think is _____ foreign language to learn?	USEFUL
	Is your English class _____ this year than last year?	EASY
	FREE TIME	
	What do you think is _____ thing to do on the weekend?	RELAXING
	What's _____ movie you've seen recently?	GOOD
	YOUR FAMILY	
	Who drives _____, your mother or your father?	SAFELY
	Who's _____ person in your family?	TALKATIVE

B

a Complete the questions with a comparative or superlative.

b Ask **A** your questions. Ask for more information.

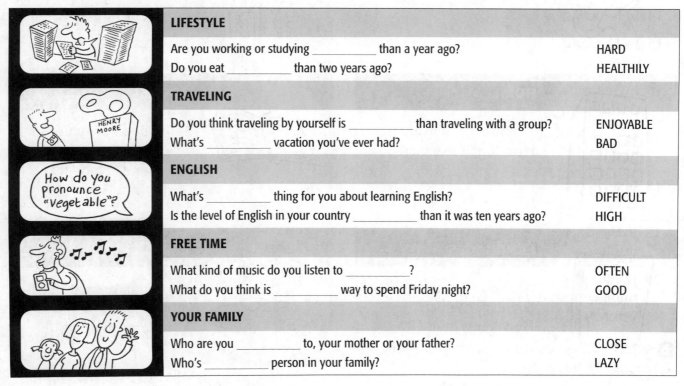

	LIFESTYLE	
	Are you working or studying _____ than a year ago?	HARD
	Do you eat _____ than two years ago?	HEALTHILY
	TRAVELING	
	Do you think traveling by yourself is _____ than traveling with a group?	ENJOYABLE
	What's _____ vacation you've ever had?	BAD
	ENGLISH	
	What's _____ thing for you about learning English?	DIFFICULT
	Is the level of English in your country _____ than it was ten years ago?	HIGH
	FREE TIME	
	What kind of music do you listen to _____?	OFTEN
	What do you think is _____ way to spend Friday night?	GOOD
	YOUR FAMILY	
	Who are you _____ to, your mother or your father?	CLOSE
	Who's _____ person in your family?	LAZY

a In pairs, read about some strange laws and customs. Five of these are false. Discuss with your partner which ones you think they are.

1 In **China**, when you use chopsticks you shouldn't leave them upright in the bowl. It brings bad luck.

2 In **Sweden**, if you drink and drive, you have to go to prison for six months.

3 In **Argentina**, when you get on a train you should shake hands with all the other people in the car.

4 In **France**, you are not allowed to call a pig "Napoleon."

5 In **Scotland**, boys have to wear a kilt to school.

6 In **Brazil**, you should never make the "OK" sign with your thumb and index finger. It is very rude.

7 In **Germany**, every office must have a view of the sky.

8 In the **Middle East**, you shouldn't admire anything in your hosts' home. They will feel that they have to give it to you.

9 In **Singapore**, you can't chew gum. It's against the law.

10 In **India**, you shouldn't thank your hosts at the end of a meal. It is an insult.

11 In **Japan**, women can't wear pants to work.

12 In the **UK**, parents don't have to send their children to school. They can teach them at home if they prefer.

13 In **Russia**, men should take off their gloves to shake somebody's hand.

14 In **Iceland**, you can't take dogs downtown.

15 In **Thailand**, you shouldn't touch a person's head (even a child's). The head is sacred.

16 In **Australia**, women must not sit on the top floor of a bus, only downstairs.

I'll never forget it again, I promise!

17 In **Samoa**, it is against the law for a man to forget his wife's birthday.

18 In **Switzerland**, you aren't allowed to wash your car or cut the grass on a Sunday.

19 In the **US**, you shouldn't tip taxi drivers. It is considered an insult.

20 In **Italy**, if you give flowers, you should give them in odd numbers, e.g., 1, 3, 5, 7, or 9. It is bad luck to give, for example, two flowers.

b Which of these customs and laws would you like to have in your country? Choose your top three.

A

Describe your picture to **B**. Find ten differences. Mark the differences on your picture.

B

Describe your picture to **A**. Find ten differences. Mark the differences on your picture.

Where? Why not? Whose? What? Where? Why? Why not? Who...with?

Find someone who...	Student's name	More information
1 would like to be able to travel more.		
2 won't be able to come to the next class.		
3 could swim before they were four years old.		
4 has been able to speak English outside class this week.		
5 can't park in very small spaces.		
6 would like to be able to speak another language.		
7 can make good cake.		
8 hasn't been able to do all the homework this week.		
9 can't ski (but would like to be able to).		
10 needs to be able to speak English in their job (or job they'd like to do).		

American English File 3 Teacher's Book
Photocopiable © Oxford University Press 2008

As soon as I know anything, …	We can't go out …	Hannah will be really angry …
You'll feel better …	I'll never finish this today …	Write that down …
He would like to retire …	I'm not going to start the class …	I'll go to the bank …
Jack won't leave home …	I can't buy the food …	We won't get a cheap flight …
If you make any noise, …	Unless we run, …	Turn off all the lights and lock the door …
We won't catch the 6 o'clock train …	You can go home …	When I graduate from high school …
… unless we make reservations early.	… if you take an aspirin.	… until I know how many people are coming to lunch.
… as soon as you finish the exercises.	… when he's 55.	… before you forget it.
… I'll call you.	… until everyone stops talking.	… before you go to bed.
… unless we take a taxi to the station.	… I want to go to college.	… you'll wake the baby up.
… as soon as it opens.	… until it stops raining.	… when she finds out.
… unless you help me.	… we won't catch the bus.	… until he gets a job.

Talk to a partner.
Say why.

> I'd prefer to live downtown.
> If I lived in a suburb, I'd have to drive
> to work every day...

If you had to choose, ...

 would you prefer to live in a small suburb or downtown in a capital city?

 would you prefer to have as neighbors a couple with five children or a couple with five dogs?

 would you prefer to live in a fourth floor apartment without a elevator or in a first floor apartment with a restaurant next door?

 would you prefer to have an enormous house with a tiny yard or a tiny house with an enormous yard?

 would you prefer to have a house with a gym or a house with a game room?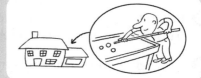

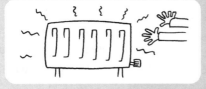 would you prefer to have central heating or a fireplace?

 would you prefer to live in a beautiful house in an ugly area or an ugly house in a beautiful area?

 would you prefer to have a vacation home at the beach or in the mountains?

A

a Write something in each circle. If it has (T) at the end, you must write something true. If it has (L), you must lie, i.e., invent something.

b Tell **B** about one of your circles. **B** will then ask you questions, and decide if you're telling the truth or lying.

c Now listen to **B** tell you about one of his / her circles. Ask questions to see if it is the truth or a lie. If it's a lie, get **B** to tell you what the true answer is!

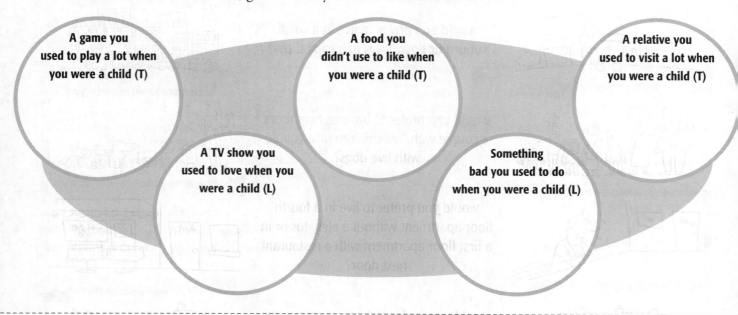

A game you used to play a lot when you were a child (T)

A food you didn't use to like when you were a child (T)

A relative you used to visit a lot when you were a child (T)

A TV show you used to love when you were a child (L)

Something bad you used to do when you were a child (L)

B

a Write something in each circle. If it has (T) at the end, you must write something true. If it has (L), you must lie, i.e., invent something.

b Listen to **A** tell you about one of his / her circles. Ask questions to see if it is the truth or a lie. If it's a lie, get **A** to tell you what the true answer is!

c Now tell **A** about one of your circles, and answer his / her questions.

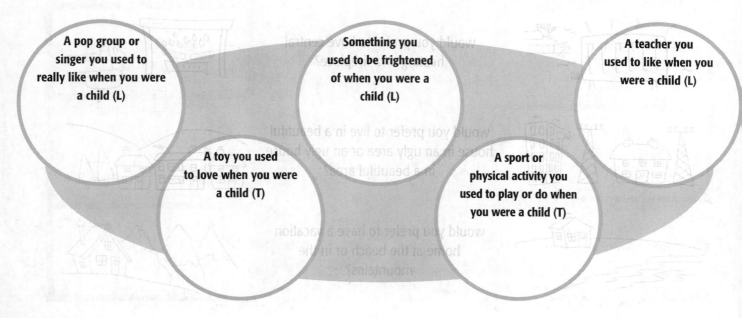

A pop group or singer you used to really like when you were a child (L)

Something you used to be frightened of when you were a child (L)

A teacher you used to like when you were a child (L)

A toy you used to love when you were a child (T)

A sport or physical activity you used to play or do when you were a child (T)

A

a Make questions with *How much* and *How many* to ask **B**. Ask for more information.

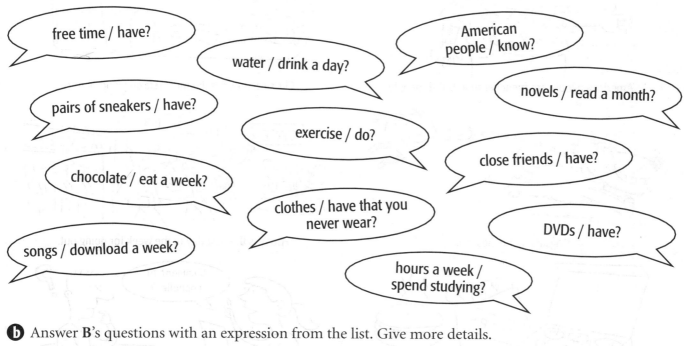

free time / have?

water / drink a day?

American people / know?

pairs of sneakers / have?

novels / read a month?

exercise / do?

close friends / have?

chocolate / eat a week?

clothes / have that you never wear?

DVDs / have?

songs / download a week?

hours a week / spend studying?

b Answer **B**'s questions with an expression from the list. Give more details.

a lot / lots   too much / many   not much / many   a few / very few
a little / very little   none   not enough

B

a Make questions with *How much* and *How many* to ask **A**. Ask for more information.

time / spend on yourself?

photos / have on your cell phone?

coffee / drink a day?

days a week / go out?

hours / usually sleep?

hours a day / spend watching TV?

fast food / eat a week?

TV / watch a day?

hot baths / take a week?

kilometers / walk a day?

time / spend on the Internet?

pairs of jeans / have?

b Answer **A**'s questions with an expression from the list. Give more details.

a lot / lots   too much / many   not much / many   a few / very few
a little / very little   none   not enough

American English File 3 Teacher's Book
Photocopiable © Oxford University Press 2008

American people are friendlier than British people.

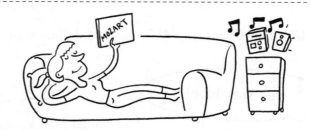

Classical music is the most relaxing kind of music.

Dogs make the best pets.

Friday is the best day of the week for going out.

Food that tastes good is usually bad for you.

Girls are better at learning languages than boys.

Italian food is the most popular in the world.

Money doesn't make you happy.

Most men today help a lot with the housework.

People who have red cars usually drive fast and aggressively.

Athletes are good role models for young people.

Women have a much better sense of style than men.

American English File 3 Teacher's Book
Photocopiable © Oxford University Press 2008

A

ⓐ Complete for your partner with a verb (phrase) in the gerund, infinitive, or base form.

I think...

When you're on your own, you enjoy _____.

When you were young, your parents didn't use to let you

_____.

A job in the house you don't mind doing is _____.

You would like to learn _____.

You're not very good at _____.

When you go on vacation, you love _____.

When you leave the house in the morning, you never forget

_____.

When you were younger, you wanted _____.

This evening you'd like _____.

When you're with your friends, you spend a lot of time

_____.

ⓑ Read your first sentence to **B**. He / She will tell you if it's true or not.

B

ⓐ Complete for your partner with a verb (phrase) in the gerund, infinitive, or base form.

I think...

On Sunday mornings you really like _____.

You're really good at _____.

In class you enjoy _____.

When you were a child, your parents used to make you

_____.

This weekend you're planning _____.

You want to give up _____.

In the future you hope _____.

Something that makes you feel good is _____.

On Saturdays you hate _____.

You are studying English to _____.

ⓑ Tell **A** if his / her sentence about you is true or not. Then read **A** your first sentence.

American English File 3 Teacher's Book
Photocopiable © Oxford University Press 2008

1 What's your favorite TV program?	**2** What kind of computer do you have?	**3** Have you ever changed a tire on a car?	**4** Are you an optimist or a pessimist?
5 Where will you be at 8 o'clock tomorrow morning?	**6** How often do you wear a hat?	**7** How long have you been studying English?	**8** What time did you wake up today?
9 How much water do you drink a day?	**10** Have you ever worked in a restaurant?	**11** Are you going out tonight?	**12** What's your favorite fruit?
13 How did you come to class?	**14** Would you like to be famous?	**15** Do you have a pet?	**16** Would you prefer to live in the city or in the country?
17 Do you support a soccer team?	**18** Are you afraid of any animals or insects?	**19** Can you play chess?	**20** What languages can you speak?

MOVIES

1 **What do these movies have in common?**
Pride and Prejudice   Bridget Jones's Diary
Charlie and the Chocolate Factory
a   They are all set in the 19th century.
b   They are all based on books.
c   They all won an Oscar for best actress.

2 **Which Oscar did all these movies win?**
Spiderman   The Lord of the Rings   The Matrix
a   best film   b   best soundtrack
c   best special effects

3 **In which movie (shot in Ireland) did an Australian actor play the part of a Scottish soldier?**
a   *Braveheart*   b   *Gladiator*
c   *Master and Commander*

PEOPLE

1 **Who played the part of James Bond in *Goldeneye*?**
a   Sean Connery
b   Roger Moore
c   Pierce Brosnan

2 **Which actor was nominated seven times for an Oscar but never won one?**
a   Richard Burton   b   Humphrey Bogart
c   Cary Grant

3 **What do these three movies have in common?**
Reservoir Dogs   Pulp Fiction   Kill Bill
a   They all star John Travolta.
b   They were all directed by the same person.
c   They were all set in New York.

PLACES

1 **Match the movies to the cities where they were set.**
a   *Lost in Translation*   b   *Notting Hill*
c   *Amélie*
Paris ☐   Tokyo ☐   London ☐

2 ***The Good, the Bad and the Ugly* is called a "spaghetti western." Why?**
a   Because most of the actors were Italian.
b   Because it was shot in Italy.
c   Because it was made by an Italian studio.

3 **What is the boarding school called in the Harry Potter movies?**
a   Hogwarts
b   Hogarths
c   Howards

FAMOUS LINES

Match the movies and these famous lines.
1   "This is my neighborhood, this is my street. My name is Lester Burnham. I'm 42 years old."
2   "I'll never let go. I'll never let go, Jack."
3   "My Momma always said life was like a box of chocolates."
4   "I'll have what she's having."
5   "May the force be with you."

a   *Star Wars*
b   *Titanic*
c   *When Harry met Sally*
d   *Forrest Gump*
e   *American Beauty*

MUSIC

1 **Which 2001 musical starred Nicole Kidman and Ewan McGregor?**
a   *Chicago*
b   *Moulin Rouge*
c   *Cabaret*

2 **Who composed the soundtrack for *Star Wars*?**
a   John Williams
b   Ennio Morricone
c   Howard Shore

3 **Which famous musical is based on the true story of the Von Trapp family?**
a   *West Side Story*
b   *The Sound of Music*
c   *Phantom of the Opera*

MOVIE TITLES

Correct these movie titles.
1   *Close Encounters of the Fourth Kind*
2   *The Chronicles of Narnia: The Lion, the Witch and the Armchair*
3   *Dead Athlete's Society*
4   *Elephant Dundee*
5   *Four Weddings and Two Funerals*
6   *The Godmother*
7   *A Hundred and Three Dalmatians*
8   *Kill Jill*
9   *Mission Improbable*
10   *Silence of the Cows*

CARD 1

a teetotaler /ˈtitoʊtlər/
1 a person who never drinks alcohol ✔
2 the card where you write your score in golf
3 _____

a nightingale /ˈnaɪtŋgeɪl/
1 a small lamp that children have on during the night
2 _____
3 a bird that sings at night ✔

a stroller /ˈstroʊlər/
1 a thing you put a small child in when you take it for a walk ✔
2 a kind of dessert that is made with apples
3 _____

CARD 2

a midwife /ˈmɪdwaɪf/
1 a woman who lives with a man but is not married
2 _____
3 a person that helps a woman when she has a baby ✔

a saucepan /ˈsɔspæn/
1 a thing made of metal that you use for cooking, for example, rice ✔
2 _____
3 a kind of tree that has very long branches

a forger /ˈfɔrdʒər/
1 a person who makes illegal copies of money or paintings ✔
2 a note that helps you remember something
3 _____

CARD 3

a widower /ˈwɪdoʊər/
1 a person who watches a TV program
2 _____
3 a man whose wife has died ✔

a lighthouse /ˈlaɪthaʊs/
1 a small building in a garden where people keep gardening equipment
2 _____
3 a tall building with a light on the top that tells ships when there is danger ✔

a sidekick /ˈsaɪdkɪk/
1 _____
2 a kick that sends the ball sideways
3 a person who is a close friend or assistant of someone important and is frequently seen with him/her ✔

CARD 4

a busybody /ˈbɪzibɑdi/
1 a person who works in show business
2 a person who is too interested in other people's lives ✔
3 _____

a lullaby /ˈlʌləbaɪ/
1 a song that you sing to a baby to make it sleep ✔
2 _____
3 a small animal like a kangaroo

a cellar /ˈsɛlər/
1 the thing you use to charge your phone
2 _____
3 a room under a house, where people keep things like wine ✔

CARD 5

an undertaker /ˈʌndərteɪkər/
1 a person who works for the subway
2 a person who organizes funerals ✔
3 _____

a jigsaw /ˈdʒɪgsɔ/
1 _____
2 a dance that is very popular in Ireland
3 a game that has pieces you put together to make a picture ✔

a greenhouse /ˈgrinhaʊs/
1 a house that uses solar energy
2 a small building made of glass where people keep plants ✔
3 _____

CARD 6

a deadline /ˈdɛdlaɪn/
1 a phone that isn't working
2 a time or date that work must be finished by ✔
3 _____

a grasshopper /ˈgræshɑpər/
1 a machine that you use for cutting the grass
2 an insect that can jump very high ✔
3 _____

a jetty /ˈdʒɛti/
1 a place where boats land ✔
2 a kind of dessert that's made with gelatin /ˈdʒɛlətin/
3 _____

American English File 3 Teacher's Book
Photocopiable © Oxford University Press 2008

START

1 The movie was in Russian. If it hadn't been subtitled, I …

2 If our best player hadn't been injured, we …

3 I got up late. I would have missed my flight if I …

4 If he had treated his wife better, she …

7 The jacket was beautiful. I would have bought it if it …

6 She wouldn't have lost her job if she …

5 We wouldn't have gotten lost in Dallas if we …

8 We would have picked you up at the airport if you …

9 If I had known it was your birthday, I …

10 You would have done better on the exam if you …

11 I would have married Sally if she …

14 You would have slept better if you …

13 If I had been able to go to college, I …

12 He wouldn't have crashed his car if he …

15 We would have gotten a table at the restaurant if we …

16 If the weather hadn't been so bad yesterday, we …

17 I would have been here on time if I …

18 He would have been a great basketball player if he …

FINISH

189

A

a You are a tourist in London. You would like to visit the Sherlock Holmes Museum and the Bloody Tower. **B** works for tourist information. Ask **B** politely for the following information, using *Could you tell me…?*

Sherlock Holmes Museum
open on Saturdays? _____
what time / close? _____
where? _____
adult's ticket? £ _____

The Bloody Tower
open on Sundays? _____
what time / open? _____
what / nearest subway (Tube) station? _____
child's ticket? £ _____

b Now you work for tourist information in London. Use the information below to answer **B**'s questions.

If you like murder mysteries and horror stories…
you must visit these places in London

The Chamber of Horrors

This is part of the world-famous Madame Tussaud's museum. Here you can see waxworks of many infamous murderers, including Vlad the Impaler, Jean-Paul Marat, Dr. Crippen, and many more.

Address	Madame Tussaud's Marylebone Road (near Baker Street Tube station) London
Opening hours	Weekdays 9:30 to 17:30 Weekends 9:00 to 18:00
Admission	Adult £23.99 Child (under 16) £19.99

The London Dungeon

This attraction recreates many of history's most horrific events. Explore the streets of Victorian London that were home to the serial killer Jack the Ripper, relive the Great Fire of London, and take a boat down the River Thames to the infamous Traitors' Gate at the Tower of London.

Address	London Dungeon 28–34 Tooley Street, London SE1 2SZ
Opening hours	Every day 9:30 a.m. to 5:30 p.m.
Admission	Adult £15.50 Child (5 to 15) £10.95

c Compare your information with **B**. You can visit just one of these places. Try to agree which one and why.

B

a You work for tourist information in London. Use the information below to answer **A**'s questions.

If you like murder mysteries and horror stories…
you must visit these places in London

The Sherlock Holmes Museum

Visit the house where Sherlock Holmes lived and where he solved many of his most famous cases!

Address	221b Baker Street, London
Opening hours	Open every day (except Christmas Day) from 9:30 a.m. to 6 p.m.
Admission	Adult £6 Child (under 16) £4

The Bloody Tower

The most famous tower in the Tower of London. This is where the Little Princes were murdered in 1483 by King Richard III and where Anne Boleyn (Henry VIII's second wife) was imprisoned before her execution. If you are lucky, you may see her ghost!

Address	Tower of London London EC3N 4AB (near Tower Hill tube station)
Opening hours	Tuesday–Saturday 9:00–18:00 Sunday, Monday 10:00–18:00
Admission	Adult £14.50 Child (under 16) £9.50

b Now you are a tourist in London. You would like to visit the Chamber of Horrors and the London Dungeon. Ask **A** politely for the following information, using *Could you tell me…?*

Chamber of Horrors
open on Saturdays? _____
what time / close? _____
what / nearest subway (Tube) station? _____
adult's ticket? £ _____

The London Dungeon
where? _____
open every day? _____
what time / close? _____
child's ticket? £ _____

c Compare your information with **A**. You can visit just one of these places. Try to agree which one and why.

American English File 3 Teacher's Book
Photocopiable © Oxford University Press 2008

1 What's the first thing you usually **ask for** when you get to a restaurant?

_____

2 Can you name a celebrity couple who have recently **broken up**?

_____

3 Can you think of two places where you have to **check in**?

_____

4 Can you think of two things you do when you **wake up**?

_____

5 How can you **find out** what movies are playing?

_____

6 Can you name three things you should **give up** if you're on a diet?

_____

7 What are two typical things young children want to be when they **grow up**?

_____

8 What do people usually say to each other when they **hang up**?

_____

9 Can you name two times of year that people normally **look forward to**?

_____

10 Can you name two books that have recently been **made into** movies?

_____

11 Can you name a person who has **set up** a famous successful company?

_____

12 When do you normally tell somebody to **slow down**?

_____

13 What can you **look up** in a dictionary?

_____

14 Can you name three things you should **turn off** before you go to bed?

_____

15 Can you name two activities you could **take up** if you wanted to get in shape?

_____

16 What's the thing you need to have when you **take** something **back** to a store?

_____

17 What do you need to fasten when a plane **takes off**?

_____

18 Can you name a thing you have to **fill out**?

_____

19 When is it important for athletes to **warm up**?

_____

20 Can you name three things you can **turn on** with a remote control?

_____

American English File 3 Teacher's Book
Photocopiable © Oxford University Press 2008

1 The movies

Think of a movie (but don't say the name). Describe it for a partner to guess.
- Where is it set?
- Is it based on a book?
- Who was it directed by?
- Who's in it?
- What's it about?

2 Your education

Tell your partner about your elementary school.
- What school did you use to go to?
- Did you use to wear a uniform?
- What subjects did you use to like?
- What subjects weren't you good at?
- What weren't you allowed to do?
- What did the teachers make you do?

3 Your family

Describe a member of your family.
- What does he / she look like? (Describe him / her.)
- What's he / she like? (Give two positive and two negative characteristics.)
- How are you similar / different?

4 Sports

Tell your partner about:
- a sport you really like watching / playing
- a sport you hate watching / playing
- a sport you used to play and why you stopped
- the sporting event / game you most remember

5 Your home

Tell your partner:
- where you live
- how long you've lived there
- who you live with
- if you get along well
- what you argue about

6 Your diet

Talk for a minute about your diet.
- Is your diet healthy or unhealthy? Why?
- Do you eat too much / not enough of anything?
- Are you trying to cut down on anything at the moment?
- What do you usually eat when you eat out?

7 Work

Think of a friend or family member who has a job. Tell your partner about the good and bad side of his / her job. Talk about:
- salary
- working hours
- the kind of contract
- vacation days
- stress

8 Transportation

Talk to your partner about the kinds of public transportation in your town.
- Which do you think is the best? Why?
- How do you get to work or school?
- How long does it take you?

9 Experiences

Tell your partner about a time when you …
- felt very frightened …
or - felt very embarrassed …
or - felt very excited …
or - felt very stressed or nervous …
or - got very angry.

10 Preferences

Tell your partner which you prefer and why:
- vacations abroad / in your country
- traveling by car / by plane
- eating at home / in a restaurant
- living in a big city / small town
- shopping in large supermarkets / small stores

1 Describing game

A card game

SS define words / phrases for other SS to guess. Copy and cut up one set of cards per pair or small group.

> **VOCABULARY** Food, sport, adjectives of personality

- Put SS in pairs or small groups. Give each group a set of cards face down or in an envelope.
- Demonstrate the activity. Choose another word or words (not on the cards) from one of the three Vocabulary Banks and describe it to the class until someone says the word, e.g., *It's an adjective. It can describe food you keep in the freezer.* **Emphasize that SS are not allowed to use the word on the card in their definition.**
- SS play the game, taking turns taking a card and describing the word / phrase. The person who is describing must not let his / her partner see what's on the card. Tell SS to wait until the person has finished his / her description before trying to guess the word.

Extra idea You could have SS play this in groups as a competitive game. The person who correctly guesses the word first keeps the card. The player with the most cards at the end is the winner.

Non-cut alternative Put SS in pairs. Copy one sheet per pair and cut it down the middle. SS take turns describing the words to their partner until he / she guesses the word.

2 Split crossword puzzle

An information gap activity

SS define words / phrases to help their partner complete a crossword. Copy one sheet per pair and cut into **A** and **B**.

> **VOCABULARY** Money, transportation, extreme adjectives (*furious*, etc.)

- Put SS in pairs, ideally face to face, and give out the sheets. **Make sure SS can't see each other's sheets.** Explain that **A** and **B** have the same crossword puzzle but with different words missing. They have to describe / define words to each other to complete their crosswords.
- Give SS a minute to read their instructions. If SS don't know what a word means, they can look it up in Vocabulary Banks **Money** and **Transportation and travel** and the vocabulary exercise on extreme adjectives in Lesson **2B** (*furious, starving*, etc.). Make sure SS understand the difference between *across* and *down*.
- SS take turns asking each other for their missing words (e.g., *What's 1 across?*). Their partner must define / describe the word until the other student is able to write it in his / her crossword. SS should help each other with clues if necessary.
- When SS have finished, they should compare their crosswords to make sure they have the same words and have spelled them correctly.

3 Pictionary

A group card game

SS draw pictures of words on cards for other SS to guess. Copy and cut up one set of cards per group.

> **VOCABULARY** Telephoning, physical description, *-ed / -ing* adjectives

- Put SS in small groups. Give each group a set of cards face down or in an envelope.
- Demonstrate the activity by picking a card and trying to draw the word / phrase from the card on the board until someone guesses the word / phrase you are trying to draw. **Emphasize that they are not allowed to say anything, but they can indicate by gesture whether the guesses are good or not.**
- SS play the game, taking turns picking a card and trying to draw the word / phrase. The person who is describing must not let anyone see what's on the card. SS can make guesses while the person is drawing. The person who correctly guesses the word first keeps the card. The player with the most cards at the end is the winner.

Non-cut alternative Put SS in pairs. Copy one sheet per pair and cut it in two horizontally. SS take turns drawing their words for their partner until he/she guesses the word.

4 What's the difference?

A team game

SS have to explain the difference between two words / phrases. Copy and cut up one set of cards.

> **VOCABULARY** Education, houses, friendship

- Divide the class into two teams (or more if you have a lot of students) and explain the activity. You give a card to each team and they have a minute to decide what the difference is between the two words or phrases. **Write the two words / phrases up on the board.** A spokesperson from the team tries to explain the difference to the rest of the class. If the explanation is correct, they get a point. If it isn't correct, the other team can try to win an extra point by explaining it correctly before having their own turn. Then give each team another card.
- Write up the teams' points on the board and add them up to see which team wins.

> A **preschool** is for very small children, e.g., 1–4 years-old.
> An **elementary school** is for young children, e.g., 4–11 years-old.
> A **subject** is something you study, e.g., math.
> **Discipline** is control, order.
> A **teacher** is a person who teaches, usually in a school, but in other situations as well.
> A **professor** teaches in a college / university. He / She is usually a senior member of the staff.

A **fireplace** is the place in the house where you light the fire.

A **chimney** is a hole in the roof out of which the smoke leaves the house.

A **coffee table** is small and usually found in the living room.

A **bedside table** is the small table next to your bed.

You open and close the **door** to leave / enter your house.

A **gate** is a door in an exterior wall, for example around a garden.

Junior high (school) usually includes grades seven to eight or nine.

High school usually includes grades nine or ten to twelve.

A **sofa** usually has room for 2 or 3 people.

An **armchair** is for one person.

A **town** is a place with many streets and buildings, houses, stores, factories, etc.

A **village** is much smaller than a town and is usually in the country. Sometimes it has only a few houses.

You **meet** someone when you see and talk to them (for the first time).

You **know someone** when you have already met them.

A **public school** is run by the government and is usually free.

You have to pay to go to a **private school**.

A **classmate** is someone who studies in your class.

A **roommate** is someone who shares a room or a house / an apartment with you.

To **review** means to study for an exam, i.e., look again and try to remember what you have studied previously.

To **learn** means to get knowledge of something.

A **penthouse** is an apartment on the top floor of a building.

A **townhouse** is a house with two or three floors, usually connected to other similar houses.

A **patio** is an outside area next to a house where you can sit and eat, etc.

A **balcony** is a kind of platform built onto the outside of the house with a wall or rail around it.

A **dishwasher** is for washing plates, cups, etc.

A **washing machine** is for washing clothes.

The **ceiling** is the top part of a room, opposite the floor.

The **roof** is the part of a house on the outside that covers the top.

The **country** is the land outside towns and cities where there are trees and plants, etc.

The **suburbs** is the area around a city (i.e., not the center) where people live.

A **friend** is someone you know and like.

A **coworker** is someone you work with (not necessarily a friend).

You **keep in touch** when you see, call, or write to a friend regularly.

You **lose touch** when you do not see, call, or write to a friend.

Non-cut alternative Put SS in pairs. Copy one sheet per pair and cut it down the middle. Set a time limit, e.g., 10 minutes, and SS take turns asking each other, *What's the difference between…?*, choosing words at random. SS decide if the explanation is correct. Finally, check answers with the whole class.

5 Pick a card

A pairwork (or group) card game

SS ask each other questions on cards to test their memory of common words and phrases. Copy and cut up one set of cards per pair or group.

VOCABULARY Work, prepositions, word building

- Put SS in pairs or small groups and give each pair / group a set of cards face down or in an envelope.
- Demonstrate the activity by picking a card and asking the group the question, e.g., *What's the missing preposition? "I'm applying ___ a job."* (Make the noise "beep" to show that there is a missing preposition.) Point out that the answer to each question is written in capital letters on the card.
- SS play the game, taking turns picking up a card and asking his / her partner or members of the group the question.

Extra idea You could divide the class into two teams and pick cards yourself and ask the questions. Keep a record of the score on the board.

Non-cut alternative Put SS in pairs. Copy one sheet per pair and cut it down the middle. SS take turns asking each other the questions.

6 Alphabet race

A pairwork vocabulary race

SS read a series of clues and write the words. Copy one sheet per student or pair of students.

VOCABULARY Shopping, professions, movies

- Put SS in pairs and give out the sheets. Set a time limit. Tell SS that they have to write as many words as they can within the time limit. Each word begins with the letter of the alphabet at the top of the circle. The pair that completes all the words correctly first is the winner.

Audience, Bargain, Comedy, Department store, Extras, Fan, Guarantee, Hero, Inventor, Just, Kind, Library, Manager, Newsstand, Online, Plot, Quit, Receipt, Sales, Thriller, Up, Violinist, Western.

7 Split crossword puzzle

An information gap activity

See instructions for **File 2 Split crossword puzzle**. The words here come from Vocabulary Bank **Phrasal verbs** and from lessons **7A** and **7B**.

VOCABULARY phrasal verbs, compound nouns, television

Review

A group card game

See instructions for **File 1 Describing game**.

VOCABULARY Review from Files 1–7

American English File 3 Teacher's Book
Photocopiable © Oxford University Press 2008

shrimp 	**a peach** 	**a menu** 	**sausage** 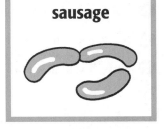
a spoon 	**a dessert** 	**an appetizer** 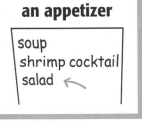	**strawberries** 
a coach 	**a referee** 	**(to) do aerobics** 	**(to) get injured** 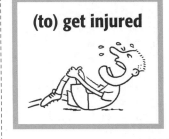
spectators 	**a stadium** 	**a team** 	**(to) tie** 
aggressive 	**messy** 	**bossy** 	**lazy** 
ambitious 	**competitive** 	**unsociable** 	**talkative** 

American English File 3 Teacher's Book
Photocopiable © Oxford University Press 2008

A

a Look at your crossword puzzle and make sure you know the meaning of all the words you have.

b Now ask **B** to define a word for you. Ask e.g., *What's 1 across? What's 2 down?* Write the word in.

c Now **B** will ask you to define a word.

B

a Look at your crossword puzzle and make sure you know the meaning of all the words you have.

b A will ask you to define a word.

c Now ask **A** to define a word for you. Ask e.g., *What's 1 down? What's 5 across?* Write the word in.

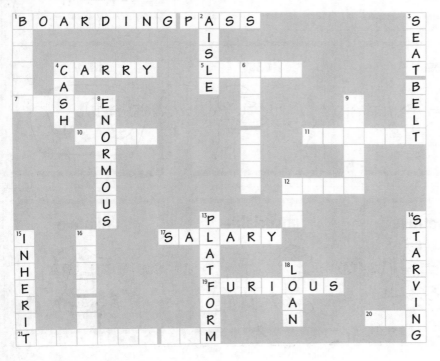

American English File 3 Teacher's Book
Photocopiable © Oxford University Press 2008

text message	beard	shoulder-length hair
depressed	overweight	ponytail
frightening	handsome	mustache
boring	bangs	ring tone
dial	straight hair	well-built
bald	excited	medium height

American English File 3 Teacher's Book
Photocopiable © Oxford University Press 2008

preschool	an elementary school	a private school	a public school
discipline	subject	classmate	roommate
a professor	a teacher	review	learn
a chimney	a fireplace	a penthouse	a townhouse
a coffee table	a bedside table	a balcony	a patio
a door	a gate	a dishwasher	a washing machine
junior high	high school	the roof	the ceiling
sofa	an armchair	the suburbs	the country
a town	a village	a coworker	a friend
meet someone	know someone	keep in touch	lose touch

What's the missing preposition? I'm applying ____ a job. **FOR**	What's the missing preposition? I work ____ a salesperson. **AS**
What's the missing preposition? He's not very good ____ cooking. **AT**	What are the missing prepositions? Don't talk ____ me ____ baseball. **TO, ABOUT**
What's the opposite of a "full-time" job? **A PART-TIME JOB**	What's another way of saying "lose your job"? get _____ **FIRED**
What's another way of saying "I work for myself"? **I'M SELF-EMPLOYED.**	What's the noun from "organize"? **ORGANIZATION**
What's the noun from "crazy"? **CRAZINESS**	What's the noun from "survive"? **SURVIVAL**
What's the missing preposition? I don't agree ____ you. **WITH**	What's the missing preposition? He's ____ charge of 50 employees. **IN**
What are the missing prepositions? I'm ____ my third year ____ college. **IN, IN**	What's the opposite of a "permanent" job? **A TEMPORARY JOB**
What's the opposite of "lend to"? **BORROW FROM**	What's another way of saying "make something smaller"? **REDUCE**
What's the word for the money you get from your job? **YOUR SALARY**	What's the noun from "govern"? **GOVERNMENT**
What's the noun from "relax"? **RELAXATION**	What's the noun from "decide"? **DECISION**

A
the people who watch a movie in a theater
_____

B
something that you buy at a very good price
_____

C
a movie that makes you laugh
_____

D
a big store, usually on several floors, where you can buy all kinds of things (two words)
_____

E
people who appear in a movie, e.g., in crowd scenes, but who don't talk
_____

F
somebody who really likes a sports team or movie star, etc.
_____

G
a written promise that a store will repair something you buy
_____

H
a brave person who people admire
_____

I
a person who invents things
_____

J
"Can I help you?" "No thanks. I'm _____ looking."

K
What _____ of movies do you like?

L
a place where you can borrow books
_____

M
a person who is in charge of a store, restaurant, or business, etc.
_____

N
the store where you can buy papers and magazines
_____

O
Many people today shop _____ (i.e., use the Internet).

P
the story of a movie
_____

Q
to leave a job
_____

R
a piece of paper they give you when you buy something
_____

S
a time when stores sell things cheaper
_____

T
a movie with a very exciting story, e.g., Hitchcock's *Psycho*
_____

U
Bill Gates set _____ a foundation to help children all over the world.

V
a person who plays the violin
_____

W
a movie about cowboys
_____

A

a Look at your crossword puzzle and make sure you know the meaning of all the words you have.

b Now ask **B** to define a word for you. Ask e.g., *What's 6 across? What's 1 down?* Write the word in.

c Now **B** will ask you to define a word.

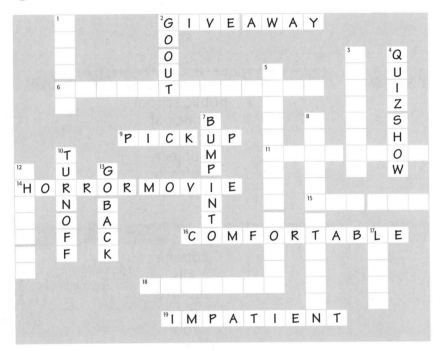

B

a Look at your crossword puzzle and make sure you know the meaning of all the words you have.

b **A** will ask you to define a word.

c Now ask **A** to define a word for you. Ask e.g., *What's 2 across? What's 2 down?* Write the word in.

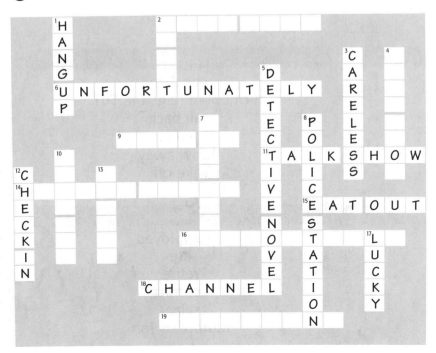

American English File 3 Teacher's Book
Photocopiable © Oxford University Press 2008

Describing people

in his mid-twenties
bald
beard
overweight
gray hair
bangs

Personality

selfish
bossy
moody
impatient
spoiled
shy

Movies

horror movie
soundtrack
dubbed
cast
sequel
plot

Education

public school
principal
schedule
subject
professor
fail an exam

Food and restaurants

seafood
spicy
check
spoon
boiled
napkin

Houses

cottage
city
suburbs
gate
roof
dishwasher

Shopping

complain
discount
customer
newsstand
refund
line

Sport

referee
coach
tennis court
beat
tie
warm up

Travel and transportation

flight
station
luggage
truck
seat belt
traffic jam

Phrasal verbs

check in
turn down (e.g., the TV)
call back
give up
throw away
take off

Money

waste (money)
inherit
loan
coin
tax
borrow

Work

unemployed
fire
retire
contract
salary
temporary job

1 C We are family 1.12 — CD1 Track 13

Correcting words

LANGUAGE Mixed vocabulary

- Give each student a sheet and focus on **a**. Go through the words in **bold** and explain that SS have to listen and decide if these words are right (what the singer sings) or wrong (different). The first time they listen, SS just have to put a check or an x in column **A**. They shouldn't try to correct the words at this stage.

- Check answers (i.e., if the words are right or wrong), but don't tell SS what the right words are.

- Now focus on **b**. Play the song again and this time SS have to try to correct the wrong words.

- Let SS compare with a partner and then check answers, going through the song line by line.

1 ✗ together	10 ✓
2 ✓	11 ✗ future
3 ✓	12 ✓
4 ✗ tell	13 ✗ depressed
5 ✗ people	14 ✓
6 ✗ close	15 ✗ things
7 ✓	16 ✗ wrong
8 ✗ love	17 ✓
9 ✗ fun	

- If there's time, have SS read the lyrics in pairs with the glossary. Help with any other vocabulary problems.

- You may want to play the song again for SS to sing along.

- Finally have SS read the **Song facts**.

3 C You can get it if you really want 3.14 CD2 Track 6

Listening for specific words

LANGUAGE Modal verbs

- Give each student a sheet and focus on **a**. Emphasize that the missing words are all verbs, but not necessarily in the base form (for example, one is a past participle).

- Give SS a minute or so to read through the lyrics once before they listen. Tell them not to worry about the meaning of the song at this stage.

- Play the recording once for SS to try to write the missing words. Have SS compare their answers with a partner and then play the song again for SS to fill in the blanks. Play specific lines again as necessary. Then check answers.

1 must	6 get
2 succeed	7 get
3 must	8 built
4 Win	9 come
5 lose	10 see

- Now have SS, in pairs, read the lyrics with the glossary and to do task **b**. Check answers. Help with any other vocabulary problems.

1 You can get it if you really want.
2 Got your mind set on a dream.
3 Rome was not built in a day.
4 Opposition will come your way.
5 The harder the battle ... the sweeter the victory.

- You may want to play the song again for the class to sing along.

- Finally, have SS read the **Song facts**.

4 B Our house 4.10 CD2 Track 22

Listening for specific words

LANGUAGE General vocabulary

- Give each student a sheet and focus on **a**. Emphasize that the clues in parentheses will help SS to decide what the missing words are when they listen.

- Give SS a minute or so to read through the lyrics once before they listen. Tell them not to worry about the meaning of the song at this stage.

- Play the recording once for SS to try to write the missing words. Have SS compare their answers with a partner and then play the song again for SS to fill in the blanks. Play specific lines again as necessary. Then check answers.

1 Sunday	6 mom
2 tired	7 late
3 downstairs	8 shirt
4 Brother	9 school
5 always	10 happy

- Now have SS, in pairs, read the lyrics with the glossary and do task **b**. Check answers. Help with any other vocabulary problems which arise.

1 His memory of his home seems to be very positive. He talks about "such a happy time" and he describes his family and home life with affection. However, one line of the song says: "Something tells you that you've got to move away from it." Perhaps this is how he felt when he was a teenager and wanted to become independent of his family.
2 busy ✓   clean ✓   crowded ✓   traditional ✓

- You may want to play the song again for the class to sing along.

- Finally, have SS read the **Song facts**.

5 B Sk8er Boi 5.12   CD2 Track 44

Listening for articles

LANGUAGE	*a* / *an*, *the*, or no article

- Give each student a sheet and focus on **a**. Then play the song once. Have SS compare answers and then play it again.

  EXTRA challenge Have SS try to fill in the blanks before they listen, and then play the song for them to listen and check. Check answers.

1 a	15 a
2 a	16 (-)
3 a	17 (-)
4 (-)	18 the
5 a	19 the
6 a	20 the
7 a	21 the
8 (-)	22 a
9 (-)	23 a
10 (-)	24 the
11 the	25 the
12 the	26 the
13 the	27 the
14 a	28 a

- Now focus on **b**. Have SS read the lyrics in pairs using the glossary and the pictures to help them. Help with any other vocabulary problems. Have each pair decide what they think the moral of the song is and elicit ideas.

  Suggested answer
  You shouldn't judge people by their appearance / social status. Losers might end up being winners, etc.

- You may want to play the song again for SS to sing along.
- Finally have SS read the **Song facts**.

---

6 C Holding out for a hero 6.11   CD3 Track 12

Listening for adjectives

LANGUAGE	Adjectives

- Give each student a sheet and focus on **a**. Then play the song once. Have SS compare answers and then play it again. Check answers.

1 good	6 fresh
2 white	7 sure
3 Late	8 soon
4 strong	9 larger
5 fast	10 wildest

- Now focus on **b**. Have SS read the lyrics in pairs, using the glossary and the pictures to help them. Help with any other vocabulary problems and get them to match the highlighted weather words to the definitions. Check answers.

1 storm	2 wind	3 thunder	4 lightning	5 flood

- You may want to play the song again for SS to sing along.
- Finally have SS read the **Song facts**.

---

7 A Ironic 7.5   CD3 Track 23

Reading and understanding a song

LANGUAGE	General vocabulary and grammar

- Give each student a sheet and focus on task **a**. Point out that they should just write the number in each box. Give SS a few minutes to read the song and try to guess the missing phrase. Then have them compare their answers with a partner.
- Focus on task **b**. Play the recording for SS to check their answers. Then check answers with the whole class.

1 B	6 C
2 J	7 H
3 G	8 E
4 A	9 I
5 F	10 D

- If there's time, have SS read the lyrics in pairs with the glossary. Help with any other vocabulary problems.

  EXTRA challenge Have SS cover the lyrics and try to remember as many examples of bad luck from the song as they can.

- You may want to play the song again for the class to sing along.
- Finally, have SS read the **Song facts**.

a Listen to the song. Are the words in bold right or wrong? Put a ✓ or an ✗ in column **A**.

b Listen again and correct the wrong words in column **B**.

We are family

		A	B
Everyone can see we're **friends**	1		
As we **walk** on by	2		
And we flock just like **birds** of a feather	3		
I won't **say** no lie	4		
All of the **women** around us they say,	5		
"Can they be that **friendly**?"	6		
Just let me state for the **record**	7		
We're giving **money** in a family dose	8		

We are family
I got all my sisters with me
We are family
Get up everybody, sing

We are family, etc.

Living life is **great** and we've just begun	9		
To get our share of this **world's** delights	10		
High hopes we have for the **summer**	11		
And our goal's in **sight**	12		
No, we don't get **sad**	13		
Here's what we call our **golden** rule:	14		
Have faith in you and the **work** you do	15		
You won't go **down**, oh no	16		
This is our family **jewel**	17		

We are family, etc.

Glossary

flock like birds of a feather = stay together, like birds of the same species

state for the record = say so that everybody knows it

dose = the amount of a medicine you have to take

delights = nice things

our goal = what we are trying to do

jewel = a valuable stone, e.g. a diamond

Song facts

The song was originally recorded in 1979 by Sister Sledge, four sisters whose last name was Sledge. The writers of the song (Bernard Edwards and Nile Rodgers) got the idea for the song from seeing how well the four sisters got along with each other.

We are family was a worldwide hit and became an anthem for women's groups, sports teams, and political parties.

a Listen to the song and fill in the missing verbs.

You can get it if you really want

You can get it if you really want,
You can get it if you really want,
You can get it if you really want,
But you ¹m_____ try, try and try,
Try and try,
You'll ² s_____ at last.

Persecution you ³ m_____ bear,
⁴ W_____ or ⁵ l_____, you've got to ⁶g_____
  your share
Got your mind set on a dream
You can ⁷ g_____ it, though hard it seems
Now

You can get it if you really want, etc.

Rome was not ⁸ b_____ in a day,
Opposition will ⁹ c_____ your way
But the harder the battle you ¹⁰ s_____,
Is the sweeter the victory
Now

You can get it if you really want, etc.

b Read the lyrics with the glossary and find a phrase that means:
1 You will get what you want in the end.
2 You have a clear idea what you want to do or get.
3 It takes a long time to do something well.
4 There will be difficulties.
5 If something is very difficult to do, you'll enjoy it
   more when you've done it.

Glossary

persecution = making someone suffer for what they believe
your share = the part that belongs to you
got your mind = you have your mind
set on = fixed on
opposition = people or things that are against you

Song facts

You can get it if you really want was written and first
recorded by the Jamaican singer Jimmy Cliff. It later
appeared on the soundtrack of the 1973 movie
The Harder They Come, which starred Jimmy Cliff and
introduced reggae music and Jamaican culture to an
international audience.

a Listen to the song and write the missing words 1–10. Use the clues (in parentheses) to help you.

Our house

Father wears his **1**_____ best *(a day of the week)*

Mother's **2**_____ she needs a rest *(adjective)*

The kids are playing up **3**_____ *(part of the house)*

Sister's sighing in her sleep

4_____'s got a date to keep *(member of the family)*

He can't hang around

Our house, in the middle of our street

Our house, in the middle of our...

Our house it has a crowd

There's **5**_____ something happening *(adverb of frequency)*

And it's usually quite loud

Our **6**_____ she's so house-proud *(member of the family, colloquial)*

Nothing ever slows her down and a mess is not allowed

Our house, in the middle of our street, etc.

(Something tells you that you've got to move away from it)

Father gets up **7**_____ for work *(adverb of time)*

Mother has to iron his **8**_____ *(something you wear)*

Then she sends the kids to **9**_____ *(a place)*

Sees them off with a small kiss

She's the one they're going to miss in lots of ways

Our house, in the middle of our street, etc.

I remember way back then when everything was true
 and when

We would have such a very good time
 such a fine time

Such a **10**_____ time *(adjective)*

And I remember how we'd play, simply waste the day away

Then we'd say nothing would come between us two dreamers

Repeat first verse (Father wears his..., etc.)

Our house, in the middle of our street, etc.

Glossary

Sunday best = best clothes

playing up = behaving badly

sighing = making a sad
 sound

has got a date = has a
 meeting (with a girl)

hang around = stay here for
 long

house-proud = a person
 who likes to keep her
 house clean and neat

you've got to = you have to

---

b Read the song with the glossary and answer the questions.

1 Do you think the singer's memory of his home is positive or negative?

2 Which of these adjectives would you use to describe his house?
 Check the boxes.

 busy ☐ quiet ☐ clean ☐ messy ☐ crowded ☐ traditional ☐

Song facts

Our house was the British group Madness's biggest international hit. Twenty years later, the musical *Our House*, based on Madness's songs, opened in London's West End and won the 2003 Olivier Award for "Best New Musical."

American English File 3 Teacher's Book
Photocopiable © Oxford University Press 2008

a Listen and fill in the blanks with *a, the* or –.

b What do you think the moral of the song is?

Sk8er Boi

He was ¹_____ boy, she was ²_____ girl

Can I make it any more obvious?

He was ³_____ punk, she did ⁴_____ ballet

What more can I say?

He wanted her, she'd never tell

Secretly she wanted him as well

But all of her friends just stuck up their nose

They had ⁵_____ problem with his baggy clothes.

He was ⁶_____ skater boy

She said "See you later boy"

He wasn't good enough for her

She had ⁷_____ pretty face

But her head was up in ⁸_____ space

She needed to come back down to ⁹_____ earth.

BALLET SCHOOL

Five years from now, she sits at ¹⁰_____ home

Feeding ¹¹_____ baby, she's all alone

She turns on TV. Guess who she sees?

Skater boy rocking up MTV.

She calls up her friends, they already know

And they've all got tickets to see his show

She tags along, but stands in ¹²_____ crowd

Looks up at ¹³_____ man that she turned down.

He was ¹⁴_____ skater boy

She said, "See you later boy"

He wasn't good enough for her

Now he's ¹⁵_____ superstar

Slamming on his guitar

Does your pretty face see what he's worth? (Repeat)

Sorry girl but you missed out

Well tough luck, that boy's ¹⁶_____ mine now

We are more than just ¹⁷_____ good friends

This is how ¹⁸_____ story ends.

Too bad that you couldn't see,

See ¹⁹_____ man that boy could be

There is more than meets ²⁰_____ eye

I see ²¹_____ soul that is inside.

He's just ²²_____ boy , and I'm just ²³_____ girl

Can I make it any more obvious?

We are in love, haven't you heard

How we rock each other's world?

I'm with ²⁴_____ skater boy, I said see ya later boy

I'll be back stage after ²⁵_____ show,

I'll be at ²⁶_____ studio

singing ²⁷_____ song we wrote

about ²⁸_____ girl you used to know. (Repeat)

Glossary

stuck up their nose = thought they were superior

baggy = very loose, not tight

rocking up = playing loud music

tags along = goes with her friends

she turned down = she said "no" (to him)

slamming on his guitar = playing his guitar loudly

missed out = lost your opportunity

tough luck = bad luck

rock each other's world = make each other happy

back stage = the place behind where the musicians play

Song facts

Sk8er Boi was originally recorded by Avril Lavigne in 2002. Some people say that the song is autobiographical (she was the skater boy!). The song was a worldwide hit.

a Listen to the song and fill in the blanks with the missing adjectives (one of them is a comparative and one is a superlative).

b Read the lyrics with the glossary. Match the highlighted words to their definitions.

1 _____ very bad weather with heavy rain, etc.

2 _____ air that is moving fast

3 _____ the loud noise that you hear during a storm

4 _____ a bright flash of light that appears in the sky during a storm

5 _____ a large amount of water (from a river, the sea, or heavy rain)

Holding out for a hero

Where have all the ¹ g_____ men gone
and where are all the gods?
Where's the streetwise Hercules
to fight the rising odds?
Isn't there a ² w_____ knight upon a fiery steed?
³ L_____ at night I toss and I turn and I dream of what I need.

I need a hero
I'm holding out for a hero till the end of the night.
He's got to be ⁴ s_____ and he's got to be ⁵ f_____
and he's got to be ⁶ f_____ from the fight.
I need a hero
I'm holding out for a hero till the morning light.
He's got to be ⁷ s_____ and it's got to be ⁸ s_____
And he's got to be ⁹ l_____ than life
(⁹)L_____ than life.

Somewhere after midnight
In my ¹⁰ w_____ fantasy
Somewhere just beyond my reach
There's someone reaching back for me.
Racing on the thunder and rising with the heat
It's gonna take a Superman to sweep me off my feet.

I need a hero, etc.

Up where the mountains meet the heavens above
Out where the lightning splits the sea
I could swear there is someone somewhere watching me.
Through the wind and the chill and the rain
and the storm and the flood
I can feel his approach like a fire in the blood.

I need a hero, etc.

Glossary

streetwise = a person who can look after himself
rising odds = the opposition, people who are against us
fiery steed = a wild horse
toss and turn = move, in bed
I'm holding out for = I'm waiting for
beyond my reach = too far away for me to touch
reaching back for me = trying to take my hand
it's gonna take a Superman = he'll have to be a Superman
to sweep me off my feet = for me to fall in love with him
chill = cold
his approach = he's coming nearer

Song facts

Holding Out For a Hero was written for Bonnie Tyler in 1982 by Jim Steinman and Dean Pitchford. Steinman also wrote all of Meat Loaf's hits as well as *Total Eclipse of the Heart* for Tyler. A version by Jennifer Saunders was the theme song to the 2004 movie *Shrek 2*.

Ironic

An old man turned ninety-eight
He [1]_____ and died the next day
It's a black fly in your Chardonnay
It's a death row pardon [2]_____
And isn't it ironic... don't you think?

It's like rain on your [3]_____
It's a free ride when you've [4]_____
It's the good advice that you just didn't take
And who would've thought...? It figures.

Mr. Play-It-Safe was afraid to fly
He [5]_____ and kissed his kids good-bye
He waited his whole damn life to take that flight
And as the plane [6]_____ he thought
"Well isn't this nice..."
And isn't it ironic... don't you think?

It's like rain, etc.

Well, life has a funny way of sneaking up on you when
You think everything's okay and everything's going right
And life has a funny way of helping you out when
You think everything's gone wrong and everything blows up
In your face.

A [7]_____ when you're already late
A [8]_____ on your cigarette break
It's like ten thousand spoons when all you need is [9]_____
It's meeting the man of my dreams
And then meeting [10]_____
Isn't it ironic... don't you think?
A little too ironic... yeah, I really do think.

It's like rain, etc.

Well, life has a funny way of sneaking up on you
And life has a funny funny way of helping you out, helping you out.

a Read the song and try to match blanks 1–10 with a phrase A–J.

A already paid ☐
B won the lottery ☐
C crashed down ☐
D his beautiful wife ☐
E no-smoking sign ☐
F packed his suitcase ☐
G wedding day ☐
H traffic jam ☐
I a knife ☐
J two minutes too late ☐

b Listen and check your answers.

Glossary

ironic = strange or amusing because it's the opposite of what you expected
Chardonnay = a kind of white wine
death row = the cells in a prison for prisoners waiting to be executed
It figures. = It makes sense.
sneaking up on you = surprising you
blows up = explodes

Song facts

Ironic was written and first recorded by the Canadian singer Alanis Morissette in 1995. It was her third single and her first top-ten hit. It was nominated for a Grammy in the category "Record of the Year" and in 1996 won the MTV Award for "Best Female Video."

WORKBOOK ANSWER KEY

1 A

1 READING

a 2 T 3 T 4 F 5 T

b 2 believe 3 currently 4 getting
  5 opt for 6 alternative to 7 growing
  8 protect

c 2 believe 3 growing 4 currently
  5 getting 6 opt for 7 protect
  8 global

2 GRAMMAR

a 2 is / 's working
  3 Do you usually get up
  4 don't usually have
  5 What are you doing
  6 love
  7 am / 'm going
  8 doesn't buy
  9 am / 'm trying
  10 feel

b 3 ✓
  4 ✓
  5 I'm talking
  6 What does this word mean?
  7 ✓
  8 It depends
  9 ✓
  10 She isn't coming

3 VOCABULARY

a 2 meat 3 Raw 4 homemade
  5 steak 6 frozen 7 meal 8 spicy
  9 chicken 10 takeout

b 1 a knife 2 a fork
  3 a napkin 4 a glass
  5 shrimp 6 fried eggs
  7 strawberries 8 salt and pepper

4 PRONUNCIATION

a /u/ c̶o̶o̶k̶ /ʊ/ m̶o̶u̶s̶s̶e̶ /u/ c̶o̶o̶k̶i̶e̶
  /ʊ/ l̶e̶t̶t̶u̶c̶e̶

b 2 salmon 3 knife 4 half
  5 wholewheat 6 chocolate

c 1 veg̶e̶tables 2 sa̶l̶mon 3 k̶nife
  4 hal̶f̶ 5 ̶whole wheat 6 choc̶o̶late

LISTENING

a 1

b 1 T 2 F 3 T 4 T 5 F

1 B

1 GRAMMAR

a 1 called, couldn't, had broken down
  2 beat, was winning, scored
  3 arrived, had finished, were sitting
  4 ran, had already left, was,
    were waiting
  5 started, was walking, stopped,
    wasn't wearing, didn't have
  6 were driving, remembered,
    hadn't turned off
  7 didn't recognize, had changed
  8 had already started, turned on,
    was losing, were playing

2 VOCABULARY

a 2 captain 3 fan 4 warm up
  5 shape 6 tennis court 7 referee
  8 ski slope 9 train 10 running track

b 2 had scored 3 tied 4 winning
  5 won 6 played

3 PRONUNCIATION

a shorts, court, sport, warm

b world, first, girl, word, worst

c **stress on 1st syllable:** marathon, final,
  basketball, spectators

  stress on 2nd syllable: celebrity,
  facilities, alternative

  stress on 3rd syllable: international,
  referee, disadvantage, recognition

4 READING

a 1 c 2 a 3 b

b 2 gradually 3 fine 4 statues
  5 major 6 ban 7 slaves 8 site
  9 revealed 10 hippodrome

c A 2 B 3 C 3

LISTENING

a 3

b 1 Physics
  2 The chemistry teacher was more
    relaxed. The physics teacher was
    stricter.
  3 Her best friend
  4 In his pencil case
  5 She got very angry and sent them
    out of the room.

1 C

1 VOCABULARY

a 2 great-grandmother
  3 cousin
  4 half-sister
  5 brother-in-law
  6 couple
  7 mother-in-law
  8 great-great-grandfather
  9 stepfather
  10 only child

b 2 patient 3 lazy 4 reliable
  5 affectionate 6 organized 7 sociable
  8 shy 9 sensitive 10 bossy

c 2 dishonest 3 quiet 4 stingy
  5 unfriendly 6 unkind 7 impatient
  8 unselfish / generous

2 HOW WORDS WORK

2 each other 3 ourselves 4 each other
5 himself 6 yourself 7 themselves

3 READING

a 2 F 3 T 4 T 5 F 6 F 7 F 8 F

4 GRAMMAR

a 2 I'm staying
  3 I'll make
  4 I'll carry
  5 We're meeting
  6 I'm going to go
  7 we'll arrive / we're going to arrive
  8 I'll call

b 1 I'll set
  2 will be ready / is going to be,
    I'll call
  3 I'm going / I'm going to go,
    What are you doing
  4 We're going to spend, will be
  5 What are you going to do, I'll work

5 PRONUNCIATION

a 2 re<u>spons</u>ible 3 i<u>ma</u>ginative
  4 un<u>friend</u>ly 5 <u>mood</u>y 6 im<u>pat</u>ient
  7 am<u>bit</u>ious 8 <u>so</u>ciable 9 ag<u>gress</u>ive
  10 dis<u>or</u>ganized

LISTENING

a 1, 3, 4

b himself: not spoiled, not selfish, not
  imaginative, responsible, organized

  his wife: affectionate, not lazy,
  hardworking, charming, not
  manipulative

  his father: responsible, bossy

Practical English 1

1 MEETING PEOPLE

2 good / nice / great   3 Welcome   4 met
5 introduce   6 How   7 heard   8 this
9 meet   10 trip / journey

2 SOCIAL ENGLISH

2 e   3 d   4 a   5 f   6 b

3 READING

a 2 Dress   3 Learn   4 Ask   5 Take
  6 Work

b 2 c   3 a   4 b   5 d   6 e

2 A

1 VOCABULARY

a 2 wasted   3 afford   4 charged
  5 pay back   6 earns   7 borrow
  8 inherited

b 2 salary   3 charge   4 save   5 cost
  6 loans   7 Mortgages   8 taxes

c 1 from   2 to   3 for   4 on   5 in, by

2 READING

a 2 lets   3 each other   4 makes   5 cash
  6 join   7 afford   8 fill out   9 monthly
  10 wait for

b 3

3 GRAMMAR

a 2 have used   3 have made   4 took
  5 Have you ever had   6 I called
  7 didn't give   8 did she borrow
  9 parked   10 have never owed

b 1 have you had, bought
  2 went, Have you been, haven't had,
    Did you buy
  3 have known, did they meet, were
  4 came, have sold, haven't sold
  5 did you live, stayed, bought,
    I've been

4 PRONUNCIATION

a 2 four and a quarter
  3 eight hundred and forty-nine
  4 one thousand five hundred
  5 six point seven three
  6 zero point five
  7 two and a half

b 2 nine hundred and ninety-nine
    dollars
  3 fourteen point five
  4 two thirds
  5 one and a half
  6 three thousand eight hundred and
    forty-two
  7 two and a half million dollars / two
    million five hundred thousand
    dollars
  8 zero point seven percent

LISTENING

a 1 D   2 E   3 A   4 B   5 F   6 C

b Check your answers with the
  audioscript on page 75.

2 B

1 GRAMMAR

a **for:** the last three days, ages,
  a long time, months and months

  since: 1992, Friday, New Year's Day, I
  last saw you, he was a child

b 1 I've been cleaning
  2 I've been working
  3 What have you been doing,
    I've been preparing
  4 he's been trying
  5 We've been thinking

c 2 been going   3 both   4 been sleeping
  5 both   6 been looking   7 had

2 PRONUNCIATION

a 2 She's been <u>learning</u> <u>Spanish</u> for <u>five</u>
    <u>years</u>.
  3 He's been <u>working</u> as a <u>tour</u> <u>guide</u>
    since he <u>left</u> <u>here</u>.
  4 They've been <u>traveling</u> around
    <u>Asia</u> for <u>two</u> <u>months</u>.
  5 We've been <u>waiting</u> for your <u>call</u>.
  6 <u>What</u> has she been <u>doing</u> since she
    <u>moved</u> to <u>Peru</u>?
  7 I've been <u>cleaning</u> the <u>house</u> all
    <u>morning</u>.

3 READING

a 2

b 2 F   3 F   4 T   5 T   6 F

c 2 take a nap   3 barefoot   4 volunteer
  5 researching   6 amazing   7 rural
  8 poverty

4 VOCABULARY

a 2 boiling   3 starving   4 filthy
  5 freezing   6 tiny

b 2 enormous / huge
  3 awful / horrible / terrible
  4 exhausted
  5 delicious / great
  6 great / wonderful / fantastic /
    amazing

5 PRONUNCIATION

a 2 b   3 e   4 a   5 f   6 c

LISTENING

a 1 D   2 B   3 F   4 E   5 A   6 C

b 1 quiet
  2 people
  3 course
  4 her bicycle
  5 discounts
  6 expensive to run

1 READING

a 1 AeroSur
  2 by bus
  3 at night
  4 No, only locally.
  5 It's slow, uncomfortable, and they don't always accept reservations.
  6 yes
  7 Because *rápido* means *fast*, but in fact it stops at every station.

b 2 drop 3 in advance 4 main
  5 option 6 cargo 7 scheduled
  8 available

2 HOW WORDS WORK

2 long, take 3 takes 4 took
5 long, take, get 6 took, get

3 GRAMMAR

a 2 much **cheaper**
  3 the same skirt **as**
  4 drives **more slowly** than
  5 as **hard** as
  6 taller **than** I am
  7 **the** most intelligent
  8 the **hottest** day
  9 the **worst** restaurant
  10 the **most boring**

b 2 Sydney is the healthiest of the three destinations.
  3 Rio de Janeiro is cheaper than Helsinki.
  4 Sydney is not as dangerous as Rio de Janeiro.
  5 Helsinki is as easy to get to as Rio de Janeiro.
  6 Sydney is the most relaxing of the three destinations.
  7 Sydney is sunnier than Helsinki.
  8 Helsinki doesn't have as many tourists as Sydney.

4 VOCABULARY

2 platform 3 parking ticket 4 card / pass 5 ticket 6 limit 7 gas 8 land
9 travel 10 gate 11 luggage 12 aisle

5 PRONUNCIATION

a 2 e 3 b 4 a 5 g 6 d 7 h 8 f

b 1 flight 2 highway 3 helmet 4 truck
  5 van

LISTENING

a 2, 3, 4

b 1 You can't concentrate on the road and have a telephone conversation at the same time.
  2 Because you stop looking at the road and look at your cell phone.
  3 Because people get angry / impatient and try to pass.
  4 Stop at traffic lights.
  5 On the sidewalk and in the middle of the road.

CAN YOU REMEMBER...?

1 does 2 had 3 'll 4 Have
5 been 6 as

PRACTICAL ENGLISH 2

1 REQUESTS AND PERMISSION

a 2 call 3 use 4 sending 5 take
  6 helping

b 2 c 3 b 4 e 5 a 6 d

2 SOCIAL ENGLISH

1 started 2 heard 3 Just 4 Let
5 How

3 READING

a Aaron ✓, Greg ✓, Steph ✗, Joseph ✗, Luke ✗

b 2 Luke 3 Helen 4 Joseph 5 Aaron
  6 Greg

1 READING

a 2 F 3 F 4 T 5 T 6 F

c 2 As well as 3 However 4 so that
  5 although

2 GRAMMAR

a 2 shouldn't 3 should 4 must
  5 should 6 have to 7 shouldn't
  8 don't have to, have to / should
  9 should 10 must not

b 2 You should **take** a rest
  3 everyone will **have to** speak
  4 ✓
  5 I **had to** stay in bed
  6 You **must not** park
  7 ✓
  8 ✓

3 VOCABULARY

2 busy 3 hang 4 dial
5 ring tone 6 call back 7 turn off
8 message, voice mail 9 hands-free
10 speed

4 PRONUNCIATION

a 2 We should <u>call</u> the <u>restaurant</u> to <u>reserve</u> a <u>table</u>.
  3 You <u>must</u> <u>not</u> <u>park</u> your <u>car</u> on the <u>sidewalk</u>.
  4 <u>Children</u> <u>shouldn't</u> <u>watch</u> <u>more</u> than <u>two</u> <u>hours</u> of <u>television</u> a <u>day</u>.
  5 Do you <u>really</u> <u>have</u> to <u>work</u> on <u>Saturday</u>?
  6 You <u>don't</u> <u>have</u> to <u>be</u> a <u>member</u> to <u>play</u> at <u>this</u> <u>club</u>.
  7 We <u>had</u> to <u>buy</u> a <u>new</u> <u>car</u> <u>last</u> <u>month</u>.

b 2 must 3 shouldn't 4 busy
  5 cell phone 6 message

LISTENING

a 1

b 1 move away
  2 bother, annoying
  3 far as, at all
  4 good manners
  5 shouldn't do, interesting

1 READING

a 2 e 3 f 4 c 5 h 6 d 7 a 8 b

b 2 advertise 3 instead of 4 basic
5 financial 6 comic books
7 characters 8 style

c 2 T 3 F 4 T 5 F 6 F 7 F 8 T

2 HOW WORDS WORK

2 ✓ 3 ✓ 4 looks 5 ✓ 6 look

3 VOCABULARY

a 2 bangs 3 look 4 bald
5 overweight 6 mid 7 gray
8 ponytail 9 slim 10 wavy

b 2 early 3 height 4 well-built
5 short 6 curly 7 blond
8 beard 9 mustache 10 twenties
11 short 12 overweight 13 long
14 straight 15 dark

4 PRONUNCIATION

a /eɪ/ ~~light~~ /aɪ/ ~~neighbor~~ /aɪ/ ~~straight~~
/aɪ/ ~~weigh~~

5 GRAMMAR

a 2 can't 3 might / may 4 can't
5 must 6 might / may

b 2 might / may rain 3 can't have
4 must feel 5 might / may come
6 can't be 7 must earn 8 can't be

LISTENING

a 1 China
2 He's in his (late) twenties or (early) thirties.
3 He's very tall and has short straight hair.
4 He's a basketball player.
5 Australia
6 She's in her (early) forties.
7 She's slim, has long blond hair and blue eyes.
8 She's an actress.

b Yao Ming, Nicole Kidman

1 GRAMMAR

a 2 could 3 can't
4 she has / 's been able to
5 to be able to 6 couldn't
7 she will / 'll be able to

b 2 must be able to 3 both 4 both
5 haven't been able to
6 used to be able to 7 both
8 not being able to 9 both 10 both
11 never been able to 12 be able to

2 PRONUNCIATION

a 2 I've never been able to play chess well.
3 She can ski better than me.
4 We weren't able to find the restaurant.
5 I'll be able to meet her family on Saturday.
6 We can't understand a word he says.
7 We could meet downtown.
8 I'd like to be able to travel more often.

b 2 1 3 2 4 1,1 5 1 6 2

3 READING

a Before: 3, 4, 5, 8, 10
During: 6, 7, 9

b 2 F 3 T 4 F 5 T 6 F 7 F 8 F
9 T 10 F

4 VOCABULARY

a 2 ✓ 3 ✓ 4 exciting 5 embarrassed
6 ✓ 7 interested 8 ✓

b 2 tired 3 worrying 4 boring
5 excited 6 interesting 7 depressing
8 embarrassed

5 HOW WORDS WORK

2 c 3 a 4 e 5 f 6 b

LISTENING

a 1, 3, 4, 6, 8

b 1 Yes.
3 I'm pretty good at it.
4 When I left home and went to college.
6 I learned by myself, by experimenting.
8 I found it quite easy.

CAN YOU REMEMBER...?

1 for 2 long 3 most 4 must not
5 can't 6 able

PRACTICAL ENGLISH 3

1 HOW TO GET THERE

2 way 3 stops 4 change 5 off 6 take
7 far

2 SOCIAL ENGLISH

2 c 3 f 4 a 5 g 6 d 7 e

3 READING

1 On foot or by subway.
2 At metro and train stations.
3 *Paris Par Arrondissements*.
4 By buying a *carnet* of ten tickets.
5 Stamp your tickets in the machine.
6 Because it's a compact city and you can feel the atmosphere change as you walk from district to district.
7 No.
8 The white light on the roof is on.
9 No.
10 Go on a river tour.

214

4A

1 VOCABULARY

Across: 2 private   4 degree   5 strict
6 preschool   8 teacher   10 math
16 grade   17 secondary   19 learn
20 information   21 exam

Down: 1 review   3 results   7 semester
9 chemistry   11 schedule   12 cheat
13 literature   14 discipline   15 principal
18 fail

2 PRONUNCIATION

a /ʌ/ ~~computer~~   /yu/ ~~study~~
/ʌ/ ~~uniform~~   /yu/ ~~subject~~

b 2 re<u>vie</u>w   3 ex<u>a</u>m   4 <u>u</u>niform
5 be<u>ha</u>ve   6 <u>di</u>scipline   7 <u>se</u>condary
8 el<u>e</u>mentary   9 pr<u>o</u>fessor   10 <u>co</u>llege

3 READING

a 2 It comes from "weblog."
3 It's an online diary.
4 To work together, to share
information and ideas.
5 What I know is.
6 Anyone.
7 The information may not be
completely correct.
8 It's the best-known wiki website.

4 GRAMMAR

a 2 f   3 e   4 a   5 c   6 b

b 2 until   3 before   4 when
5 unless   6 as soon as   7 if   8 until

c 2 Will you take, fail
3 I'll do, ends
4 are, won't be able to
5 won't leave, graduates
6 get, I'll call
7 I'll come, go
8 We'll be, hurry up
9 speak, won't know
10 won't pass, don't review

LISTENING

a 2, 3

b 1 look the same   2 easier
3 much quicker, get ready
4 on their own
5 feel more confident   6 behave better

4B

1 GRAMMAR

a 2 ✓
3 even if someone **offered** them
4 If he **didn't** like the job so much
5 ✓
6 I'**d** be a journalist
7 ✓
8 if we **had** the time

b 2 I'll meet   3 you'll lose   4 weren't
5 Would you retire   6 get married
7 wouldn't be   8 went out
9 I'll learn   10 I'd learn

2 PRONUNCIATION

a 2 <u>chi</u>mney   3 resi<u>den</u>tial
4 re<u>fri</u>gerator   5 <u>town</u>house
6 <u>ba</u>lcony   7 <u>ga</u>rage   8 <u>co</u>ttage
9 in<u>ha</u>bitant   10 <u>su</u>burbs
11 <u>dish</u>washer   12 a<u>part</u>ment

b 2 I <u>would</u>n't <u>work</u> if I <u>didn't need</u> the
<u>money</u>.
3 If you <u>went</u> to <u>bed earlier</u>, you'd <u>feel</u>
<u>better</u>.
4 She'd <u>call</u> if she <u>couldn't</u> come.
5 We'd <u>get there faster</u> if we <u>took</u> a
<u>taxi</u>.

3 VOCABULARY

a 2 suburb   3 downtown   4 yard
5 garden   6 patio   7 garage   8 steps
9 armchairs   10 coffee table
11 dishwasher   12 sink   13 bathrooms
14 shower   15 bedrooms

b 2 floor   3 steps   4 residential
5 chimney   6 townhouse   7 balcony
8 suburbs   9 roof   10 country

4 READING

a 2 c   3 b   4 a   5 b   6 b

c 2 extraordinary   3 giant
4 ultramodern   5 invisible
6 minimalist   7 open-plan

LISTENING

a 1 C   2 F   3 A   4 B   5 E   6 D

b 1 Kenya or Tanzania because he's
always wanted to go on safari.
2 A Ferrari because it's a lot of fun.
3 Tennis so that he could beat
his friend.
4 He'd be a news anchor because the
money is good and he would have to
work for only one hour every day.
5 To cook properly so that he could
cook for his friends.
6 He would buy a house in Arizona
and go there in the winter.

4C

1 VOCABULARY

a 2 known   3 get along
4 have in common   5 argue
6 keep in touch   7 lost touch
8 stay friends

b 2 old friends   3 new friends
4 coworkers   5 close friends

2 GRAMMAR

a 2 ✓   3 ✓
4 He **used** to be very overweight
5 ✓   6 doesn't **usually** drive
7 did you **use** to work   8 ✓

b 2 used to eat out
3 usually visit
4 Did you use to wear
5 used to go
6 didn't use to like
7 Do you usually work
8 used to be
9 Did they use to go
10 don't usually have

3 READING

a 1 Marie   2 David   3 Richard   4 Ana

b 1 B   2 D   3 C   4 A   5 D   6 A
7 C   8 B

4 PRONUNCIATION

2 /s/   3 /z/   4 /z/   5 /s/   6 /z/   7 /z/
8 /s/   9 /s/   10 /z/

5 HOW WORDS WORK

2 get along   3 got to   4 get
5 get to know   6 get in touch
7 got rid of   8 getting

LISTENING

a 1, 3, 4

b 1 When they were 16.
2 After college.
3 He was rude and didn't explain
things well.
4 She failed French.
5 She wasn't in good enough shape
to play it anymore and her friend
always beat her.
6 It's less competitive and more fun.

CAN YOU REMEMBER...?

1 had / used   2 must   3 Will   4 unless
5 Would   6 used

215

PRACTICAL ENGLISH 4

1 MAKING SUGGESTIONS

2 How about **going** out?
3 ✓
4 ✓
5 How about **going** to
6 ✓
7 let's **go**

2 SOCIAL ENGLISH

2 looks   3 could do me   4 Aren't you
5 Hang on

3 READING

a 2 Red Hot Chilli Peppers
  3 Jennifer Lopez
  4 Elton John
  5 Whitney Houston
  6 Coldplay
  7 Van Halen
  8 Jane's Addiction

1 GRAMMAR

a **Large quantity:** many
  Small quantity: a little, very few
  Less than you want / need: not enough (people), not (long) enough
  More than you want / need: too (fast)
  Zero: no

b 2 too much   3 very few   4 lots of
  5 too   6 many

c 2 a little, much
  3 no / little, any / much
  4 too many, big enough
  5 few, many
  6 little, enough
  7 enough money, too expensive

2 PRONUNCIATION

a /ɔ/ enough   /ʌ/ although
  /ɔ/ through   /ɔ/ laughed
b 1 cough   2 naughty   3 drought
  4 doughnut   5 rough

3 VOCABULARY

a 2 imagination   3 information
  4 survival   5 prediction   6 argument
  7 decision   8 proposal
b 2 happiness   3 similarity
  4 possibility   5 minority   6 ability

4 READING

b 3
c 1 Because we live too fast.
  2 No.
  3 Depressed and overweight.
  4 He wants us to look for quality
    ingredients and to take pleasure in
    eating.
  5 Eight weeks.
  6 No.
  7 We will have healthy bodies.

LISTENING

a 1 D   2 A   3 C   4 B   5 E
b 1 food is unhealthy
  2 personal responsibility
  3 people leave
  4 nowhere to
  5 much nicer
  6 to sit

1 GRAMMAR

a 2 (–), (–)   3 a   4 (–)   5 the, the
  6 (–)
b 2 work
  3 ✓
  4 left home
  5 **an** electrician
  6 ✓
  7 What **a** cold day!
  8 ✓
  9 twice **a** month
  10 **the** UN president
  11 next Friday

2 PRONUNCIATION

a 2 /ðə/   3 /ðə/   4 /ði/   5 /ðə/   6 /ðə/
b /ð/: they, together, although, the, there,
  that, those, clothes
  /θ/: months, math, think, worth,
  thanks, thousands, healthy

3 READING

a clothes 6, 8
  housework 10, 14
  technology 3, 4
  children 11, 15
  cars and driving 7, 9
b B 15   C 16   D 1   E 7   F 11   G 6
  H 13   I 2   J 12
c 1 amount   2 effortlessly   3 curtains
  4 run out   5 outfit

4 HOW WORDS WORK

1 a   2 b   3 a   4 a   5 b

5 VOCABULARY

2 at, for   3 as   4 from, in, to
5 about, with   6 to, for   7 at, in / for
8 of   9 for   10 for, from

LISTENING

a reading and shopping
b 1 Science fiction and action novels.
  2 Novels about feelings, emotions, and
    personal relationships.
  3 Science fiction novels.
  4 Shopping.
  5 She finds shopping boring.

5 C

1 VOCABULARY

a B Responsibilities   C Working hours
  D Qualifications   E Training
  F Opportunities   G Salary

b 2 full-time   3 hours   4 overtime
  5 experience   6 part-time
  7 multinational   8 promoted   9 earn
  10 apply for   11 send in   12 résumé

c 2 in   3 of   4 contract   5 temporary
  6 quit   7 responsible   8 retire

2 READING

a 2

b 2 T   3 T   4 F   5 T   6 F   7 T   8 T

3 PRONUNCIATION

a 2 employee   3 multinational
  4 unemployment   5 psychologist
  6 temporary   7 university
  8 permanent   9 promotion
  10 experience   11 career   12 scientist
  13 interview   14 retire   15 apply

b /aɪ/ responsible   /æ/ apply
  /ər/ experience   /ɑ/ overtime
  /ə/ full-time

4 GRAMMAR

a 2 c   3 g   4 h   5 d   6 e   7 a   8 b

b 2 not going   3 to train   4 sending in
  5 being   6 to give   7 typing
  8 to include

c 2 ✓   3 ✓   4 interviewing   5 ✓
  6 studying   7 to move   8 Working

LISTENING

a She's a cardiac surgeon. She doesn't
  have enough time for her son.

b 1, 3, 4, 6, 9, 10

CAN YOU REMEMBER...?

1 won't   2 were   3 use   4 no   5 an
6 watching

PRACTICAL ENGLISH 5

1 GIVING OPINIONS

2 opinion   3 think   4 absolutely
5 agree   6 Personally   7 sure   8 with
9 That's

2 SOCIAL ENGLISH

2 unfair   3 turn   4 What's   5 kidding
6 deal   7 Let's

3 READING

a 1 No, you get one with your entrance
    ticket.
  2 The Mona Lisa.
  3 In the morning, because you have
    more energy then.
  4 In one of the cafes.
  5 Relax and find surprises.
  6 Yes.
  7 Yes.
  8 Which stand you got it from, so that
    you can get your credit card or
    passport back.

---

6 A

1 GRAMMAR

a 2 told me   3 she bought   4 it was
  5 hadn't bought   6 whether
  7 had to go   8 worked
  9 told them, might   10 if I could

b 2 I told her (that) I didn't like
    shopping at sales.
  3 She asked me how much I had paid /
    'd paid (or I paid) for my bag.
  4 They said (that) they would buy /
    they'd buy their plane tickets on the
    Internet.
  5 The salesperson asked me if /
    whether I had the receipt.
  6 I asked the man where the restrooms
    were.

2 VOCABULARY

a 2 customers   3 receipt
  4 shopping cart   5 discount
  6 cash register   7 manager   8 sale
  9 department store   10 bargain
  11 complain   12 line   13 refunds
  14 salesperson

b 1 newsstand   2 bakery
  3 drugstore or pharmacy
  4 department store   5 shopping mall

3 PRONUNCIATION

a /g/: drugstore, goods, guarantee
  /dʒ/: vegetable, travel agency, register
  /k/: cash, complain, market
  /ʃ/: shoe store, shopping, stationery
  /tʃ/: cheese, chocolate, watches

4 READING

a 1 What are the most common fakes?
  2 How can you identify fakes?
  3 Why should you avoid buying fakes?

b 2 c   3 a   4 e   5 d   6 b

c 2 rash   3 global   4 bargain   5 strap
  6 Goods

5 GRAMMAR

2 She told me to come back next week /
  the following week.
3 He told me not to forget my free gift.
4 I asked the salesperson to call the
  manager.
5 She told me to keep my receipt.
6 I asked him to give me a bag.
7 He asked me not to touch the fruit.

LISTENING

1 F   2 F   3 F   4 T   5 T   6 T   7 F   8 F
9 T   10 F

1 GRAMMAR

a 2 It will be shown in theaters next year.
3 It rained all the time the movie was being made on location.
4 The extras have been sent to the wrong place.
5 Auditions are being held all day.
6 The movie is going to be dubbed into other languages.
7 The movie was made in France.
8 It is based on a book.

b 1 is directed   2 was shot   3 tells
4 are changed   5 plays   6 is played
7 starts   8 was occupied   9 ends
10 has been based   11 was composed
12 wrote   13 was nominated
14 can be seen   15 shouldn't be missed

2 PRONUNCIATION

a /aɪ/: subtitles, dialogue, writer, island
/ɪ/: script, filmed, trilogy, thriller

b 1 based   2 filmed   3 voted
4 destroyed

3 READING

a **Advantages:**
1 It's a job you can do as well as your full-time job. (You can be an extra just a few days a year.)
2 You meet the stars in the movie.
3 It's unique and fun.

Disadvantages:
1 It isn't well-paid.
2 You have to work long hours (often doing nothing, just waiting).
3 You don't get much recognition for your work.

b 2 F   3 T   4 T   5 F   6 F   7 T   8 T

c 2 glamorous   3 waiting around
4 average   5 tips   6 had an urge
7 annoy   8 suits

4 VOCABULARY

Across: 1 dub   4 plot   5 horror
7 sequel   10 science fiction   11 comedy
12 action   14 cast   15 scene

Down: 1 director   2 role   3 soundtrack
6 musical   8 effects   9 filmed   13 on
14 crew   15 set

LISTENING

a 1 F   2 G   3 B   4 D   5 A   6 C   7 E

b 1 When they were making a TV movie in her hometown.
2 When it's a film she thinks she's really going to like.
3 So that she can hear the actors' voice and tone.
4 It made her laugh.
5 Chile.
6 Because it's her favorite movie.

218

1 GRAMMAR

a 2 which / that   3 who / that
4 whose / where   5 which / that
6 whose   7 who / that   8 which / that
9 whose   10 where

b Sentences 5 and 7

c 2 *Psycho*, which was directed by Hitchock, is my favorite horror film.
3 ✓
4 The new stadium, which cost millions to build, is already too small.
5 ✓
6 My oldest sister, whose husband is a lawyer, has an enormous house.
7 ✓
8 The village of Salzburg, where Mozart was born, gets millions of tourists every year.
9 Sean Connery, who used to play James Bond, was born in Scotland in 1930.

2 READING

a 2 B   3 E   4 A   5 C

b 2 treaty   3 approximately
4 tuberculosis   5 nationalist
6 teenager   7 assassinate   8 empire

3 VOCABULARY AND PRONUNCIATION

a 2 cyclist   3 composer   4 soccer player
5 violinist   6 sculptor   7 painter
8 inventor

b 2 scientist   3 conductor   4 musician
5 director   6 photographer
7 designer

c **stress on 1st syllable:** cyclist, soccer player, sculptor, painter, scientist
stress on 2nd syllable: composer, inventor, conductor, musician, director, photographer, designer
stress on 3rd syllable: politician, violinist

LISTENING

a 1 1836   2 painter   3 24   4 life   5 sea
6 popular   7 expensive   8 1910

CAN YOU REMEMBER...?

1 few   2 the   3 to   4 not   5 were
6 whose

1 GIVING AND REACTING TO NEWS

2 believe   3 you sure   4 joking / kidding
5 telling   6 incredible / amazing

2 SOCIAL ENGLISH

2 funny   3 would be   4 see you either
5 at all

3 READING

b 1 F   2 T   3 F   4 T   5 F   6 F   7 F
8 T

1 READING

a 1 a   2 c   3 c   4 b
c 2 a   3 f   4 c   5 b   6 e
d 2 likely   3 statistics   4 puzzling
   5 occur   6 casualties   7 rushing

2 GRAMMAR

a 2 would have arrived
  3 had offered
  4 wouldn't have served
  5 hadn't recommended
  6 Would you have gone
  7 had known
b 2 we would have gone
  3 he had been interested in the movie
  4 I hadn't had so many calls
  5 they wouldn't have moved
  6 it hadn't been so cold

3 PRONUNCIATION

a **stress on 1st syllable:** effort, instinct
  stress on 2nd syllable: unhappy,
  advantage, mistake
  stress on 3rd syllable: optimistic,
  opportunity, realistic
b /ʌ/: bump, comfortable, lucky, unhappy
  /ɛr/: airport, careful, there, vary
  /eɪ/: fail, mistake, patient, pain
  /i/: routine, scream, seem
  /oʊ/: control, focus, goal, over

4 HOW WORDS WORK

2 ✓   3 ✓   4 what   5 that   6 ✓

5 VOCABULARY

a 1 lucky, happy
  2 fortunate
  3 comfortable
  4 helpful, successful, careful
b 2 Luckily / Fortunately
  3 unfortunately
  4 uncomfortably
  5 carefully
  6 successfully
  7 helpfully

LISTENING

a 1
b 1 T   2 F   3 F   4 F   5 T

---

1 READING

a 1 T   2 F   3 T   4 T   5 F   6 F   7 F
  8 T   9 F   10 T
b 1 armchair detectives
  2 horror movie
  3 crime scene
  4 time machine
  5 science fiction
  6 television documentary

2 GRAMMAR

a 2 were you   3 didn't you   4 haven't you
  5 aren't you   6 can you   7 won't he
  8 isn't it   9 hasn't he   10 wouldn't you
b 2 aren't you   3 isn't it   4 doesn't he
  5 didn't they   6 has she   7 isn't he
  8 won't you

3 PRONUNCIATION

a 2 violent   3 machine   4 convince
  5 investigation   6 achieve   7 royal
  8 police
b 1 murderer   2 mysterious   3 famous
  4 fictional   5 continue

4 GRAMMAR

a 2 why she went back
  3 where the nearest bank is
  4 how much it costs
  5 what she wants to do
  6 if we have arrived yet
b 2 Do you know if she has ever been to
    Vietnam?
  3 Can you tell me if this train goes to
    Quebec?
  4 Could you tell me what time the
    show starts?
  5 Do you know who this pen
    belongs to?
  6 Could you tell me how long he's
    lived there?

5 VOCABULARY

1 train station
2 boarding card, credit card
3 golf course, training course
4 strawberry jam, traffic jam

LISTENING

a 1 F   2 T   3 T   4 T   5 F   6 F   7 F
b 1 Ruth Rendell writes crime novels.
  5 One of his daughters is jealous of
    the other.
  6 He always solves the crime.
  7 He's just an ordinary person who's
    good at his job.

---

1 VOCABULARY

2 Life in 21st Century China
3 Sports File
4 Tom and Jerry
5 The World at Seven
6 Jonathan Ross
7 Big Brother 10
8 Laugh a Minute
9 Main Street
10 Want to be Rich?
11 Ben Hur

2 GRAMMAR

a 2 go out on Friday evenings
  3 both
  4 find out the truth
  5 Put them on
  6 get along with my neighbors
  7 both
  8 Turn them off!
  9 both
  10 Please go away
b 2 turn it up   3 set it up
  4 throw them away   5 look for them
  6 turn it off   7 take it off   8 ask for it

3 PRONUNCIATION

a /ʃ/ fortunate   /ɪ/ knife   /k/ receipt
  /aʊ/ grow   /ər/ sports   /θ/ them

4 READING

a 3
b 2, 3, 7
c 1 keep on   2 meet up with
  3 cut back   4 work out   5 take up
  6 put up with

5 VOCABULARY

a 2 take   3 turn   4 warm   5 use   6
  call   7 sold   8 find
b 2 turn it on   3 taken any money out
  4 checked in   5 come in   6 speed up

LISTENING

a 1 Three.
  2 In the living room.
  3 He prefers to read everything in the
    newspaper.
  4 Channel 4 because it has the most
    interesting programs.
  5 Mexican TV so he could practice
    his Spanish.
  6 One hour every evening on
    weekdays.
  7 Because there are more interesting
    things to do.

CAN YOU REMEMBER...?

1 had   2 by   3 which   4 would   5 isn't
6 turn

1 APOLOGIZING

2 I'm really sorry.
3 That's all right.
4 How could I be so stupid?
5 I'm terribly sorry.
6 It was my fault.
7 I just wasn't concentrating.
8 Don't worry.

2 SOCIAL ENGLISH

1 hopeless at   2 now or never
3 must have been   4 blame me
5 hear a word   6 confirm your reservation

3 READING

a 1 Eiffel Tower   2 Gare d'Orsay
   3 Notre Dame   4 Egyptian Obelisk
   5 Louvre   6 Place de la Concorde
   7 Ile de la Cité